Tired of sitting in ill-planned, unproductive meetings that accomplish little more than allowing more work to pile up while you waste precious time?

Ever wish you could wave a magic wand and make those ineffective meetings just plain disappear?

Or perhaps say "Hocus Pocus" and give your meetings some focus?

Fact is, you don't need a wand or mystical chant to become a meeting magician!
All you need are the secrets of

Meeting Magic
revealed!

The Secrets of

Tony Jeary and George Lowe

To order additional copies of
The Secrets of MEETING MAGIC Revealed
or for information on other
WALK THE TALK® products and services,
contact us at
1.888.822.9255
or visit our website at
www.walkthetalk.com

The WALK THE TALK® Company

*Helping organizations achieve success
through Ethical Leadership and
Values-Based Business Practices*

ISBN 1-885228-40-6

Printed in the United States of America
10 9 8 7 6 5 4 3

Printed by MultiAd

This book is **dedicated** to two special people
      Tammy and Marj
who have stuck with Tony and George, despite
the fact that even writers' wives don't fully
appreciate that we are working while looking
out the window.

Special thanks to **Eric Harvey,
Steve Ventura, and the rest of the
WALK THE TALK team** for their enthusiastic
reception, support, and patience.

Big kudos to **Todd McDonald**
for his excellent creative and editorial advice.

Acknowledgments

The tips and tricks in this book have been developed
and polished over years of hard work in meeting
rooms across the land. Our thanks go to the people –
meeting participants and leaders – who have helped
us learn our craft.

*T*his book is for both meeting leaders and participants. The fundamentals found here will work for any meeting – big or small, corporate or field location – and for all kinds of issues.

As you read on, much of what you'll discover touches on the subject of leadership. Our basic philosophy is that successful organizations leverage leadership at all levels and through all kinds of activities – including the meetings they have. When people are empowered and encouraged to act, the burden of leadership is shared. And it's that shared leadership that can make your meetings *magical*!

Have you ever seen a famous magician perform? Seemed like you were watching a one-person show, didn't it? But you weren't. In reality, you were watching a TEAM perform: stage assistants, lighting and special effects people, sound technicians, etc., as well as the magician. Sure, the magician may wave the wand and pull the rabbit out of the hat, but the real secret to making magic is a bunch of people all working together.

A meeting is a lot like a magic show. You have a group of people trying to reach a common goal. If you have good leadership and share the work, you can produce results that appear magical.

If you're someone who routinely calls meetings, **your role is providing skilled leadership**. You need to endorse, sponsor, and follow an effective meeting management process. And, you must promote a culture that values diverse views, solicits fresh perspectives, and demonstrates respect for people's time.

If you're someone who mostly participates in meetings that others call, you have your own unique opportunities for making a difference. You need to model positive behaviors by being prepared, by being an enthusiastic and involved participant, and by being willing to provide candid feedback on how future meetings can be even more productive.

Over the years, we've learned that while meetings are a fact of business life, *bad* meetings don't have to be.

You *can* get more done in less time – with much less frustration. All you need is a skilled leader, a willing team, and … a little bit of magic.

The universe is full of magical things, patiently waiting for our wits to grow sharper.

–Eden Phillpotts

Your First Trick:
How to use this book

The Secrets of Meeting Magic Revealed is full of key ideas, strategies, and tested processes that will drive big improvements in the meetings you lead or attend. But, as in stage magic, there's more to it than meets the eye. So you'll need to be a careful observer … and a diligent student!

We recommend that you begin by first reading the entire book with a colored pen and highlighter in hand. Mark items that stand out to you:

> Remember to send written thanks

Jot down questions or question marks in the margin next to items that aren't clear on the first pass:

> *What's a "desired outcome"?*

Then, go back and work through the book with a "live" example – a meeting you're planning or one you have just attended. As in pulling rabbits from hats, Meeting Magic requires that you study and practice the tricks before going on stage!

Use the book to prepare for the next ten meetings you're involved with. As you develop understanding of the nuances of each phase, mark the text pages with a big checkmark!

Practice our tricks. Learn how to: build your own meeting agendas with desired outcomes and timing, evaluate each session, and handle difficult meeting situations with ease. When you begin to receive high scores for your meetings, you will know that you're well on your way to becoming a master

Meeting Magician!

Table of Contents

Beginnings: **The Magic Formula** 1

Chapter One: **Meet or Not?** 3

Chapter Two: **Agenda** 7

Chapter Three: **Guidelines** 17

Chapter Four: **Involvement** 23

Chapter Five: **Clarity** 29

Your Trick Bag: **Meeting Magic Forms** 37

Beginnings:
The Magic Formula

About Stage Magic

People *want* to believe in Magic. However, anyone past 12 years of age knows that it's the elaborate preparation, practice, good props, and some showmanship that permit the magician to make it look easy on stage.

Audience participation is often encouraged or even required to make the trick work.

About Meeting Magic

Meeting Magic embodies the same concept in that people *want* to believe that meetings will be both efficient and effective; they want their leaders to orchestrate meetings that seem to make the impossible *possible* and get the work done easily. And, leaders want to believe that they'll receive help in creating the Magic.

As in stage magic, preparation, practice, good material, and excellent front-of-the-room talent is needed to achieve the desired outcomes. Precise techniques – with lots of practice and audience involvement – will make each new performance better than the last. In reality, our "secrets" aren't really secrets at all. Of course, if you attend a lot of typical meetings, you might think they are. As in the theater, a bad show is a waste of time and money.

Just as the magician enlists the audience, skilled meeting leaders and attendees collaborate to achieve the right level of participation from each and make it look easy to all. The better the magician <u>and</u> the audience, the better the show.

Stage magic is about fun, entertainment, and believing in illusion. Our Magic is about making your reality a bit more fun and making meetings a lot more productive.

The Meeting Magic Formula:

$$M + A + G + I + C = \textbf{Success}$$

M eet or Not?
Determine whether or not a meeting is the best way to accomplish your goal.

A genda:
With the end in mind, prepare carefully to get what you want.

G uidelines:
Set and follow "the rules" that will allow you to conduct the meeting with confidence.

I nvolvement:
Participate and encourage others to do the same. (That is, after all, why you have meetings.)

C larity:
Communicate clearly to help ensure success!

Chapter One
Meet or Not?

Determine whether or not a meeting is the best way to accomplish your goal.

This chapter is about careful decision making, early on, that can help you avoid an all-too-common mistake: Expending money and valuable time on meetings that really aren't necessary. There are several questions you should answer before calling meetings, or before agreeing to attend those that you have a choice about:

 What is the overall objective? Is the purpose ...
        ... to ANNOUNCE/INFORM?
        ... to INFLUENCE?
        ... to CREATE?
        ... to DECIDE?

 What needs to be accomplished? Creating a desired outcome statement (e.g., "Develop a plan to have all order-taking computers installed, networked, and staffed by February 1st.") can help you (and eventually others) focus on what is needed to get the job done.

 Is there another approach that would work as well as, or better than, a meeting? Many issues can be effectively discussed and resolved through less costly means such as a conference call or a series of short one-on-one meetings with those involved.

✔️ **Can the work be done by a group?** Groups are not well suited to some kinds of work. This is especially true for writing. You can save time by having key documents drafted by one or two individuals with writing skills and experience.

✔️ **What is needed for the group to do the work?** Determine what information is critical to achieving the desired outcomes, and whether it can be acquired when needed. If important data isn't available, any meeting will probably be ineffective.

✔️ **When is action required? When are the desired outcomes needed?** Determine whether more effective non-meeting methods will allow you to meet existing deadlines.

✔️ **Who *really* needs to attend?** Think about the sub-questions below before you "round up the usual suspects" and possibly include people who may not be needed to get the work done:
- Who are the key stakeholders?
- Who has the knowledge, experience, or information needed to develop the issues?
- Who will make the final decisions?
- Whose support is critical to achieving the goal?
- Who will be upset if not invited?

✔️ **Do *you* need to attend?** If it's not your meeting and attendance is not mandatory, think through the need to be present. Can someone else convey your views? Empowered representatives can extend your reach and save you time. In some cases, your perspectives on a subject can be provided to the meeting leader in advance – eliminating the need to attend or be represented.

✔️ **Do you need to attend the *entire* meeting?** For extended meetings, participants who are needed only for specific segments may not have to stay for the entire session. If this is the case, agree to attend only those portions for which you are truly needed.

What will the meeting cost … and will achieving the desired outcomes be a good "return on investment"?

Meetings are expensive – a fact often overlooked by the people who call them. Typical costs include: salaries, meeting facilities, refreshments and equipment, "travel and living" for out-of-town participants, etc. In addition to these factors, the careful meeting planner will consider the *opportunity* costs – what people would have done with their time (sales, production, etc.) if they weren't in the meeting.

Even "small" meetings can be costly. Too often, people call meetings, rather than pursue alternatives, in order to save *themselves* time (e.g., "It's much easier *for me* to get people together instead of taking the time to write a lengthy report.") With few exceptions, those behaviors are selfish … and just plain bad business.

Don't have a meeting if …

- You haven't prepared
- You have incomplete information
- There's no real need for group interaction
- People who need to be there can't make it
- The objective is already accomplished
  (e.g., Don't have a decision-making meeting if you've *really* already made the decision)
- There's a more efficient alternative such as:
  - having a conference call
  - sending an e-mail or voice mail
  - distributing an announcement, report, or memo
  - requesting individual input
- There's sufficient time to pursue alternatives.

Need help organizing your "to meet or not to meet" decision-making process? You'll find a DECISION WORKSHEET (page 39) – along with other *Meeting Magic Forms* – in the back of this book. Reproduce and use them as needed. Seem a little too much for smaller meetings? Just take the ideas and modify them to suit your needs.

One man's "magic"
is another man's
        engineering.
"Supernatural" is
a null word.

Excerpt from the notebooks of Lazarus Long,
from Robert Heinlein's *Time Enough for Love*

Chapter Two

Agenda

With the end in mind, prepare carefully to get what you want.

Before "the show" begins ...

Once you've decided that a meeting is appropriate, you need to "set the stage" and plan the event. This chapter is about the work that both leaders and participants can do ahead of time to make the meeting more productive and less frustrating.

Good meetings, like good magic, require some work in advance of the show! Here's our quick "sell" on why you need to invest in pre-work:

■ The salary clock starts ticking when people come into the room. If one person does "homework" on behalf of 20 and saves 30 minutes of meeting time, you jointly save 10 hours. Additionally, if the leader has his or her "act" together, participants will be more likely to step up to the challenges before them.

■ You can save immense amounts of time by gathering facts, organizing issues, and developing "straw person" (trial) solutions before the session. This allows discussions to focus on real issues instead of arguments over un-researched "facts."

■ Planning *how* to address the material can save time and significantly improve results. You'll be prepared to employ the right methods in dealing with the issues at hand.

On the next several pages, you'll find a step-by-step guide to agenda preparation that considers all of the ideas on the previous page and builds the foundation you need for "bringing your act to the stage." For many of the steps, we've provided a hypothetical example ... and space for you to *apply* the information by adding your own "real-world" example of a meeting you're planning or one you've already conducted.

Agenda Preparation Steps

Your meeting agenda planning actually began with the questions you answered when deciding to have a meeting in the first place. You'll need to revisit those questions – along with a few others – and answer them with specific detail.

Step One: Determine the meeting overview components:

■ What is your meeting subject?

Our example: *New Product Plan*
Your example:

■ What is/are your overall objective(s)?

Our example: *Resolve open issues and set production plan*
Your example:

■ What is/are your desired outcome(s)?

Our example:	Understand customer requirements, Develop product plan
Your example:	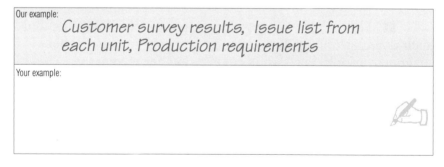

■ Who are the stakeholders/key participants?

Our example:	VP - Product Development, Sales Manager Chief Engineer, Manufacturing Manager
Your example:	

■ What information will be needed?

Our example:	Customer survey results, Issue list from each unit, Production requirements
Your example:	

■ When are the desired outcomes needed ("timing")?

Our example:	All work to be completed by May 3
Your example:	

Step Two: Segment and sequence your meeting. Separate your desired outcomes into meeting sub-topics, segments or elements, and determine which meeting participant will take the lead in each segment.

Our example:
> 1. *Customer requirements – Sales Manager*
> 2. *Prod. development timing – Chief Engineer*
> 3. *Production plan – Manufacturing Manager*

Your example:

Step Three: Determine the TIME and HOW for each segment:

■ Establish realistic TIME allocations for each element. It's better to plan too much time than too little; meetings that end early are always well received.

■ For each HOW, consider using a variety of meeting tools such as brainstorming, breakouts for problem solving, fishbone diagrams, prioritizing – using colored dots for voting, etc.

Our example:
> 1. *Customer requirements – Sales Manager*
> *10 min.   Present, analyze, and discuss*
> 2. *Prod. development timing – Chief Engineer*
> *10 min.   Present and brainstorm alternatives*

Your example:

Step Four: Prepare the invitation list. Build your invitation list with people who must be involved in order to achieve the desired outcomes. Remember that each stakeholder may not need to personally attend. Some may send representatives, others may be polled for their views prior to the meeting.

Step Five: Identify the specific information required for the meeting and any pre-work that will be involved.
  - What should be provided to attendees in advance ... and when?
  - Who will prepare the data, information, or analyses, etc.?

Our example:
> 1. *Sales Mgr. to distribute cust. specs to attendees day before meeting.*
> 2. *Manufacturing Mgr. to supply production flowchart at meeting.*

Your example:

Step Six: Identify the equipment and materials needed. Write down such needs as:
  - flip charts and easels, laptop word processor, writing pads and pens, etc.
  - long-lead time items such as projectors, video cameras, and sound systems
  - samples or props for the discussion.

Identify the people who will be responsible for arranging each item. Then follow up with them, prior to the meeting, to confirm they've completed their assignments.

Step Seven: Establish plans for meeting minutes or notes. Determine the type of post-meeting documentation required. Consider the following:

- Simple notes for participants only.
- Transcriptions of flip chart notes.
- Detailed minutes with exhibits, summary of findings, conclusions, and work plans.

■ Appoint a recorder in advance or solicit a volunteer at the start of the meeting. For more formal records, consider using a videographer or court recorder who can produce verbatim notes.

Step Eight: Select/reserve the meeting facility and determine the appropriate room layout. With your invitee list and desired outcomes in mind, pick a room that will suit your purposes. Here are some considerations:

- Sessions that require a high degree of interaction need room layouts that allow the leader or facilitator to move around. Use the classic horseshoe for groups of 25 or fewer.

- Circles, with or without tables, are the most egalitarian of layouts and are excellent for subjects requiring high levels of participation by all attendees.

- Rectangular layouts have "power ends" and work best when communications are primarily one way.

- For larger groups, try "crescent rounds" (round tables with chairs removed so that everyone faces the center or front of the room).

Step Nine: Decide on refreshments – as appropriate.
Consider ages, lifestyles, and special requirements (e.g., fat vs. no fat, caffeine vs. "decaf," etc.) when making your selections. A good mix is always a safe bet. At a minimum, provide coffee and water.

That concludes the planning phase. Your "act" has been designed, and now it's time to invite "the audience."

To assist you in agenda development, we've provided an *AGENDA PLANNER FOR MEETINGS* form in the back of the book (page 40). Reproduce and use it ... or consider developing your own version.

Meeting Announcement and Agenda

Once planning is complete, the next step is to create and distribute a meeting announcement and agenda – the written document that notifies/invites participants and lets them know what to expect. This can be done using a pre-developed form or written in plain memo format.

Here are some tips on creating your announcement:

■ Review your plan one final time and cross out any items or activities that you now determine aren't needed.

■ Add items such as: provisions for breaks, a closing segment to recap agreements and assignments, and a brief evaluation period.

■ Check your time allocations to ensure that you'll be able to get the work done that you've outlined.

A sample Meeting Announcement and Agenda – in memo format – is provided on the next page. Use it as a guide to develop your own version. Prefer a pre-developed form to fill out? You'll find one in the back of the book (page 41) to reproduce and use.

Sample Meeting Announcement and Agenda

To: Jack Johnson, Chief Engineer   Christine Fox, Sales Mgr.
Sarah Masterson, Manufact. Mgr.   Fred Smith, Admin.
Sally Winston, Planning   Pat Jones, Engineering

From: John O'Malley, VP - Product Development

Subject: **New Product Plan Meeting**

Date: 1/25   Time: 7:30 a.m. (coffee & bagels at 7:15)
Duration: 2 hours   Place: Engineering Conference Room #1
Facilitator: John   Projection: Fred   Recorder: Pat

I've set a meeting for the 25th with the following desired outcomes: 1) Understand Customer Requirements for new product. 2) Determine Product Development Plan for new product. 3) Determine Production Plans.

In order to get this important work done as efficiently as possible, there is some pre-work required. Here's what we need and when:
- Customer Specifications (Jack): Day before meeting
- Product Development Issues List (John): Day before meeting
- Production Schedule (Sarah): At meeting
- Prototype (Sally): At meeting

Order of Agenda

What	Time	Who	How
Agenda Review/Ground Rules	:05	John	Present/Discuss
Customer Specifications	:15	Jack	Present/Discuss
Product Development Issues	:15	John	Present
Product Dev. Resolution Ideas	:30	Group	Brainstorm
Break	:10		
Product Dev. Resolution Plan	:15	John/Grp.	Discuss/Agree
Production Schedule	:20	Sarah/Grp.	Discuss/Agree
Recap & Evaluation	:10	John/Grp.	

Preparing for Your Meeting

 Distribute the agenda and confirm attendance.

■ For simple meetings, you should distribute the agenda several days in advance. For critical sessions that require pre-work, distribute agendas at least a week to ten days ahead of time.

■ Don't assume that everyone invited will attend. Request RSVP's and do follow-up contacts to confirm that key stakeholders will be present or represented.
Note: If you have major "holes" in your planned group, you'll need to decide if you should proceed or reschedule.

■ Highlight any pre-work required in your meeting notice or cover letter and be clear and specific about who needs to do what in advance of the meeting.

Minimize stage fright through preparation. The best way to avoid being overly nervous at show time is by being prepared. Understand the issues; have all the information you'll need with you; be clear in your mind about how you will conduct the meeting. Being totally familiar with your agenda will help you achieve each desired outcome.

Check your venue. If you haven't used the facility previously, make sure you examine the room for unpleasant surprises BEFORE people arrive. Here are some considerations:
- ■ Environmental noise, coupled with poor acoustics, can be a major problem. If there's any doubt as to whether speakers can be heard, use a PA system.
- ■ Confirm that the heating or air-conditioning system is set at a comfortable temperature and is noise free.
- ■ Confirm food and beverage arrangements in advance. Re-confirm just prior to the start of the meeting.

**There is no magic
in magic,
   it's all in the
details.**

–Walt Disney

Chapter Three
Guidelines

Set and follow the "rules" that will allow you to
conduct the meeting with confidence.

This chapter is about how you can execute a well-planned meeting if you're the leader, and how to make important contributions if you're a participant. Clear guidelines and ground rules allow difficult matters to be dealt with in an organized way and keep controversy over process matters to a minimum. We'll illustrate these disciplines by walking through the steps of conducting a meeting.

Be ready to start. Timeliness is rule #1. As a participant, it's important to arrive several minutes early to demonstrate that you are engaged and ready. For leaders, it's vital that you establish a positive presence by arriving early and by beginning on time. This is a reinforcing signal to those who arrived promptly that you respect their time and are ready to get to work.

Welcome the group warmly. Introduce yourself and quickly recap the meeting title and purpose. This allows people who are in the wrong meeting room to pull their own Houdini act and escape without major embarrassment. (Don't laugh ... it happens more often than you might think!)

■ Thank people for taking time from their busy schedules to attend, and ask them to introduce themselves.

■ If it's a group that doesn't work together regularly, ask them to fill out name tags or place cards.

Set the ground rules. The following is a generic list of common sense ground rules that you can use as a starting point. However, it's very important that group members agree to the rules at the outset and are given the opportunity to add some of their own. Take the time to get the rules established, and it will pay off as you work your way through the agenda.

Ground Rules

1. Everyone participates.
2. One person speaks at a time, and side comments will be limited.
3. Active listening is encouraged.
4. No personal attacks. Discuss positions, not people.
5. Please turn off cell phones and pagers or set them on silent. Wait for the break to return calls.
6. We will stick to the agenda and scheduled times.
7. If the group wants to extend a discussion or add a topic, everyone must agree to extend the meeting or defer other topics.
8. If we slip off the agenda, we'll "park" issues for discussion at the end, if time permits.
9. It's okay to call for a "process check" if you think we're getting off track.

Address housekeeping issues. For meetings longer than an hour, people need to know:
- When the breaks will be. If you don't schedule breaks about every 60-90 minutes, people will license themselves to leave and disrupt your meeting. Put breaks on your agenda; most people will hang in if they know that a break is coming.
- Where the restrooms and telephones are located.
- When the meeting will conclude.

Review and confirm the agenda. Even though you've provided the agenda in advance, it's important to take a quick trip through it now to orient the group.

■ Review the objectives and desired outcomes. Ask for participants' agreement that these are clear and doable within the meeting time available.

■ Ask for participants' assistance in staying on task. Say something like, "I know you've all been in meetings that wasted time. Let's make today different. Can we all agree to filter questions and comments in our minds first, so we can maximize our time and stay focused on the objectives?"

■ Confirm that you have the right people in the room to get the work done, that you have the necessary information, and that the requested pre-work has been completed.

■ Identify people in key supporting roles (e.g., timekeeper, recorder) and review your plan for meeting minutes or notes.

Once you have the right people and the necessary information at hand, you're ready to begin. If you're missing a key player or critical data, consider postponing until they are available.

Begin working the agenda. Your agenda is the guide for the work at hand and needs to be treated seriously by both leader and participants. A key requirement of Meeting Magic is the ability to focus on the desired outcomes <u>for each segment of the meeting</u>. These segments are key building blocks that must be completed on time and in the sequence listed.

Enlist participants. We'll talk more about involvement in the next chapter, but here are some basics to keep in mind as you work through the meeting agenda:

- Remember that people do things for their reasons, not yours.
- Well-defined desired outcomes will resonate with everyone. The meeting leader needs to monitor reactions to keep the group focused and away from polarizing personal or parochial views.
- Quiet or reserved people need to be drawn out: "Fred, what do you think about this?" "Sarah, do you have a different view from what Pete just said?"
- Dominant people need to be moderated: "Chris, we have a good grip on your solution. If you'd bear with us for a few minutes, I believe there are others with thoughts that we need to hear before we finalize a course of action."

Stay on track. You don't want to bring in the "meeting police," but it's extremely important to avoid lengthy digressions. Here are three time-eating situations you're likely to face, along with some Meeting Magic tricks for dealing with them:

■ *Interesting but off-agenda discussions.* Intervene and put the topic or issue on a flip chart to revisit. Agree to come back to it if time permits or to address it in a separate session.

■ *Too much detail.* At times, individuals may have extensive information about a topic in question that's not really needed to achieve a desired outcome. Gently suggest that the information be provided to participants afterwards via a memo or e-mail.

■ *Arguments **intended** to derail the meeting.* Revisit the desired outcomes and enlist key stakeholders to support a shut-off approach that essentially says: "We're familiar with this view, and repeating it now isn't helping us reach a positive solution. Can you find a slightly different approach that will help us achieve what we need to do?"

✓ **Close out topics when agreement is reached.** Continuing conversation on a topic after everyone has been heard and agreement has been reached ("selling past the close") may risk an unwinding of the agreement. Once you have consensus, move on.

✓ **Document agreements.** It's important to record all agreements and assignments as they are made. Keep a flip chart list of specific agreements (or use the *MEETING AGREEMENTS and ASSIGNMENTS* form supplied on page 42). And when a topic is finalized, create a "who does what by when" chart to help summarize and move the issue from good idea to *ACTION*.

✓ **Wrap up.** The end of a meeting is another opportunity to add value by confirming the results and evaluating how the work was accomplished. Here are the key ingredients:

- *Recap* what you've accomplished and what actions are to be taken following the meeting.
- *Evaluate* the meeting **results** (achievement of desired outcomes) and **process** (participation, candor, timeliness, etc.). Remember that evaluation is the last group activity on the agenda. Make sure you allow enough time for people to complete it before you adjourn.

Written evaluations are best because they tend to produce more detailed and candid feedback. You'll find a Meeting Evaluation form in the back of this book (page 43). Reproduce and use it ... or develop your own version.

- *Thank* the group and support staff for their work. If there are "heroes" who made unique contributions, make sure they get special recognition.

✓ **End on time ... and formally!** If you need to run long, get permission from the group to extend. Conclude the meeting with a formal declaration that you're done. This lets everyone know that it's okay to leave without feeling obligated to stay and listen to sidebar conversations that may be continuing.

An idea can turn to dust
or magic,
depending on the talent
that rubs against it.

–William Bernbach

Chapter Four
Involvement

Participate and encourage others to do the same.
(That is, after all, why you have meetings.)

This chapter is about getting all attendees truly involved in the work of the meeting. It is unquestionably one of the most important tricks you need to master in order to be a Meeting Magician.

Why is involvement so important? Because ...

■ With few exceptions, the best solutions have input from a number of people who are informed and engaged in the task.

■ People tend to support solutions they help create.

■ Decisions and plans can be derailed if people who must implement them are not "brought up to speed" and involved.

Throughout the meeting process, there are several opportunities for building involvement:

Build involvement *before* the meeting. Fostering participation actually begins when you determine who will be invited. Time spent here can pay big dividends by ensuring that people who have a stake in the matter – or who know something about the issue – are brought into the discussion.

All too often, work done in meetings is wasted because someone wasn't invited. The damage can be caused simply by not having the right data from a key expert. More complex problems can be created by the absence of people with strongly held views and a big say in the decision process.

For the meeting leader, the best protection from these unforeseen land mines is to broaden the list of potential stakeholders and attendees at the outset, and then allow people to "opt out" at their discretion. Even if the people who choose not to participate have concerns about your meeting results, they'll likely be easier to deal with because they had the opportunity to be involved.

For invitees who are somewhat involved in the matter but don't believe they need to attend, a pre-meeting contact with the leader may provide a viable alternative. They can briefly discuss the matter, provide input, and offer support for the outcomes. This approach allows involvement without attendance.

Consider brief pre-meeting contacts with selected people to build involvement and head off potentially difficult situations. Are people coming to the session who you suspect won't agree to work toward your desired outcomes? Will people be attending who don't agree that there's a problem, or who have preconceived notions that may be counterproductive to meeting the goals? "Pre-sell" work with these individuals can be a wise investment of your time. If nothing else, you'll find out where they stand and be better prepared to address their issues at the meeting.

"Walk the talk" with *personal* preparation. Woody Allen once said: "Showing up is ninety percent of life." When it comes to meetings, some people take his comment way too literally. Sure, it's important to be there and to be there on time. But effective meetings require more than filled seats. Leaders and participants need to demonstrate their involvement by coming to the meeting prepared and ready to work. This means reading the background material, doing pre-work assignments (if any), and walking in with a positive, productive, "I'm here to contribute" attitude.

Build involvement *during* the meeting. Unless your purpose is merely to give information, participant involvement is critical … it's the reason you're meeting in the first place. Here are some Meeting Magic tips for encouraging involvement:

- Don't try to do it all yourself. Enlist participants as recorders, timekeepers, and facilitators in defined roles.
- Use a variety of techniques that require participation (e.g., brainstorming, breakout sessions, etc.).
- Use topical, tailored, and tasteful humor.
- Do periodic process checks ("Are we on track?") to create opportunities for participant feedback.
- Target interaction: Ask for input from specific people.
- Reward active participation with acknowledgments and simple "thank you" comments.
- Act swiftly on disruptors and dominators.

If you're a meeting participant rather than a leader, there are many ways to demonstrate your involvement and help the group along:

- Come prepared. Do all required pre-work and familiarize yourself with the agenda beforehand.
- Introduce yourself or say hello to the leader and other participants when you arrive.
- Volunteer to serve as recorder, timekeeper, etc.
- Pay attention, take notes, listen attentively, and ask questions that help clarify issues and build understanding.
- Provide nonverbal reinforcement to others' comments.
- Leave sarcasm and skepticism outside the meeting room.
- Help the leader deal with negative behaviors in others by calling for process checks and help draw out and reinforce the "quiet types."
- If problems emerge, don't join the "feeding frenzy."
- Don't waste time with off-track monologues.
- Contribute to the development of action plans to ensure that what's agreed to is feasible.

☑ **Continue building involvement *after* the meeting.** Moving from mere good ideas to *ACTION* requires follow-up work. Your goal is to maintain the involvement and commitment you achieved before and during the meeting.

■ *Send thank-you notes.* Even for less complex meetings, short thank you notes – handwritten or e-mailed – are very helpful in maintaining involvement. For maximum impact, they should go out within 24 hours of the session to people who helped prepare for the meeting as well as the participants.

Besides expressing your appreciation, you can use thank-you notes to summarize agreements and action plans, and to communicate results (via "cc") to those not in attendance. For example:

> To: Joe, Sally & Chris
> cc: Allison, Fred & Pat
>
> Thanks for taking the time yesterday to meet on the ACME sales presentation plan. Chris, your slide layouts are great! I look forward to our rehearsal, next Tuesday at 9:30 a.m., and the client meeting on Wednesday at 2 p.m.

For meetings involving more details, session notes or minutes can be attached to the thank you – along with any action plans that were developed.

■ *Do targeted follow-up as needed.* You'll definitely need to follow up with people who are <u>tentative</u> in their agreements and plans. Here are some typical agreement statements that signal the need for targeted follow-up:
- "I think we can do this by Friday, but I'll need to get Larry and Alice on-board."
- "I need to study this to determine if we can support your deadline of ten days."
- "I think I can pull this off, but I have lots of other demands right now. Mary may not want me to push this ahead of other priorities."

"Pay no attention to the man behind the curtain,"

said the Wizard of Oz when unexpectedly confronted by Dorothy and her friends.

The Meeting Magician often faces a similar challenge to respond quickly and creatively to unplanned turns of events. You can increase your effectiveness in handling these situations by:

- Being familiar with the audience and the topic
- Staying alert to emerging problems
- Remaining flexible enough to go with the flow
- Being willing to say "I don't know"
- Being honest in expressing your concern or discomfort
- Asking others to jump in
  and when all else fails
- Calling for a break (to allow yourself thinking time).

As you gain experience, you will develop skills in "on-the-fly" adaptation and be able to add coping strategies to your Magic act.

*There is real magic
in enthusiasm.
It spells the difference
between mediocrity
and accomplishment.*

–Norman Vincent Peale

Chapter Five
Clarity

Communicate clearly to help ensure success!

Clarity in communication is integral to the success of any meeting. Without it, the only things you'll be pulling out of your hat are misunderstanding, misinterpretation, and a lot of confusion.

This chapter is about bringing clarity to the meeting process. It's about ensuring that all participants are "on the same page" during the session and leave with a common understanding. And it all begins with clear thinking.

Clarify with questions. You can develop a habit of clear thought by reminding yourself to use the "news reporter questions": Who? What? When? Where? Why? How? These questions can be used in the planning phase and during the meeting itself.

Clarify language. Words don't always mean the same things to people from different backgrounds. Vocabulary can be a **BIG** problem for diverse and cross-functional groups. Here are some tips for building clarity in language:

- Use pictures, charts, and other visuals.
- Explain any unique terms or acronyms that you use and remind others to do the same.
- Provide a glossary of new or technical terms.
- Ask participants to paraphrase discussions.
- Encourage questions about unclear language.

☑ Clarify action items. Being specific about agreements and commitments reached during the meeting is another angle on the clarity issue. Do we *really* have agreement? Do people who signed up to do things know *when* they are to be done? Are there any doubts about *how* things are to be accomplished or *who* has the lead? In such areas, the best way to avoid fuzziness is simply to list agreements and action plans on a flip chart and ask the group for confirmation that the information is correct.

Leaders need to distribute the minutes or notes to all participants soon after the meeting concludes. Timely communication will reinforce the next steps to be taken and thereby increase the likelihood that you'll achieve the results you need.

Be sure you encourage folks to contact you with any post-meeting questions about agreements or action-plan components. And if you're a participant who's unclear on what needs to happen next, don't be bashful … contact the meeting leader for clarification.

☑ Build clarity through continuous improvement. A good meeting evaluation process, coupled with a continuous improvement mentality, can be a major contributor to clarity over the longer term. Understanding *why* people may have had trouble addressing past issues (e.g., lack of facts, confusing presentation, lack of a clear desired outcome, inefficient meeting process, etc.) can equip you to do better the next time.

Building lessons learned into the next show is a hallmark of top-notch Meeting Magicians. The reputations of business individuals, teams, and work groups are often driven by how well they perform in meetings. Is this a "can-do," well-organized outfit that learns from experience or a bunch of bureaucratic foot-draggers who are stuck in their ways?

The concept of Kaizen, or continuous improvement (striving to be better than you were yesterday in small but important ways), is one of the most important ideas in Meeting Magic.

The foundation of continuous improvement in meeting management is *actionable* evaluation information. As we mentioned earlier, most meetings should be evaluated by all participants from two viewpoints:

Results: the extent to which desired outcomes were achieved;
Process: the quality of actions that led to the results (participation, candor, timeliness, etc.).

The following is a brief run-down on how to process your evaluation information effectively so that clarity through continuous improvement is achieved and recognized:

■ *Review written evaluations as soon as possible.*
  ■ Do the participant comments match your perception of the meeting outcomes?
  ■ For things that went well, do you understand why they were viewed positively?
  ■ For things that did not go so well, do you understand what may have caused the problem(s)?
If clarification is needed on any of the above, re-contact participants while the meeting is fresh in their memory.

■ *Diagnose poor "results" ratings.* If you have low ratings on meeting results, here are some suggestions on how to diagnose the problem(s):
  ■ Examine your agenda and meeting process. Look for common problems such as insufficient time allocations for certain topics, lack of appropriate data or information, and missing stakeholders.
  ■ Reflect on your facilitation. Did a dominant voice inhibit the group from reaching the solutions needed?
  ■ Still not sure? Talk to others who attended and ask for help in determining what may have gone wrong.

■ *Diagnose poor "process" ratings.* If you have low ratings on meeting process, here are some ideas on how to assess the cause(s):

   ■ Check your time management for common problems such as failure to start and end on time, inadequate breaks, and digressions into irrelevant topics.

   ■ Check "environment" issues: Was the room too hot or cold? Were there negative comments about the refreshments? Were the chairs uncomfortable or was the A/C too noisy? Pay attention to all comments – even those that may seem trivial. As the old saying goes, "The mind can absorb no more than the seat can endure."

Lack of full participation and involvement can show up in low ratings for both results and process. You may believe you have a solid agreement but receive a low process or results rating from someone that suggests otherwise. If there are hints that domination or lack of participation were problems for some attendees, you need to investigate and adjust your facilitation approach accordingly.

   ■ *Make noticeable changes at the next meeting.*
   ■ Include a brief comment in your opening remarks on preparation or process changes you've incorporated.
   ■ Thank people for their candid comments on prior meeting evaluations.
   ■ Cite examples of how your meetings are improving based on participants' input and ask them to continue providing the valuable feedback that will make your meetings even better in the future.
   ■ Carefully review evaluations from the most recent meeting – checking to see if participants recognize the changes you've made.

**The basics of MEETING MAGIC
can be taught quickly, but ...**

... to get started, you'll probably need to overcome a certain amount of inertia (a.k.a., "the way we've always run meetings"). And, as with any change that's effectively implemented, you have to *want* to change ... get others to *want* to change, too.

So how do you do all that? How do you overcome inertia and strengthen your (and others') commitment to change? You begin by posing *the* initiating question:

> ## Am I consistently satisfied with the meetings we have here?

If your answer is "yes," you're truly fortunate, and the most we can hope for is that you get a couple of usable ideas from this book. However, if – like most people – your answer is "no" (or something stronger), you have more than enough reason to give these suggestions a try. What do you have to lose?

To move forward, you need to select a starting point, examine your own commitment to the work, and get others involved. If you're the "boss," you can gather critical mass faster by mandating a trial of the Meeting Magic techniques presented in this guide. And you'll increase receptivity by prefacing your activities with an explanation of the benefits to be gained by all ("What's in it for you!").

If you're not the boss, recruit others who share your frustration (over ineffective meetings that waste time and don't achieve desired results) to help demonstrate the benefits of good meetings and "spread the Magic." In other words, don't wait for others to take the lead.

If you've ever complained about poor meetings, do something to make them better!

In stage magic, David Copperfield doesn't use the <u>exact</u> same methods as Siegfried & Roy. Each has perfected their own special brand of magic. The situation is similar for meeting management: no single method is "the only right way."

The methods you use need to fit the mission and the constraints of your organization.

Nevertheless, it's important to select *one* framework as a starting point, and then experiment with others as you gain experience and skill. Start with the recommendations in this book, modify them to suit your needs, and then add your own tricks that play well with your unique audience. We realize that not every suggestion we offer will be right for every circumstance. But the general principles upon which our suggestions are based *are* right for EVERY organization!

Finally, remember that despite your best efforts, not all participants will immediately see the value and benefits of improved meetings. The administrative aspects of good meetings may appear unduly bureaucratic to some. Others may be threatened by the higher standards for discipline and preparation that are implied. Over time, however, usually even the strongest skeptics come around as they experience the Magic at work.

Be persistent!

It's *your* time … don't let it be wasted.

A wizard cannot do everything –
a fact most magicians are reticent to
admit, let alone discuss with prospective
clients.

Still, the fact remains that there are
certain objects, and people, that are, for
one reason or another, completely
immune to any direct magical spell.

It is for this group of beings that the
magician learns the subtleties of using
indirect spells. It also does no harm, in
dealing with these matters, to carry a
large club near your person at all times.

–The Teachings of Ebenezum, Volume VIII

Your Trick Bag
Meeting Magic Forms

Here are several forms to help make your meetings more efficient and effective. Reproduce and use them as needed, or make up your own versions.

1. Meeting Magic Summary Checklist

2. Decision Worksheet

3. Agenda Planner for Meetings

4. Meeting Announcement and Agenda

5. Meeting Agreements and Assignments

6. Meeting Evaluation

Enlarge and reproduce these forms on a photocopier or recreate them with modifications to fit your needs.

MEETING MAGIC Summary Checklist

M — Meet or Not?
Deciding that a meeting is (or isn't) the best tool for the job

- [ ] Best method?
- [ ] Work group can do?
- [ ] Cost effective?
- [ ] Attend or be represented?

A — Agenda
With the end in mind, prepare carefully and get what you want

- [ ] Desired outcomes?
- [ ] Who is needed?
- [ ] Time required?
- [ ] Materials required?
- [ ] Facilities and equipment?

G — Guidelines
Conducting the meeting with confidence

- [ ] Start on time
- [ ] Establish "ground rules"
- [ ] Work the agenda
- [ ] Document agreements
- [ ] Evaluate and close on time

I — Involvement
The most common reason for meeting

- [ ] Make pre-meeting contacts
- [ ] Build involvement during the meeting
- [ ] Build a team that's "in on the tricks"

C — Clarity
Communication throughout leads to success

- [ ] Build clarity through questions
- [ ] Establish a common language
- [ ] Clarify required actions through timed work plans
- [ ] Use written evaluations to continuously improve

DECISION WORKSHEET

Meeting Subject:	
Overall Objective(s):	
Desired Outcomes:	
Key Stakeholders:	
Key Information:	
Timing:	
Nature of Work:	

COSTS

Salaries: (preparation and meeting time X people X average salary or daily fee)	
Opportunity Costs: (lost sales, lost production, etc.)	
Facilities and Food Service:	
Travel and Lodging:	
TOTAL COST:	

Decide and Act:

☐ YES, Plan Meeting   ☐ NO, Don't Meet

AGENDA PLANNER FOR MEETINGS

Meeting Subject:	
Overall Objective(s):	
Desired Outcomes:	
Key Stakeholders:	
Key Meeting Participants:	
Key Information:	
Timing:	

#	WHAT Desired Outcomes	WHO Discussion Leader	TIME Allocation per segment	HOW Process to address segment

PRE-WORK AND INFORMATION REQUIRED

What	Who	When	Assigned

EQUIPMENT AND MATERIALS REQUIRED

What	Who	When	Done

DOCUMENTATION PLAN

Recorder/Scribe:	Type of Documentation:

Facilities and Layout:

MEETING ANNOUNCEMENT and AGENDA

Subject:_____

_____

Called by:_____
Phone:_____

Questions to:_____
Phone:_____

Day:_____
Date:_____
Time:_____
Duration:_____
Location:_____

DESIRED OUTCOMES:	

1. _____

2. _____

3. _____

Facilitator:

_____

Recorder:

_____

Timekeeper:

_____

Participants:

Pre-Work:

Order of Agenda

WHAT	TIME	WHO	HOW

MEETING AGREEMENTS and ASSIGNMENTS

AGREEMENTS

1.

2.

3.

4.

5.

	ASSIGNMENTS	Lead Person	Timing
1.			
2.			
3.			
4.			
5.			
6.			
7.			

Meeting Evaluation

Meeting Name (Subject):_____

Meeting Date:_____

Things That WENT WELL:	Opportunities TO IMPROVE:

RESULTS Rating (circle one)	5 4 3 2 1 great okay poor
PROCESS Rating (circle one)	5 4 3 2 1 great okay poor

Comments:

The Authors

Tony Jeary

As the founder and CEO of **High Performance Resources, Inc.**, Tony has personally coached corporate leaders wishing to improve their speaking, meeting management, and presentation skills. His expertise has been sought out by the CEOs and top executives of such corporations as American Airlines, Ford Motor Company, New York Life, Shell Oil, Texaco, and Wal-Mart.

His reputation as a premier speaking coach – along with his nine popular books on the subject – have earned him the title of Mr. Presentation™. His signature book, *Inspire Any Audience*, has been hailed as "the ultimate presenter's guide" by Zig Ziglar. Now in its sixth printing, it continues to be one of the best-selling books on public speaking worldwide.

George Lowe

George Lowe has spent thirty-plus years in the automotive business with one of the big three manufacturers, holding leadership positions in the U.S. and Mexico. He has led global organizations and numerous cross-functional teams and now has an independent consulting practice.

His expertise in meeting management processes is founded on years of study and real-world experience in leading and participating in thousands of meetings. The concepts contained in this book have been validated in a wide array of work settings in both technical and non-technical functions, and from the perspective of both the meeting leader and the participant.

The Publisher

Since 1977, **The WALK THE TALK Company's** clear mission has been to help individuals and organizations achieve success through ethical leadership and values-based business practices. To learn more about our other high-impact publications, training resources, keynote presentations, and consulting and training services, call **1.888.822.9255** or visit **www.walkthetalk.com**.

Other WALK THE TALK® Resources

Walk The Talk...And Get The Results You Want – $12.95
Bring values to life in your organization and shape a positive business environment.

Monday Morning Leadership – $14.95
Offers unique encouragement and direction that will help you become a better manager, employee, and person.

The Leadership Secrets of Santa Claus™ – $14.95
Help all your leaders accomplish "big things" by giving them clear goals, solid accountabilities, ongoing feedback, coaching, and recognition in your "workshop."

180 Ways To Walk The Recognition Talk – $9.95
The proven techniques and practical strategies found in this book will get EVERYONE in your organization walking the recognition talk.

175 Ways to Get More Done in Less Time — $9.95
This handbook is packed with 175 tips to help you get things done faster so you can accomplish more of your long-term goals.

136 Effective Presentation Tips — $9.95
This is a powerful handbook providing 136 practical, easy-to-use tips to make every presentation a success!

144 Ways To Walk The Talk – $9.95
Quick reference handbook packed with 144 techniques and strategies to help you build a positive work environment.

Walking The Talk Together – $9.95
Focusing on shared responsibility, this easy-read handbook encourages employees to be accountable for values-driven business practices.

180 Ways To Build A Magnetic Culture — $9.95
How-to handbook packed with tactical and practical techniques to "magnetize" the best, brightest, and most productive people to you and your organization.

180 Ways To Walk The Customer Service Talk — $9.95
Packed with 180 proven strategies and tips, this unique guide will help employees at all levels deliver the best customer service possible.

Call us today!
1.888.822.9255

Please send me extra copies of: *The Secrets of Meeting Magic Revealed*

1-99 copies $9.95 each   100-499 copies $8.95 each   500+ copies please call

The Secrets of Meeting Magic Revealed	_____ copies X	_____	=$_____

Other Resources

Walk The Talk...And Get The Results You Want	_____ copies X	$ 12.95	=$_____
Monday Morning Leadership	_____ copies X	$ 14.95	=$_____
The Leadership Secrets of Santa Claus™	_____ copies X	$ 14.95	=$_____
180 Ways To Walk The Recognition Talk	_____ copies X	$ 9.95	=$_____
175 Ways To Get More Done In Less Time	_____ copies X	$ 9.95	=$_____
136 Effective Presentation Tips	_____ copies X	$ 9.95	=$_____
144 Ways To Walk The Talk	_____ copies X	$ 9.95	=$_____
Walking The Talk Together	_____ copies X	$ 9.95	=$_____
180 Ways to Build a Magnetic Culture	_____ copies X	$ 9.95	=$_____
180 Ways to Walk the Customer Service Talk	_____ copies X	$ 9.95	=$_____

Product Total	$_____
*Shipping & Handling	$_____
Subtotal	$_____

(Sales & Use Tax Collected on TX & CA Customers Only)

Sales Tax:

Texas Sales Tax – 8.25%	$_____
CA Sales & Use Tax	$_____
Total (U.S. Dollars Only)	$_____

*Shipping and Handling Charges

No. of Items	1-4	5-9	10-24	25-49	50-99	100-199	200+
Total Shipping	$6.75	$10.95	$17.95	$26.95	$48.95	$84.95	$89.95+$0.25/book

Call 972.243.8863 for quote if outside continental U.S. Orders are shipped ground delivery 7-10 days. Next and 2nd business day delivery available – call 888.822.9255

Name_____ Title_____

Organization_____

Shipping Address_____

City_____ (No PO Boxes) State_____ Zip _____

Phone_____ Fax_____

E-Mail_____

Charge Your Order: ❑ MasterCard   ❑ Visa   ❑ American Express

Credit Card Number_____Exp. Date_____

❑ Check Enclosed (Payable to The WALK THE TALK Company)

❑ Please Invoice (**Orders over $250 ONLY**)   P.O. Number (required)_____

Accts. Payable Contact_____ Phone_____

PHONE	FAX	MAIL
1.888.822.9255 or 972.243.8863 M–F, 8:30-5:00 Cen.	**972.243.0815** **ON-LINE** www.walkthetalk.com	WALK THE TALK Co. 2925 LBJ Fwy., #201 Dallas, TX 75234

Prices effective November 2005 are subject to change.

BED & BREAKFAST

...Vacation or a romantic getaway... La Petite Auberge Les Bons Matins!

Your host, Harold Côté

www.bonsmatins.com

STE-CATHERINE

RENÉ-LÉVESQUE

GUY

ARGYLE

CRESCENT

B&B

Centre Bell

METRO
Lucien L'Allier

ST-ANTOINE

Interac
PAIEMENT DIRECT

VISA

MasterCard

Diner's Club
enRoute

AMERICAN EXPRESS

1393, Argyle ave. Montréal (Québec) H3G 1V5

Tel.: (514) 931-9167   Fax : (514) 931-1621

Welcome to the North Coast of Québec
At 15 minutes distance from Tadoussac

4 seasons
Location activities
Duration : 2 to 3 hours
Spring, Summer, Fall

- Whale watching cruise
- Quad excursions in the mountains
- Canoeing on lakes or rivers
- Sea kayaking on the Fjord du Saguenay
- Fishing (trout, salmon)
- Hiking trails and mountain biking
- Nature observation (black bear and beaver)
- Contact with the wolves
- Museums

Winter

- Snowmobiling or dog sledding (a possibility for long journeys)
- Sleep in igloos with cariboo skins
- Ice fishing
- Slides
- Sugar shack, toffee on the snow and traditions
- Snowshoeing and cross country skiing trails along the Saguenay

Special Packages — Ferme 5 étoiles

1. Discovery of nature
(2 days – 1 night)
Included : one location activity at your choice, depending on the season :

- The gratuities of the Ferme 5-Étoiles
- One night lodging
- One wholesome breakfast
- One home-cooked supper

84$ /pers./at the farm
94$ /pers./in cottage

2. Nature Exploration :
(3 days – 2 nights)
Included : two location activities at your choice depending on the season :

- The gratuities of the Ferme 5-Étoiles
- Two nights lodging
- Two wholesome breakfasts
- Two home-cooked suppers

99$ /pers./at the farm
169$ /pers./in cottage

Free for our customers :
Guided visit of the farm and of the sugar shack, care of the animals with the kids' participation, hiking trails, swimming pool, tennis, playground, campfire, BBQ

Children below 12 years old accompanied by parents :
20% discount on adults' tarification for double occupancy (taxes not included).

Group tarification (11 persons and more)

Informations – Reservations

Tél : (418) 236-4833 *toll free : 1-877-236-4551
*Fax. : (418) 236-4551
Ferme 5 étoiles. 465 rte 172 north, Sacré-Coeur (Qc) G0T 1Y0
Web site: www.ferme5etoiles.com E-mail: info@ferme5etoiles.com

For me, it's all right here in

Québec

Bonjour Québec.com

- The most extensive bank of tourist information on Québec
- Secure and confidential reservations
- More than 700 accommodation establishments
- More than 250 packages means there's something for everyone

Information and reservations:
www.bonjourquebec.com
1 877 BONJOUR (1 877 266-5687)

Gift certificate

Photograph taken at the Auberge l'Air du Temps, Chambly, Montérégie (Photo : Sandra Fabris) Concept/Spin design

Inns and Bed & Breakfasts

For a gift that's sure to please,
offer a delightful getaway...

ACCREDITED BY
AGRICOTOURS
QUALITY ❖ COMFORT

GÎTES ET AUBERGES DU PASSANT™MC

Marque déposée par
Fédération des Agricotours du Québec

Information: 1-877-869-9728

Inns and Bed & Breakfasts in Québec 2003

This guide offers the largest quality network of Bed & Breakfasts and Country Inns in Québec

It features a selection of rented homes as well as various agrotourism activities.

This guide is divided into two large sections:

I. Agrotourism
(included: Country-Style Dining, Farm Shops, Farm Explorations, Farm Stays and Country Home at the Farm)

II. Bed & Breakfasts and Country Inns
(including Country and City Homes)

Find out who won the Prizes for Excellence on the following pages!

Project Coordinators
Odette Chaput
Director General
(Fédération des Agricotours
du Québec)
André Duchesne
(Ulysses Travel Guides)

Page Layout
Alain Berthiaume

Computer Graphics
André Duchesne

Collaboration
Odile Bélanger
Diane Drapeau
Andrée Lyne Allaire
Annie Dupriez
Diane Lamoureux

Cartography
Isabelle Lalonde

Illustrations
Marie-Annick Viatour
Lorette Pierson
Myriam Gagné

Illustrations (Cont'd)
Émilie Desmarais
Vincent Desruisseaux

Photography
Cover:
Sandra Fabris
Establishment:
Auberge l'Air du Temps
Chambly, Montérégie

Canadian Cataloguing in Publication Data

Main entry under title:
    Inns and bed & breakfasts in Quebec
    (Ulysses Travel Guide)
    Translation of : Gîtes et auberges du passant au Québec
    ISSN 1701-7610
    ISBN 2-89464-632-1

1. Bed and breakfast accommodations - Quebec (Province) - Directories. 2. Farms - Recreational use - Quebec (Province) - Directories. I. Fédération des Agricotours du Québec II. Series.
TX907.5.C22Q8   647.94714'03   C2002-390008-3

DISTRIBUTORS

CANADA: ULYSSES TRAVEL GUIDES, 4176 ST. DENIS STREET, MONTRÉAL, QUÉBEC,
H2W 2M5, ☎(514) 843-9882, EXT.2232, 800-748-9171, FAX: 514-843-9448, INFO@ULYSSES.CA,
WWW.ULYSSESGUIDES.COM

GREAT BRITAIN AND IRELAND: World Leisure Marketing, Unit 11, Newmarket Court, Newmartket
Drive, Derby DE24 8NW, ☎1 332 57 37 37,
Fax: 1 332 57 33 99, office@wlmsales.co.uk

SCANDINAVIA: Scanvik, Esplanaden 8B, 1263 Copenhagen K, DK,
☎(45) 33.12.77.66, Fax: (45) 33.91.28.82

SWITZERLAND: OLF, P.O. Box 1061, CH-1701 Fribourg, ☎(026) 467.51.11,
Fax: (026) 467.54.66

U.S.A.: BHB Distribution (a division of Weatherhill), 41 Monroe Turnpike, Trumbull, CT 06611,
☎1-800-437-7840 or (203) 459-5090, Fax: 1-800-557-5601 or (203) 459-5095

OTHER COUNTRIES: Contact Ulysses Travel Guides, 4176 St. Denis Street, Montréal, Québec,
H2W 2M5, ☎(514) 843-9882, ext.2232, 800-748-9171,
Fax: 514-843-9448, info@ulysses.ca, www.ulyssesguides.com

For information on the Fédération des Agricotours network:

Fédération des Agricotours du Québec
4545, av. Pierre-de-Coubertin, C.P. 1000, Succursale M.
Montréal (Québec) H1V 3R2
(514) 252-3138
Fax: (514) 252-3173
Internet: http://www.agricotours.qc.ca
http://www.giteetaubergedupassant.com
E-mail: info@agricotours.qc.ca

© April 2003, Ulysses Travel Guides.
All rights reserved
Printed in Canada
ISBN 2-89464-632-1

TABLE OF CONTENTS

INTRODUCTION   3

SEVEN ACTIVITY AND HOLIDAY PACKAGES   4

PRACTICAL INFORMATION   5

"HÉBERGEMENT QUÉBEC" CLASSIFICATION   7

HOW TO USE THIS GUIDE   8

TABLE OF SYMBOLS   9

PRIZES FOR EXCELLENCE 2002   10

NEW ESTABLISHMENTS   12

VISIT OUR WEB SITE   14

SECTION I: AGROTOURISM   15

    ❑ Country-Style Dining 16
    ❑ Farm Shops 33
    ❑ Farm Explorations 50
    ❑ Farm Stays and Country Homes at the Farm 64

SECTION II : BED & BREAKFASTS AND COUNTRY INNS
(Including Country and City Homes)   75

    ❑ Abitibi-Témiscamingue 76
    ❑ Bas-Saint-Laurent 79
    ❑ Eastern Townships (Cantons-de-l'Est)................................. 92
    ❑ Centre-du-Québec 109
    ❑ Charlevoix 113
    ❑ Chaudière-Appalaches 127
    ❑ Côte-Nord... 136
    ❑ Gaspésie 144
    ❑ Île-de-la-Madeleine 160
    ❑ Lanaudière 162
    ❑ Laurentides 167
    ❑ Laval... 184
    ❑ Mauricie 187
    ❑ Montérégie 198
    ❑ Montréal Region 207
    ❑ Outaouais... 220
    ❑ Quebec City Region 227
    ❑ Saguenay-Lac-Saint-Jean.. 256

INDEX

    ❑ By name of establishment.. 269
    ❑ Location 277
    ❑ By tourist region... 282

EVALUATION FORMS   297

28 years of hospitality
1975 – 2003

For 28 years, the host members of the
Fédération des Agricotours du Québec have been
committed to offering you genuine, high-quality choices
for accommodation and agricultural tourism.

This has made Agricotours the largest
high-quality network in Quebec, and
your confidence has helped in its success.

For this reason, our network host members
hope that they may, with their traditional
warm welcome, continue to help you discover
the best of Quebec for many more years to come.

You'll always feel welcome in the Agricotours network.

The Fédération des Agricotours
du Québec

www.inns-bb.com
www.agricotours.qc.ca

INTRODUCTION

INNS AND BED & BREAKFASTS IN QUÉBEC 2002

For 28 years, the Fédération des Agricotours du Québec has been proud to offer travellers its selection of bed and breakfasts and country inns in Québec.

Moreover, it invites you to enjoy various agro-tourism activities offered by local farmers, making your trip all the more enjoyable. Last but not least, those seeking a self-catering stay will be happy to choose from among its rental city and country homes. *Inns and Bed & Breakfasts in Québec 2003*, divided into two large sections, features 612 quality properties.

Section I: Agrotourism

For fun, dining or staying at a farm, discover our:

24 Country-Style Dining (Tables Champêtres™)*
26 Farm Shops (Relais du Terroir™)*
19 Farm Explorations
30 Country Home on a Farm

Section II: Bed and Breakfasts and Country Inns*

For authentic accommodations, choose among our:

363 Bed and Breakfasts (Gîtes du Passant™)*
80 Country Inns (Auberges du Passant™)*
70 Country and City Homes

For a definition of these categories, refer to the following page.

Inns and Bed & Breakfasts in Québec is the perfect way to discover the best of Québec. This guide is a very useful tool, comprising practical information, reservation advice, tourist maps, colour photos and useful information about each establishment (illustration, price, directions, details about rooms, bathrooms, menus, activities, etc.).

*Mark of certification and trademark registered by the Fédération des Agricotours du Québec. Only members may use this designation.

ANNUAL REVISION OF THE GUIDE

Though the guide is revised every year, all information contained herein is subject to change without notice (i.e. increase in taxes). However, the prices listed are valid throughout 2003.

GIFT CERTIFICATES

Would you like to offer someone special a stay in a B&B or a Country Inn? For more information: 1-877-869-9728 (see ad at end of guide).

QUALITY CONTROL

A guarantee of quality for an enjoyable experience!

All owners wishing to have their establishment featured in this guide must submit a request for accreditation to the Fédération des Agricotours du Québec. Once their request is granted, they must agree to respect a code of ethics, as well as hospitality, accommodation and food-service standards of quality. To ensure consistent quality, each establishment is inspected every two years and an ethics committee reviews guests' comments. Moreover, every establishment prominently displays a sign and certificate confirming that it has been accredited by Agricotours and consistently meets its standards of quality.

EVALUATION FORMS

Do not hesitate to complete an evaluation form at the end of the book, and available in guest rooms (or dining rooms in Country-style Dining establishments), to let us know how you enjoyed your Agricotours experience. We need your feedback, suggestions and criticism to continue to improve the quality of the network and the services provided.

AWARD OF EXCELLENCE

Each year, the Fédération honours its members with two different categories of awards. You will find a list of the 2002 prize winners on the following pages.

- The "Special Favorite" category: awarded to member-hosts who have distinguished themselves for their consistent hospitality.

- The "Success" category: awarded to member-hosts who have distinguished themselves in their efforts to develop, promote and offer quality service.

WIN A STAY

By filling out and sending in your evaluation form, you get the chance to win a two-night stay for two people in one of our member-establishments.

SEVEN ACTIVITY AND HOLIDAY PACKAGES

SEVEN ACTIVITY AND HOLIDAY PACKAGES

BED AND BREAKFASTS

Bed and breakfast in a private residence in the country, on a farm, in the suburbs or in the city. Bed and Breakfasts (B&Bs) offer up to five rooms per residence. Whether for a long or short stay, choose one of our featured bed and breakfasts; so many B&Bs, so many ways to be welcomed and to discover Québec and its people.

COUNTRY INNS

Bed and breakfast in a small, quintessential country inn with cachet. These establishments offer up to 20 rooms, and most also provide additional meals in the dining room. Although country inns accommodate more people than do B&Bs, they always offer guests attentive service and a personalized welcome.

COUNTRY AND CITY HOMES

House, cottage, apartment or studio fully equipped for a self-catering stay in the city, in the country or on a farm. These country and city homes cater to your every need, ensuring a pleasant stay. Some country homes offer a program of farm-related activities. Bedding and bath towels are provided. Monthly, weekly, weekend and daily rates available.

FARM STAY

Bed and breakfast in a farmer's private home. Farm-related activities are offered and vary according to the type of farm and the animals raised there. Choose one of our farm stays to enjoy a unique experience on a farm while sharing in the passion of farmers for this way of life.

NOTE: If a bed and breakfast or a country inn does not offer a private bathroom, the following criteria apply:

- 1 shared bathroom for up to 6 people
- 1 shared bathroom and 1 shower room for 7 to 9 people
- 2 shared bathrooms for 10 to 12 people
- etc...

COUNTRY-STYLE DINING

Food service whose menus mainly feature farm products. Meals are served in the intimacy of a farmhouse dining room or tastefully and authentically decorated outbuilding. The hosts of country-style dining establishments invite you to sample their delicious farm products and to share in their passion by taking part in a guided farm tour.

FARM SHOPS

Sales of traditional farm and regional goods, providing an introduction to the various production and processing methods that go into making these products, by means of a narrated farm tour. Farm shops thus offer visitors a taste of local products and typical Quebec fare.

FARM EXPLORATIONS

Different recreational and educational activities are offered by farmers to promote farm life. Farm Excursions fall under the following categories:

Interpretive Centre: activities program centred on the making of farm products or food processing.

Farm Outing: walking, horseback-riding or motor-vehicle tour exploring farm production and the environment.

Hunting and Fishing: hunting in an enclosed area or fishing in a pond or lake.

Teaching Farm: guided or self-guided farm tour, or custom-made training program for school groups.

Garden Tour: guided or self-guided tour.

PRACTICAL INFORMATION

BED AND BREAKFASTS, COUNTRY INNS AND COUNTRY AND CITY HOMES

☐ **Reservations:**

It is always advisable to reserve in advance to be sure of getting the type and size of accommodation desired, especially during peak season (July and August). For reservations, contact the establishment directly, either by mail, by telephone or by e-mail. Since each place is different, it is usually a good idea to confirm details with your hosts: the type of room, the number of beds per room, the size of beds, what restaurant facilities are nearby, your time of arrival, the precise time until which your room will be held in case of delay. Also, if you have any special requirements (for example, if you are allergic to pets), it is strongly recommended you advise your hosts before making a reservation.

☐ **Methods of payment:**

Payment is usually made with travellers cheques or cash. Establishments that accept credit cards or debit cards (Interac) display the following pictograms: **VS, MC, AM, ER, IT.**

☐ **Taxes:**

As per federal and provincial laws, customers may have to pay the federal Goods and Services tax (7%) and the provincial tax (7.5%). Deposits are also subject to these taxes.

According to provincial law, some tourist regions (Montréal, Laval, Québec City, Charlevoix, Outaouais and Saguenay-Lac-Saint-Jean) must charge an additional tax of $2 per night for each unit rented. This tax goes toward a partnership fund that is used to promote the regions' tourist attractions.

☐ **Deposit and cancellation:**

For Bed and Breakfasts and Country Inns: it is important to get precise details about an establishment's deposit and cancellation policies. Should the establishment not have specific deposit and cancellation policies, those of the Fédération des Agricotours du Québec may apply, namely: a maximum deposit of 40% ($20 minimum) to confirm a reservation. In the case of a cancellation, the specified fee received as a deposit will be retained by the establishment for damages according to the following rules:

8 to 15 days' notice: 50% of deposit is retained.

7 days or less: entire deposit is retained.

If your stay must be cut short, 40% of the cost of the unused portion of your stay may be retained. It is therefore advisable to postpone rather than cancel your reservation to avoid losing your deposit.

For Country and City Homes: check with the owners of country homes for their individual deposit and cancellation policies.

SMOKING POLICY

Since December 17, 1999, the tobacco law obliges establishments that permit smoking to set aside smoking sections. Moreover, several establishments prohibit smoking in their guest rooms.

FOR EUROPEAN CUSTOMERS

There are several ways to book your stay in advance: contact the establishment directly, consult a travel agency that offers packages including stays in bed and breakfasts or country inns accredited by the Fédération des Agricotours du Québec, visit our Web site (**www.inns-bb.com**) or contact Hospitality Canada or Tourisme Chez l'Habitant in France.

☐ **Hospitality Canada**

For a stay of **2 nights or more**, you can reserve through the Hospitality Canada network, at no charge from France, Belgium or Switzerland, by calling ☎0-800-90-3355. From North America, call 1-800-665-1528.

Reservations can also be made upon arrival by telephone or by visiting the network's offices, located in **Montréal** and **Québec** tourist information centres:

Tel: (514) 287-9049
Fax: (514) 287-1220
Internet: www.hospitality-canada.com
E-mail: hosp.can@iq.ca

In person:
Centre Infotouriste
1001 Square Dorchester
Montréal
(corner Ste-Catherine & Peel)

Maison du Tourisme
12, rue Sainte-Anne
Vieux-Québec
(opposite the Château Frontenac)

☐ **Tourisme Chez l'Habitant**

Reservations can be made by mail or by telephone with a credit card. All arrangements and payments are made in advance, allowing you to take immediate occupation. An additional charge is added to the price for all reservation services. Information is sent free of charge.

Tourisme Chez l'Habitant
15 rue des Pas Perdus, B.P. 8338
95 804 - Cergy St-Christophe Cedex
Tel: 01 34.25.44.44,
Fax: 01 34.25.44.45
Internet: www.tch-voyage.fr
E-mail: informations@tch-voyage.fr

6.

COUNTRY-STYLE DINING

☐ **Menus:**

The menus featured in this guide merely provide examples of the types of meals served. In addition to the standard menu, member-hosts may also offer diners a variety of other, variously priced dishes, always prepared with farm- fresh products.

You can bring your own wine in most of the establishments, but this policy should be verified when making your reservations.

At the request of member-hosts, the menus have been left in their original French to preserve their authenticity.

☐ **Number of people:**

The number of people admitted during the week and on weekends is provided for each establishment. The minimum may vary according to the season. Note that some hosts can accommodate more than one group at a time. In such cases, depending on the minimum number of people stipulated by the owners, it is possible to reserve the whole establishment for your group.

☐ **Rates:**

Prices vary according to the menu chosen and do not include service charges.

☐ **Reservations, deposit and cancellation:**

Reservations must be made directly through member-hosts, preferably several weeks in advance. A maximum deposit of 50% of the total price may be required to confirm a reservation.

If you cannot honour your reservation, note that some establishments have flexible cancellation policies. It is a good idea to get these policies in writing. However, if there is no written agreement, policy stipulates that if a cancellation is made within 30 days of the reservation date, the entire deposit is retained. It is therefore advisable to postpone rather than cancel your reservation to avoid losing your deposit.

FARM SHOPS

☐ **Operating Hours and Seasons:**

It is important to take note of operating hours and seasons.

☐ **Methods of payment:**

Establishments that accept credit cards and debit cards (Interac) display the following pictograms: **VS, MC, AM, ER, IT.**

FARM EXPLORATIONS

☐ **Reservations, deposit and cancellation:**

Reservations are made directly through each of the farms. A 40% deposit ($20 minimum) may be required to confirm a reservation.

If you cannot honour your reservation, note that some establishments have flexible cancellation policies. It is a good idea to get these policies in writing. However, if there is no written agreement, the specified fee received as a deposit will be retained by the member-host for damages according to the following criteria:

8 to 15 days notice: 50% of the deposit will be retained ($20 minimum);

Within 7 days of the reservation date: the entire deposit will be retained.

It is therefore advisable to postpone rather than cancel your reservation to avoid losing your deposit.

ACCREDITED BY AGRICOTOURS

All bed and breakfasts and country inns in this guide have been accredited by the Fédération des Agricotours du Québec. This accreditation is the most important thing to look for, as it ensures that each establishment conforms to high standards of quality relating to hospitality, meals and facilities. Moreover, every owner undertakes to respect a code of ethics.

In order to avoid confusion, we have included the following clarification with regard to certain establishments that do not post a grading result. There are two reasons for which no result may be posted:

- the establishment has opted not to post its grading result
- the establishment has not been graded yet: ❧

CLASSIFICATION «HÉBERGEMENTS QUÉBEC»

CLASSIFICATION LEGEND	
BED AND BREAKFAST	
❀	B&B offering basic comfort
❀❀	Comfortable, quality B&B
❀❀❀	Very comfortable, good-quality B&B
❀❀❀❀	Quality B&B offering superior comfort
❀❀❀❀❀	Comfortable, refined and luxurious B&B of exceptional quality
COUNTRY INNS	
★	Establishment offering basic comfort whose facilities and services conform to quality standards
★★	Comfortable establishment with good-quality facilities, as well as some services and amenities
★★★	Very comfortable establishment with excellent facilities, as well as many services and amenities
★★★★	Establishment offering the highest level of comfort, with top-notch facilities and a wide range of services and amenities
★★★★★	Exceptional establishment in terms of comfort, facilities and the many amenities and exemplary services offered
COUNTRY AND CITY HOMES	
★	Tourism home with accommodations that meet minimum classification standards.
★★	Tourism home with accommodations and services that provide basic comfort and meet quality standards.
★★★	Tourism home with accommodations and some services and features that provide a good level of comfort and quality.
★★★★	Tourism home with accommodations and several services and features that provide a very good level of comfort and quality.
★★★★★	Tourism home with accommodations and a wide range of services and features that provide a superior level of quality.

The various grading schemes are administered and applied by the Corporation de l'Industrie Touristique du Québec. For all comments, call 1-866-499-0550.

HOW TO USE THIS GUIDE

For BED AND BREAKFASTS or INNS

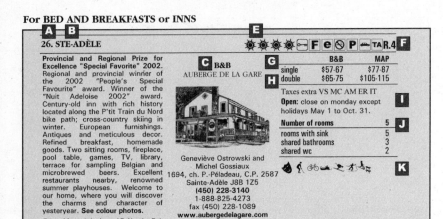

A **B** **E**

26. STE-ADÈLE ☀☀☀☀ ⊡ F e ⊘ P ⟵ TA R.4 **F**

Provincial and Regional Prize for Excellence "Special Favorite" 2002. Regional and provincial winner of the 2002 "People's Special Favourite" award. Winner of the "Nuit Adeloise 2002" award. Century-old inn with rich history located along the P'tit Train du Nord bike path; cross-country skiing in winter. European furnishings. Antiques and meticulous decor. Refined breakfast, homemade goods. Two sitting rooms, fireplace, pool table, games, TV, library, terrace for sampling Belgian and microbrewed beers. Excellent restaurants nearby, renowned summer playhouses. Welcome to our home, where you will discover the charms and character of yesteryear. **See colour photos.**

From Montréal, Aut. 15 North, Exit 69, 370 East 4km.

C B&B
AUBERGE DE LA GARE

Geneviève Ostrowski and Michel Gossiaux
1694, ch. P.-Péladeau, C.P. 2587
Sainte-Adèle J8B 1Z5
(450) 228-3140
1-888-825-4273
fax (450) 228-1089
www.aubergedelagare.com
gossiauxm@qc.aira.com

G
	B&B	MAP
single	$57-67	$77-87
double	$65-75	$105-115
H

Taxes extra VS MC AM ER IT
Open: close on monday except holidays May 1 to Oct. 31. **I**

Number of rooms	5	**J**
rooms with sink	5	
shared bathrooms	3	
shared wc	2	

K

For COUNTRY or CITY HOMES

D

44. WOTTON ★★★ F P R5 M4

Cosy cottage with old-fashioned charm and magnificent view of the lakes. Activities include pedal-boats, canoeing, snowmobiling, hiking through forests and fields. Cross-country skiing, snowshoeing, golf and swimming close by. 4km from Asbestos.

From Montréal, Aut. 20 East, Exit 147. Rte 116 East twd Danville, Rte 255 South twd Wotton. 4km after crossing Rte 249, left on Route des Lacs, 2km.

COUNTRY HOME
LA MAISON DES LACS

Monique Mercier
28, chemin des Lacs
Wotton J0A 1N0
(819) 346-3575
(819) 573-9478
www.tourisme-cantons.qc.ca/maisondeslacs

No. houses	1
No. rooms	5
No. people	10
WEEK-SUMMER	$600
WEEK-WINTER	$600
W/E-SUMMER	$300
W/E-WINTER	$300
Open year round	

L

Legend

A. Number corresponding to the one on the regional map

B. Localization of house

C. Type of service offered

D. Hotel classification

E. Classification of Bed and Breakfasts

F. See table of symbols on next page.

G. Rate table *(see below)*

H. Information about additional taxes and accepted methods of payment

I. Dates open and reduced rate period

J. Room and bathroom information

K. Nearby activities, see next page

L. House information and table of rates

G. Rate Table These rates are set according to the number of people occupying the same room. The two-person rate thereby applies to double occupancy.	**B&B** Bed and Breakfast **MAP** Modified American Plan: breakfast and supper	***Child** 12 years and younger staying in parents' room *When two prices are given, they refer to the comfort level of the room and not to high and low seasons.*

TABLE OF SYMBOLS

Services

Secure reservation service through the Internet www.bonjourquebec.com

Bed and Breakfast classification (see p 9)

Country Inn classification (see p 9)

NC Non-classified establishment

F French spoken fluently

f Some French spoken

E English spoken fluently (55% of establishments)

e Some English spoken

Guest are requested to refrain from smoking

Assisted wheelchair access

Wheelchair access

Sign language

P Private parking

Pick-up from public transportation with or without additional charge

Pets on premises

Swimming on site

Restaurant on site

R3 Distance (km) from nearest restaurant

M3 Distance (km) from nearest grocery store

AV Establishment that works with travel agencies and accepts B&B and Country Inn gift-certificates

Method of Payment

VS Visa

MC MasterCard

AM American Express

ER En Route

IT Interac payment

Activities

Art gallery, museum

Summer theatre

Cruise

Swimming

Golf

Hiking

Kayaking

Whale-watching

Wildlife-watching

Fishing

Skating

Bike path

Horseback riding

Snowmobiling

Downhill skiing

Cross-country skiing

Dog sledding

Farms Exploration Categories

Teaching Farm

Farm Outing

Garden Tour

Hunting and Fishing

Interpretive Centre

Prizes for Excellence 2002

« People's Special Favorite »
Category

« Congratulations to these hosts and hostesses for the remarkable welcome and service they have consistently offered their guests. »

Accommodation Sector
The Provincial Grand Prize-Winner is

Auberge de la Gare
Geneviève Ostrowski et Michel Gossiaux
Sainte-Adèle, LAURENTIDES
(Bed & Breakfast)

Country-Style Dining Sector
The Provincial Prize-Winner is

Domaine de la Templerie
Roland Guillon et son fils François
Huntingdon, Godmanchester
MONTÉRÉGIE

Accommodation Sector
The Regional Prize-Winners are

BAS-ST-LAURENT :
La Maison au Toit Bleu
Daria Dumont, Saint-Alexandre-de-Kamouraska

CANTONS-DE-L'EST :
Au Virage
Louise Vachon et Jean Barbès, Magog

CHARLEVOIX :
L'Eider Matinal,
Annie-Christine Laliberté et Stéphane L'Écuyer,
Saint-Irénée
**Finalist for the Provincial Grand Prize
« People's Special Favorite »

CHAUDIÈRE-APPALACHES :
Auberge de la Visitation,
Ginette L'Heureux et Martin Bergeron, Lévis

CÔTE-NORD :
La Maison Fleurie,
Germina et Thérèse Fournier
Sainte-Anne-de-Portneuf

GASPÉSIE :
Le Panorama,
Marie-Jeanne et Hector Fortin
Saint-Luc-de-Matane

LANAUDIÈRE :
Auberge du Vieux Moulin,
Sylvie et Yves Marcoux
Sainte-Émilie-de- l'Énergie

LAURENTIDES :
Auberge de la Gare,
Geneviève Ostrowski et Michel Gossiaux
Sainte-Adèle

MAURICIE :
À L'Arrêt du Temps
Serge Gervais et René Poitras
Sainte-Anne-de-la-Pérade

MONTÉRÉGIE :
Le Virevent
Johanne Jeannotte
Saint-Marc-sur-Richelieu
**Finalist for the Provincial Grand Prize
« People's Special Favorite »

MONTRÉAL (région de) :
Gîte Maison Jacques
Micheline et Fernand Jacques
Pierrefonds

QUÉBEC (région de) :
La Maison du Vignoble
Lise Roy, Île d'Orléans, Saint-Pierre
**Finalist for the Provincial Grand Prize
« People's Special Favorite »

SAGUENAY-LAC-ST-JEAN :
Gîte de la Rivière aux Sables
Marie et Jean Eudes Girard
Jonquière

Prizes for Excellence
2002

« Achievement »
Category

« Congratulations to these hosts and hostesses for the remarkable way they have developed, promoted and offered high-quality services. »

Agrotourism Sector
The Provincial Prize-Winner is

Les Élevages Ruban Bleu
Denise Poirier Rivard
Saint-Isidore-de-Laprairie
MONTÉRÉGIE
(Farm Shops)

Accommodation Sector
The Provincial Prize-Winner is

Le Gîte Saint-Michel
Robert Burelle et Michel Desjardins
Saint-Michel-des-Saints,
LANAUDIÈRE
(Bed & Breakfast)

Special Mention by the jury

Notre Maison sur la rivière
Viviane Charbonneau et Serge Gaudreau
Saint-François, LAVAL
(Bed & Breakfast)

Fédération des Agricotours du Québec
28 years of hospitality
1975 – 2003

www.inns-bb.com
www.agricotours.qc.ca

New establishments 2003

ABITIBI-TÉMISCAMINGUE

Val d'Or
• Auberge de L'Orpailleur, *Country Inn*

BAS-SAINT-LAURENT

L'Isle-Verte
• Au Pays des Rêves, *Bed & Breakfast*

Notre-Dame-du-Portage
• La Halte du Verger, *Bed & Breakfast*
• Gîte Chute Couette et Café, *Bed & Breakfast*

Trois-Pistoles
• Gîte Chez Nico, *Bed & Breakfast*

CANTONS-DE-L'EST

Bolton
• L'Iris Bleu, *Bed & Breakfast*

Coaticook
• Séjour Nadeau
  Country Home at the Farm

Cowansville
• Gîte Masypa, *Bed & Breakfast*

Danville
• Maison Mc Cracken, *Bed & Breakfast*

Farnham
• Les Matins de Rosie, *Bed & Breakfast*

Frelighsburg
• À la Girondine, *Country-Style Dining,
  Farm Shops, Farm Explorations, Bed & Breakfast*
• La Ferme du Wapiti, *Farm Explorations*

Granby
• Aux Abords, *Bed & Breakfast*
• Chez Marie B&B, *Bed & Breakfast*

Magog
• À la Colline aux Chevaux
  Bed & Breakfast and Farm Stay
• Au Gré du Vent, *Country-Style Dining*
• Le Vignoble le Cep d'Argent, *Farm Shops*
• Le Vignoble les Chants de Vignes, *Farm Shops*

Mansonville
• Le Magestik, *Bed & Breakfast*

North-Hatley
• Le Cachet, *Bed & Breakfast*

Stanstead
• Domaine Félibre, *Farm Shops*

Sutton
• Auberge Altitude 2000, *Bed & Breakfast*

CHARLEVOIX

Baie-St-Paul
• Auberge la Grande Maison, *Country Inn*
• Auberge La Muse, *Country Inn*
• Au Bonhomme Sept Heures, *Bed & Breakfast*
• Gîte À L'Ancrage, *Bed & Breakfast*

La Malbaie
• La Maison sous les Lilas, *Bed & Breakfast*

Les Éboulements
• Gîte de la Basse-Cour, *Bed & Breakfast*
• Les Finesses de Charlevoix, *Farm Shops*

Petite-Rivière-St-François
• Auberge la Côte D'or, *Country Inn*

St-Hilarion
• Élevage de la Butte aux Cailles, *Farm Explorations*

St-Irénée
• Auberge des Sablons, *Country Inn*

GASPÉSIE

Matane
• Gîte des Îles, *Bed & Breakfast*

LANAUDIÈRE

Rawdon
• Ferme Guy Rivest, *Farm Shops*

LAURENTIDES

La Macaza
• Gîte du Temps qui Passe, *Bed & Breakfast*

Mont-Tremblant
• La Belle au Bois Dormant, *Bed & Breakfast*

Ste-Agathe-des-Monts
• Ancestral B&B, *Bed & Breakfast*

Ste-Agathe-Nord
• Gîte aux Champs des Elfes, *Bed & Breakfast*

Ste-Lucie-des-Laurentides
• Chez Grand-Mère Zoizeaux, *Bed & Breakfast*

MAURICIE

Bastican
• Le Gîte au Bois Dormant, *Bed & Breakfast*

Lac-aux-Sables
• Auberge Marcil, *Bed & Breakfast*

Shawinigan
• Gîte du Manoir Kane, *Bed & Breakfast*

St-Prosper-de-Champlain
• Ferme la Bisonnière, *Farm Shops*

St-Rock-de-Mekinac
• Auberge le Montagnard, *Country Inn*

Trois-Rivières
• Appartement du Centre-Ville, *City Home*,
  Bed & Breakfast

MONTÉRÉGIE

Huntingdon, Godmanchester
• Domaine de la Templerie, *Bed & Breakfast*,
  Country-Style Dining

Iberville
• Vignoble Dietrich-Jooss, *Farm Shops*

St-Jean-sur-Richelieu
• Aux Chants D'Oiseaux, *Bed & Breakfast*
• Fromagerie au Gré des Champs, *Farm Shops*

St-Paul-d'Abbotsford
• Vignoble Artisans du Terroir, *Farm Shops*

St-Simon
• Gîte à Claudia
  Bed & Breakfast and Farm Stay

St-Théodore-d'Acton
• Verger Cidrerie Larivière, *Farm Shops*

Ste-Victoire-de-Sorel
• Gîte à la Ferme du Rang
  Bed & Breakfast and Farm Stay

OUTAOUAIS

Aylmer
• La Rivière au Bois Dormant, *Gîte du Passant*
• L'Escapade B&B, *Bed & Breakfast*

Gatineau
• Le Pommier D'Argent, *Country-Style Dining*

Hull
• Au 55 Taché, *Bed & Breakfast*
• Gîte Fanny et Maxime, *Bed & Breakfast*

MONTRÉAL (RÉGION DE)

L'Île-Bizard
• Le Quai du Rêve, *Bed & Breakfast*

Montréal
• À la Bonne Heure, *Bed & Breakfast*
• Anne ma Sœur Anne, *City Home*
• Appartements les Bons Matins, *City Home*,
  Bed & Breakfast
• Au Gîte le Rayon Vert, *Bed & Breakfast*
• Azur Résidences de Tourisme, *City Home*,
  Bed & Breakfast
• Héritage Victorien, *Bed & Breakfast*
• L'Atome, *Bed & Breakfast*

QUÉBEC (RÉGION DE)

Boischatel
• Le Royal Champêtre, *Bed & Breakfast*

Cap-Santé
• Gîte Nicolas le Jardinier, *Bed & Breakfast*

Château-Richer
• Direction Mont Ste-Anne, *Country Home*,
  Bed & Breakfast

L'Île-d'Orléans, Ste-Pétronille
• Auberge la Goéliche, *Country Inn*

Neuville
• Au Gré des Saisons, *Bed & Breakfast*

Portneuf
• Auberge de la Baronnie de Portneuf
  Bed & Breakfast

Québec
• Acacias, *Bed & Breakfast*
• Château des Tourelles, *Bed & Breakfast*
• Château du Faubourg, *Bed & Breakfast*

Québec, Lac Delage
• Le Gîte Delageois, *Bed & Breakfast*

Québec, Ste-Foy
• Chez Anick et Patrick, *Bed & Breakfast*

St-Alban
• Gîte Chez France, *Bed & Breakfast*

St-Casimir
• Gîte B&B pour les Amis, *Bed & Breakfast*

Ste-Catherine-de-la-Jacques-Cartier
• Gîte du Sous-Bois, *Bed & Breakfast*

SAGUENAY-LAC-SAINT-JEAN

Chicoutimi
• Le Gîte au Bois Dormant, *Bed & Breakfast*

Dolbeau-Mistassini
• La Magie du Sous-Bois Inc., *Farm Shops*

St-Henri-de-Taillon
• L'Eau Berge du Lac, *Bed & Breakfast*

St-Honoré
• Accueil du Randonneur, *Farm Explorations*

Ste-Rose-du-Nord
• Fromagerie la Petite Heidi enr., *Farm Shops*

Visit
our establishments
via the Internet

More than 2000 photos...
4 efficient search engines...

www.inns-bb.com
Including Country and City Homes
(secure online booking service)

www.agricotours.qc.ca
**(Including Country-Style Dining,
Farm Shops, Farm Explorations,
Farm Stays, Country Homes at the Farm)**

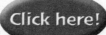

Click here!

Agrotourism

- Country-Style Dining
- Farm Shops
- Farm Explorations
- Farm Stays
  and Country Homes
  on the Farm

Country-Style Dining

COUNTRY-STYLE DINING

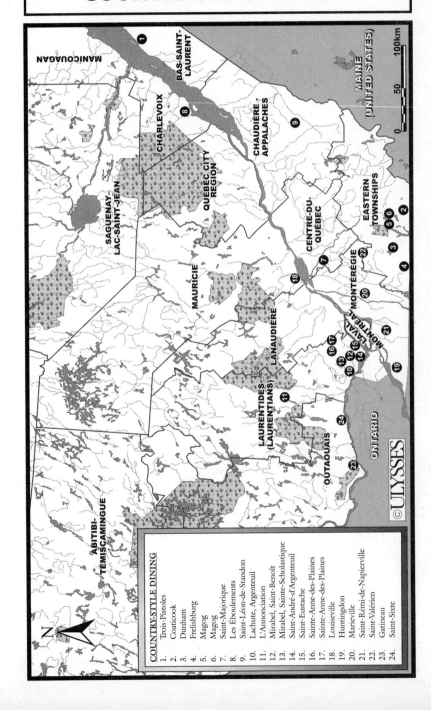

COUNTRY-STYLE DINING

1. Trois-Pistoles
2. Coaticook
3. Dunham
4. Frelishburg
5. Magog
6. Magog
7. Saint-Majorique
8. Les Éboulements
9. Saint-Léon-de-Standon
10. Lachute, Argenteuil
11. L'Annonciation
12. Mirabel, Saint-Benoit
13. Mirabel, Sainte-Scholastique
14. Saint-André-d'Argenteuil
15. Saint-Eustache
16. Sainte-Anne-des-Plaines
17. Sainte-Anne-des-Plaines
18. Louiseville
19. Huntingdon
20. Marieville
21. Saint-Rémi-de-Napierville
22. Saint-Valérien
23. Gatineau
24. Saint-Sixte

© ULYSSES

1. TROIS-PISTOLES

LA BERGÈRE, GÎTE ET COUVERT
Céline Cyr and Robert Forest
171, Rang 2 Est
Trois-Pistoles G0L 4K0
(418) 851-4478
www.inns-bb.com/bergere

In our lovely Bas-St-Laurent region, in Trois-Pistoles, home of the Bouscotte TV series, enjoy a dining experience with a special emphasis on lamb. Let yourself be tempted by our menus, which vary according to the season, available products and the shepherds inspiration. Our home is the perfect haven for an unforgettable stay in the region. B&B and country-dining package available.

Aut. 20 East, Rte 132, at traffic light, right twd the 293. After 1km, left on 2nd Rang East, 7km.

Open: Oct. 15 to June 15
Includes: visit of the farm in season

Saucisse à l'agneau ou foie à l'orange ou pâté en croûte
Consommé à l'orge ou crème du potager
Galantine au romarin ou feuilletée aux épinards
Sauté d'agneau aux herbes de Provence ou gigot au
romarin ou au sirop d'érable
Granité au citron et vodka
Salade de feta ou d'agneau fumé
Strudel aux pommes et poires ou tartelettes au sirop
d'érable et bleuets sauvages

Meal: 30 $

week: 6 to 8 people   w/e: 6 to 8 people

2. COATICOOK

LA FERME MARTINETTE
Lisa Nadeau and
Gérald Martineau
1728, chemin Martineau
Coaticook J1A 2S5
tel/fax (819) 849-7089
1-888-881-4561
www.lafermemartinette.com
martinet@abacom.com

In our hundred-year-old maple grove, enjoy a creative gourmet cuisine of farm and regional products in an enchanting setting. Lamb, rabbit, duck, red deer, smoked trout; berries and vegetables from the family garden; maple products with a hint of sweet cream; edible flowers and fine herbs grown with love; menus of all colours and flavours depending on the season; tempting spit-roasted lamb barbecue over a wood fire; in March and April, traditional sugar-shack meals combined with a tour of the farm and maple taffy on the snow... Welcome to our table! **Farm Explorations p 52. Farm Shops p 35. Country Home p 107.**

From Montréal, Aut. 10 Exit 121, Aut. 55 Exit 21. Rte 141 South, 1km before Barnston. Right at Chemin Madore, left at Chemin Martineau.

Open year round
Includes: visit of the farm in season

Baluchons de truite fumée des Bobines
au fromage de chèvre chaud
Velouté de courgettes jaunes aux arômes du potager
Porc farci des produits du terroir
Gigot d'agneau mariné à la fleur d'ail
Cuissot de cerf rouge des Cantons
Sauce au concassé des quatre poivres
Sauce fruitée du verger au vin blanc
Sauce à la menthe de rose, gelée de menthe orange, gelée de cèdre
Pommes de terre au four, petites fèves du jardin
Salade jardinière et sa vinaigrette framboise et fines herbes
Fantaisie de légumes marinés
Salade de tomates tricolores à la fleur du Petit Mas de Ste-Edwidge
Chutney aux fruits rouge et vert
Tarte à la crème d'érable de La Martinette
Poires flambées au brandy et leur bleu
Autres menus sur demande

Meal: 17-60 $ Taxes extra VS MC IT

week: 4 to 100 people w/e: 4 to 100 people

Can accommodate more than 1 group / 2 dining rooms (exclusive use depends on season, nb. of people).

3. DUNHAM

LA CHÈVRERIE DES ACACIAS
Renée Ducharme and
Gérard Landry
356, chemin Bruce (rte 202)
Dunham J0E 1M0
(450) 295-2548
fax (450) 295-2447
www.chevrerie.ca
info@chevrerie.ca

On the road to the vineyards, our homestead is a major goat-breeding, fodder-crop and poultry farm. The originality of the food served in the ambiance of a last century house will charm you. Our menu constitutes a gastronomic adventure orchestrated around our farm products combined with those of our neighbours. Our home is just the place to end an unforgettable day in the region.

Located 1 hour from the Champlain bridge. From Montréal or Sherbrooke, Aut. 10, Exit 68 twd Cowansville Rte 139. Then Rte 202 twd Dunham. In the village, Chemin Bruce, Rte 202 at the corner of "Boni-Soir". The goat farm is 1.2km from the village.

Open year round
Includes: visit of the farm

Canapés de fromage au pesto
Pâté de chevreau sur bruschetta
Mosaïque de légumes au frais de chèvre
Potage de carottes, parfumé à l'orange
Gigot de chevreau, sauce aux cerises de terre
Ou cuisses de canard aux pruneaux
Accompagnés de choux rouge à l'érable
Et feuilles de vigne farcies
Granité aux trois melons
Salade de betteraves à l'aïoli
Meringue aux fruits des champs
sur crème anglaise

Meal: 35 $ Taxes extra

week: 12 to 35 people w/e: 12 to 35 people

Can accomodate more than 1 group / 2 dining rooms available (exclusive use depends on season, nb. of people).

4. FRELIGHSBURG

À LA GIRONDINE
Françoise and François Bardo
104, Route 237 sud
Frelighsburg J0J 1C0
(450) 298-5206
fax (450) 298-5216
www.netc.net/lagirondine
lagirondine@netc.net

Nestled in the bosky bower of the magnificent village of Frelighsburg, La Girondine invites you to experience the magic of a trip to France. Taste our regional cuisine and be transported to the southern French countryside, where the aroma of fried escalope de foie gras (the house specialty) blends with the seductive fragrance of lapin à la moutarde. In a barn with double pitch roof that can seat up to 55 people, savour our own farm-raised duck and enjoy delicate rabbit, quail and guinea fowl. La Girondine is an escape to the land of a thousand flavours! **B&B p 96. Farm Shops p 36. Farm Explorations p 52.**

Aut. 10, Exit 22, Aut 35 South to the end. Left twd St-Alexandre to Bedford, Rte 202 about 7km. Right at the sign for Frelighsburg. Turn right and continue 1km after crossing the village.

Open year round
Includes: visit of the farm

Potage du jour
Assiette Landaise ou le foie gras sur canapé
Mesclun avec timbales de chèvre
Salade de cœurs de canards aux champignons sauvages et vinaigrette de cidre
Salade tiède aux gésiers confits
Feuilleté aux foies de lapin
Granité maison
Confit de canard ou d'oie
Cassoulet ou Garbure landaise
Brochettes de canard aux échalottes
Lapin à la moutarde ou Lapin à la girondine
Fricassée de lapin en salmis au thym
Suprême de pintade au brandy, hachis parmentier
Magret de canard en aiguillettes, sauce aux mûres ou nectar d'abricot
Aiguillettes de canard et ananas
Escaloppe de foie gras déglacé au vin de glace, pommes caramélisées
Foie gras aux raisins au caramel de loupiac
Salade et plateau de fromage
Choix de dessert
Autres menus sur demande

Meal: 36 $ Taxes extra VS MC IT

week: 6 to 55 people w/e: 6 to 55 people
Can accommodate more than 1 group.

5. MAGOG

AU GRÉ DU VENT
Patrick Bélanger
225, chemin Roy
Magog J1X 3W3
(819) 843-9207
(819) 843-9301
www.agricotours.
qc.ca/anglais/augreduvent

Let your senses guide you through the magnificent panoramas of our region, as you are surrounded by Mont Orford and the majestic Lac Memphrémagog. You'll be seduced by the aromas and flavours of our kitchen, where we prepare delicious veal, rabbit and poultry dishes, as well as many other delicacies. Enjoy our rooms for longer stays and participate in a multitude of nearby activities. There is a bike path on our property, and the town is Magog is a mere 3km away.From Montréal, Aut. 10 twd Sherbrooke, Exit 118, Rte 141 South, first road to the right, Chemin Couture, to the end. Left on Chemin Roy, first house to the left.

From Québec City, Aut. 20 East, Aut. 55 twd Sherbrooke, Aut. 10 twd Magog, Exit 118, Rte 141 South...

Open year round
Includes: visit of the farm in season

Salade et ses médaillons de volaille
Terrine de veau aux pommes et noisettes
Mousse de foie au cognac et poivre
Velouté de courgettes à la ciboulette
Le Boucanier
Croustillant de lapin sauce au miel
Rissolé de foie de volaille au porto
Aumônière de truite à la fleur d'ail
Blanquette de veau campagnarde
Râble de lapereau braisé à la moutarde
Filet de porc à la duxelles
Suprême de volaille poché florentine
Gâteau mousse au chocolat et framboise
Autres menus sur demande

Meal: 40 $ Taxes extra MC IT

week: 4 to 16 people w/e: 14 to 16 people
Can accommodate more than 1 group.

6. MAGOG

Just steps away from Magog and Orford, you will succumb to the charm of the surrounding countryside, the warmth of our century-old house as well as the "pure delights" we have in store for you. Our dishes are concocted from our various farm-bred animals, organic vegetables and edible flowers. Do not resist, but rather prolong your pleasure, whether alone or as a group, by taking advantage of the hospitality of our B&B. Ulysses favourite (2000/2001). Packages from $92 per person, double occupancy. Bring your own wine. **Inns p 103. See colour photos. Ad back cover.**

From Montréal, Aut. 10 East, Exit 115 South-Magog/ St-Benoît-du-Lac, 1.8km. Right on Chemin des Pères twd St-Benoît-du-Lac/Austin, 6.1km. From Québec City, Aut. 20 West, 55 South and 10 West, Exit 115 twd St-Benoît-du-Lac.

Open year round
Includes: visit of the farm in season

AUX JARDINS CHAMPÊTRES
Monique Dubuc and Yvon Plourde
1575, chemin des Pères, R.R. 4
Canton-de-Magog J1X 5R9
(819) 868-0665
1-877-868-0665
fax (819) 868-6744
www.auxjardinschampetres.com
auxjardinschampetres@
qc.aira.com

Salade au confit de canard et vinaigrette tiède balsamique ou
Rillettes de lapin au moût de pommes
Potage aux poires et cresson
Aumônière de poireaux sauce cheddar et coulis de poivrons rouges ou
Croustade de lapin aux pistaches et au Pineau des Charentes
Granité au calvados
Magret de canard au genièvre et Porto ou
Scalopini de volaille aux cerises de terre ou
Médaillon de cerf rouge à la crème de pleurotte
Crêpes glacées aux pommes et figues ou
Gâteau à la pâte d'amande ou
Péché mignon aux marrons et chocolats sauce Sabayon au Grand Marnier
Autres menus sur demande

Meal: 29-42 $ Taxes extra VS MC IT

week: 1 to 60 people w/e: 1 to 60 people

Can accommodate more than 1 group / 4 dining rooms (exclusive use depends on season, nb. of people).

7. ST-MAJORIQUE

FLEUR EN BOUCHÉE
Edith Fleurent and
Robert Boucher
1915, boul. Lemire Ouest
Saint-Majorique J2B 8A9
(819) 477-7760
tel/fax (819) 477-8197
**www.agricotours.qc.ca/
anglais/fleur_en_bouchee**
robert@9bit.qc.ca

The birds have composed lovely melodies for you. Although we are located near the city, we can offer you the harmony of nature in a verdant setting. It is our great pleasure to receive you in our cosy, candlelight family dining room, where we serve our lovingly prepared local products. We specialise in grain-fed veal; also available are free-range chicken and pork. Our desserts are euphoria to your taste buds. A certified pastrycook and chef, Edith is first and foremost a devotee of good, authentic cooking, a passion we share with you. Come and enjoy the pleasures of life by taking part in this gastronomic experience.

Aut. 20, Exit 175, 4.5km twd St-Bonaventure.

Open year round
Includes: visit of the farm

Mousse de légumes au trois saveurs
ou
Paté de campagne aux pruneaux
Crème Washington
ou
Potage Parmentier aux deux pommes
Quiche aux asperges
ou
Crêpe citronnée au veau sauce crémeuse à l'avocat
Granité canneberge et mousseux
Paupiette de veau farci sauce au vin, Gratin Dauphinois
ou
Pomme de terre duchesse.
Légumes fraîcheurs saisonnière
Laitue panachée du jardin, sauce aux agrumes.
Miroir aux fraises
ou
omelette Norvégienne
Vous pouvez modifier le contenu du menu avec des canapés
ou plateau de fromages
Autres menus sur demande

Meal: 35-40 $ Taxes extra

week: 10 to 30 people   w/e: 10 to 30 people

Can accommodate more than 1 group / 2 dining rooms
(exclusive use depends on season, nb. of people).

8. LES ÉBOULEMENTS

LES SAVEURS OUBLIÉES
Régis Hervé and Guy Thibodeau
350, rang Saint-Godefroy, rte 362
Les Éboulements G0A 2M0
(418) 635-9888
(418) 635-2682
fax (418) 439-0616
agneausaveurscharlevoix.com
saveurs.oubliees.com@sympatico.ca

"Les Saveurs Oubliées" country-style dining from Ferme Éboulmontaise (Lucie Cadieux et Vital Gagnon), located in the heart of the Réserve Mondiale de la Biosphère at the foot of Mont des Éboulements and facing the majestic St. Lawrence River, offers you the opportunity to discover the sheep breeding in Charlevoix. After visiting the sheepfold and organic gardens or hiking in a bucolic decor, you will be cordially invited to our table. You will then discover the many aspects of our regional cuisine at its best. A taste to discover.

From Québec, Rte 138 twd Ste-Anne- de-Beaupré and Baie-St-Paul. At Baie-St-Paul, scenic Rte, 362, 1km after Les Éboulements village.

Open year round
Includes: visit of the farm

Apéritif et amuse-bouche
Rillette de canard au confit d'oignon,
Gâteau de presse d'agneau et Salade folle au goût du jour
ou carpaccio d'agneau à l'huile de tomates séchées et râpe de parmesan
Soupière du moment ou verdurette des jardins
et croûtons de fromage Le Ciel de Charlevoix
Tartiflette à la truite fumée des Éboulements
Foie d'agneau poêlé aux pommes et tombée de choux rouge
Assiette d'agneau de la maison sur le grill
Navarin d'agneau Éboulemontaise
Souris d'agneau et sa pipérade au cari
Carré d'agneau à ma façon et salsa rhubarbe maïs
Lapereau aux petits lardons, vin rouge et pomme cloutée
Jambonneau de canard confit, caramel d'érable
Mes coups de cœur sucrés, Café-Mignardises
Autres menus sur demande

Meal: 36-45 $ Taxes extra VS MC AM IT

week: 2 to 50 people w/e: 2 to 50 people

Can accommodate more than 1 group / 1 dining room
(exclusive use depends on season, nb. of people).

9. ST-LÉON-DE-STANDON

FERME LA COLOMBE
Rita Grégoire and
Jean-Yves Marleau
104, rang Sainte-Anne
Saint-Léon-de-Standon G0R 4L0
(418) 642-5152
fax (418) 642-2991
www.fermelacolombe.qc.ca
r.gregoire@globetrotter.net

Agrotourism "Realisation" 2000 award of excellence, special mention; Grand Prix du Tourisme 1997. One hour from Québec City, in the heart of the Appalachians, come experience the culinary adventure offered by the Ferme La Colombe. You'll savour every moment in our cosy hewn-timber dining room, made all the more charming by the crackling fireplace and the beautiful panoramic view from the window. You'll be won over by our exotic cuisine, composed of guinea fowl, rabbit, trout and prominently featured edible flowers. Garden and country-dining package available. **Farm Explorations p 56.**

From Québec City, Aut. 20 East, Exit 325 twd Lac-Etchemin, Rtes 173 South and 277 South St-Léon-de-Standon, Rue Principale, 0.9km past the church, cross Rte 277 at the stop sign, left on Rte du Village, 4km. Right on Rang Ste-Anne, 2km.

Open year round
Includes: visit of the farm in season

> *Fromage frais aux fleurs d'onagre*
> *Terrine de canard à l'estragon*
> *Velouté de citrouille et fromage de chèvre*
> *Aumônière de pintade ou Râble de lapin au*
> *cidre de pomme ou*
> *Poitrine de poulet de grain à l'abbaye*
> *Pomme de terre noisette*
> *Tonnelle de courgette*
> *Salade fleurie*
> *Délice roulé à la fleur de rose*
> *Fondant au chocolat et*
> *coulis de gadelles noires*
> ***Autres menus sur demande***

Meal: 30-34 $ Taxes extra

week: 8 to 30 people w/e: 8 to 30 people

Can accommodate more than 1 group / 1 dining room
(exclusive use depends on season, nb. of people).

10. LACHUTE, ARGENTEUIL

AU PIED DE LA CHUTE
Émilie Kervadec and
Yves Kervadec
273, Route 329 Nord
Lachute J8H 3W9
tel/fax (450) 562-3147
www.pieddelachute.com
info@pieddelachute.com

Right at the edge of a wooded area, our home offers charm, comfort and personalized service. Authentic cuisine where duck, deer, guinea-fowl, pheasant and capon are the specialties. The lake, falls and river add to the charm of our property. Come and enjoy the culinary delights and reception that have made our reputation.

From Montréal, Aut. 15 North, Exit 35. Aut. 50 twd Côte St-Louis, right Rte 158 West, left Rte 329 North. At the flashing yellow light, right for exactly 1.5km. It's on your left.

Open year round
Includes: visit of the farm

Amuse-bouche de bienvenue
Champignons de nos sous-bois en feuilleté ou
terrine de daim aux cèpes, rémoulade de céléri ou
Salade gourmande au fromage de chèvre frais ou
Foie gras de canard en terrine pointes d'asperges
Crémeuse provençale pesto de basilic et olives ou
Velouté de pintade et moelleux à l'estragon
Cuisse de daim rôtie, jus au vinaigre de cassis ou
Fricassée de chapon aux lardons et oignons ou
Poitrine de canard de barbarie à la sariette ou
Gigot d'agneau émulsion de tomates et marjolaine ou
Poitrine de pintade et pleurotes au porto ou
Suprême de faisan, civet de cuisse à l'estragon
Raclette d'Argenteuil et mesclun à l'érable
Tarte Fondante au chocolat à l'orange confite ou
Mousse de Fromage et bleuets, jus "Balsamico"
Café, thé, tisane
Autres menus sur demande

Meal: 35-39 $ Taxes extra

week: 10 to 28 people w/e: 16 to 28 people

Only 1 group at a time. Min. nb. of guests required.

11. L'ANNONCIATION

LA CLAIRIÈRE DE LA CÔTE
Monique Lanthier and
Yves Bégin
16, chemin Laliberté
L'Annonciation J0T 1T0
(819) 275-2877
www.inns-bb.
com/clairieredelacote

In the Hautes Laurentides, you are invited to our table to spend some peaceful hours in the clearing of a forest of varied species. We live in harmony with nature amongst a variety of small animals (lambs, rabbits, grain-fed chickens, calves and deer), which become succulent dishes accompanied by fresh vegetables from our organic gardens. **Farm Stay p 69. B&B p 169.**

From Montréal, Aut. 15 North and Rte 117 twd L'Annonciation. 4.3km beyond the hospital. Left on Chemin Laliberté.

Open: Dec. 1 to Mar. 31, May 1 to Oct. 31
Includes: visit of the farm

Rougette crémière
Foie gras poulette
Pesto en pâte
Velouté de saison
Tournedos dindonneau au fouillis jardinier
Verdoyant potager, crémerie de fines herbes
Fromagerie raisinet
Fruiterie sauvagine en velours
Pouding paysan sirop d'érable
Autres menus sur demande

Meal: 30 $

week: 6 to 20 people w/e: 6 to 20 people

Only 1 group at a time.

12. MIRABEL, ST-BENOÎT

AU GIBIER DU ROI
France Couture and
Guy Arseneault
6015, Rang Saint-Vincent
Saint-Benoît, Mirabel J7N 2T5
(450) 258-2388
fax (450) 258-3970
www.augibierduroi.com
augibierduroi@hotmail.com

It will be our pleasure to welcome you into our home to share our passion for our farm-bred red deer, pheasants and partridges. In a setting reminiscent of both the wilderness and the charming countryside, we offer you a locally flavoured culinary adventure. Experience the tastes and flavours of game offered by our "Table du Roi" (king's table), an eight-course tasting menu. A walk along our breeding pens will allow you to admire the nobility of our deer and learn a little more about this coveted "Gibier des rois" (game fit for a king). **Farm Shops p 42.**

From Montréal, Aut. 13 or 15 North, Aut. 640 West and Boul. Arthur-Sauvé Exit 11 twd Lachute, 17km and left on St-Vincent twd St-Placide, 6km away. You will find us on the right.

Open year round
Includes: visit of the farm in season

Bouchées de bienvenue
Terrine aux abricots et mousse de foie
Potage du jardin
Feuilleté de perdrix des sous-bois au porto
Pâtes maison farcies de cerfs au pesto de tomates séchées
Roulade de faisan aux canneberges
et noix de pin sauce au rhum
Granité du Roi
Médaillons de cerf rouge
à la gelée de cèdre et poire caramélisée
Ou Poulet fermier au miel et au thym
Rouleau de verdures et ses mayonnaises
Gâteau mousse à l'érable et fromage
Aussi disponible : Capucino, Espresso
et plateau de fromage
Autres menus sur demande

Meal: 39-47 $ Taxes extra VS IT

week: 10 to 24 people   w/e: 2 to 44 people

Can accommodate more than 1 group / 2 dining rooms (exclusive use depends on season, nb. of people).

13. MIRABEL, ST-SCHOLASTIQUE

LES RONDINS
Lorraine Douesnard and
François Bernard
10331, côte Saint-Louis
Mirabel J7N 2W4
(514) 990-2708
(450) 258-2467
fax (450) 258-2347
www.lapetitecabane.com
laptitecabane@sympatico.ca

Located a few km from Mirabel airport, Les Rondins henceforth welcomes you to their saphouse, situated on the edge of a vast maple grove, with trails laid out for walks. Farm-bred Barbary Coast ducks and grain-fed chickens are found here alongside Belgian horses. Antique furnishings and the piano create a warm and friendly ambiance in the two dining rooms, where guests savour our refined dishes, prepared in the adjoining kitchen. At Les Rondins, a peaceful, enchanting site is yours to enjoy.

From Montréal, Aut. 15 North, Exit 35, Aut. 50 West, Exit 272, Chemin Côte St-Louis. Left at the stop sign, 3km. Les Rondins and the "P'tite Cabane d'la Côte" are on the left.

Open year round
Includes: visit of the farm in season

Bouchées d'avant
Roulade de chapon farcie
Potage de saison et pain maison
Salade tiède au confit de canard
Mille feuilles de cerf rouge
Suprême de volaille farci sauce aux framboises
Mijoton de veau au parfum de basilic
Suprême de pintade sauce raisins et vin rouge
Canard de Barbarie à l'estragon et orange
Fromage fermier
Verdure et 2 fromages chauds
Gâteau rhubarbe mousse au sirop d'érable
Crème glacée-sorbet maison
Autres menus sur demande

Meal: 35-42 $ Taxes extra

week: 10 to 50 people w/e: 15 to 50 people

Min. nb. of guests may vary depending on the season / Can accommodate more than 1 group / 2 dining rooms (exclusive use depends on season, nb. of people).

14. ST-ANDRÉ-D'ARGENTEUIL

LA FERME DE CATHERINE
Marie Marchand and
Robert Dorais
539, Route du Long-Sault rte 344
St-André-d'Argenteuil J0V 1X0
(450) 537-3704
fax (450) 537-1362
**www.agricotours.qc.ca/
anglais/fermedecatherine**
fermecatherine@videotron.ca

In the beautiful region of Oka, Marie, Catherine and Robert invite you to come enjoy family ambiance and country cooking close to the old wood stove whose warmth mixes with the warmth of the hosts. Robert will take you around the farm and you can admire a superb view of Lac des Deux-Montagnes and surroundings. If you love good food, have a seat and let the feast begin.

From Montréal, Aut. 13 or 15 to Aut. 640 twd Oka. From Oka, take Aut. 344, 19km. On the 344 it's 6km after St-Placide. The road gets narrower and winding as you arrive at La Ferme de Catherine.

Open year round
Includes: visit of the farm

Crémant de pomme
Saucisse deux viandes sur
tombée de tomates au basilic ou
Terrine de bison au confit d'oignons
et vinaigre de framboises
Velouté du fermier
Médaillon de bison
Veau de grain braisé,
sauce aux cidre et gingembre
Suprême de volaille farci de canard
Plateau de fromages avec panaché de laitue
Délices de la saison au coulis fruités
Autres menus sur demande

Meal: 38-42 $

week: 12 to 40 people w/e: 12 to 40 people

Only 1 group at a time.

---

15. ST-EUSTACHE

LE RÉGALIN
Réjean Brouillard
991, boul. Arthur-Sauvé, route 148 Ouest
Saint-Eustache J7R 4K3
tel/fax (450) 623-9668
1-877-523-9668
www.regalin.com
regalin@videotron.ca

Winner "Pétale d'Or" Comité d'embellissement du conseil des Arts de St-Eustache. Less than 30 min from Montréal, in the maple area of St-Eustache, a beautiful, typical old house with dormer windows overlooking a large orchard extending as far as the eye can see. Farm animals (rabbits, pheasants, guinea fowl, geese, ducks and ostriches) inspire the planning of our menus. We offer dinner-concerts where you don't have to be in group. 2 separate dining rooms, for your exclusive use, are available at each end of the house.

From Montréal, Aut. 15 North, Exit 20 West, Aut. 640 West, Exit 11. Boul. Arthur-Sauvé twd Lachute. 5km from the Exit, 8 houses after the tree nursery Eco-Verdure, on the right side.

Open year round
Includes: visit of the farm in season

Mousse de foies de lapereau et pain maison
Feuilleté de faisan au poivre vert ou
Aumônières de pintade à l'érable
Potage de saison
Lapin aux abricots, au cidre ou à l'érable ou
Rotisson d'autruche à l'hydromel ou
Suprême de faisan au poivre rose
Salade verdurette
Plateau de fromages fins
Profiteroles au chocolat ou
Gâteau mousse aux abricots
Autres menus sur demande

Meal: 38-45 $ Taxes extra

week: 12 to 50 people w/e: 15 to 50 people

Min. nb. of guests may vary depending on the season /
Can accommodate more than 1 group / 2 dining rooms
(exclusive use depends on season, nb. of people).

16. STE-ANNE-DES-PLAINES

F E ⊘ ♿ P ✕

BASILIC ET ROMARIN
Jocelyne Parent
12, boul. Normandie
Sainte-Anne-des-Plaines
J0N 1H0
(450) 838-9752
www.agricotours.qc.ca/
anglais/basilicetromarin
basilicetromarin@sympatico.ca

Barely 45 min from downtown! And there you are in the heart of a maple grove, the sweet cocoon of Basilic et Romarin. The dining experience awaits you in the solarium that opens out on the kitchen garden and a magnificent forest. The farmyard, maple grove, vegetable garden and regional products provide the raw materials for our creativity, inspired by a six-year journey through both the American and European continents. Are your taste buds curious, insatiable and ready to be surprised? Then come sample our original flavours in small groups of two to six people. The menu varies according to our whims throughout the year as well as the evening. Two different menus are served to each two guests.

Aut. 15, Exit 31. Head East for 14km along Victor, then Lepage. Right, twd South for 500m to Boul. Normandie.

Open year round
Includes: visit of the farm in season

Gravad lax à la coriande et lime
Rillettes de lapin aux noisettes
Mousse de légumes sur coulis de poivron rouge
Potage au zucchini et basilic
Feuilleté de mousse de foie à l'oseille
Tourte de cailles et d'amandes
Pâté de lapin sur coulis de champignons
Granité de vin blanc et de lime
Lapin farci à la courgette et pacanes avec sauce à l'estragon
Pintades avec sauce à l'orange et aux canneberges
Caille au riz sauvage et oignons caramélisés
Faisan aux petits fruits
Gâteau à la mousse d'érable
Marquise au chocolat sur crème anglaise
Gaufrette farcie de crème glacée au basilic
Tuile de mascarpone et framboises
Autres menus sur demande

Meal: 45 $

week: 2 to 22 people w/e: 2 to 22 people

Can accommodate more than 1 group of 6 people / 1 dining room (exclusive use depends on season, nb. of people).

17. STE-ANNE-DES-PLAINES

F E ♿ P ✕

LA CONCLUSION
Chantal and Gilles Fournier
172, rang La Plaine (rte 335)
Sainte-Anne-des-Plaines
J0N 1H0
(450) 478-2598
fax (450) 478-0209
www.laconclusion.com
conclusi@qc.aira.com

Prize for Excellence "Special Favorite" Provincial 2000. By a stroke of good fortune, this elegant house caught our eye. We chose it in order to continue our adventure and receive you in a rural setting and relaxed atmosphere. In harmony with the seasons, you will enjoy refined cuisine made up of fresh products from our farm-bred animals. Our different cultures add flavour and colour to your dish. You are invited to share a moment in the country and let yourself be pampered by the Fournier family. In "conclusion", you will appreciate the warm welcome that has made our name, and you may hear the tale of our adventure...

From Montréal, Aut. 15, Exit 31. After the light, right at the stop sign on Rue Victor, 10.7km. Left at the flashing light, 7.7km, Rte 335 North.

Open year round
Includes: visit of the farm

Potage ou crème du jardin
Pain maison aux cinq grains
Caille glacée au vinaigre de framboises ou
Gâteau de lapin au vin blanc ou
Aumônière de foies de lapin à la crème ou
Assortiment de pâtés
Lapin aux pommes et raisins ou
Lapin farci aux abricots ou
Lapin chasseur aux olives ou
Cailles rôties, sauce porto et raisins verts
Salade de saison
Tarte aux framboises glacée au sirop d'érable
ou Gâteau mousse aux fraises et à la rhubarbe
ou Crêpes de blé au Cointreau et bleuets ou
Gâteau moka et mousse d'amandes
Crème glacée maison et gourmandises
Autres menus sur demande

Meal: 30-46 $

week: 2 to 34 people w/e: 2 to 34 people

Min. nb. of guests may vary depending on the season / Can accommodate more than 1 group / 2 dining rooms (exclusive use depends on seasons, nb. of people).

18. LOUISEVILLE

LA TABLE DE LA SEIGNEURIE
Michel Gilbert
480, chemin du Golf
Louiseville J5V 2L4
(819) 228-8224
fax (819) 228-5576
www.agricotours.qc.ca/
anglais/gitedelaseigneurie
m.gilbert@infoteck.qc.ca

60 min from Montréal, La Seigneurie looks forward to spoiling you in its cosy home! You'll delight in our 9- course meal composed of produce from our small traditional farm. The vegetable garden, flower beds and herb garden make our food healthy, while the colours make for an attractive presentation. After a feast complemented by wine what could be better than joining Morpheus in one of our B&B's cosy rooms. **B&B p 190. Country Home La Maison du Jardinier p 196.**

From Montréal or Québec City, Aut. 40 Exit 166, Rte 138 East, 2.4km to Rte 348 West. At the light, left twd Ste-Ursule, 1.5km, 1st road on the right, 1st house tucked away behind the trees.

Open year round
Includes: visit of the farm in season

Bouchées cordiales à l'apéritif
Feuilleté de filet de perchaude
du Lac Saint-Pierre
Soupière de Bortsch ou du terroir (sarrasin)
Granité Bienfaisant
Le porc, le veau, le lapin ou
l'agneau de la Seigneurie sont à l'honneur
Légumes potagers
Laitue, vinaigrette «Fin Palais»
Éphémère triangle de fromages
Bagatelle «Seigneuriale» au sherry
Douceurs inoubliables
Autres menus sur demande

Meal: 39 $ Taxes extra

week: 2 to 36 people w/e: 2 to 36 people

Min. nb. of guests may vary depending on the season /
Can accommodate more than 1 group / 3 dining rooms
(exclusive use depends on season, nb. of people).

19. HUNTINGDON

DOMAINE DE LA TEMPLERIE
Denise Asselin, Roland
Guillon and son fils François
312, chemin New Erin
Godmanchester (Huntingdon)
JOS 1H0
tel/fax (450) 264-9405
www.agricotours.
qc.ca/anglais/templerie

Provincial Prize for Excellence "Special Favorite" 2002. Provincial 1999 Excellence Prize. Nestled in fields and woods, our ancestral home awaits you. Walking in the forest, visiting the sugar shack, outdoor activities. At your discretion: soccer field, volleyball court, "pétanque" and horseshoes space. Our farm-bred geese, guinea fowl, pheasants and ducks will treat you to an unforgettable concert. You will enjoy succulent dishes prepared by your host, who has some thirty years' cooking experience, in a relaxed ambiance. **B&B p 202.**

From Montréal, Rte 138 West twd Huntingdon. 9km after the stop in Ormstown, right at the ch. Seigneurial, 4.7km, left on ch. de la Templerie, 350m. At the stop sign, New Erin, 1km.

Open year round
Includes: visit of the farm in season

Petits fours apéritifs, Velouté en cachette
Charcuteries fines: volaille fumée
Terrine de faisan aux pistaches, boudin d'oie
Entrée chaude au choix: ris de veau aux poires
Escalope de truite Normande-Tourte de canard
Feuilleté de langue de veau sauce piquante
Timbale de faisan au madère-quiche Victoria
au choix
Confit de canard
Filet d'oie sauce bordelaise-civet de lapereau
Gigot d'agneau aux fines herbes
Pintadeau rôti forestière
Caille aux raisins, suprême de faisan
Rotisson d'autruche, jardinière de légumes
Salade Plateau de fromage
2 desserts par personne: choux croque en bouche coupe de
la templerie
Tarte au sirop d'érable
Soufflé à l'érable et calvados
Bombe glacée, profitérole au chocolat

Meal: 36-48 $ Taxes extra

week:12 to 38 people w/e: 12 to 38 people

Min. nb. of guests may vary depending on the season /
Only 1 group at a time.

20. MARIEVILLE

L'AUTRUCHE DORÉE
Chantale and Michel Noiseux
505, Ruisseau St-Louis Ouest
Marieville J3M 1P1
tel/fax (450) 460-2446
www.autruchedoree.com
autruchedoree@hotmail.com

Treat yourself to the exoticism of ostrich, in Montérégie. L'Autruche Dorée, nestled between the St-Hilaire and Rougemont mountains, 25 min from Montréal, will stimulate all your senses. The beauty and peacefulness of the countryside will enchant you immediately on arrival. In a warm setting, discover and savour delicious ostrich meat in all its guises to the soothing sounds of the African savannah. During the meal, if you so desire, it will be our pleasure to share our passion with you for this majestic, noble African bird, which has been nesting in Montérégie since 1994. Available guided tour in season.

From Montréal, Aut. 10, Exit 37, twd Rte 227 North. At the light, left on Rte 112, right on 1st Rang, 4km. L'Autruche Dorée is in the cul-de-sac.

Open year round

Autruche fumée et sa garniture
Parfum d'autruche aux perles du jardin
Phylo d'autruche framboisine
Médaillons d'autruche aux oignons caramélisés sauce au
Porto
Bouquet de feuilles tièdes au confit d'autruche
Délices du pâtissier
Autres menus sur demande

Meal: 17-37 $ Taxes extra VS MC ER IT

week: 15 to 80 people w/e: 15 to 80 people

Can accommodate more than 1 group / 1 dining room
(exclusive use depends on season, nb. of people).

21. ST-RÉMI-DE-NAPIERVILLE

FERME KOSA
Ada and Lajos Kosa
1845, rang Saint-Antoine
Saint-Rémi-de-Napierville
JOL 2L0
tel/fax (450) 454-4490
www.agricotours.
qc.ca/anglais/kosa

On the wide expanses of the Rive-Sud, only 15 min from Montréal, come experience true gastronomy. A charming entrance, lined with apple trees and forest, a dining room redolent with the wonderful smell of well-browned chicken at the edge of a property near a pond provide a warm and soothing ambiance. While we prepare a feast for you, what could be better than an early evening drink on the terrace whose charm is only enhanced by your presence.

From Mercier bridge, Exit Kanawake Rres 207 and 221 twd St-Rémi, right on Rte 209, 3km, right 1st road St-Antoine, 4km. From the Champlain bridge, Aut. 15 twd the U.S.A., Exit 42, Rte 132. At the 5th light, left on Rte 209 South, about 15km. In St-Rémi from the light, 3km. Right 1st road St-Antoine, 4km.

Open year round
Includes: visit of the farm in season

Punch
Canapés
Crème de légumes
Terrine de lapin aux kiwis ou Terrine de canard à l'orange
ou Rillette d'oie
Gnocchi à la Romaine ou Tagliatelle aux asperges ou
Feuilletés aux petits légumes
Magrets de canard aux poires et raisins ou Confit de
canard au chou braisé ou Aiguillettes de canettes aux
griottes ou Pintade à la mandarine ou aux pommes
Pomme de terre mousseline et légumes du potager
Salade et Fromages
Crêpe farcie aux fruits avec crème anglaise ou Charlotte
aux poires ou Framboisier au fromage blanc
Autres menus sur demande

Meal: 35 $ Taxes extra

week: 10 to 40 people w/e: 14 to 40 people

Min. nb. of guests may vary depending on the season /
Only 1 group at a time.

22. ST-VALÉRIEN

LA RABOUILLÈRE
Pierre Pilon, Denise
Bellemare and Jérémie Pilon
1073, rang de l'Égypte
Saint-Valérien JOH 2B0
(450) 793-4998
fax (450) 793-2529
www.rabouillere.com
info@rabouillere.com

Provincial Excellence Prize "Success" 2001 agrotourism. Depending on the season, you will greeted by our gardens or a fire in the hearth. Rabbit is on the menu, as well as lamb, goat and farm birds. Edible flowers brighten or flavour our dishes. Get here early, as there is so much to see. Consult our Web site for our packages. **B&B p 205. Farm Explorations p 60. Farm Stay p 70. See colour photos.**

From Montréal, Aut. 20 East, Exit 141 twd St-Valérien, about 20km. In the village, at 1st flashing light, straight ahead, 3km. At 2nd flashing light, right, 1.3km. From Québec City, Aut. 20 West, Exit 143 twd St-Valérien... Or Aut. 10, Exit 68, Rte 139 twd Granby, Rtes 112 and 137 North twd St-Hyacinthe. After St-Cécile, right on Ch. St-Valérien, left at 1st flashing light.

Open year round
Includes: visit of the farm

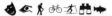

Dégustation de canapés
Trio de charcuteries maison et son mesclun
Potage provençal, pesto et chèvre frais
Feuilleté aux rognons de lapin, sauce porto
Granité aux fruits de saison
Râble de lapin farci, sauce à l'estragon
Carré d'agneau, sauce aux cerises de terre
Magret de canard au vinaigre de framboise
Suprême de pintade, sauce aux pommes
Plateau de fromages de la région
Gâteau mousse au chocolat et fromage
Crème brûlée au gingembre et romarin
Crêpe aux fruits de saison
Autres menus sur demande

Meal: 30-60 $ Taxes extra VS IT

week: 8 to 100 people w/e: 15 to 100 people

Min. nb. of guests may vary depending on the season /
Can accommodate more than 1 group / 4 dining rooms
(exclusive use depends on seasons, nb. of people).

23. GATINEAU

LE POMMIER D'ARGENT
Philippe Salmon and
Thérèse Desjardins
793, Montée McLaren
Gatineau J8R 3C5
(819) 669-5417
(819) 661-5550
**www.infonet.
ca/pommierdargent**
pommierdargent@infonet.net

15min from the heart of Gatineau, Le Pommier d'Argent is one of the most beautiful farms in the Outaouais region. It can be seen from a distance, with its lovely Canadian-style house and farm buildings. The long entranceway, lined with majestic trees, flowers and a wonderful pond, will simply seduce you. We will delight your tastebuds with our fine French cuisine composed of savoury products from our farm, as the warm decor of our intimate and friendly dining room awaits you. We guarantee that the wild-boar tongue and liver will live on in your memory!

From Ottawa, Aut. 50 East, de l'Aéroport Exit, then left on Boul. Industriel. At Montée McLaren, northbound, continue 3.5km. The farm is to your left. From Montréal, Rte 148 to Masson, Aut. 50 West, de l'Aéroport Exit...

Open year round
Includes: visit of the farm in season

Prusciutto de sanglier
Mousse de foie de chapon ou de bison
Terrine de lapereau Charentaise
Ballottine de chapon aux petits légumes
Consommé de volaille Vichyssoise
Médaillons de langue de sanglier sauce ravigote
Confit de notre basse- cour et fondue de poireaux
Aiguillettes de foie de sanglier ou bison en persillade
Lapereau braisé à la moutarde et au Porto
Estouffade de chapon à l'ancienne
Surlonge de bison sauce demi glace Bordelaise
Brie ou chèvre chaud et verdure à la française
Le royal chocolat et crème anglaise
Crème brûlée à la vanille des îles
Soufflé glacé à l'amaretto
Mousse de fruits sauvages et coulis de fraise

Autres menus sur demande

Meal: 29-45 $ Taxes extra VS IT

week: 12 to 30 people w/e: 6 to 30 people

Only 1 group at a time.

24. ST-SIXTE

FERME CAVALIER
Gertie and Marc Cavalier
39, montée Saint-André
Saint-Sixte J0X 3B0
(819) 985-2490
**www.agricotours.
qc.ca/anglais/cavalier**
marc.cavalier@sympatico.ca

In our beautiful valley, beside the Rivière St-Sixte, lamb and poultry from our farm are served in the two traditions: the richness of French gastronomy and the exotism of Moroccan cuisine. Give in to temptation with our changing menu, depending on the seasons and available products and the vision of your hosts. And don't forget our package including accommodation in a cosy and comfortable B&B.

One hour from Hull, 2 from Montréal. From Hull, Aut. 50 twd Masson, Rte 148 twd Thurso. Rte 317 North, 18km right on Montée Paquette, left on Montée St-André.

Open: May 1 to Mar. 31
Includes: visit of the farm in season

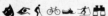

Potage "Harira" aux petits légumes à la coriande
Feuilleté à la pintade et aux herbes : la "pastilla"
Dégustation de sept salades traditionnelles
Tajin d'agneau aux oignons et amandes
Coquelet, farce au couscous, sauce au miel et cannelle
Épaule d'agneau à la vapeur, dorée au safran, couscous aux oignons et miel
Keftas d'agneau aux tomates, risotto au safran
Pastilla J'agneau
Briouats au miel et salade d'orange
M'hencha : gâteau traditionnel aux amandes
Pain "Kesra" au sésame et anis
Nous pouvons vous aider à planifier vos occasions spéciales.
Autres menus sur demande

Meal: 25-35 $ Taxes extra

week: 10 to 40 people w/e: 15 to 40 people

Min. nb. of guests may vary depending on the season / Only 1 group at a time.

Farm Shops

FARM SHOPS

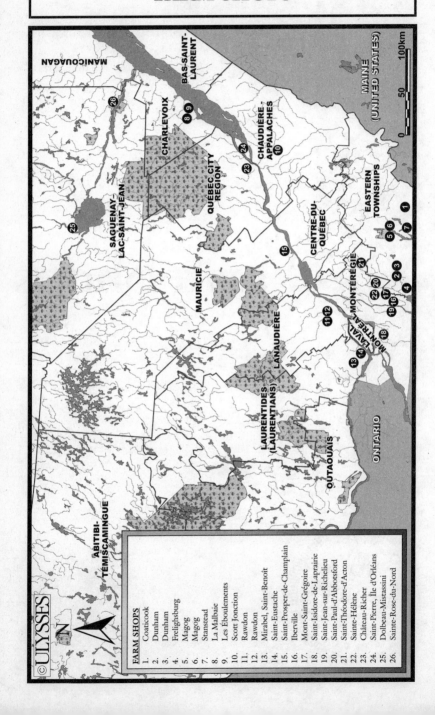

FARM SHOPS
1. Coaticook
2. Dunham
3. Dunham
4. Frelighsburg
5. Magog
6. Magog
7. Stanstead
8. La Malbaie
9. Les Eboulements
10. Scott Jonction
11. Rawdon
12. Rawdon
13. Mirabel, Saint-Benoît
14. Saint-Eustache
15. Saint-Prosper-de-Champlain
16. Iberville
17. Mont-Saint-Grégoire
18. Saint-Isidore-de-Laprairie
19. Saint-Jean-sur-Richelieu
20. Saint-Paul-d'Abbotsford
21. Saint-Théodore-d'Acton
22. Sainte-Hélène
23. Château-Richer
24. Saint-Pierre, Île d'Orléans
25. Dolbeau-Mistassini
26. Sainte-Rose-du-Nord

1. COATICOOK

LA FERME MARTINETTE
Lisa Nadeau and
Gérald Martineau
1728, chemin Martineau
Coaticook J1A 2S5
tel/fax **(819) 849-7089**
1-888-881-4561
www.lafermemartinette.com
martinet@abacom.com

In the heart of a century-old maple grove, discover a sugar shack that produces maple syrup in the spring and processes maple products all year. A charming gift shop offers the delights of the Québécois tradition. Of high quality both in terms of content and presentation, the refined maple goods of La Ferme Martinette will guarantee pure enchantment to the lucky recipient. Maple syrup, butter, caramel, sugar and candy. **Farm Explorations p 52. Country-Style Dining p 19. Country Home p 107.**

From Montréal, Aut. 10 Exit 121, Aut. 55 Exit 21. Rte 141 South 1km before the village of Barnston. Right on Chemin Madore, left on Chemin Martineau. 10 km from Coaticook - 25 km from Magog - 40 km from Sherbrooke.

Products: Regional products sold on the premises. Corporate gift-wrapping. Country dining and dining room (reservations required). Picnic area. Horseshoe game.

Services : Stroll through the farm. Guided tour of the farm. Lodging in a suite or room at the country house.

VS MC IT

Open: Year round. Every day by reservation individual or group.

2. DUNHAM

DOMAINE DE LA CHEVROTTIÈRE
Monique Bouchard and
Gilles Vennes
326 C, Bruce
Dunham J0E 1M0
(450) 295-3584
1-877-295-3584
fax (450) 295-1237
www.domainedelachevrottiere.com
chevrottiere@hotmail.com

Located in Dunham, 1hr from Montréal, Domaine de la Chevrottière will delight all of your senses. Come and share our passion for goat farming and homemade natural cosmetics. Let us offer you respite amidst lush, generous vegetation.

From Montréal, Champlain bridge, Aut. 10 twd Sherbrooke, Exit 68 twd Cowansville, Rte 139. At the 2nd light, right Rte 202 twd Dunham. At the stop sign, right twd Bedford Rte 202, 0.9km to the Domaine. From Lafontaine tunnel, Aut. 30 twd Brossard, Aut. 10 twd Sherbrooke... From Sherbrooke, Aut. 10, Exit 68 twd Cowansville... 35 km from Granby - 25 km from Bromont - 20 km from Sutton.

Products: Le Domaine de la Chevrottière offers visitors a wide array of high-quality natural products, such as goat's-milk and bee's wax cosmetics: soap, moisturizing lotion, body milk, shampoo and conditioner, lipstick and glosses, etc; honey products: liquid and creamy honey; and even maple products: syrup, taffy and butter. Come see, smell and taste these delicious treats that were created especially for you...

Services : In addition to natural products, we offer our guests a guided tour of the goat farm and the sugar shack, and we allow free access to footpaths. Visitors can also enjoy observing local wildlife from the top of the tower that was designed for this very purpose. A rest stop with panoramic view will allow you to admire the magnificent landscape of the Eastern Townships.

VS

Open: June to Oct.: seven days a week, from 10am to 5pm; the rest of the year, open weekends only, from 10am to 5pm, or weekdays by reservation.

3. DUNHAM

F E &P

**LA CIDRERIE FLEURS
DE POMMIERS**
Hélène and Steve Levasseur
1047 rue Bruce (rte 202)
Dunham J0E 1M0
(450) 295-2223
tel/fax (450) 298-5319
**www.agricotours.qc.ca/anglais
/fleurs_de_pommiers**
hlevasseur@acbm.net

Cidrerie Fleurs de Pommiers is located along the "Route des vins of the Dunham Valley" and Montérégie cider Route and is the only cider mill in Quebec which has a woman for cellar master. Our products have won several medals at the national and international levels, the latest being a Gold Medal, from the "Coupe des Nations 2002" and a Silver Medal from Intervin International in 2001 for the Pommeau d'Or, our aperitif cider. This last one is also a favourite of Daniel Vézina, the famous chef at the Laurie Raphaël Restaurant in Québec City. A refreshing stop with a warm welcome. Hope to see you soon!

Only 1 hr from Montréal and Sherbrooke. Aut. 10, Exit 68, take Rte 139 South twd Cowansville. In Cowansville right on Rte 202 at 2nd light twd Dunham. At the stop sign, right, 4km. The Cidrerie is on your left at the corner of Godbout Road. Follow the blue signs - Vignobles de Dunham. 100 km from Montréal - 35 km from Granby - 100 km from Sherbrooke.

Products: Ciders: Cuvée de la Pommeraye - sparkling, Réserve - light semi-dry, Blanc de Pomme - light sweet, Clé des Champs and Cuvée de Noël - flavored, Pommeau d'Or - liqueur. Old-fashioned vinegar: aged in oak barrels for one year, non-filtered, non-pasteurisez. 500ml, 1L, 2L, 4L in dark glass bottles. Flavored cider vinegars with blackberries, currant, raspberries, cranberries, red currant, oranges, blueberries etc. and fine herbs, mustards and vinaigrettes. Apple products: jellies, jams, apple butter and syrup, pickles, chocolates, pies and fresh cider. Regional procuts: terrines, pâtés, vegetable jellies, honey, maple products and apple must.

Services : Tasting. Guided tours (advance booking required). U-pick. Picnic table. Walks in the 70 acres orchard. Exceptional site and view. Gift baskets. Corporate gifts.

VS MC IT

Open: May, Nov., Dec. - Sat. and Sun., 11am to 5pm. June to end of Oct., everyday from 10am to 5pm. Jan. to May, on demand.

4. FRELIGHSBURG

F e

À LA GIRONDINE
Françoise and François Bardo
and Yannick Lemée
104, Route 237 sud
Frelighsburg J0J 1C0
(450) 298-5206
www.netc.net/lagirondine
lagirondine@netc.net

La Girondine is housed in a beautiful building with double pitch roof in which you will find a meat shop, a gift shop and a superb reception hall. Here, your hosts prepare the traditional recipes of their native France from their own raised mulard ducks, guinea fowl, rabbits and quails. These dishes are served in regional dining and sold at the boutique in various formats. **Country-Style Dining p 20. Farm Explorations p 52. B&B p 96.**

Aut. 10, Exit 22, Aut. 35 South to the end. Left twd St-Alexandre to Bedford, Rte 202 about 7km. Right at the sign for Frelighsburg. Turn right and continue 1km after crossing the village. 24 km from Cowansville - 48km from Granby - 48km from St-Jean.

Products: We offer a sublime foie gras, cooked or terrine, rillettes, pâtés, smoked cutlet, duck thigh, sausage and other products composed of various meats. Ready-made meals: conserves, cassoulets and meat pies; fresh and frozen meat. Consult the list on our Web site: www.netc.net/lagirondine

Services : Observe ducks and stroll through the orchard and the forest to spot a deer or two. You can also take a break near the lake and enjoy a picnic. The kids will love the idea of running around and feeding the roaming hens.

VS MC IT

Open: Shop open year round except Tues. 10am to 6pm. May to Oct. picnic bask on request. We take order and deliver with min. buy.

5. MAGOG

F E ♿

LE VIGNOBLE LE CEP D'ARGENT
Denis Drouin
1257, chemin de la Rivière
Magog J1X 3W5
(819) 864-4441
1-877-864-4441
fax (819) 864-7534
www.cepdargent.com
cep@netrevolution.com

In the heart of the picturesque Eastern Townships, Le Cep d'Argent reveals its secrets and shares its passion with thousands of visitors from the world over. An enticing and pleasurable experience for both eyes and tastebuds! Vignoble Le Cep d'Argent was founded in 1985, when 10,000 vines were planted; today, the vineyard includes 60,000 vines of six types. During the past few years, Le Cep d'Argent's team has made major investments in the infrastructures to ensure that its clientele enjoys the best service and top-quality products.

From Montréal, Aut. 10, Exit 118 twd Magog. In Magog, Rte 108 East, left on Chemin de la Rivière. 7 km from Magog - 15 km from Sherbrooke - 80 km from Granby.

Products: White wine: Domaine Le Cep d'Argent, Cuvée des Seigneurs
Red wine: Délice du Chais, Réserve des Chevaliers
Kir: Fleur de lys
Late harvest: Le Fleuret
Pineau des Charentes: Le Fleuret
Port: L'Archer
Champagne method: Sélection des Mousquetaires.

Services : Guided tours and sampling. Great gift shop (open 7 days). Air-conditioned reception halls for special events. Terrace for refreshments and light lunch meals. Personalized corporate gifts.

VS MC AM IT

Open: June-Oct. from 9am to 6pm, Oct. to Dec. from 10am to 5pm, Jan. to May from 10am to 4pm.

6. MAGOG

F E ♿

LE VIGNOBLE LES CHANTS DE VIGNES
Valérie Martel
459, chemin de la Rivière
Magog J1X 3W5
(819) 847-8467
fax (819) 847-2940
www.chantsdevignes.com
chantsdevignes@qc.aira.com

Coming to Le Vignoble Les Chants de Vignes, you'll know what we are : Smaller and even more passionate. Maybe hard to find, but even harder to forget. You come for a smile. That, you'll get as a greeting. You also come for the smile that comes to your face, eyes and heart when you sample our wines. Located halfway between lake Magog and Memphrémagog, Le Vignoble Les Chants de Vignes offers you a graceful hymn of the Magog-Orford region. Our different grape varieties bloom in a respectful way of growing grapes. The fruit of our work is available for sampling on the premises, or at our boutique. The smiling and welcoming guides will escort you through the vineyard while you observe the life of winemakers.

From Montréal, aut. 10, exit 55 South. Exit 32 ch. De la Rivière. 100 km from Montréal - 30 km from Sherbrooke - 30 km from Newport (U.S.A.).

Products: White wine: Le Canon Blanc Cuvée Spéciale 1999. Red wine: Le Canon Rouge. Rosé: Le Régale. Raspberry kir: Le Kyrié. Late harvest: L'O de Gamme. White port: L'Opéra. Red port: Le Port'O'Chant.

Services : Sampling, guided tour, reception hall, evening entertainment, "Murder Mystery" night, catering service, gift-wrapping, fundraising, personalized activities and service.

VS MC IT

Open: Year round weekdays 9am to 5pm except sunday 10am to 4pm.

7. STANSTEAD

F **E** ♿

DOMAINE FÉLIBRE
Catherine Hébert and
Gilles Desjardins
740, chemin Bean
Stanstead J0B 3E0
(819) 876-7900
www.produitsdelaferme.
com/felibre
felibre@abacom.com

In the Upper Townships, between Stanstead and Coaticook, at an altitude of 425m, Domaine Félibre occupies an exceptional site. The panorama takes in Mont Orford and reaches all the way to the edge of the Appalachians. Here, savour our delicious cider, wine and our absolutely amazing wild-cherry liqueur. Learn about the history of alcohol in your region and see how we make new delicious beverages from still.

From Montréal, Aut. 10 twd Sherbrooke, Exit 121. Aut. 55, Exit 21, Rte 141 South twd Coaticook. 2km past Rte 143, turn right on Chemin Way's Mills. At Way's Mills, Rue Isabelle, left on Rue Provencher, right on rue Davis, which becomes Bean. 35 km from Magog - 60 km from Sherbrooke - 165 km from Montréal.

Products: CRU DES VALLONS, dry white wine, 12.5% alc.
SANS SOUCIS, apple and grape wine, 11% alc.
POMMÉ, dry hard cider, 10% alc.
FRUIT DÉFENDU, mildly effervescent cider, 10% alc.
VICE CHACHÉ, ground-cherry liqueur, 30% alc.

Services : Free tour and sampling, picnic table, playground for children. For groups of 8 to 15 people, we offer country meal by reservation. It is best to reserve in advance for groups of over 8 people (by e-mail or telephone).

IT

Open: May 15 to Sep 15, everyday 11am to 5pm.
Rest of the year: Sat. and Sun. 11am to 5pm.

🏛 👁 🎿 🚶 🚴 🐎 ⛸ 🛶

8. LA MALBAIE

F **E** 🦽 **P**

LA VALLÉE DES CERVIDÉS
Suzanne D. Rousselle and
Gratien Potvin
394, Chemin des Loisirs
La Malbaie G5A 1Y3
(418) 665-2409
(418) 633-2162
fax (418) 665-2410
**www.agricotours.qc.ca/
anglais/vallee_des_cervides**

Wild venison in Charlevoix. How to describe the pleasure of a visit to the Vallée des Cervidés, a whitetail-deer breeding farm. Magnificent creatures that remain wild yet dare to let visitors pamper them. A guided introduction to these animals offers a return to nature, tranquillity and well-being. An incomparable experience in an enchanting setting. **Farm Explorations p 54.**

From Québec City, via Ste-Anne-de-Beaupré. In La Malbaie cross the bridge, left and follow the signs twd the Grand-Fond ski resort. 8km from the beginning of Ch. des Loisirs. 158 km from Québec - 58 km from Baie St-Paul - 12 km from La Malbaie - Pointe au Pic.

Products: Farm products. Garden products in season. Vacuum-packed cuts of meat at the Veau de Charlevoix Enr. slaughterhouse. Cold cuts and ready-cooked meals. Grain-fed chickens. Homemade pastries. Preserves of all kinds. Products available on premises.

Services : Walks in the wild on trails made by the deer. Snowshoeing and cross-country skiing. Tour and information on the life of whitetail deer.

Open: Open year round Wed. to Sun. 10am to 5pm by reservation.

9. LES ÉBOULEMENTS

F **E**

**LES FINESSES
DE CHARLEVOIX**
Nathalie Savard
378, St-Godefroy
Les Éboulements G0A 2M0
(418) 635-1407
(418) 635-1393
**www.finessesdecharlevoix.
com**
*finessesdecharlevoix@
qc.aira.com*

Les Finesses de Charlevoix has won several regional and provincial awards, and is the best place to find regional Charlevoix products. Located in the heart of the World Biosphere Reserve, we look forward to welcoming you to our shop, in our home offering a breathtaking view of the majestic St. Lawrence River and mountains. In addition to discovering regional treasures, you will have the opportunity of enjoying a picnic on site.

From Québec City, Rte 138 twd Ste-Anne-de-Beaupré and Baie-St-Paul, panoramic Rte 362, 2.5km past the village of Les Éboulements. 18 km from Baie St-Paul - 26 km from La Malbaie - 150 km from Québec.

Products: We produce a line of over 150 homemade products, such as jam and low-sugar jam, jelly, marmalade, fruit sauce, fruit syrup, vinaigrette, fruit and fine-herb mustard, flavoured oil and vinegar, butter and dip, sauce, honey and maple products, picnic items and other products available on the premises.

Services : We offer gift-wrapping and personalized service throughout the year. Sampling is possible by reservation. Picnic service with panoramic view of the river available in summer and fall.

VS MC IT

Open: Year round 9:30am to 9pm. Unless otherwise specified.

10. SCOTT JONCTION

F E ♿ P

LA CACHE À MAXIME
Gina Cloutier
265, rue Drouin, C.P. 929
Scott G0S 3G0
(418) 387-4781
(418) 387-5060
fax (418) 387-1826
www.lacacheamaxime.com
service@lacacheamaxime.com

La Cache à Maxime is an agrotourism centre that you can contemplate, savour and even bring back home with you. First and foremost a vineyard, La Cache is also a country compound where regional history and culture are omnipresent. Take a guided tour of the vineyard or of the Miel d'Émilie beehives and visit our shop specializing in country products, arts and crafts and regional treasures. Also: terrace, café-bistro, porto-tasting room, cigar room, etc.

From Québec, Aut. 73 South, Exit 101, left on Rue Carrier, left on Rte Kennedy, right on Rue Drouin, 1km. From the U.S., Rte 173 North, Aut. 73 North, Exit 101, right on Rte Kennedy, right on Rue Drouin, 1km. 10 km from Sainte-Marie - 43 km from Québec - 56 km from Lévis.

Products: Le Jarret Noir - red wine, Le Jarret Noir - white wine, Le Rosé de Maxime - pinkish wine.

Services : Sampling, guided tour, group reservations, large terrace, porto-tasting room, cigar room, picnic area, country and crafts shop, gift wrapping, fish-filled lake, garden, "Les douceurs de Maxime" café-bistro, public market, guided tour of the Miel d'Émilie beehives and many more activities.

VS MC IT

Open: Early Apr. to late Jan. Every weekdays 10am to 10pm.

11. RAWDON

F e

FERME GUY RIVEST
Louise and Guy Rivest
1305, Laliberté
Rawdon J0K 1S0
(450) 834-5127
fax (450) 834-7367
**www3.sympatico.
ca/guy.rivest/index.html**
guy.rivest@sympatico.ca

At the award-winning Ferme Guy Rivest, strawberries are more than a simple fruit. Production and processing is done on site; share the liveliness and enthusiasm of owners who are not afraid to enjoy life's finest things. Here, stock up on strawberries and discover wines and liqueurs that will enchant you thanks to their strawberry bouquet and summery flavours. In season, you can even pick your own berries and have a fun family picnic.

From Montréal, Aut. 25 North and Rte 125 North, Exit 337, Rte 348 East, Chemin Laliberté 1km. From Trois-Rivières, Aut. 40 West, Exit Berthier, Rtes 158 and 345 twd Notre-Dame-de-Lourdes about 30km. Rte 348, Chemin Laliberté. 50 km from Montréal - 16 km from Joliette - 95 km from Trois-Rivières.

Products: Strawberry wines: "La Libertine" dry aperitif - "Le Libertin" semi-sweet aperitif - "La Courtisane" sweet aperitif- "Mistelle de fraises" strawberry liqueur – strawberry-wine jelly – fresh and frozen strawberries - jam - sauce – gift-wrapping.

Services : Pick your own berries or buy them at the farm kiosk; gift-wrapping, picnic area. Guided tour with wine and strawberry-liqueur sampling (minimum of 10 people) by reservation. $2 per person.

Open: May to Aug. every day 9am to 8pm. Low season from thurs. to Sun. 10am to 6pm.

12. RAWDON

F e P

LES SUCRERIES DES AÏEUX
Guylaine Léveillé and
Guy Breault
3794, Chemin de Kildare
Rawdon J0K 1S0
(450) 834-4404
tel/fax (450) 834-6454
www.multimania.com/aieux/
*sucreries-des-aieux@
efferent.net*

Les Sucreries des Aïeux, a reputed maple-processing plant, will reveal the many different aspects of sap. This ancestral maple grove will enchant you with its modern equipment, while the processing plant will seduce you with its maple-treat shop. 5 min from Dorwin falls, discover our natural treasure, the maple tree.

From Montréal, Aut. 25 North and Rte 125 North, Exit 337, Rte 348 East, 6.4km. From Trois-Rivières, Aut. 40 West Exit Berthier Rtes 158 and 345 twd N.D-de-Lourdes, about 30km. Rte 348, 10km. 50 km from Montréal - 16 km from Joliette - 95 km from Trois-Rivières.

Products: Pure maple butter – pure maple candy – soft maple sugar – firm maple sugar – granulated maple sugar – pure maple syrup – pure maple taffy – maple peanuts – hard candy and lollipops – maple-filled Belgian chocolates – maple caramel – maple-taffy cones – maple jelly – maple-sugar pie – maple mustard – gift-wrapping – etc.

Services : Products sold at the kiosk and the farm, gift-wrapping, etc. Open year-round. By reservation: guided tour of the maple grove and processing plant with sampling of maple products. Rate: Guided tour $2 per person with sampling (min. 8 people).

Open: Open year round. Mon. to Fri., 9am to 6pm. Sat. from 9am to 5pm. Sun. 12am to 5pm (march only).

13. MIRABEL, ST-BENOÎT

F E & P X

AU GIBIER DU ROI
France Couture and
Guy Arseneault
6015, Rang Saint-Vincent
Saint-Benoît, Mirabel J7N 2T5
(450) 258-2388
fax (450) 258-3970
www.augibierduroi.com
augibierduroi@hotmail.com

The "La Cerferie shop at this red-deer farm features various cuts of stag meat and a wide array of homemade products for you to discover: pâtés, liver mousse, sausages, etc. The stags are raised in harmony with nature and fed with grain and forage, which produces a highly natural red meat. Through various activities, learn more about the breeding of this coveted "game of kings" and how to serve it in your own home! **Country-Style Dining p 26.**

From Montréal, Aut. 13 or 15 North, Aut. 640 West, Exit 11 Boul. Arthur-Sauvé twd Lachute. After 17km, left on St-Vincent twd St-Placide, 6km. 22 km from St-Eustache - 22 km from Lachute - 35 km from Laval.

Products: Here, red deer is the specialty. Meat cuts: Medallion, steak, roast, filet, fondue, kebab cubes, ground, loin, etc. Homemade products: Various pâtés, liver mousse, various sausages, stuffed pasta. Other products: Free-range chicken, fresh eggs, pickles, partridge, pheasant.

Services : Country-style dining on Thursdays, Fridays and Saturdays (reservations required). 2 dining rooms for your convenience. Tour of the farm (by request during the week). Recipes and culinary demonstrations by request.

VS IT

Open: Open year round. Weekdays by reservation. Sat. and Sun. 11am to 5pm.

14. ST-EUSTACHE

F E & P X

VIGNOBLE DE LA RIVIÈRE DU CHÊNE
Isabelle Gonthier and
Daniel Lalande
807, Rivière Nord
Saint-Eustache J7R 4K3
(450) 491-3997
(450) 473-3357
fax (450) 473-0112
www.agricotours.qc.ca/anglais /vignoble_riviere_duchene
latza@total.net

Visit the Vignoble de la Rivière du Chêne and discover of a wide array of remarkable products, a warm reception and an exceptional setting. In 1998, Daniel Lalande and Isabelle Gonthier decided to dedicate themselves to viniculture and now care for 20,500 vines on their 8.9ha family property.

Aut. 640 West, Exit 11 twd Lachute Rte 148. Past the hospital, left on Boul. Industriel twd Chemin Rivière-Nord. Right, 5km. Follow the blue "Route des Vins" signs. 50 km from Montréal - 30 km from Laval - 70 km from Longueuil.

Products: Cuvée William (white): Well-elaborated, fruity wine. Excellent balance of sugar and acidity. 2001 MAPAQ gold medal. Cuvée William (red): Surprising wine with great character and rich expression. Accompanies seasoned red meat and game. Cuvée Glacée des Laurentides: An explosion of intense aromas and exquisite softness. Gold medal in Tremblant and 2001 MAPAQ bronze medal. L'Adélard: Maple-syrup-flavoured wine. Full and round, generous character, ideal with appetizers, brunch and dessert. Vendange des Patriotes: Its dark-red colour is due to non-filtration. Supple attack, fruity with wood flavours. 2001 MAPAQ silver medal. Accompanies red meat and game.

Services : Wine for sale on the premises. Guided tours. Tastings. Picnic tables. Activities for children in fall. Tasting room for wine and farm products (max. 50 people, by reservation, for all types of events).

VS IT

Open: Sat. and Sun.12am to 5pm. Weekdays by reservation.

15. ST-PROSPER-DE-CHAMPLAIN

FERME LA BISONNIÈRE
Daniel Gagnon and
Sylvie St-Arneault
490, rang Ste-Élisabeth
St-Prosper-de-Champlain
G0X 3A0
(418) 328-3669
fax (418) 328-8668
**www.letremplin.
qc.ca/bisonniere**

To see grazing bison from a safe distance, follow the road to St-Prosper, rain or shine. Here, stock up on prepared meals and frozen meat (standard cuts). On a unique tractor-trailer, see what it feels like to get up close to some 100 heads of cattle. A day at La Bisonnière is a day of discovery, adventure and top-quality products in a family atmosphere that will brighten your day.

Aut. 40 (30min from Trois-Rivières and 1hr from Québec City), Exit 236. 7km on Rte 159 North and right on Rang Ste-Elizabeth. Continue 0.5km to Ferme La Bisonnière. 50 km from Trois-Rivières - 100 km from Québec - 200 km from Montréal.

Products: Ferme La Bisonnière offers visitors top-quality natural meat in the best cuts, such as sirloin steak, roast, Chinese and meat fondue, ground meat or burger, filet mignon, T-bone, tournedos, meat pie, sausage, tongue, liver, heart, tail and even complete carcass and half-carcass for groups. We also offer various products derived from the bison, such as leather, skulls and floral arrangements with horns, bone and wood sculptures, paintings, jewellery, etc.

Services : Buffet-style meal featuring bison, meat pies and sausages... One-hour guided tour: $5 per adult, $3 per child. Guided tour and sampling $10, by reservation. Guided tour and meal (buffet): $18 per adult, $10 for children aged 2 to 11, by reservation.

Open: Open year round, 7 days, 9am to 9pm.

16. IBERVILLE

F e 🦽

VIGNOBLE DIETRICH-JOOSS
Victor and
Christiane Dietrich-Jooss
407, Grande Ligne
Iberville J2X 4J2
tel/fax (450) 347-6857
www.dietrich-jooss.qc.ca
info@dietrich-jooss.qc.ca

The vineyard is located in Iberville (30min southeast of Montréal) and was founded in 1986 by Victor and Christiane Dietrich-Jooss (French wine growers). We produce white, red, rosé, sparkling, late-harvest and ice wines in the purest tradition of our native region, Alsace. With over 115 medals and awards, our vineyard has won the most international medals in Québec thanks to the quality and originality of our wines.

From Montréal, Aut. 10, Exit 22, then Aut. 35 South. At the end of Aut. 35, turn left at the lights twd St-Alexandre, to 407 Grande Ligne. 50 km from Montréal - 4 km from St-Jean sur Richelieu - 40 km from Chambly.

Products: White wine: Réserve du Vigneron. White wine: Cuvée Spéciale. White wine: Storikengold. Rosé: Rosé d'Iberville. Red wine: Réserve des Tonneliers. Late-harvest white wine: Cuvée Stéphanie. White ice wine: Sélection Impériale. White wine: Dionysos. Sparkling wine: Crémant d'Iberville.

Services : Sampling, sale, shop, guided or independent tour, reception hall, picnic table.

VS MC AM IT

Open: May to Dec.: Wed. to Sun include 10am to 5pm or by reservation. On Jan. to Apr.: Thurs. to Sun. include: 10am to 5pm.

🏛 🍷 ⛵ 🛶 ⛷ 🚶 🚴

17. MONT-ST-GRÉGOIRE

F E 🦽 P

CLOS DE LA MONTAGNE
Denise Marien
330, de la Montagne
Mont-Saint-Grégoire J0J 1K0
(450) 358-4868
fax (450) 358-5628
www.agricotours.qc.ca/
anglais/clos_de_la_montagne
aryden@videotron.ca

Named "Clos de la Montagne" because it is located barely 1km from Mont St-Grégoire, this property was purchased in 1988 by former Montrealers Denise-Andrée Marien and Aristide Pigeon. What makes this site charming is both the layout and the reception room, which is decorated with stained glass made by the wine growers themselves. Le Clos de la Montagne is part of the Montérégie Cider Route and the Québec Wine Route. It is also included in the maple-grove route in spring and the orchard route in autumn.

Aut. 10 twd Sherbrooke, Exit 37, Rte 227 to De la Montagne or via Rte 104 twd Cowansville, 0.5km from the Rue De la Montagne stop sign. 10 km from St-Jean d'Iberville - 35 km from Montréal - 32 km from Longueuil.

Products: Red wine: St-Grégoire, Cuvée Versailles. White wine: St-Grégoire, Cuvée Joffrey. Red-wine aperitif: Grégorio Rouge. White-wine aperitif: Grégorio Blanc. Hard cider: La Drupa. Sparkling cider: Méthode Champenoise. Aperitif ciders: Le Maceron, Pomme sur lie, Cuvée Réserve. Rosé: Le Bouquet du Clos. Vinegars: cider vinegar, raspberry vinegar.

Services : Guided tour. Tasting sessions. Picnic areas. Fruit picking. By-products. On-site sales. Distributor of oak casks. Family or business reception (max. 32 people).

VS MC IT

Open: Open year round, 10am to 6pm.

18. ST-ISIDORE-DE-LAPRAIRIE

LES ÉLEVAGES RUBAN BLEU
Denise Poirier Rivard
449, Saint-Simon
Saint-Isidore-de-Laprairie
JOL 2A0
tel/fax (450) 454-4405
www.rubanbleu.net
chevre@rubanbleu.net

Excellence Prize "Achivement" 2002 Agrotourism. For 20 years, Denise Poirier Rivard has made it her duty and her joy to confect a wide array of delicious 100% homemade goat's-milk cheeses in the most traditional fashion. That's why a good regional wine must always accompany them. During your wine-and-goat's-cheese-tasting session, you will be warmly welcomed by passionate people who will tell you all about the goat world, from the birth of the kid to the processing of pure goat's milk cheese...some of the best in Canada. For all amateurs of fine gustatory experiences and those who simply love goats! **Farm Explorations p 59. See colour photos.**

Rte 132, Aut. 30 West, Exit 86, left at the stop sign, take Rte 221 twd St-Rémi. 1km past the 1st stop sign, right on rang St-Simon, 3km. 15 km from Châteaugay - 15 km from Montréal - 25 km from Longueuil.

Products: Our sale kiosk is open throughout the year and offers 21 kinds of the most popular cheeses, such as La P'tite Chevrette: this soft cheese with flourished crust is pyramid-shaped and creamy, melts in your mouth and lingers on the palate; Le St-Isidore: soft with flourished crust, Camembert or Brie-type; Le St-Isidore Cendré: soft cheese with flourished crust wrapped in vegetable charcoal; Le Pampille: soft, unripened, fine texture, delicate; Le Chèvre d'Or: baked crust, surface-ripened.

Services : Wine & Cheese Tasting Session. 3 sittings:assortment of Ruban Bleu goat's cheese (unlimited), regional wines, quality bread, fruit, coffee, etc. Included: guided tour, video. Rate: $25 per person (tax included). For groups of 20 to 50 people year round (by reservation). Cheese gift baskets and gift certificate available.

Open: Farm-shop operating hours: year round: Wed. to Fri., 10am to 6pm; Sat.and Sun., 10am to 5pm; closed Mon and Tue. Narrated tours: May 1 to Oct. 31. For groups: year round (by reservation).

19. ST-JEAN-SUR-RICHELIEU

FROMAGERIE AU GRÉ DES CHAMPS
Suzanne Dufresne and
Daniel Gosselin
400, rang St-Edouard
St-Jean-sur-Richelieu J2X 4J3
(450) 346-8732
www.inns-bb.com/gredeschamps
gredeschamps@qc.aira.com

This cheese dairy specializes in the production of cheeses made from the freshest milk. At Daniel Gosselin, Suzanne Dufresne, Marie-Pier and Virginie's farm, you will find a unique flavour, aroma and character that results from strict guidelines in the quality of all the cheese-making elements, from the field of blossoming, aromatic plants to the heard of Brown Swiss cows. Organic farming techniques are used to enhance the soil and transmit its characteristics to the milk and cheese.

Aut. 10 twd Sherbrooke, Exit 22, Aut. 35 twd St-Jean-sur-Richelieu, Exit 6. Left at the first stop sign, Av. Conrad-Gosselin. Left at the second stop sign, Rang St-Édouard. 30min from the Champlain bridge. 30 km from Montréal - 32 km from Longueuil.

Products: Le D'Iberville: made from raw milk, this farm cheese is semi-hard with a washed crust. Matured for over two months, it offers a magnificent taste of herbs and flowers.
Le Gré des champs: this farm cheese, made from raw milk, is hard with a mixed crust. It matures for over three months. During its processing and maturation, a selection of its natural flora allows it to offer a delicious hazelnut flavour.

Services : Sample our own cheese, as well as other farm and handmade cheeses from Québec. Picnic areas. Visit at your leisure. Observe the processing and maturation of cheese. We also sell regional products.

VS

Open: Apr. to Dec. Thur. to Fri. 1pm to 6pm. Sat. and Sun. 10am to 5pm. Close on Jan. Feb. and Mar. : Sat. 10am to 5pm.

20. ST-PAUL-D'ABBOTSFORD

**VIGNOBLE ARTISANS
DU TERROIR**
Céline and Réjean Guertin
1150, Rang de la Montagne
St-Paul-d'Abbotsford J0E 1A0
(450) 379-5353
fax (450) 379-2004
**www.agricotours.qc.ca/
anglais/artisansduterroir**
artisansduterroir@qc.aira.com

At the foot of Mont Yamaska, we invite you to enjoy culinary delights at our vineyard and jam factory. Let yourself be tempted by over 20 products that will please your tastebuds. Enjoy the beauty and tranquillity of the countryside during your visit to the Artisans du Terroir vineyard. Welcome to the Guertin family's home!

From Montréal, Aut. 10, Exit 55. Left on Rte 235, follow the directions to Pépinière Abbotsford to Rte 112. Turn right, past the Pépinière 0.5km, turn left, follow the blue signs to the vineyard. From Granby, Rte 112 East twd St-Paul, follow the blue signs. From Ste-Hyacinthe, Rte 235 South left Rte 112, follow the blue signs. 10 km from Granby - 60 km from Montréal - 20 km from St-Hyacinthe.

Products: 1999 white wine -Artisans du Terroir: 2000 white wine-La Vrillée: 2000 red wine - Artisans du Terroir: 2001 red wine-Prémices d'automne and Daumeray: 2001 white wine - Prémices d'automne, winner of the 2002 Grappe de Bronze: aperitif wine -Tourbillon 365. Selection of jellies and jams of various flavours: blackcurrant, currant, blackberry, raspberry, ground cherry and more. To accompany meat, we prepare fruit ketchups and rhubarb chutney. Apple pie in season.

Services : Sample our wine, jelly, jam, ketchup and chutney, all handmade on site. In season, taste the various kinds of apples and dessert grapes that are grown on our farm. Personalized gift-wrapping and corporate gifts available. Guided tour by reservation. Country-style shop on an ancestral road. It is also possible to hike on the mountain and the farm site.

IT

Open: In season : Mid May to Dec. 23. Tues. to Sun. 10am to 5pm. Close on Mon. Low season: Jan. to Mid-May. Reservation (450) 379-5353.

21. ST-THÉODORE-D'ACTON

VERGER CIDRERIE LARIVIÈRE
Monique and Clément Larivière
1188, 8ième Rang
St-Théodore-d'Acton J0H 1Z0
(450) 546-3411
fax (450) 546-4938
www.clementlariviere.com
clementlariviere@hotmail.com

A few kilometres from Acton Vale and accessible via the bike path, come experience an educational and delicious adventure! In the orchard, we grow 10 kinds of apples and have over 5,000 apple trees, as well as 5,000 vines. We make our products, such as natural apple juice, cider and liqueurs, on the premises thanks to traditional methods. Shop on site for all our products as well as regional products.

Aut. 20, Exit 147 twd Acton Vale, Rte 139 North to 8e Rang in St-Théodore d'Acton. 20 km from Drummondville - 25 km from St-Hyacinthe - 35 km from Granby.

Products: La Ruée vers l'Or: hard cider. La Fête au village: sparkling hard cider. La Cidraise: strawberry aperitif cider. L'Eden: apple mistelle; apple juice, 10 kinds of apples.

Services : Sampling, guided or independent tour of the orchard, guided tour of the cider factory, rides by group reservation, picnic tables, pick your own apples, gift-wrapping, Kéroul-adapted establishment.

IT

Open: Aug. to Dec.: Mon. to Sat. from 9am to 5pm. Sun 10am to 4pm. Jan. to July from Mon. to Fri. from 9am to 5pm. Sat. 9am to 12.

22. STE-HÉLÈNE

F e & P

ÉRABLIÈRE L'AUTRE VERSAN
Hélène Belley and Stéphan Roy
350, 4ᵉ Rang
Sainte-Hélène J0H 1M0
(450) 794-2524
(450) 261-6271
fax (450) 794-2081
**www.agricotours.
qc.ca/anglais/
erabliere_autre_versan**

We fell in love at first sight with this 25ha dream property, a warm and intimate place in the heart of a farming region. A walk in the forest, tasting and a tour of our maple products facilities will charm you. A 50-person dining room is open for meals at sugaring-off time.

From Montréal, Aut. 20 twd Québec City. Exit 152 Ste-Hélène. Left at the intersection, 2km, right on Rang 4.3km. 15 km from St-Hyacinthe - 15 km from Drummondville - 48 km from Montréal.

Products: Maple products: syrup, butter, sugar, toffee, jelly, caramel, cones, candy, lollipops, chocolate, maple "fudge", ice cream, pie, maple-sugar rolls, ketchup, fruit jam, gift-wrapping.

Services : Typical, family-run sugar shack that can accommodate up to 50 people. Tasting. Guided or self-guided tour. Dining room. Forest walk. Rest area. Gift-wrapping.

Open: Open year round by reservation.

23. CHÂTEAU-RICHER

F E   P

MOULIN DU PETIT PRÉ
Isabelle Longpré
7007, ave. Royale
Château-Richer G0A 1N0
(418) 824-7007
1-877-449-4411
fax (418) 824-7017
www.moulin-petitpre.com
ilongpre@moulin-petitpre.com

The "Moulin du Petit Pré" vineyard is located on a historic site that is over 300 years old and whose picturesque setting and exceptional view of the St. Lawrence River will win you over. The boutique features wine products, regional delicacies and great gift ideas. On-site wine tasting, tour, self-guided tour of the vineyard and picnic area. Multi-purpose room for presentation and workshop, cocktail parties or meeting. **Farm Explorations Musée de l'Abeille p 62.**

From Québec City, Aut. 40 twd Ste-Anne-de-Beaupré. Follow the blue Tourisme Québec sign. 20 km from Québec - 15 km from Ste-Anne-de-Beaupré.

Products: White wine, rasberry liqueur and cream, "Saveurs du Village" products.

Services : For individuals and families: free admission. Tasting sessions of our wine products and Saveurs du Village. Wine-and-cheese samplings. Group rates with guided tour and slide show. "Festival des Vendanges" (wine harvest) package in mid-September.

VS MC AM IT

Open: Open year round June 22 to Oct. 14, 10am to 5pm.

24. L'ÎLE-D'ORLÉANS, ST-PIERRE

F e   P

DOMAINE ORLÉANS
Jacques Paradis
285, Chemin Royal
Saint-Pierre-de-l'Île-d'Orléans G0A 4E0
(418) 828-9071
fax (418) 828-2935
www.domaineorleans.com
jparadis@domaineorleans.com

This agrotourism site is located near the downtown area (10 min by car) and offers views of the Île d'Orléans bridge, Chutes Montmorency and Côte de Beaupré. Devoted to the promotion and conservation of fish, Domaine d'Orléans features a wide array of rainbow- and speckled-trout products, tours, tastings, fishing and a museum. School groups and business receptions held under large tents. Alcoholic apple beverages, apple picking, ice fishing, overnight stays in igloos, dog-sledding.

Île d'Orléans bridge, right at the light, right 1km. Located 15 min from Mont Ste-Anne, 30 min from Stoneham ski station, 5 min from shopping malls, restaurants and accommodations. 10 km from Québec - 20 km from Beaupré - 150 km from Trois-Rivières.

Products: Fish farm: rainbow and speckled trout for breeding. Smoked trout marinated in our cider vinegar and white wine or cider, mousse, smoked-trout pizza, trout pâté. Apple products: light and hard cider, ice cider, mistelle, apple and blackcurrant liqueur, apple and cranberry liqueur, cider vinegar in various flavours (raspberry, blackberry, rosemary), apple butter, apple and strawberry/raspberry/blueberry butter, jellies (apple cider, raspberry, rose petal), fresh apple juice, maple butter, maple jelly, syrup and taffy.

Services : Tasting sessions, picnic, boutique offering gift-wrapping, play area, guided tour of the fish farm and fishing museum, Loto-Québec fireworks. Apple picking, pond fishing and ice fishing, overnight stays in igloos and campfire with breakfast, dog-sledding.

VS MC IT

Open: Jan. 1 to Apr. 30 as well as Nov. and Dec. Everyday 9am to 5pm except Mon. and Tues. May to Oct., every day, 9am to 5pm.

25. DOLBEAU-MISTASSINI

LA MAGIE DU SOUS-BOIS INC.
Lucina and Mariette Beaudet
801, 23ᵉ avenue
Dolbeau-Mistassini G8L 2V2
(418) 276-8926
fax (418) 276-9447
www.agricotours.
qc.ca/anglais/magiesous-bois
magiedusousbois@qc.aira.com

La Magie du Sous-Bois, an ancestral property, is an ecological centre for the cultivation of Nordic berries and processing of regional products. 10km of hiking trails with wild-flora interpretation stations and bird watching; an Aboriginal tepee awaits you in the heart of this boreal forest. Small lake that is ideal for calm and relaxation. Organic blueberry products. Massages, well-being and spirituality. Guide available for outdoor excursions. Pick your own berries for an unforgettable experience and sample products that are a treat for the tastebuds.

From Dolbeau-Mistassini, Rte 169 twd Normandin, left on 23ᵉ Av. and continue 2km. 34 km from St-Félicien - 124 km from Chicoutimi (Saguenay) - 82 km from Alma.

Products: Spreads - blueberry: "Plaisir Divin", blueberry/raspberry: "Audace", blueberry jelly: "Inspiration." Sauces - blueberry: "Volupté", raspberry: "Délice." Syrups - blueberry: "Séduction", raspberry: "Désir", Saskatoon berry: "Opulence." Blueberry candies. Fresh berries (blueberries, raspberries, Saskatoon berries, blackberries). Pères Trappistes chocolate, organic vegetables. Blueberry pies, sorbets, juices, teas.

Services : Pick your own Saskatoon berries, blueberries, raspberries and blackberries from mid-July to mid-September. Taste regional products. Independent or guided tour of the blueberry museum and pedestrian trails. Picnic tables, shelters, benches along the trails. Gift-wrapping. Reception hall, farm kiosk, tepee, showshoe rental. Relaxation services: massage therapy, reiki, intuitive therapy.

Open: May 1 to Oct. 31 9am to 6 pm. Dec. 25 to Mar. 15 from 10am to 4pm, every day.

26. STE-ROSE-DU-NORD

FROMAGERIE LA PETITE HEIDI ENR.
Line Turcotte and
Rhéaume Villeneuve
504, boul. Tadoussac
Ste-Rose-du-Nord G0V 1T0
tel/fax (418) 675-2537
www.agricotours.
qc.ca/anglais/petiteheidi

In the Saguenay Lac St-Jean region, in Sainte-Rose-du-Nord, a small village nestled between the mountains and the sea that is also known as the "pearl of the fjord," Fromagerie La Petite Heidi is a unique experience. We have been welcoming visitors since 1996 and offer various goat-milk cheeses.

From Québec City, Rte 175 North twd Chicoutimi, Rte 172 East twd Ste-Rose-du-Nord. From Tadoussac, Rte 138 East, 7km, left on Rte 172 twd Ste-Rose-du-Nord. 40 km from Ville Saguenay - 75 km from Tadoussac - 100 km from Alma.

Products: Goat's-milk cheese.

Services : Visit the farm, sample products and purchase your favourites. Picnic area. Various cheeses to taste. $2.50 per adult; $1.50 per child.

Open: Year round 9am to 6pm except Friday 9am to 4pm.

Farm
Explorations

RECOGNIZED BY
AGRICOTOURS
QUALITY ❀ COMFORT

FARM EXPLORATIONS

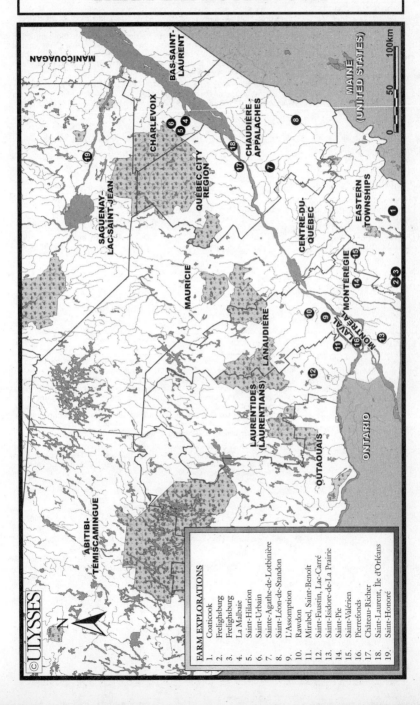

© ULYSSES

N

MANICOUAGAN

BAS-SAINT-LAURENT

CHARLEVOIX

QUÉBEC CITY REGION

CHAUDIÈRE-APPALACHES

MAINE (UNITED STATES)

SAGUENAY–LAC-SAINT-JEAN

EASTERN TOWNSHIPS

MAURICIE

CENTRE-DU-QUÉBEC

MONTÉRÉGIE

LANAUDIÈRE

LAVAL

MONTRÉAL

LAURENTIDES (LAURENTIANS)

OUTAOUAIS

ONTARIO

ABITIBI-TÉMISCAMINGUE

0   50   100km

FARM EXPLORATIONS

1. Coaticook
2. Frelighsburg
3. Frelighsburg
4. La Malbaie
5. Saint-Hilarion
6. Saint-Urbain
7. Sainte-Agathe-de-Lotbinière
8. Saint-Léon-de-Standon
9. L'Assomption
10. Rawdon
11. Mirabel, Saint-Benoît
12. Saint-Faustin, Lac-Carré
13. Saint-Isidore-de-La Prairie
14. Saint-Pie
15. Saint-Valérien
16. Pierrefonds
17. Château-Richer
18. Saint-Laurent, Île d'Orléans
19. Saint-Honoré

1. COATICOOK

LA FERME MARTINETTE
Lisa Nadeau and
Gérald Martineau
1728, chemin Martineau
Coaticook J1A 2S5
tel/fax **(819) 849-7089**
1-888-881-4561
www.lafermemartinette.com
martinet@abacom.com

La Ferme Martinette opens its door to reveal the fascinating world of pure-bred Holstein dairy production as well as cultivation, small animals, the family orchard, flowers, history... The old-fashioned-tractor ride will take you to the sugar shack where you will learn about the production and processing of maple products in the heart of a maple grove that is over 100 years old. Country-style dining and regional-product gift shop. The tour is included in overnight stays. **Country-Style Dining p 19. Farm Shops p 36. Country Home p 107.**

From Montréal, Aut. 10 Exit 121, Aut. 55 Exit 21. Rte 141 South, 1km before the village of Barnston. Right on Chemin Madore, left on Chemin Martineau. 10 km from Coaticook - 25 km from Magog - 40 km from Sherbrooke.

❀ - ❀ -❀-❀ -❀ -❀ -❀-❀

For families and groups.
- Picnic area
- Horseshoe game
- Hiking in the maple grove
- 45 min guided tour of the farm, snow-hardened maple taffy.10% less school group (march to Apr.)
- Guided tour of the farm and the maple grove, 2hrs (May to late Oct.)
- Children's playground
- Mini labyrinth (sunflower field)

RATES

Adult: $5-$5.50
Child: $5-$5.50
School group: discount 10%

Rates vary according to age, number of people, selected activities, etc.

Taxes extra VS MC IT

Open: Mar. to end of Oct. Every day by reservation. Individual and group.

2. FRELIGHSBURG

À LA GIRONDINE
Françoise and François Bardo
and Yannick Lemée
104, Route 237 sud
Frelighsburg J0J 1C0
(450) 298-5206
fax (450) 298-5216
www.netc.net/lagirondine
lagirondine@netc.net

At La Girondine, discover a traditional farm where ducks are raised in outdoor enclosures, similarly to the tradition of southern France. A guided tour will allow you to learn about our duck, whose foie gras is served in the finest cuisine. These magnificent, large white birds share their space with geese, guinea fowl and other animals. During your visit, you will also discover the forest's riches and diversity and walk through an orchard overlooking Mont Pinacle. Our on-site shop features regional products and gift ideas. The tour is included in overnight stays. **Country-Style Dining p 20. Farm Shops p 36. B&B p 96.**

Aut. 10, Exit 22, Aut. 35 South to the end. Left twd St-Alexandre to Bedford, Rte 202 for about 7km. Right at the sign for Frelighsburg. Turn right and continue 1km after crossing the village. 24 km from Cowansville - 48km from Granby - 48km from St-Jean.

❀ - ❀ -❀-❀ -❀ -❀ -❀-❀

- For families and groups: from May to late October
- Picnic area
- Hiking.

RATES

Guided tour: 30 to 45 min $7 includes sampling from May to October. Reservation only.

Open: Year round except tuesday from 10 am to 6pm (boutique).

3. FRELIGHSBURG

LA FERME DU WAPITI
Lise Bourgoin
50, chemin des Bouleaux
Frelighsburg J0J 1C0
tel/fax (450) 298-5335
1-800-391-5466
**www.agricotours.
qc.ca/anglais/wapiti**

La Ferme du Wapiti offers guided tours describing how we raise and care for our cattle and explaining animal behaviour. We will teach you the various steps to incubating emu, wild turkey and pheasant eggs. Observe the quality of life of our animals and learn how we make ham and smoked meat from wapitis and bison. Those who wish to relax in a natural setting can do so in the forest, where a picnic area has been set up in an enclosure.

From Montréal, Aut. 10, Exit 22 St-Jean-sur-Richelieu, Rte 35 South and 133 South. Past the village of Pike River/St-Pierre-de-Vérone, continue about 5km. Turn left at the flashing light on Chemin St-Armand, continue 15km. Left on Chemin des Bouleaux. 24 km from Cowansville, 48km from Granby, 48km from St-Jean.

- Farm visit
- Learn about the breeding process. Picnic area either in the woods or surrounded by animal enclosures.

RATES

Adult:	$4
Child:	$2

Open: Apr. to Dec. from Wed. to Sun. from 11am to 4pm.

4. LA MALBAIE

LA VALLÉE DES CERVIDÉS
Suzanne D. Rousselle and
Gratien Potvin
394, Chemin des Loisirs
La Malbaie G5A 1Y3
(418) 665-2409
(418) 633-2162
fax (418) 665-2410
**www.agricotours.qc.ca/
anglais/vallee_des_cervides**

Wild venison in Charlevoix. How to describe the pleasure of a visit to the Vallée des Cervidés, a whitetail-deer breeding farm. Magnificent creatures that remain wild yet dare to let visitors pamper them. A guided introduction to these animals offers a return to nature, tranquillity and well-being. An incomparable experience in an enchanting setting. **Farm Shops p 39.**

From Québec City, via Ste-Anne-de-Beaupré. In La Malbaie, left after the bridge follow the signs twd the Grand-Fond ski resort. 8km from the beginning of Ch. des Loisirs. 158 km from Québec - 58 km from Baie St-Paul - 12 km from La Malbaie - Pointe au Pic.

* Walks in the wild on trails made by the deer
* Snowshoeing and cross-country skiing
* Tour and information on the life of whitetail deer.

RATES
Adult: $3
Child 3 to 16 years: $2
Group 10 to 20 people

Open: Year round. From Wed. to Sun., 10am to 5pm. By reservation.

5. ST-HILARION

**ÉLEVAGE DE LA BUTTE
AUX CAILLES**
Claude Riel Lachapelle
70, Rang 5
St-Hilarion G0A 3V0
(418) 457-5050
1-866-457-5050
**www.agricotours.qc.ca/
anglais/butteauxcailles**

This pheasantry features raising and hunting infrastructures in a natural habitat. Here, visitors are given complete information on the pheasant (history, habitat, traditions, raising, gastronomy and hunting.) On site, traditional restaurant renowned for its pâtés, grilled pheasant and partridge, and Bourgogne wines. The restaurant and terrace are open in summer every day from 1pm to midnight (reservations are preferred). Groups welcome. Farm tours from Tuesday to Sunday, 2pm to 4pm. Hunting from September to October. Pheasant hunting with dogs.

From Québec City, Rte 138 East twd Baie-St-Paul. Past Baie-St-Paul, about 25km on Rte 138, left on 4e-5e Rang.

* Video on breeding: from the chick to maturity and hunting.

RATES
Free for all. Except for hunting.
Price on request

Open: Visit of the farm from June 24 to Sep.1 from tuesday to sunday from 2pm to 4pm.

6. ST-URBAIN

i F e ♿ P

**CHEZ GERTRUDE CENTRE
DE L'ÉMEU DE CHARLEVOIX**
Raymonde Tremblay
706, Saint-Édouard, rte 381,
C.P. 293
Saint-Urbain G0A 4K0
(418) 639-2205
1-866-639-2205
fax (418) 639-1130
www.emeucharlevoix.com
raymondetremblay@videotron.ca

The Centre de l'Émeu de Charlevoix is the largest emu farm in Québec, with over 250 emus of all ages and a rhea who really enjoys visitors. Our guides are available every day during summer and will teach you about the world of ratites and the emu industry in Québec. This visit will fascinate both children and adults. **B&B p 125. Farm Stay p 68. See colour photos.**

From Québec City, Rte 138 East. About 10km past Baie St-Paul, Rte 381 North, 3km. Take the entrance behind B&B Chez Gertrude. 10 km from Baie St-Paul - 45 km from La Malbaie - 100 km from Québec.

- Observation of emus of all ages
- Learn the difference between emus, ostriches and rheas, as well as their habitat and habits
- Discover the various products derived from emus (oil, soap, body lotion, painted shell, meat and by-products, etc.)
- Video on the hatching of chicks
- Samplings
- On-site shop
- Possibility of meals for groups.

RATES
Adult: $3
Child 2 to 12 years: $2
Group 10 to 45 people: $5
Group 46 and more: $2

Rates vary according to age, number of people, selected activities, etc.

Open: Every day, 9:30am to 4:30pm from Jun. 20 to Aug. 24 and Aug. 30 to Sept. 2. Every sat. and sun. of Sep. 10am to 3pm. Rest of the year or group: by reservation.

7. STE-AGATHE-DE-LOTBINIÈRE

FERME PÉDAGOGIQUE
MARICHEL
Louise Fortin
809, Rang Bois Franc
Sainte-Agathe-de-Lotbinière
G0S 2A0
(418) 599-2949
fax (418) 599-2959
www.clic.net/~marichel
marichel@clic.net

From the earth to your plate... La Ferme Pédagogique Marichel's goal is to promote awareness on such issues as farming, ruralism, the environment and development. Since 1994, we have been welcoming groups to our farm with an emphasis on quality and authenticity. Marichel is a diverse farming business that includes ovine and porcine production, a small apiary and several other animals. We care for the environment and practice organic farming in our fields. Overnight stays with meal (max. 35 people): from $45/person. Other services and rates on demand.

From Québec, Aut. 20 West, Exit 305, twd St-Gilles, Rte 218 West twd Ste-Agathe-de-Lotbinière. From Montréal, Aut. 20 East, Exit 278, South twd Ste-Agathe-de-Lotbinière. 50 km from Québec city bridges - 40 km from Ste-Marie-de-Beauce - 50 km from Thetford Mines.

- Dairy production, lambing, "time-travelling" (tepee and log cabin), tractor rides, bread-making, candles, apple juice, butter, animal care, wool processing, sheep-shearing, hay games, beekeeping, campfires, gardening, farm crafts, scarecrows...
- Our programs are adapted to your needs
- Welcoming groups and families (with or without overnight stay)
- Farm classes
- Summer camp
- Sale of farm products
- Meals composed of farm products
- Also for training, meetings, anniversaries...

RATES

Adult: $10
Child: $10
Group 15 to 60 people: $10

Rates vary according to age, number of people, selected activities, etc.

Taxes extra

Open: Year round. Summer camp June to Aug. Groups, schools and families Sep. to June. By reservation only.

8. ST-LÉON-DE-STANDON

JARDINS DES TOURTEREAUX
DE LA FERME LA COLOMBE
Jean-Yves Marleau
104, rue Sainte-Anne
Saint-Léon-de-Standon
G0R 4L0
(418) 883-5833
(418) 642-5152
fax (418) 642-2991
www.fermelacolombe.qc.ca
r.gregoire@globetrotter.net

"Success" 2000 Special Mention for Excellence. Nestled in the mountains, this garden will allow you to discover farm animals, aviaries and over 600 plant species laid out in 12 themes. The tour will rouse your every sense and add a touch of romance and reverie to your days. Order a gourmet picnic basket of local flavours or bring your own. By taking advantage of the "Table Champêtre", you will be able to better enjoy our gardens. **Country-Style Dining p 24.**

From Québec City, Aut. 20 East, Exit 325 twd Lac-Etchemin, Rtes 173 South and 277 South twd St-Léon-de-Standon. At the stop sign, 0.9km from the church, cross Rte 277, left on Rte du Village, 4km. Right on Rang Ste-Anne, 2km. 90 km from St-Georges-de-Beauce - 100 km from Québec - 70 km from Lévis.

- Horticultural farm: tending and reproduction of plants (20 species)
- Theme gardens: edible flowers (75 species), fragrances, colours, birds, indigenous plants, aquatic (6 ponds, 1 lake and 3 streams), berries, (samplings)
- Nature-interpretation relay. Tree nursery (sale of rare and perennial shrubs)
- School groups: "Tour of Noah's Ark"*
- Groups: Plant reproduction
- Sampling of flower-based products*
- Dinner at the farm*
- Gourmet picnic basket*
*By reservation, additional charge

RATES

Adult: $5
Seniors: $4
Student: $3
Child 2 to 6 years: $2
Group 20 to 80 people: $5

Open: For families and small groups: mid-June to early Sept. For groups of 20 to 80 people: May to Oct.

9. L'ASSOMPTION

ÉRABLIÈRE DES PATRIOTES
Mario Lavoie
573, Montée Ste-Marie
L'Assomption J5W 5E1
(450) 588-7206
fax (450) 588-1837
www.erabliere-des-patriotes.
qc.ca
erabliere_des_patriotes@
hotmail.com

Close to Montréal, the Érablière des Patriotes was founded in 1995. We raise exotic breeds on our multifunctional farm while preserving our heritage and the memory of our past. Our period characters will share their knowledge with you through various educational activities related to farming.

From Montréal, Aut. 40 East, Exit 108, at the 2nd access Rte 343 North twd Joliette. At the church, cross the bridge (Montée Ste-Marie), 2.9km. We are on the left side of the road. 30 km from Montréal - 10 km from Repentigny - 10 km from Joliette.

Choice of 7 different themes with characters dressed in period costumes.
- Discovery of the maple grove, the farm and deer, inhabitants, lumberjacks, Aboriginal woman, Aboriginal man and trappers
- Country-style dining by reservation
- Indoors or under tents
- Farm boutique
- Groups by reservation
- Capacity: 160 people

RATES

Adult: $5
Child: $3

Taxes extra

Open: Year round, 7 days a week, by reservation.

---

10. RAWDON

ARCHE DE NOÉ
Bernard Boucher
4117, ch. Green
Rawdon J0K 1S0
(450) 834-7874
(450) 834-3934
fax (450) 834-5090
www.agricotours.
qc.ca/anglais/archedenoe

You can begin your stroll immediately upon your arrival by visiting the 26 different animals, some of which run free. The flower gardens and landscaping will enhance your visit, while lovely footpaths will guide you through our valleys to peaceful picnic areas. We can organize special events.

From Montréal, Aut. 25 North twd Rawdon. Rte 337 North, left on Rue Queen (at the IGA). Cross the village right on 11th Av., left at the Chemin Morgan. About 7km farther, on the left, is Chemin Green. We are at the end of the road. 55 km from Montréal - 65 km from Longueuil - 30 km from Joliette.

- Hiking trails and site for up to 200 people
- Giant covered sandbox for children
- Various animals: ostriches, emus, wild boars, horses, vietnamese pigs, sheep, large and miniature goats, Limousin cows, guinea pigs. Several species of aquatic birds: ducks and geese. Aviary for winged birds: pheasants, guinea-fowl, peacocks, etc
- Our unforgettable landscape and family ambiance will brighten your day!

RATES

Adult: $6
Child over 1 year: $5
Group 2 to 200 people: $5
Rates vary according to age, number of people, selected activities, etc.

Open: May 1 to Nov. 1. Every day 9am to 5pm.

11. MIRABEL, ST-BENOÎT

⛤ 🐄 ♿ i F E ♿ P

INTERMIEL
Viviane and Christian Macle
10291, rang de La Fresnière
Saint-Benoît, Mirabel J7N 3M3
(450) 258-2713
fax (450) 258-2708
www.intermiel.com
intermiel@sympatico.ca

In St-Benoît, visit the largest beekeeping area in Québec. The guided tour includes a visit of our mead cellar, a video, demonstrations, an educational play area and a "bee safari" in season. Our shop offers a original array of honey and maple goods...come in for a taste! The educational tour includes a jar of honey and a light snack. The group rate includes a 2hr educational tour and 4 workshops.

From Montréal, Aut. 15 North, Exit 20, Aut. 640 West, Exit 8. Follow the blue tourist information signs, 18km. 15 km from Saint-Eustache - 45 km from Montréal - 25 km from Mirabel airport.

❀ - ❀ -❀-❀ -❀ -❀ -❀-❀

- Movie on the beekeeping activities of the farm
- Information on bees. Observation of living hives (wall of bees)
- Handling of an active hive by the beekeeper (in summer)
- Demonstration of production technique
- Tour of the mead cellar
- Educational play area. Puppet show (school groups)
- Sampling of honey products (ganache, caramel, etc) and hydromel (honeywine)
- Country store (candles, gifts, cosmetics, maple products, maple liquor, etc)
- Picnic area (indoor area in case of rain)
- Mini-farm

RATES

Adult: $3
Child: $1
School Group: $6 or $8/people (with guided tours of mini-farm and specific work-group by reservation).

Open: Year round, 7 days a week 9am to 6pm.

12. ST-FAUSTIN, LAC CARRÉ

⛤ 🐄 ♿ i F E ♿ P

FERME DE LA BUTTE MAGIQUE
Diane Gonthier
1724, ch. de la Sauvagine
Saint-Faustin-Lac-Carré
J0T 1J2
tel/fax (819) 425-5688
www.infodesing.com/ bmagique
fermedelabuttemagique@ hotmail.com

On a typical Laurentides property, a herd of "multicoloured" sheep brightens the landscape, while on our picturesque farm, artisan shepherds take pleasure in modernizing ancestral techniques with abounding creativity. Our tours combine farming and art; our "tailored" programs are highly educational. We even offer spinning and felting classes. Come discover the varieties of wool produced by our five breeds of sheep. There are also hens, pigs, dogs and cats!

From Montréal, Aut. 15 North. In St-Faustin, 2km past Mont Blanc, left on Chemin La Sauvagine, 7km. From St-Jovite, Rte 327 South twd Arundel, 2km. Left on Chemin Paquette, 6km. 25 km from Mont-Tremblant - 115 km from Montréal - 180 km from Ottawa.

❀ - ❀ -❀-❀ -❀ -❀ -❀-❀

First package
Guided farm tour (2hrs)
- Discover the diversity of the shepherd lifestyle; from animal care to wool processing to the "attic of memories"

Second package
The sheep's bounty from every angle (1 day)
- An exciting "picnic day" with choice of interactive workshops
- Tour of the wool-washing pavilion, the carding workshop and a collection of spinning wheels...
- Make your own souvenir
- Presentation on the history of spinning
- Excursion to the Butte Magique
- Characteristics of ewe's milk
- Guided farm tour.

RATES

Adult: $6 to $15
Child 2 to 12 years: $4 to $8
Group child 10 to 50 people: $4 to $8
Rates vary according to age, number of people, selected activities, etc.

Open: Year round: for groups of all ages (minimum of 10 people), by reservation only.

13. ST-ISIDORE-DE-LAPRAIRIE

LES ÉLEVAGES RUBAN BLEU
Denise Poirier Rivard
449, Saint-Simon
Saint-Isidore-de-Laprairie
J0L 2A0
tel/fax (450) 454-4405
www.agricotours.qc.ca/
anglais/elevagesrubanbleu
chevre@rubanbleu.net

Excellence Prize "Achivement" 2002 Agrotourism. Recipient of the Montérégie Grand Prize of Tourism 2000, category tourist attraction for less than 100,000 visitors. 10 min from the Mercier bridge, come pet the adorable goats who are the first to greet you on site! Also, discover some 21 kinds of handmade cheeses offered yearound in our on-site shop. And if the goat world intrigues you, take part in the narrated tour in our interpretive centre, the Ruban Bleu pavilion, where you will learn everything about goats, from breeding to cheese. **Farm Shops p 45. See colour photos.**

Rte 132, Aut. 30 West, Exit 86, left at the stop sign, take Rte 221 twd St-Rémi. 1km past the 1st stop sign, right on rang St-Simon, 3km.
15 km from Châteauguay - 15 km from Montréal - 25 km from Longueuil.

- Independent walk through the site. Feeding and petting the goats. Close contact with the animals
- "From breeding... to cheese" narrated tour. Video, Commentaries, sampling of goat's milk and cheese, May, Jun, Sep, Oct: Sat and Sun 2pm, July and Aug: Wed to Sun 2pm
- Educational school program
- Farm shop: 21 kinds of goat's-milk cheese; goat's-milk bubble bath, bath milk and soaps; mohair socks
- Wine-and-cheese tasting by reservation

RATES

Adult: $5
Child 0 to 5 years: free with parent
Child 6 to 12 years: $2.50
Group 10 to 55 people: $5
Autobus: 2 people free

Open: Farm-shop operating hours: year round: Wed. to Fri., 10am to 6pm; Sat.and Sun., 10am to 5pm; closed Mon and Tue. Narrated tours: May 1 to Oct. 31. For groups: year round (by reservation).

14. ST-PIE

FERME JEAN DUCHESNE
Diane Authier and
Jean Duchesne
1984, Haut-de-la-Rivière Sud
Saint-Pie J0H 1W0
(450) 772-6512
fax (450) 772-2491
www.geocities.
com/fermejeanduchesne

2000 "Success" Award of Excellence. Our farm will make little farmers of your children since everything had been designed with them in mind. A day filled with fun, interaction and learning about the significant breeds of Québec farms or our 2 main productions. The adventure is crowned with a personalized "farmer for a day" certificate of merit.

Aut. 20, Exit 123. At the stop sign, left on Rte 235 South, at the 2nd flashing light, left on Rang Emille Ville, at the end left on Rang Haut-de-la-Rivière South, left at the stop sign. Aut. 10, Exit 55 Ange-Gardien, Rte 235 North, right at the flashing light on Rang Emille Ville. Left at the stop sign, then left at the next stop sign. 60 km from Montréal - 20 km from St-Hyacinthe - 15 km from Granby.

- Our five-hour guided tour features educational, recreational and interactive programs adapted to group age (possibility of adjusting time for groups).
- Presentation of various breeds such as the cow and its dairy, the rabbit and its hutch, etc
- Possibility of feeding animals
- Farm games and many surprises!
- Picnic areas and games for rainy days
- Certificate of merit for all little farmers
- Parties for children, private receptions
- Hay rides to the sheep farm and maple grove*. What an adventure in the woods! Apple picking*, water slide*, camping.*

*Additional charge

RATES

Adult: $6.50
Child: $6.50
Group 25 to 180 people: $6
One adult free per 10 children for school, kindergarden and day camp

Taxes extra

Open: Apr. to Oct.: every day 10am to 3pm. By reservation only. One free admission for every adult with 10 children, school, daycare centre, day camp.

15. ST-VALÉRIEN

🐂🏠F e♿P✕

LA RABOUILLÈRE
Pierre Pilon, Denise
Bellemare and Jérémie Pilon
1073, rang de l'Égypte
Saint-Valérien J0H 2B0
(450) 793-4998
fax (450) 793-2529
www.rabouillere.com
info@rabouillere.com

Provincial Excellence Prize "Success" 2001 agrotourism. La Rabouillère is a farm with a difference. An amazing array of animals in an exceptional setting. Ideal for weddings, anniversaries, etc. **Country-Style Dining p 31. B&B p 205. Farm Stay p 70. See colour photos.**

From Montréal, Aut 20 East Exit 141 twd St-Valérien 20km. In the village, 1st flashing light, straight ahead 3km. At the 2nd flashing light, right 1.3 km. From Québec City, Aut. 20 West Exit 143 twd St-Valérien... 80 km from Montréal - 20 km from St-Hyacinthe - 20 km from Granby.

❀ - ❀-❀ -❀ -❀ -❀ -❀ -❀ -❀-❀ -❀ -❀ -❀ -❀ -❀ -❀ -❀ -❀ -❀ -❀ -❀ -❀ -❀ -❀ -❀-❀ -❀ -❀-❀

- In the garden: perennial and edible flowers, fine herbs, water garden
- Farmyard: more than 70 bird species
- Sheepfold: rare breeds, four-horned Jacob, Barbados and Katahdin (without wool)
- Miniatures: horses, donkeys, goats
- In the rabbit hutch: giant and dwarf rabbits, Angora
- Exotic animals: llama, alpaca, deer
- Other activities: pony rides, pool, volleyball, music*, campfire, sampling of farm products*, spit-roasted lamb barbecue, brunch*
- Doves available for release during weddings.

*Additional charge

RATES

Adult: $7
Child: $5
Group 15 to 30 people: $5
Group 31 to 120 people: $4.50

VS IT

Open: May to Oct. Every day by reservation, 10am to 4pm. Family or group (up to 120 people). By reservation only.

16. PIERREFONDS

**CORPORATION D-TROIS-
PIERRES/FERME ÉCOLOGIQUE**
183, ch. du Cap-Saint-Jacques
Pierrefonds H9K 1C6
(514) 280-6743
fax (514) 624-0725
www.d3pierres.com
info@d3pierres.com

Agrotourism-reintegration business. Close to Montréal, delve into the universe of organic farming. We are the only farm in Canada that is associated with the international association of educational farms. We have over 15 species, a greenhouse, an organic garden and cultivated fields — everything to initiate young and old to the world of agriculture. We also offer a wide array of complementary services. Our country ambiance will win you over! Parking: $4.

Aut. 40, Exit 49. Follow the blue signs. The park entrance is located at 20009 Boul. Gouin West. In the park, follow the directions to the "ecological farm". 30 km from Montréal - 100 km from Joliette - 180 km from Hull.

- Guided tours: educational/recreational programs adapted to group age
- Over 15 animal species
- Organic garden and greenhouse: identification of cultures, composting
- Interpretation centre
- General store, regional products
- Restoration
- Footpaths and picnic site, cross-country skiing
- Special programs*: sugar shack, farm, beach, Halloween, carriage rides
- Play area, theme parties, harvest parties* (2nd Sunday in August)
- Complementary services*: country dining, children's parties, carriage rides
- Rental of sites and rooms
*Additional charge

RATES

Open: Year round. Self-guided tours for all. Guided tours for groups of 10 to 120 people.* Feb. 15 to Oct. 31. Sugar shack*: Feb. 15 to Apr. 15, tour and traditional meal*. By reservation.

17. CHÂTEAU-RICHER

i F E & P

**MUSÉE DE L'ABEILLE -
ÉCONOMUSÉE DU MIEL**
Redmond Hayes
8862, boul. Sainte-Anne
Château-Richer G0A 1N0
(418) 824-4411
1-877-449-4411
fax (418) 824-4422
www.musee-abeille.com
info@musee-abeille.com

An unforgettable experience awaits young and old alike at the honey economuseum. At the Bee Safari, observe a beekeeper at work in a real apiary. Giant glassed-in beehives. "Bees and Humans" exhibit, interactive quiz, bee rally. Savour dry or sweet, light or frothy, mead, "the nectar of the gods", produced on site. Shop abounding in beehive products, gift wrapping. Honey-chocolate and pastry shop, healthy meals on the terrace in season. Multipurpose room for presentations, workshops, happy hour or functions. Group rates (20 to 70 people) upon request. **Farm Shops Moulin du Petit Pré p 48.**

From Québec City, Aut. 40 twd Ste-Anne-de-Beaupré. Follow the blue Tourisme Québec roadsigns. 30 km from Québec - 5 km from Ste-Anne-de-Beaupré - 5 km from Château-Richer.

For individuals and families:
- Free admission to the exhibit and shop year-round
- Sampling of our seven kinds of mead (honey wine)
- Bee Safari from St-Jean-Baptiste (June 24) to Thanksgiving for individuals and families
- Educational activities for school groups year-round
- Candle workshop
- Honey-chocolate workshop
- Humorous presentation for groups of adults
- Coffee break, top-of-the-range pastries and dessert plates
- Package with individual gift (wine, chocolate, etc.)
- Wine-and-cheese tasting
- Bistro and gourmet meal
- Cocktail and snack
- Lunch-box service

RATES

Adult: $2.61
Child 0 to 11 years: free with parent
Child over 12 years: $2.61

Rates vary according to age, number of people, selected activities, etc.

Taxes extra VS MC AM IT

Open: Year round, June 24 to Oct. 31, 9am to 6pm. Nov. 1 to June 23, 9am to 5pm.

18. L'ÎLE-D'ORLÉANS, ST-LAURENT

 F E & P

**LAC DE PÊCHE LA SEIGNEURIE
DE L'ÎSLE AUX SORCIERS**
Herman Bédard
1870, chemin Royal
Saint-Laurent-de-l'Île-d'Orléans G0A 3Z0
(418) 692-2425
(418) 828-2163
fax (418) 692-2528
**www.agricotours.qc.ca/anglais
/lacdepecheauxsorciers**
*lacdepecheauxsorciers@
qc.aira.com*

Discover the most beautiful natural spot on the island, the only 5-star spotted-trout-fishing club in the entire Metropolitan Québec City area. Our trout feeds on insects and other foods provided by nature itself. Savour your trout on the premises (steamed, with olive oil or butter, or BBQed). Rediscover tranquillity, serenity, peace of mind, birds, rustling leaves, forests and their inhabitants (foxes, deer, muskrats, racoons, squirrels, grass snakes, tree frogs, etc.). Observe market gardeners (60-acre farm) working in the fields. Trout: $0.75 per inch. $5 is deduced from the fishing bill.

From Québec, Rte 138 East twd Ste-Anne-de-Beaupré, Exit Île d'Orléans, from light, 7km, it's at your left. 18 km from Québec - 32 km from Ste-Anne-de-Beaupré - 36 km from l'Ancienne Lorette.

- Market garden
- Spotted-trout fishing (license not required)
- Equipment and boats provided
- Banquet hall
- Picnic areas
- Free trout-cooking and dishes
- Frozen lake measuring 1/3 of a mile
- Diverse forests and bogs; marked footpaths with bird-feeding dishes
- Volleyball and other games
- Collection of nature posters (over 100)
- Fishing pavilion

RATES

Adult: $5
Child: $5

Rates vary according to age, number of people, selected activities, etc.

Open: Early May to late Oct., 7 days a week from 9am to 6pm. Our activities cater to families, small and large groups, schools, daycare centres, senior citizens, etc.

19. ST-HONORÉ

🏠 F e ♿ P

ACCUEIL DU RANDONNEUR
Bertrand Robitaille
5490, boul. Martel
St-Honoré G0V 1L0
(418) 673-3956
(418) 673-4410
fax (418) 673-6017
**http://quebecweb.
com/lamartingale**

Accueil du Randonneur is located on an enchanting site that allows you to relax while soaking in the natural setting. We are located near Ferme La Martingale, which offers horseback rides (20 horses). Our establishment features a dining room where travellers and hikers can savour regional cuisine. There is also a small farm for children to commune with nature. We welcome organisations, social clubs and school groups for unforgettable moments in the wilderness. Visit the dairy farm, go for a horseback ride by the hour or the day, up to five days. Possibility lodging on the premises.

From Chicoutimi, past the Dubuc bridge, left on Boul. Ste-Geneviève, at the 5th light, left on Boul. Boivin, which becomes Martel. 5km past the church. 15 km from Chicoutimi - 55 km from Alma - 42 km from La Baie.

❀ - ❀ -❀-❀ -❀ -❀ -❀-❀

- We welcome groups and families (babies too!)
- Enjoy our equestrian trails
- In winter, horse-drawn carriage rides
- Small farm
- Fishing pond
- Picnic area
- Visit the stable and dairy farm
- Sample our regional products
- Summer camp
- Campfire.

RATES

Adult: $10
Child 1 to 4 years: $6
Child 4 to 12 years: $8
School group $8 all day, $6 half day
With animation $8/day

Taxes extra VS AM IT

Open: Year round. Group, school, family by reservation. Various prices depend age, number of people and choice of activities.

Farm Stays and Country Homes on the Farm

FARM STAYS AND
COUNTRY HOMES ON A FARM

FARM STAYS
1. Rimouski
2. Saint-Jean-de-Dieu
3. Courcelles
4. Magog
5. Wickham
6. Saint-Urbain
7. Saint-Cyprien
8. Saint-Damien-de-Buckland
9. Sacré-Cœur
10. Saint-René-de-Matane
11. L'Annonciation
12. Hérouxville
13. Howick
14. Saint-Simon
15. Saint-Valérien
16. Sainte-Agnès
17. Sainte-Victoire-de-Sorel
18. Gatineau
19. Vinoy, Chénéville
20. Neuville
21. Stoneham, Saint-Adolphe
22. Hébertville
23. La Baie
24. Métabetchouan, Lac-à-la-Croix
25. Normandin

COUNTRY HOMES
ON A FARM
26. Île-Nepawa
27. Coaticook
28. La Baie

FARM STAYS

		RATES			ANIMALS	ACTIVITIES
		1 meal	2 meals	3 meals		
BAS-SAINT-LAURENT						
Rimouski LA MAISON BÉRUBÉ tel/fax (418) 723-1578	single double child	$45 $60 $5-15	--- --- ---	--- --- ---	The Ferme Flots Bleus is a dairy farm, with a herd of 60 cattle, including 30 purebred dairy cows, plus bulls and calves.	The small farm behind the bed & breakfast is made up of hens and ducks as well as Cannelle the goat and Mylène the ewe. Two horses, Tristan and Bel-Ami, are waiting for you to come pet them. During the summer season, I invite you to help out with farm chores, such as milking the cows, tending the animals, gathering eggs, haymaking, harvesting and gardening. If this work proves too hard, I propose you take a stroll in the fields or along the river. **B&B p 86.**
Saint-Jean-de-Dieu LA FERME PAYSAGÉE (418) 963-3315	single double child	$35 $50 $5-15	$45 $70 $5-15	--- --- ---	Deer, lamas, ponies, lambs, sheeps, goats, rabbits, ducks, cows, peacocks, golden pheasant.	Breathe in the fresh country air while bringing the cows in from pasture and learning how to milk them. You can also feed the small animals and gather fresh chicken and quail eggs. And why not end the day by taking a stroll through the fields to watch the sunset? **B&B p 90.**

		RATES			ANIMALS	ACTIVITIES
		1 meal	2 meals	3 meals		
EASTERN TOWNSHIPS						
Courcelles L'AUBERGE D'ANDROMÈDE tel/fax (418) 483-5442	single double child	$45 $70 $15	$70 $140 $35	--- ---	Adorable racehorses: Percheron, Canadian, Quarter-Horse and a cute little pony, Bambi. Two fun dogs, Dalmatienne and "Tobby la Terreur"; four gentle cats; lovely Angora goats; hens that produce morning-fresh eggs, and geese and ducks quacking in harmony.	Come discover the fantastic world of animals. The horses graze in the fields and are ready to initiate you to horseback riding. Come feed the animals with me after breakfast. For adults we offer, in summer: romantic equestrian package in green forests and lush landscapes. In winter, the carriage package features an amazing carriage ride through the woods. Later, enjoy our delicious table d'hôte, composed of farm and garden products. Here, raspberries abound. **B&B p 94.**
Magog À LA COLLINE AUX CHEVAUX (819) 843-2401	single double child	$60-90 $70-110 $15	$95-105 $130-150 $25	--- ---	We breed Paint horses: stallions, mares and foals. Dogs: Pitoune and Pom (Bernese mountain dogs), cat; laying hens of various races, sheep, calves, rabbits. Lake with trout. Many wild animals (deer, moose, beavers...)	On our magnificent 250-acre property, discover our Paint horses. We will proudly show you our foals. Activities, depending on the season: picking of berries, mushrooms and eggs. Gathering of hay. Campfires, stargazing. In fall, be enchanted by magical colours. In winter, escape by going snowshoeing or cross-country skiing. Direct access to the B&B by skidoo and all-terrain vehicle (Trans-Canada 55, local 55 south.) Bird-watching. **B&B p 101.**
CENTRE-DU-QUÉBEC						
Wickham LA FERME DE LA BERCEUSE (819) 398-6229 (819) 398-6411 fax (819) 398-6496	single double child	$60 $70 $12	$75 $115 $20	--- ---	Laying hens, goats, northern bobwhites, partridges, guinea fowl, wild turkeys, dog and cat.	We invite you to share a moment of sheer delight in a bountiful space. A small organically certified farm, we grow 80 different varieties of more than 25 vegetables, herbs and raspberries. Take part in an educational tour, stroll through the woods or simply laze around on the farm. Renew your connection to the earth and sample the joys of the countryside. La Ferme de la Berceuse, a shared passion. **B&B p 111.**

| | | RATES | | | ANIMALS | ACTIVITIES |
		1 meal	2 meals	3 meals		
CHARLEVOIX						
Saint-Urbain CHEZ GERTRUDE CENTRE DE L'ÉMEU DE CHARLEVOIX (418) 639-2205 1-866-639-2205 fax (418) 639-1130	single double child	$40-50 $55-65 $15	--- --- ---	--- --- ---	The largest specialized emu farm in Québec. Over 350 emus of all ages, from chicks to breeders to a rhea who loves visitors.	The guided tour (1hr) allows you to observe emus of all ages, to tell the differences between emus, ostriches and rheas, to learn about their habitat and habits and to discover the benefits of the many products derived from emus (oil, soap, body lotion, painted eggshell, meat and by-products, etc.). Shop and sampling on premises. Schedule of visits: June 20 to August 24 and August 30 to September 2. Reservations are needed any other time. Dining available for groups. Visit only: $3/adult and $2 for children under 12. **B&B p 125. Farm Explorations p 55. See colour photos.**
CHAUDIÈRE-APPALACHES						
Saint-Cyprien, Barré LE JARDIN DES MÉSANGES tel/fax (418) 383-5777	single double child	$45 $60 $5-10	$57 $84 $15-20	--- ---	Charlot the pony, cows, calves, ox, pigs, hens, grain-fed chickens, turkeys, rabbits, goats, Blanchette the cat and everyone's favourite, Café the dog.	As the seasons drift by, discover different activities. In spring, participates in maple-syrup making in our sugar shack. In summer, discover the organic garden and it's original produce, as well as the flowers and the birds. Help take care of the animals. Visit the region on the bike paths. Enjoy the beautiful colours of automn while hiking, wood cutting or picking mushrooms. In winter, skate on the lake or do some snowshoeing. B&B accessible by skidoo. In summer, baby-sitting for a small additional charge. **B&B p 131.**
Saint-Damien-de-Buckland CASSIS ET MÉLISSE (418) 789-3137	single double child	$40 $55 $5-15	$50 $75 $15-25	--- ---	Goats, rabbits, hens, ducks and, if you come at the right moment, ducklings. Grain-fed chickens, quails, Laïka the Labrador and Grisouille the Cat.	The sun adds a touch of perfume to our herbs, our chickens follow the children, the wind caresses our fields and brings blackcurrants to our kitchen, while a cozy fire ushers in the evening and the aroma of fresh bread welcomes the morning. You will be seduced by the rhythm of our certified-organic farm. Accompany our family as we care for the animals and gardens and share our daily life with you! **B&B p 132.**

CÔTE-NORD

		RATES			ANIMALS	ACTIVITIES
		1 meal	2 meals	3 meals		
Sacré-Coeur FERME 5 ÉTOILES (418) 236-4833 1-877-236-4551 fax (418) 236-4551	single double child	$40 $50 $10	$55 $88 $29	$65 $110 $39	Arctic wolves, buffaloes, stags, cows, sheep, horses, birds and many other farm animals for young and old... over 32 species.	Tour of the farm and animals, sugar shack, excursions: horseback riding, cycling, "Quad" vehicles, fishing, camping, bear observation, canoeing, whale-watching, kayaking on the Saguenay fjord, hydroplane. **B&B p 139. Country Homes p 142. Ad end of region Côte-Nord and Saguenay-Lac-St-Jean. Ad start of the guide.**

GASPÉSIE

		RATES			ANIMALS	ACTIVITIES
		1 meal	2 meals	3 meals		
Saint-René-de-Matane GÎTE DES SOMMETS (418) 224-3497	single double child child alone	$35 $50 $15 $20	$45 $70 $20 $30	$55 $90 $25 $40	Goat farm, chickens, rabbits.	Guided tours of the farm, hikes on the well-marked and maintained trails. Fishing in the brook, mountain biking, picnics, campfires, mushroom picking, wild-berry picking, photo safari. Mountain climbing, visit to beaver pond. In winter season: snowshoeing, cross-country skiing, sliding, skidooing (equipment not provided). **B&B p 150.**

LAURENTIDES

		RATES			ANIMALS	ACTIVITIES
		1 meal	2 meals	3 meals		
L'Annonciation LA CLAIRIÈRE DE LA CÔTE (819) 275-2877	single double child	$35-50 $50-65 $15	$65 $90 $20-25	$70 $100 $30	Cows, calves, goats, sheeps, rabbits, grain-fed chickens, turkeys, geese, dogs and cats.	Visit of the farm. Forest walks (300 acres). Organic gardens, fine herbs, flowers, greenhouse. See chicks hatch. Transformation of farm products. Smoking of meat and fish. Rest areas. Campfires. Games. Life on the farm is busy. **B&B p 169. Country-Style Dining p 25.**

MAURICE

		RATES			ANIMALS	ACTIVITIES
		1 meal	2 meals	3 meals		
Hérouxville ACCUEIL LES SEMAILLES (418) 365-5190	single double child	$45 $55 $12	$55 $75 $18	$65 $95 $24	Cattle, horses, miniature horses, goats, sheep, rabbits, kittens, ducks, geese, pheasants, turkeys, hens, grain-fed chickens, guinea pigs.	Feeding the animals, gathering eggs, horseback riding, petting kittens and playing in the hay barn will put a smile on any child's face. A herd of 200 cattle allows you to immerse yourself in the farmer's daily life, in keeping with the passing seasons. Finally, take advantage of our outdoor facilities: swimming pool, volleyball court, sandbox, horseshoes, campfire, vegetable garden and swings. **B&B p 189.**

MONTÉRÉGIE

		RATES 1 meal	RATES 2 meals	RATES 3 meals	ANIMALS	ACTIVITIES
Howick HAZELBRAE FARM (450) 825-2390	single double child	$35 $60 $10	$40 $80 $15	$45 $90 $12-30	Cows and variety of small animals. Dairy farm.	Campfire, hay ride, inground pool, cycling, farm activities. Observe the milking of the cows, haymaking, collect the eggs. Stroll the spacious lawn and view the many flower gardens. Quiet area for country walks. Dairy Farm. **B&B p 201.**
St-Simon GÎTE À CLAUDIA (450) 798-2758 (514) 953-0673	single double child	$50-100 $65-115 $15	$70-120 $105-155 $25	--- --- ---	Écurie Kanadian features a young herd of purebred registered horses. Originally from Brittany and Normandy, the Canadian horse was the only horse in Lower Canada for a long time. Mini-farm with a variety of small animals.	Located in a maple grove with a traditional sugar shack; old-fashioned method of collecting sap (with buckets) and boiling it on a wood fire. Activities abound: caring for horses and small animals, care of the garden and flowers. Your participation is welcomed. Savour the quietude, breathe in the country air and simply relax; stroll through the maple grove, jump in the pool, take a nap on the veranda. Our home awaits you! **B&B p 205.**
Saint-Valérien LA RABOUILLÈRE (450) 793-4998 fax (450) 793-2529	single double child	$55-75 $70-90 $20	$80-100 $120-140 $30-45	--- --- ---	Exotic animals (llama, donkeys, miniature horses, Bourbados sheep, Katahdin sheep, Jacob sheep, Boer and pigmy goats, pot-bellied pigs). Rabbit hutch (100 females, 10 varieties), fowl (50 bird species, peacocks, pheasants, geese, ducks, hens, pigeons, etc.).	Animal observation and care, egg gathering, incubator, births. Tour of the gardens and organic gardens, forest walks, mushroom and berry picking, fishing, pool, play area, summer theatre, zoo, bike paths, campfires. **B&B p 205. Country-Style Dining p 31. Farm Explorations p 60. See colour photos.**
Ste-Agnès-de-Dundee LE GÎTE CHEZ MIMI (450) 264-4115 1-877-264-4115	single double child	$45 $55 $10	$55 $90 $25	$70 $120 $35	Bullock, cows, dogs, cats, hens, rabbits.	Taking care of the garden and flowers. Feed the rabbits, collect eggs, make hay, pick vegetables. Bird-watching, river fishing, golf courses, snowmobile stopovers, horseback riding, country walks, bike paths, archeology. **B&B p 205.**

		RATES			ANIMALS	ACTIVITIES
		1 meal	2 meals	3 meals		
MONTÉRÉGIE						
Ste-Victoire-de-Sorel GÎTE À LA FERME DU RANG (450) 782-2967 (450) 743-7899 fax (450) 782-3215	single double child	$30 $50 $20	$55 $90 $25	$70 $120 $35	Laying hens, rabbits and grain-fed calves.	Get acquainted with the small animals; stroll through the garden; spend a day at the maple grove (organic syrup); pick your own organic blueberries. **B&B p 206.**
OUTAOUAIS						
Gatineau FERME DE BELLECHASSE (819) 568-3375 (819) 775-7549	single double child	$50-75 $65-90 $15	--- --- ---	--- --- ---	Breeding of Colombian Paso Fino horses renowned for their ease and refinement. Rearing of goldfish in the farm's artificial pond.	Charming site where you can feed, admire and tend to the horses, stroll through the flowery gardens, relax by the goldfish pond, savour the peacefulness of the countryside right near the city, pick edible flowers, or lounge with a good book in front of the fireplace. **B&B p 222. See colour photos.**
Vinoy, Chénéville LES JARDINS DE VINOY (819) 428-3774 fax (819) 428-1877	single double child	$50-65 $65-80 $10	$69-84 $103-118 $19	$78-93 $120-150 $29	Goats, pigs, rabbits, sheep, geese, guinea-fowl, ducks, hens, chickens, dogs, cats.	Old-world charm with modern comfort. Animal care, old-fashioned sugar shack, dogsledding, soap making, jams, preserves, bread, spinning, medicinal plants, footpaths, cross-country skiing, snowshoeing, play area, campfires, organic garden, regional cuisine and thematic dining. **B&B p 226. See colour photos.**

		RATES			ANIMALS	ACTIVITIES
		1 meal	2 meals	3 meals		
QUÉBEC (RÉGION DE)						
Neuville LA FERME L'ÉMEULIENNE (418) 876-2788 fax (418) 876-3280	single double child	$50 $60 $15	$70 $100 $25	--- --- ---	Three ratites: ostriches, emus, Rheas and their young. Pony, 10 varieties of hens, ducks, geese, rabbits, dogs, cats, sheep, goats, Vietnamese pigs, pheasant, peacocks, pigeons...	Guided tour of the farm. Visit the incubation room, observe the development of an embryo, feed the animals, tame an animal, gather eggs, pick berries. Smoke and savour emu meat. Take part in a rally. Campfire, play area: volleyball, bowls, badminton. Have a picnic. Enjoy an old-fashioned dinner with emu meat*. Play with Ti N'homme the dog. Babysitting available for children*. Explore the region by bicycle. Experience a therapeutic "Swedish" massage*. Familly special: 2 adults + 2 children $84/B&B $125/PAM. *Extra charge. **B&B p 237.**
Saint-Adolphe, Stoneham AUBERGE DE LA FERME ST-ADOLPHE (418) 848-2879 fax (418) 848-6949	single double child	$45 $55 $15	--- --- ---	--- --- ---	Sheep, rabbits, ducks, hens, egg incubation, speckled trout. Wildlife observation in the forest of animals such as moose, deer, hares, partridges eagles and herons.	Guided tours of the farm, wildlife observation, river fishing, rest area in a pergola, heated swimming pool. In the spring, take part in the making of maple products. In winter: snowshoeing. The delicious farm products (eggs, maple syrup, maple jams) will win you over at breakfast. Packages on request: guided visit to the sugar shack with sampling of maple toffee, speckled-trout fishing and cooking area. **B&B p 253. See colour photos.**
SAGUENAY-LAC-SAINT-JEAN						
Hébertville FERME CAROLE ET JACQUES MARTEL tel/fax (418) 344-1323	single double child	$35 $45 $10	--- --- ---	--- --- ---	Cows, heifers, calves, dogs, cats, fowl.	Tour of the farm and observation of farm activities (milking, maintenance, etc.) Grain farming square and round hay baling. Computerize feeding for the cattle. Capacity: 10 people. **B&B p 258**

		RATES			ANIMALS	ACTIVITIES
		1 meal	2 meals	3 meals		
SAGUENAY-LAC-SAINT-JEAN						
La Baie CHEZ GRAND-MAMAN (418) 544-7396 (418) 697-0517	single double child	$45-50 $60-65 $10-15	--- --- ---	--- --- ---	Cows, calves, chickens, hens, turkeys, cats, dogs.	Try milking a cow. Feed the animals and see to their care. Walk along the shores of the Baie des HA! HA!. Outdoor fireplace, pool, and ice-fishing during winter. **B&B p 260.**
Métabetchouan-Lac-à-la-Croix CÉLINE ET GEORGES MARTIN tel/fax (418) 349-2583	single double child	$35 $45 $13	$50 $75 $18	--- --- ---	Cows, heifers, calves, dog.	Visit of the farm. **B&B p 263.**
Normandin LES GÎTES MAKADAN tel/fax (418) 274-2867 1-877-625-2326	single double child	$50 $60-80 $15	--- --- ---	--- --- ---	Goats, sheep, rabbits, hens, partridges, cats, dogs, etc.	Charming little farm where everyone can feed and tend to the small animals, gather eggs and cuddle these oh-so-engaging little creatures. **B&B p 264.**

74. FARMS STAYS

COUNTRY HOME ON A FARM

	RATES	ANIMALS	ACTIVITIES
ABITIBI-TÉMISCAMINGUE			
Île Nepawa FERME VACANCES HÉLÈNE WILLE (819) 333-6103	Activities included in the rental rate of the Country Home.	Cattle, dog.	Feed the animals. Help with the farm work. Harvest the hay. Aquatic activities, hunting and fishing, hiking trails. **Country Home p 78**
CANTONS-DE-L'EST			
Coaticook SÉJOUR NADEAU tel/fax (819) 849-3486 (819) 849-9932	Activities included in the rental rate of the Country Home.	Cows, goats, cats, dog.	Feed the animals, observe the milking of cows, work in the garden, help gather hay. **Country Home p 107.**
SAGUENAY-LAC-SAINT-JEAN			
La Baie LA MAISON DES ANCÊTRES (418) 544-2925 fax (418) 544-0241	Activities included in the rental rate of the Country Home.	Dairy farm.	Snowmobile trails run through the farm, snowshoeing, cross-country skiing on the farm, ice fishing... **Country Home p 268.**

Bed & Breakfasts
and Country Inns
including Country
and City Homes

ABITIBI-TÉMISCAMINGUE

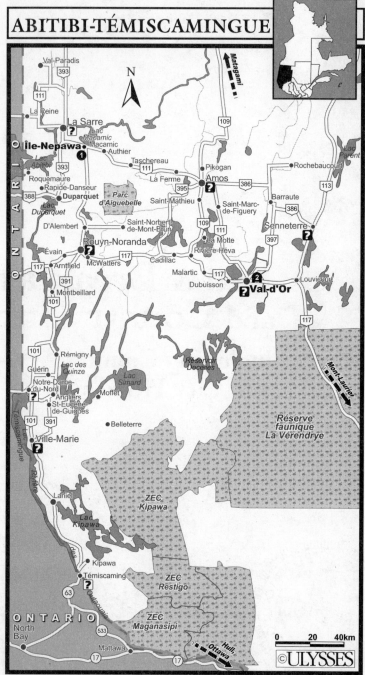

1. VAL D'OR

A former boarding house that used to welcome miners from Europe, L'Auberge de l'Orpailleur will let you relive the days of the Abitibi gold rush. The inn is ideally located in the historic mining village of Bourlamaque, steps away from Cité de l'Or, and features 60 log cabins. Varied and hearty homemade breakfasts. Snowmobiling, snowshoeing, dog-sledding, canoe-camping and trekking packages offered.

From Montréal, Rte 117, at the roundabout, Rue St-Jacques and left on Rue Perreault (follow the directions to "Cité de l'Or").

INN
AUBERGE DE L'ORPAILLEUR

Anne Cazin and Bruno Hugues
104, rue Perreault
Val-d'Or J9P 2G3
(819) 825-9518
fax (819) 824-7653
**www.geocities.
com/auberge_orpailleur**
wawate@cablevision.qc.ca

	B&B
single	$45
double	$55
triple	$70
child	$0-15

Taxes extra VS
Open year round

Number of rooms	6
rooms with sink	6
shared bathrooms	1
shared wc	4

2. ÎLE-NEPAWA

★ F E P R30 M10

Three comfortable chalets in the wilderness on the shores of Lac Abitibi, including a Swiss-style with fireplace, as well as two bungalows. We raise cattle, goats and horses. Water sports, hunting and fishing. Near the Aiguebelle conservation park. Come and enjoy a visit with Quebecers of German descent. **Country Home on a Farm p 74.**

From Rouyn, Rte 101 twd La Sarre. 3km past La Sarre, follow the signs twd Ste-Hélène and Île Nepawa, half-paved gravel road. 1st house on the right after the bridge to the island.

COUNTRY HOMES
FERME VACANCES
HÉLÈNE WILLE

Hélène Wille
695, Île-Nepawa, R.R. # 1
Clerval
JOZ 2TO
(819) 333-6103
www.inns-
bb.com/fermevacances

No. houses	3
No. rooms	2-3
No. people	6-8
WEEK-SUMMER	$250
W/E-SUMMER	$125
DAY-SUMMER	$50

Open: May 1 to Oct. 31

AGROTOURISM

Country Home on a Farm:

2   FERME VACANCES HÉLÈNE WILLE, Île-Nepawa.. *Page 74*

BAS-SAINT-LAURENT

The numbers on the map refer to the establishments described in the text.

1. BIC, LE

★★★ F e ⊘ P ⟵ R.2

Winner of the 1999 regional "Special Favourite" Award of Excellence. This century house deep in the country offers beautiful sunsets on the Rivière-Hâtée cove. A covered terrace with wood stove. Alcohol license. Ambiance where flowers meet the magic of Christmas. Queen-size beds and private bath, old-fashioned or healthy breakfast, picnic baskets, mountain and seashore hiking trails. Winner of the 2000 Grand Prix du Tourisme Bas-St-Laurent.

From Québec City, Aut. 20 East, Rte 132 East, East Bic Exit, left at flashing light on Rte 132, 2km. From Ste-Flavie or Mont-Joli, Rte 132 West twd Bic.

INN
AUBERGE CHEZ MARIE-ROSES

Jacqueline Caron
2322, Route 132 Est
Le Bic G0L 1B0
(418) 736-5311
(418) 736-4954
fax (418) 736-5955
www.marie-roses.qc.ca
marieroses@globetrotter.net

	B&B
single	$65-75
double	$75-85
child	$10

Taxes extra VS MC IT

Reduced rates: Oct. 15 to May 1
Open: Mar. 1 to Jan. 1

Number of rooms	7
rooms in basement	1
rooms with private bath	5
shared bathrooms	1
shared wc	1

2. BIC, LE

☼ ☼ ☼ F e ⊘ P ⟵ 🦌 ✕ R5

Quintessential Québec house dating back to 1830. This home offers four rooms with sink and two shared bathrooms. Small reading room. Dining-room service by reservation. Located between Le Bic and Rimouski, where outdoor activities and festivals abound. Open in winter. Packages: meal, overnight stay and breakfast; call for more information.

From Québec City, Aut. 20 and Rte 132 East. At the Bic East Exit, left on Rte 132, about 4km.

B&B
AUX 5 LUCARNES

Johanne Desjardins
2175, Route 132 Est
Le Bic G0L 1B0
tel/fax (418) 736-5435
1-866-582-2763
www.cam.org/~bsl/lucarnes/
jojodesj@globetrotter.net

	B&B
single	$50
double	$60
triple	$85
quad.	$110
child	$15

Taxes extra VS MC
Open year round

Number of rooms	4
rooms with sink	4
shared bathrooms	2

3. BIC, ST-FABIEN

☼ ☼ ☼ F e ⊘ P ⟵ ✕ R3

At the gates of Parc du Bic, come experience the charm of yesteryear, modern comfort, tranquillity (away from Rte 132) and a lavish breakfast of homemade bread and jam. Warm welcome. We love company!

Going to Gaspé, Rte 132 East. In St-Simon, 11km from Petro Canada. Left on Rang 1 West. Going to Montréal, Rte 132 West. 3km from St-Fabien tourist office. Right on Rang 1.

B&B
CLAIREVALLÉE

Marguerite Voyer
178, Rang 1 Ouest
Saint-Fabien G0L 2Z0
tel/fax (418) 869-3582
www.inns-bb.com/clairevallee
margvoyer@globetrotter.net

	B&B	MAP
single	$45-55	$65-75
double	$60-70	$100-110
triple	$80-90	$140-150
quad.	$100-110	$180-190

VS
Open year round

Number of rooms	5
rooms with private bath	1
shared bathrooms	3

4. CABANO

★★★ F E P ⇌ ✕ TA R.3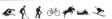

Located near Lac Témiscouata and the bike path, guests at the Auberge du Chemin Faisant enjoy our fine Magdalen Island-style cuisine, as well as our delectable breakfasts. Your host will entertain you on the piano, and the fireplace completes the cosy atmosphere. A great place for rest and relaxation.

From Québec City, Aut. 20 East, at Rivière-du-Loup, Rte 185 South. At Cabano, 1st Exit, Rue Commerciale 1km, then right in Rue du Vieux Chemin.

INN
AUBERGE DU CHEMIN FAISANT

Liette Fortin and
Hugues Massey
12, rue du Vieux Chemin
Cabano G0L 1E0
(418) 854-9342
1-877-954-9342
www.cheminfaisant.qc.ca
info@cheminfaisant.qc.ca

	B&B	MAP
single	$60-95	$86-120
double	$60-95	$111-146
triple	$70-105	$146-181
quad.	$80-115	$182-217
child	$10	$35

Taxes extra VS MC

Reduced rates: $10/night, Oct. 15 to May 1
Open year round

Number of rooms	6
rooms with private bath	4
rooms with sink	2
shared bathrooms	1
shared wc	1

---

5. CABANO

☀☀☀ F e ⊘ P ⇌ R.4

Located a few min from superb Lac Témiscouata, our B&B gives you direct access to the Le Petit Témis bike path (provincial snowmobile trail in winter). As our guests, you'll enjoy personalized service, cosy rooms and gourmet breakfasts in a warm atmosphere, as well as. A terrace and balcony to kick back and relax. Your hosts Lise and Roger will lavish you with attention. (Dinner served on request.) Getting to know you will be a pleasure.

From Québec City, Aut. 20 East, at Rivière-du-Loup, Rte 185 South. At Cabano, 1st Exit, Rue Commerciale, opposite city hall.

B&B
AUBERGE ST-MATHIAS

Lise and Roger Chamberland
70 rue Commerciale
Cabano G0L 1E0
(418) 854-5473
1-800-345-3614
fax (418) 854-3492
www.inns-bb.com/st_mathias
*auberge-st-mathias@
globetrotter.net*

	B&B
single	$50-60
double	$55-65
triple	$75-80

Taxes extra VS MC

Reduced rates: Oct. 15 to Apr. 15
Open year round

Number of rooms	5
rooms with private bath	3
shared bathrooms	1
shared wc	1

---

6. CACOUNA

☀☀☀ F e ⊘ P ≈ 🐖 R.2

La Berceuse is the pendulum swinging back, a bit of equilibrium in our busy lives. A warm, century-old house with many comforts and the joy of living, ideal for getting back to one's roots. Cozy queen-size beds, gourmets breakfasts, swimming pool, outdoor fireplace and rocking chairs! Now that's a real vacation!

Aut. 20, twd Cacouna Exit 514. Left at the stop sign. Rte 132 to the heart of the village. 12 min from the Rivière-du-Loup ferry.

B&B
GÎTE LA BERCEUSE

Julie Gendron and
Jean-Luc Potvin
45, rue Principale Ouest
Cacouna G0L 1G0
(418) 868-1752
www.laberceuse.qc.ca
info@laberceuse.qc.ca

	B&B
single	$40-50
double	$50-60
triple	$75
quad.	$90
child	$10-15

VS MC
Open: Apr. 1 to Oct. 31

Number of rooms	4
rooms with bath and sink	1
rooms with shower and sink	3
shared bathrooms	2

7. DÉGELIS

☀☀☀ F E ⊘ P ⛱ 🚣 🐾 R1.5

Located in a forest by Lac Témiscouata. Great comfort, clear panoramic view of the lake, famous à-la-carte breakfast. Come nightfall, around a fire on the beach, the song of the loon and golden sparks meeting the stars make up nature's sound and light show. Reserve from Oct. 15 to May 15.

Aut. 20, Exit 499, Rte 185 South. In Dégelis, Rte 295 North twd Auclair, 6km. By bike, cross the Dégelis dam and follow the 295 North, left and ride 2.5km.

B&B
GÎTE AU TOIT ROUGE

Dominique Lagarde and
André Demers
441, Route 295
Dégelis G5T 1R2
(418) 853-3036
(418) 853-2294
www.inns-
bb.com/giteautoitrouge
andr.demers3@sympatico.ca

	B&B
single	$50-55
double	$65-75
triple	$75-85
quad.	$90-100
child	$5-12

Reduced rates: 10 % 5 nights and more and Oct. 15 to May 15
Open: Jan. 6 to Dec. 20

Number of rooms	4
rooms with private bath	1
rooms with sink	3
shared bathrooms	1

8. DÉGELIS

☀☀☀ F e P ⛱ R.1

Welcome to our hospitable B&B where rest and relaxation are guaranteed. Our oasis of peace features a water garden and falls, park benches, a swing and a gazebo for family picnics, amidst fragrant flowers. Direct access to the lovely "Le Petit Témis" bike path. Private entrance and large parking lot. Bike shed. Balcony, living room, TV and refrigerator. Hearty breakfast served in the sunroom. Restaurant nearby. Children welcome. We look forward to greeting you.

From Québec City, Aut. 20 East twd Riv.-du-Loup, Rte 185 South. In Dégelis, 1st Exit on left on Av. Principale. From New Brunswick Rte 185 North. In Dégelis, 1st Exit on right, Av. Principale.

B&B
LA BELLE MAISON BLANCHE

Monique and André Lavoie
513, avenue Principale
Dégelis G5T 1L8
(418) 853-3324
fax (418) 853-5507
www.labellemaisonblanche.com
monand@icrdl.net

	B&B
single	$45-55
double	$55-65
triple	$75-85
quad.	$85-95
child	$15

Reduced rates: Nov. 1 to Apr. 30
Open year round

Number of rooms	5
shared bathrooms	2
shared wc	1
shared showers	1

9. KAMOURASKA

☀☀☀ F e P ✕

Situated on a hilltop, the Auberge des Îles has a magnificent view of the Kamouraskan Islands and the sunsets. In the evening, whether you're in the dining room, solarium or in your room, the twinkling lights on the north coast will captivate you. A cordial welcome with a touch of class, as well as some little extras, will make your stay a memorable one.

Aut. 20, Exit 465, twd Kamouraska. Once in the village, left on Av. Morel (Rte 132), 1.5km.

INN
AUBERGE DES ÎLES

Liette and Rita Lévesque
198, avenue Morel
Kamouraska G0L 1M0
(418) 492-7561
fax (418) 492-7695
www.iquebec.com/aubergedesiles
aubergedesiles@iquebec.com

	B&B
single	$45-55
double	$55-65
child	$15

Taxes extra VS MC IT
Open: May 1 to Oct. 12

Number of rooms	5
rooms with private bath	2
rooms with sink	1
shared bathrooms	1
shared wc	1

10. KAMOURASKA

☀ ☀ ☀ **F** e 🚫 📷 **P** 🛏 **TA** R.6

A bed and breakfast in the heart of the village of Kamouraska, one of the most beautiful villages in Québec, "Au Petit Bonheur" welcomes you yearound. Comfortable rooms, living room with TV and kitchen. Period decor and warm ambiance. Magnificent view of the river. All-you-can-eat breakfast in a relaxing, convivial atmosphere. Various services 0.6km away: bank, bakery, museum, restaurant. "Come to 116, by the St.Lawrence River."

Aut. 20, Exit 465, twd Kamouraska. In the village, left on Av. Morel (Rte 132).

B&B
GÎTE AU PETIT BONHEUR

Céline and Jean-Guy Charest
116, avenue Morel
Kamouraska G0L 1M0
tel/fax **(418) 492-3247**
www.inns-bb.com/aupetitbonheur

	B&B
single	$50-55
double	$60-65
triple	$75-80

Reduced rates: Oct. 1 to May 31
Open year round

Number of rooms	4
rooms with private bath	2
rooms with sink	2
shared bathrooms	2

---

11. LA POCATIÈRE

☀ ☀ ☀ ☀ **F** e **P** 🛏 🏊 **TA**

Regional Prize for Excellence "Special Favorite" 2001. More than an B&B this is a place where we get to know our guests. A place whose charm and landscape inspires peace and love, where the aromas of regional dishes mingle with the fragrances of the ancient woods. Discounts for longer stays. Children welcome; 3km from various attractions.

One hour from Québec City, Aut. 20 East, Exit 436, right at the stop, 1500 ft. From Gaspé, Exit 436...

B&B
AUBERGE AU DIABLO-VERT

Manon Brochu and Luc Gagnon
72, Route 132 Ouest, C.P. 9
La Pocatière G0R 1Z0
(418) 856-4117
fax (418) 856-5161
www.quebecweb.com/diablovert
diablove@globetrotter.net

	B&B
single	$55
double	$65
triple	$75

Reduced rates: 20% 3 nights and more, Sept. 1 to May 31
Open year round

Number of rooms	5
shared bathrooms	3

---

12. LA POCATIÈRE

☀ ☀ ☀ ☀ **F** E 🚫 📷 **P** 🛏 🏊 🦌 ✕ **TA** R5

Five min from the city, discover a haven of peace and harmony where it warms our hearts to welcome you. For your pleasure: wide open spaces, comfort and beauty; view of the St. Lawrence River and Charlevoix region. Flower garden. Large, tastefully decorated rooms. Refined, lavish breakfasts, home-made goods. Excellent five-course dinner. Bikes, swimming pool, "pétanque", pergola, playground, swing.

Aut. 20, Exit 439, after the church, follow 1st street, left Rue de la Gare, follow the railway, at the end, right on Martineau. At the top of the hill, left on Chamberland.

B&B
LA CHEVRIÈRE

Louise and
Jean-Philippe Tirman
105, rue Boucher
La Pocatière G0R 1Z0
(418) 856-4331
www.iquebec.com/lachevriere
lachevriere@iquebec.com

	B&B	MAP
single	$45-65	$65-85
double	$50-75	$95-115
triple	$90	$150
child	$10	$20

VS

Reduced rates: 20% 3 nights consecutive and more or Oct. 1 to May 15
Open year round

Number of rooms	5
rooms with private bath	2
shared bathrooms	1

13. L'ISLE-VERTE

Those who long for calm and relaxation will enjoy watching magnificent sunsets on the river from our gazebo. This enchanting site has won several awards and is located near the family farm. After a night of sweet dreams in this antique-filled B&B savour a delicious breakfast of various homemade goods. Warm, thoughtful hosts await you!

From Québec City, Aut. 20 East. Rte 132 for 6.7km, right, at the 2nd stop sign, right and continue 0.7km. From Rimouski, Rte 132 West, after the L'Isle Verte flashing light, 2.7km, left. Right at the 2nd stop sign and continue 0.7 km.

B&B
AU PAYS DES RÊVES

Gisèle Lagacé and
Benoit Charron
100, ch. Côteau-des-Érables
L'Isle-Verte G0L 1L0
(418) 898-6358
www.inns-bb.com/paysdesreves

	B&B
single	$45
double	$55
triple	$75
child	$10

Open: May 1 to Oct. 31

Number of rooms	2
shared bathrooms	2

---

14. L'ISLE-VERTE

La Grande Ourse is a 19th century Anglo-Norman house. The babbling Rivière Verte is just a stone's throw away from our flower garden, where birds congregate. In winter, warm up by the hearth before going off to your cosy bed. In the morning, a hearty breakfast awaits. Welcome to La Grande Ourse!

From Québec City, Aut. 20 East, Rte 132 East. After the Rivière Verte bridge, right and then right again. From Rimouski, Rte 132 West, L'Isle Verte Exit, straight until end of the village, then left.

B&B
LA GRANDE OURSE

Martine Girard and
Paul-André Laberge
6, rue du Verger
L'Isle-Verte G0L 1K0
(418) 898-2763
fax (418) 898-3717
www.inns-bb.com/grandeourse

	B&B
single	$45-60
double	$55-70
triple	$65-85
quad.	$75-100
child	$0-10

Open year round

Number of rooms	5
shared bathrooms	2
shared wc	1

---

15. L'ISLE-VERTE

A Victorian-style house with centenary charm that extends a warm and genuine welcome. Large tree-lined property. In the early morning wake up to the crowing of the cock and birdsong mingled with the aroma of a hearty breakfast. View of the river and access to nearby leisure activities. Make yourselves at home.

From Québec City, Aut. 20 East, Rte 132 East. In the village, right at the caisse populaire. House on the left, on the hill. From Rimouski, Rte 132 West, left at the caisse populaire...

B&B
LA MAISON ANCESTRALE

Diane Lévesque and
Joseph-Marie Fraser
5, rue Béland
L'Isle-Verte G0L 1K0
(418) 898-2633
(418) 898-2053
lamaisonancestrale.iquebec.com

	B&B
single	$45
double	$55

Open: June to Sep. 15

Number of rooms	4
shared bathrooms	2
shared wc	1

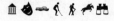

16. L'ISLE-VERTE

☀ ☀ **F P** ⟵**TA R.5**

On L'Isle Verte, choose Les Capucines for the warm welcome of your hosts Marie and Yvon, and for the tranquility and comfort. After a good night's sleep, enjoy a delicious and hearty homemade breakfast. The charming setting and flower gardens will en-chant you. We have been welcoming guests to our home for 15 years. Lounge, living room are available for your convenience. See you soon.

From Québec City, Aut. 20, Rte 132 East. At L'Isle Verte, after the flashing light, 0.5km. Left on Rue Louis-Bertrand. From Rimouski, 2nd street on the right.

B&B
LES CAPUCINES

Marie-Anna and Yvon Lafrance
31, ch. Louis-Bertrand, C.P. 105
L'Isle-Verte G0L 1K0
(418) 898-3276
www.inns-bb.com/capucines

	B&B
single	$45
double	$55
triple	$70
quad.	$80
child	$10
Open year round	
Number of rooms	**3**
rooms in semi-basement	1
shared bathrooms	2

---

17. NOTRE-DAME-DU-PORTAGE

☀ ☀ ☀ **F e ⊘ P R.25**

Facing the majestic St. Lawrence River, Gîte Chute Couette et Café welcomes you to one of the most beautiful villages east of Québec City. Panoramic view of the river. Five spacious rooms, three bathrooms, hearty breakfast, family ambiance. Nearby activities: saltwater pool, bike path, golf, whale-watching excursions, hiking on the islands, health resorts, horseback riding, etc. Guests have access to a kitchen to prepare dinner meals. Come and relax to the soothing sounds of waves and cascading waterfalls. Unforgettable moments guaranteed!

200km east of Québec City via Aut. 20 or Rte 132. Exit Notre-Dame-du-Portage, on Route du Fleuve, 1km east of the church.

B&B
GÎTE CHUTE COUETTE ET CAFÉ

Francine Pelletier and
Colbert Lebel
408, Route du Fleuve
Notre-Dame-du-Portage G0L 1Y0
(418) 862-5367
1-888-739-5367
fax (418) 862-2548
www.chutecouettecafe.com
chute@qc.aira.com

	B&B
single	$45
double	$60
triple	$75
quad.	$90
child	$10
VS MC	
Reduced rates: $5 less Nov. 1 to May 1 except Christmas / New Eve and Easter holidays	
Open year round	
Number of rooms	**5**
shared bathrooms	3

---

18. NOTRE-DAME-DU-PORTAGE

☀ ☀ ☀ **F E P** ⟵ 〰 **R.25**

La Halte du Verger, a country home decorated with woodwork, offers peace, quiet, beauty and a warm atmosphere. Admire majestic sunsets on the patio while breathing in the sea air. All of this, in addition to massage therapy, will make your stay a most pleasant one. Relax by the fireplaces in both living rooms. Our breakfasts will satisfy even the fussiest palate.

Aut. 20, Exit 496, right at the stop sign, Rte 132 twd Rivière-du-Loup, about 2km to your left, on the river side.

B&B
LA HALTE DU VERGER

Léo Poussard and Yves Poussard
341, Route de la Montagne
Notre-Dame-du-Portage G0L 1Y0
(418) 863-5726
1-866-863-5726
www.lahalteduverger.com
la.halte.duverger@qc.aira.com

	B&B
single	$55-60
double	$70-74
triple	$85-89
quad.	$100
child	$10
VS MC IT	
Reduced rates: from 11% and 18% Jan. 1 to Apr. 18 and Sept. 15 to Dec. 31	
Open year round	
Number of rooms	**4**
rooms in basement	2
rooms with sink	2
shared bathrooms	2
shared wc	1

19. POINTE-AU-PÈRE

★★★ F e P ✕

Come to our Victorian home, built around 1860, and dream of travelling. Former property of Sieur Louis-Marie Lavoie, known as "Louis XVI", who was master-pilot on the St. Lawrence and upriver for the city of Québec. This charming home has since become an inn where you'll be spoiled by serenity and a warm welcome.

From Québec City, Aut. 20 East, Rte 132 twd Rimouski, Rte 132 twd Pointe-au-Père,1km past the church.

INN
AUBERGE LA MARÉE DOUCE

Marguerite Lévesque
1329, boul. Sainte-Anne
Pointe-au-Père, Rimouski
G5M 1W2
(418) 722-0822
fax (418) 723-4512
www.inns-bb.com/mareedouce

	B&B	MAP
single	$115-135	$135-175
double	$125-140	$160-185
triple	$140-155	$220
quad.	$155-160	$260

Taxes extra VS MC IT
Open: May 1 to Oct. 31

Number of rooms	9
rooms with private bath	9

---

20. POINTE-AU-PÈRE

☀☀ F E ⊘ P ⇌ TA R.5

Magnificent location, panoramic view, warm welcome, comfortable bed, affable host, nearby restaurant, quiet walks, sunsets, beach campfires, starry nights, northern lights, lapping waves, deep sleep. Quiet mornings, fragrant coffee, talks... Activities: kayaking, museum, cycling, hiking... Enjoy your stay! André, sculptor.

Drop anchor at the end of the 20! Past Rimouski, Rte 132 East, between Bic and Métis, below the Pointe-au-Père lighthouse, Rue du Phare.

B&B
GÎTE DE LA POINTE

André Gamache
1046, rue du Phare
Pointe-au-Père G5M 1L8
(418) 724-6614
(418) 750-3332
www.inns-bb.com/pointe
gamhbnb@globetrotter.net

	B&B
single	$50-70
double	$60-75
triple	$70-85

Taxes extra VS

Reduced rates: $10 the night Sep. 15 to June 15
Open: Jan.15 to Dec. 15

Number of rooms	5
rooms in semi-basement	4
rooms with private bath	1
shared wc	4

---

21. RIMOUSKI, BIC

☀☀☀ F e P ⇌ 🐑 TA R6

An ancestral home
A family farm
A friendly ambiance
Amazing breakfasts
Enticing eggs, crepes
That young and old alike will enjoy
The house, the rooms, the stay
Are lovingly decorated
So that you will always remember
That at La Maison Bérubé
You are like family
Who visit us yearly. **Farm Stay p 66.**

3 hours from Québec City, Aut. 20 East, Rte 132 East. At the Eastern Bic Exit, at the flashing light left Rte 132, 6.4km to the left. 11.5km from Rimouski.

B&B
LA MAISON BÉRUBÉ

Louise Brunet and
Marcel Bérubé
1216, boul. Saint-Germain Ouest
(rte 132)
Rimouski G5L 8Y9
tel/fax (418) 723-1578
www.inns-bb.com/maisonberube
maisonberube@globetrotter.net

	B&B
single	$45
double	$60
triple	$80
quad.	$100
child	$5-15

VS
Open year round

Number of rooms	5
rooms with sink	1
shared bathrooms	2
shared wc	1

22. RIMOUSKI, ST-NARCISSE

Rural, family-style setting in a rustic home with log interior; warm and quiet. Indoor and outdoor fire-place, small private lake, picnic table, swimming and free canoeing included. Close to wildlife observation. Near Portes de l'Enfer, the highest footbridge in Québec. A great vacation spot only 15 min away from Rimouski. Welcome to our home... come and relax!

From Québec City, Aut. 20 East, Exit 610, Rte 232 West, 16km, left on Chemin de l'Écluse, 1km.

B&B
DOMAINE
DU BON VIEUX TEMPS

Hélène Rioux
89-1, chemin de l'Écluse
Saint-Narcisse, Rimouski
G0K 1S0
(418) 735-5646
**www.inns-
bb.com/bonvieuxtemps**

	B&B
single	$60
double	$70
triple	$135
child	$10-15

VS

Open year round

Number of rooms	1
shared bathrooms	1
rooms with toilet and sink	1

---

23. RIVIÈRE-DU-LOUP

A superb 1895 Victorian house. Come and admire the sunsets from the solarium while breathing the fresh, salty air. Rest in the shade of hundred-year-old trees. Two living room perfect for relaxation. Prime Ministers John A. MacDonald and Louis St-Laurent once stayed in the neighbourhood. Magnificent surroundings!

Via Aut. 20, Exit 503, left at the stop sign, 11th house on the left. Located on Rte 132 between Notre-Dame-du-Portage and Rivière-du-Loup.

B&B
AUBERGE LA SABLINE

Monique Gaudet and
Jean Cousineau
343, rue Fraser Ouest
Rivière-du-Loup G5R 5S9
(418) 867-4890
www.inns-bb.com/sabline

	B&B
single	$65-85
double	$70-90
triple	$85-105
child	$10

Taxes extra VS MC

Reduced rates: 20% Sep. 3 to June 21
Open year round

Number of rooms	4
rooms with private bath	2
shared bathrooms	1
shared wc	1

---

24. RIVIÈRE-DU-LOUP

Prize for Excellence "Special Favorite" Regional 1997-98 and the "small tourist business" Grand Prix du Tourisme Bas-St-Laurent. Home sweet home! Charming, antique-furnished house with rustic decor, terrace and garden, river view and lavish breakfast with homemade bread and jams. Near the ferry, whale-watching cruises, museum, summer theatre and good restaurants. Come share in our happiness—the only thing missing is you.

Aut. 20, Exit 503, right at the stop sign, 1.4km to Rue Fraser.

B&B
AU TERROIR DES BASQUES

Marguerite Filion and
Pierre-Paul Belzile
197, rue Fraser
Rivière-du-Loup G5R 1E2
tel/fax (418) 860-2001
1-877-647-8078
**www.inns-
bb.com/terroirdesbasques**
marpierre@sympatico.ca

	B&B
single	$50
double	$60
triple	$80
child	$10

Open: June 15 to Sep. 15

Number of rooms	3
rooms in basement	1
shared bathrooms	2

25. RIVIÈRE-DU-LOUP

Summer residence of Canada's first Prime Minister, Sir John A. Macdonald from 1872 to 1890. Magnificient heritage house which gives visitors a splendid view across the St. Lawrence River to the mountainous north shore. Enjoy your stay in a quiet and peaceful environment, as well as our delicious home-made breakfast. Many activities and day trips nearby.

Aut. 20 twd Rivière-du-Loup then West on Rte 132 twd St-Patrice.

B&B
LES ROCHERS

Meredith Fisher, hôtesse
336, rue Fraser
Saint-Patrice-de-la-Rivière-
du-Loup G5R 5S8
(514) 393-1417
(418) 868-1435
fax (514) 393-9444
www.inns-bb.com/rochers
chq@total.net

B&B	
single	$60-80
double	$75-90
triple	$90-105
quad.	$105-120

VS MC

Open: June 20 to Sep. 7

Number of rooms	5
rooms with private bath	2
rooms with sink	3
shared bathrooms	3

---

26. RIVIÈRE-DU-LOUP, ST-ANTONIN

Located less than 5km from Rivière-du-Loup, on the road to Edmunston, "La Maison de Mon Enfance" awaits you. A perfect stopping place on the way to the Maritimes or Gaspésie. Whale-watching cruises, museums, theatre, golf. Only 1km from the Petit Témis bike path; motorcycle/bicycle garage, free parking. See you soon, Roseline.

Aut. 20, twd Rivière-du-Loup. Rte 185, in St-Antonin, at the flashing light, turn twd the Trans Canadien restaurant, it's at the stop sign. From Rivière-du-Loup, twd Edmunston, Jct. 185, straight ahead, 4km.

B&B
LA MAISON DE MON ENFANCE

Roseline Desrosiers
718, ch. Rivière-Verte
Saint-Antonin G0L 2J0
(418) 862-3624
fax (418) 862-8969
**www.infobelix.com/
maisonenfance**
maisonenfance@iquebec.com

B&B	
single	$45-55
double	$55-65
triple	$70-75
quad.	$95
child	$10

VS

Open: June 15 to Sep. 15

Number of rooms	5
shared bathrooms	2
shared wc	1

---

27. ST-ALEXANDRE, KAMOURASKA

Enjoy a warm welcome in a spacious house in the heart of the village. It's a quiet place on a large property with fruit trees, vegetable gardens and flowers, and a large solarium for your relaxation. Sizeable, well-equipped rooms with queen-size beds, lavish breakfast with homemade jams, healthy meals. Welcome!

From Québec City, Aut. 20 East, Exit 488 twd St-Alexandre, Rte 289. After the church, right on Av. Marguerite D'Youville.

B&B
GÎTE DES FLEURS

Alice and Julien Ouellet
526, av. Marguerite D'Youville
Saint-Alexandre G0L 2G0
(418) 495-5500
www.inns-bb.com/desfleurs

B&B	
single	$45
double	$60
triple	$75
quad.	$100
child	$10

Reduced rates: Sept. 1 to May 31, 3 nights and more
Open year round

Number of rooms	3
shared bathrooms	2
shared wc	1

28. ST-ALEXANDRE, KAMOURASKA

Regional Prize for Excellence "Special Favorite" 2002. Spend your holidays in the beautiful ancestral home of Marie-Alice Dumont, first professional photographer in Eastern Québec. Mouthwatering breakfasts served by the stained-glass window of the former photography studio. The warmest of welcomes awaits. Prize for Excellence "Special Favorite" Regional 1994-95.

From Québec City, Aut. 20 East, Exit 488 twd St-Alexandre. 1st house left, at the junction of Rte 230.

B&B
LA MAISON AU TOIT BLEU

Madame Daria Dumont
490, avenue Saint-Clovis
Saint-Alexandre G0L 2G0
(418) 495-2701
tel/fax (418) 495-2368
**www.inns-
bb.com/maisonautoitbleu**

	B&B
single	$45
double	$60
child	$10
Open year round	
Number of rooms	**3**
shared bathrooms	1
shared wc	1

---

29. ST-ANDRÉ, KAMOURASKA

A charming inn with romantic decor and inviting atmosphere, La Solaillerie welcomes you with open arms. Very comfortable country-style rooms, indoor and outdoor sitting rooms, balconies, easy access to the river. La Solaillerie also offers the best dining in the Kamouraska region, offering creative, refined and generous local cuisine; organic vegetables from the garden. Québec Tourism Grand Prix: 2002 "Fine Dining," 1999 "Tourist Services." **See colour photos.**

Aut. 20, Exit 480 twd St-André. In the village, right on Rue Principale. Or direct acces with "Route des Navigateurs" (Rte 132).

INN
AUBERGE LA SOLAILLERIE

Isabelle Poyau and Yvon Robert
112, rue Principale
Saint-André, Kamouraska
G0L 2H0
(418) 493-2914
fax (418) 493-2243
www.aubergelasolaillerie.com
lasolaillerie@globetrotter.net

	B&B
single	$80-100
double	$89-119
triple	$139
Taxes extra VS MC IT	
Open: May 1 to Oct. 31	
Number of rooms	**10**
rooms with private bath	8
rooms with bath and sink	2
shared bathrooms	1

---

30. ST-ÉLOI

Come share the comfort and tranquility of a former presbytery, built in 1863, where you can relive a bygone era. Located in a wonderful, peaceful village. Breathe in the fresh air and admire amazing sunsets on the St. Lawrence River. The inn is decorated with canvases painted by your hostess. Choose your own evening meal and breakfast. Snowmobile path nearby. Spend a night with us and you'll be in heaven. Children welcome.

From Québec City, Aut. 20 East to the end, then 19km along Rte 132. Right on Rte St-Éloi, 5km. Left on Rue Principale.

INN
AU VIEUX PRESBYTÈRE

Raymonde and Yvon Pettigrew
350, rue Principale Est
Saint-Éloi G0L 2V0
(418) 898-6147
1-888-833-6147
**www.iquebec.ifrance.
com/vieuxpresbytere**
aubergeauvieux@qc.aira.com

	B&B	MAP
single	$40-50	$55-65
double	$55-65	$85-95
triple	$70-80	$100-110
quad.	$85-95	$115-125
child	$10	$18
Taxes extra VS MC IT		
Reduced rates: Nov. 1 to May 1		
Open year round		
Number of rooms		**4**
rooms with sink		4
shared bathrooms		2

31. ST-JEAN-DE-DIEU

☀☀☀ **F** **P** R4

Located 20 min from the St. Lawrence River, our family is happy to welcome you to our dairy farm. Enjoy our animals, such as deer, llamas, sheep, goats, geese and peacocks. Our specialty is a crepe breakfast with maple syrup, homemade bread and jam... for a warm atmosphere and healthy fare. Families welcome. **Farm Stay p 66.**

From Québec City, Aut. 20 East, Rte 132 East twd Trois-Pistoles. Rte 293 South twd St-Jean-de-Dieu, 4km past the church.

B&B
LA FERME PAYSAGÉE

Gabrielle and Régis Rouleau
121, Route 293 Sud
Saint-Jean-de-Dieu G0L 3M0
(418) 963-3315
www.fermepaysagee.com
rouls@globetrotter.net

	B&B	MAP
single	$35	$45
double	$50	$70
child	$5-15	$5-15
Open year round		
Number of rooms		3
shared bathrooms		2

---

32. ST-LOUIS-DU-HA! HA!

☀☀☀☀ **F** **e** **P** TA R6

Prize for Excellence "Special Favorite" Regional 2000, this typical 1920s house located in the heart of the mountains offers a magnificent view. Situated on the road to the Maritimes and in the middle of the "Le Petit Témis" bike path. Shuttle service, bike shed, luggage carrying services. Our priorities: welcome, warm ambiance, comfort, cleanliness and a delicious breakfast. You'll want to come back.

From Québec City, Aut. 20 twd Riv.-du-Loup. Rte 185 South, 60km. At flashing light, right 1.6km. Left on Rang Beauséjour, 5km.

B&B
AU BEAU-SÉJOUR

Louiselle Ouellet and
Paul Gauvin
145, rang Beauséjour
Saint-Louis-du-Ha! Ha! G0L 3S0
(418) 854-0559
**www.multimania.com/
gitebeausejour/**
lgauvin@sympatico.ca

	B&B
single	$50
double	$60-70
triple	$85
quad.	$100
child	$10
VS	
Open year round	
Number of rooms	4
shared bathrooms	2

---

33. STE-LUCE-SUR-MER

F **E** **P** X

Right on the beach and just a few km from the Jardins de Métis, we offer an oasis of peace in harmony with the rhythm of the seas. In concert with the setting sun and our fine regional cuisine (included in the menu), you will experience a magical sound and light show. **See colour photos.**

From Québec City, Aut. 20 East, Rte 132 twd Ste-Flavie. After Pointe-au-Père, watch for "Camping La Luciole", 500 ft. and turn left, then right on Route du Fleuve.

INN
AUBERGE DE L'EIDER

Johanne Cloutier and
Maurice Gendron
90, Route du Fleuve Est
Sainte-Luce-sur-Mer G0K 1P0
tel/fax (450) 448-5110
(418) 739-3535
www.inns-bb.com/l_eider

	B&B
single	$72-90
double	$75-95
triple	$105-115
quad.	$135
child	$15
Taxes extra VS MC	
Reduced rates: June 1 to June 15 and Sept. 9 to Sept. 20	
Open: June 1 to Sep. 20.	
Number of rooms	14
rooms with private bath	14

34. STE-LUCE-SUR-MER

On the banks of the St. Lawrence, charming 1920 house with country colours, landscaped grounds and private beach. Creative "eye-catching" breakfast will whet your appetite. Relaxing gazebo. Unforgettable evening show as the fiery sun kisses the sea. Cocktail hour. 15 min from Jardins de Métis, Parc du Bic, Côte-Nord ferry.

Mid-way between Rimouski and Mont-Joli via Rte 132. Enter the picturesque village of Ste-Luce along the river; we are 0.2km West of the church, near the river.

B&B
MAISON DES GALLANT

Nicole Dumont and Jean Gallant
40, rue du Fleuve Ouest, C.P. 52
Sainte-Luce-sur-Mer G0K 1P0
(418) 739-3512
www.inns-bb.com/gallant
jean.gallant@cgocable.ca

B&B	
single	$60
double	$70
triple	$95
child	$10

Open year round	
Number of rooms	3
shared bathrooms	1
shared wc	1

35. TROIS-PISTOLES

We await you at our lovely, quaint and cozy B&B located in the heart of Trois-Pistoles, facing the ferry, next to the Maison des Notaires (painting exhibits). Summer playhouse, museum, bike path, whale-watching expeditions and much more...

From Québec City, Aut. 20, Rte 132 twd Gaspésie, at the lights twd the St. Lawrence River, right at the church.

B&B
GÎTE CHEZ NICO

Nicole Pelletier
160 Notre-Dame est C.P. 1336
Trois-Pistoles G0L 4K0
tel/fax **(418) 851-1297**
www.inns-bb.com/cheznico
giteanico@hotmail.com

B&B	
single	$50
double	$60
child	$20

Open year round	
Number of rooms	4
shared bathrooms	2

AGROTOURISM

Farm Stays:

🌑 *21*   LA MAISON BÉRUBÉ, Rimouski .... *Page 66*

🌑 *31*   LA FERME PAYSAGÉE, Saint-Jean-de-Dieu .... *Page 66*

Country-Style Dining:

🌑 *36*   LA BERGÈRE, GÎTE ET COUVERT, Trois-Pistoles .... *Page 18*

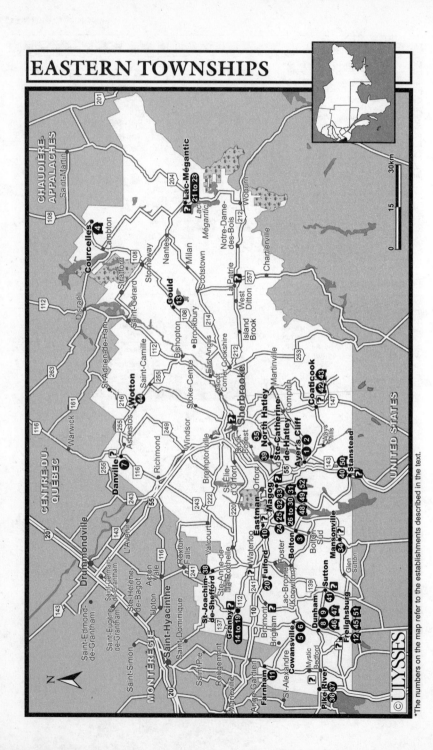

EASTERN TOWNSHIPS

*The numbers on the map refer to the establishments described in the text.

CHAUDIÈRE-APPALACHES

CENTRE-DU-QUÉBEC

MONTÉRÉGIE

UNITED STATES

30km

0   15

N

Courcelles **4**

Lac-Mégantic **? 21 to 23**
Lac Mégantic

Notre-Dame-des-Bois

Saint-Martin

Lambton

Stratford

Stornoway

Milan

Scotstown

La Patrie

West Ditton

Chartierville

Gould **13**

Nantes

Bishopton

Brookbury

East Angus

Cookshire

Island Brook

Danville **? 7**

Wotton **14**

Saint-Camille

Sawyerville

Compton

Coaticook **? 42 43**

Stanstead **50**

40

? ?

Ayer's Cliff **1 2**

Ways Mills

Ste-Catherine-de-Hatley **55**

North Hatley

35

39

Magog **62 63 ? 31 52 48 49**

Sherbrooke **?**

Rock Forest

Windsor

Richmond

Asbestos

St-Adrien-de-Ham

Warwick

Bromptonville

Stoke-Centre

Ste-Élie-d'Orford

Orford

Eastman **10 ?**

24 25 26 to 30

Bolton **3**

Bolton Sud

Mansonville **34 ?**

Drummondville

L'Avenir

Roxton Falls

Valcourt

Ste-Anne-de-la-Rochelle

Waterloo

Fulford **20**

Lac-Brome (Knowlton)

Foster

Sutton **41 ?**

Glen Sutton

St-Joachim-de-Shefford **? 38**

Granby **14 to 19**

Bromont

Brigham

Cowansville **5 6**

Dunham **8 9 46 47**

Frelighsburg **12 45 51**

Acton Vale

Upton

Ste-Hélène-de-Bagot

St-Germain-de-Grantham

Saint-Edmond-de-Grantham

Saint-Eugène-de-Grantham

Saint-Simon

Saint-Pie

Saint-Dominique

Saint-Hyacinthe

Rougemont

Marieville

Ange-Gardien

Farnham

St-Alexandre

Bedford

Mystic **11**

Pike River **36 37**

1. AYER'S CLIFF

Hundred-year-old house in the country, panoramic view, quiet place. Home cooking. Swimming in Lake Massawippi 3km away, summer theatre, Coaticook Gorge, cross-country skiing, downhill skiing 15 min. away, 8 min. from golf, 200 ft. from skidooing. Near North Hatley, Mont Orford and Magog. Horseback riding 15 min. away. Ideal for hiking and cycling.

From Montréal, Aut. 10 East, Exit 121. Aut. 55 South, Exit 21, Rte 141 South. About 2.5km after intersection of Rte 143, left on Chemin Audet. Big white house on the hill.

B&B
GÎTE LAUZIER

Cécile Lauzier
3119, ch. Audet, Kingscroft
Ayer's Cliff J0B 1C0
(819) 838-4433
www.inns-bb.com/cecilelauzier

	B&B
single	$50
double	$55-65
triple	$85
Open year round	
Number of rooms	5
shared bathrooms	2

---

2. AYER'S CLIFF

Unique Norwegain-style log house surrounded by 7 acres of private woods and field. 2 large bedrooms with fireplace and TV or grand piano. Whirlpool and sauna in house. Landscaped pond, brook and water-lily garden. Kitchen access for long stays. Picniking anytime. The phone number 866 is toll free.

From Montréal, Aut. 10 East, Exit 121, Aut. 55 South, Exit 21, Rte 141 South twd Coaticook. 2km after crossing Rte 143, right on Way's Mills road. Drive to village, then staight ahead, 3km on Ballbrook road.

B&B
LA CHAUMIÈRE
EN PAIN D'ÉPICES

Claudine Trudel
1488, ch. Ballbrook, Way's Mills
Ayer's Cliff J0B 1C0
tel/fax (819) 876-2686
1-866-276-2686
www.inns-
bb.com/chaumiereenpaindepices
chaumiere@sympatico.ca

	B&B
single	$75
double	$95
child	$20
Open year round	
Number of rooms	2
rooms with sink	2
shared bathrooms	1
shared wc	2

---

3. BOLTON

You'll be seduced by our New England-style residence (circa 1850) surrounded by a large park, a wooded area, a river and a flower-filled garden. Step inside and discover books, music, sparkling colours, inviting aromas, flowers...we await you! Our spacious rooms are comfortable and soundproof, and our hearty breakfasts can be enjoyed in the sunroom or under the apple tree. Perfumed Mediterranean cuisine and plenty of wine are served by a roaring fire. Bike shelter, Eastern Townships paths nearby. Golf/ski/spa packages and gift certificates available.

Aut. 10, Exit 106, Route 245 South twd Mansonville for 12km. Last house in the village, on the left.

B&B
L'IRIS BLEU

Ginette Breton and
Jérôme Dal Santo
895, chemin Missisiquoi Rte. 245
Bolton J0E 1G0
(450) 292-3530
1-877-292-3530
www.irisbleu.com
bbliirisbleu@qc.aira.com

	B&B	MAP
single	$75-85	$100-110
double	$100-125	$150-175
triple	$160-185	$235-260
quad.	$195-230	$295-320
child	$20	$35

Taxes extra VS MC

Reduced rates: 20% 3 nights and more Nov. 1 to May 31 (except long week-end and school break)

Open: Dec. 1 to Nov. 15

Number of rooms	3
rooms with private bath	3
shared wc	2

4. COURCELLES

F E P �　🚣　🐾　✕ TA

Wonderfully located with a view of valleys, forests, flowers and horses. Regional cuisine, including homemade foie gras and conserve of duck. Old-fashioned rooms. Come meditate in peace and well-being in the country. Pedestrian, equestrian and mountain-biking paths. Heated pool on site. Snow-shoeing and cross-country skiing paths from the B&B. Golf near Parc du Mont Mégantic and Parc Frontenac. Bring your own wine. Warm welcome. Dog-sledding packages. **Farm Stay p 67.**

From Montréal, Aut. 10, East Angus Exit twd Lac-Mégantic. Rte 108 West twd Courcelles.

B&B
L'AUBERGE D'ANDROMÈDE

Gina Hallée and Gilles Leclerc
495, rang 6
Courcelles G0M 1C0
tel/fax (418) 483-5442
www3.sympatico.
ca/andromedetour
andromedetour@sympatico.ca

	B&B	MAP
single	$45	$70
double	$70	$140
child	$25	$35

Taxes extra VS
Open year round

Number of rooms	3
rooms with private bath	3

🦆 🏃 🚲 🐎 🛷 ⛷ 🐟

5. COWANSVILLE

☀☀☀☀ F E P 🚣 TA R.5

Prize for Excellence "Special Favorite" Regional 1999. Enchanting site near Bromont and Lac Brome. Discover our paradise on a 10-acres hill, overlooking Lac d'Avignon with view over the mountains. Flowery expanses, pond, footpaths, in-ground pool, VIP suites, hearty and varied breakfasts. Near cultural and sports activities. Gift certificates and "golf, bike, relaxation, ski" packages available. "Sheer bliss".

From Montréal or Sherbrooke, Aut. 10, Exit 74, Boul Pierre Laporte twd Cowansville. Facing hospital, left on Rue Principale, 0.5km.

B&B
DOMAINE SUR LA COLLINE B&B

Nicole and Gilles Deslauriers
1221, rue Principale
Cowansville J2K 1K7
(450) 266-1910
1-888-222-1692
fax (450) 266-4320
www.surlacolline.qc.ca
info@surlacolline.qc.ca

	B&B
single	$70-100
double	$75-125
triple	$145
quad.	$155
child	$10-20

VS MC

Reduced rates: 10% Jan. 12 to May 15 and Nov. 1 to Dec. 15
Open year round

Number of rooms	4
rooms with private bath	2
shared bathrooms	1
shared wc	1

 🦆 🏃 🚲 🐎 🎿 ⛷ 🔭

6. COWANSVILLE

☀☀☀☀ F E 🅴 P 🚣 R2

European-style residence attrac-tively decorated with wood from our farm. The beauty of the Appalachians, the flower-filled gardens and the fish in the ponds will seduce you. Share the tranquility of the countryside with us, and treat yourself to our delicious breakfasts, served indoors or, in summer, on the veranda. Pool, gift certificates and packages available. Welcome to our home!

From Montréal or Sherbrooke, Aut. 10, Exit 68, Rte 139 twd Cowansville. After traffic lights, turn right on Rue Beaumont and left on Montée Lebeau.

B&B
GÎTE MASYPA

Jacqueline and Pierre Caron
500, Montée Lebeau
Cowansville J2K 3G6
(450) 263-6403
1-888-244-6403
fax (450) 263-3434
www3.sympatico.ca/masypa
masypa@sympatico.ca

	B&B
single	$55-60
double	$65-70
child	$15

Taxes extra VS

Reduced rates: long stay
Open: May 1 to Oct. 31

Number of rooms	3
shared bathrooms	1
shared wc	1

 🦆 🚣 🏃 🚲 🐎 🔭

7. DANVILLE

 R.3

Located in one of the most beautiful villages of the Eastern Townships, this elegant Victorian home is entirely renovated and furnished with antiques. Our warm reception will enchant you. Sitting room, fireplace, solarium, garden, homemade breakfast.

From Montréal, Aut. 20 East, Exit 147, Rte 116 East. In Danville, first street to your right, Rue Daniel Johnson to the square, left on Rue Grove. From Québec City, Aut. 20 West, Exit 253, Rte 116 West. In Danville, second street to the left, Rue Daniel Johnson. At the square, left on Rue Grove.

B&B
MAISON MC CRACKEN

Nicole Marcq Jousselin
126, Grove C.P 749
Danville J0A 1A0
(819) 839-2963
1-866-839-2963
www.maison-mc-cracken.ca.tc
maison-mc-cracken@ca.tc

B&B	
single	$60
double	$70
triple	$85
child	$10
Open year round	
Number of rooms	**3**
rooms with sink	2
shared bathrooms	1
shared wc	1

---

8. DUNHAM

 R4

A great find, "with a lovely name... A superb house run by a young couple. The stately trees along the road here form a leafy tunnel... It's just like being in Vermont... lavish breakfast..." (Pierre Foglia, La Presse). Heated pool, hiking trails, maple grove. If you stay 3 nights, get maple product for free. Free tour of the L'Orpailleur vineyard (May-Oct).

Aut. 10, Exit 68, Rte 139 South, 20km. In Cowansville, right at 2nd light on Rte 202 South twd Dunham, 2km. Left on Chemin Fitchett, 2km, then left on Chemin Vail, 2km.

B&B
AU TEMPS DES MÛRES

Marie-Josée Potvin and
Pierre Cormier
2024, chemin Vail
Dunham J0E 1M0
(450) 266-1319
1-888-708-8050
fax (450) 266-1303
www.tempsdesmures.qc.ca

B&B	
single	$55-75
double	$70-85
child	$15-25
Taxes extra VS MC	
Reduced rates: 3 nights consecutive and more. Nov. 1 to May 1	
Open year round	
Number of rooms	**5**
rooms with private bath	3
shared bathrooms	1

---

9. DUNHAM

 R.2

Located amidst orchards and vineyards in a village that has preserved its heritage, this sumptuous Victorian home will seduce you with its charm, warmth, comfort and hospitality. Culinary delights are only a few steps away, and in the morning, aromas and tastes will satisfy your every craving!

Aut. 10, Exit 68, Rte 139 twd Cowansville, 18km. At traffic light, Rte 202 twd Dunham, 8km. 200m past the corner store, left Rue du Collège.

B&B
AUX DOUCES HEURES

Lyette Leroux Dumoulin and
André Dumoulin
110, rue du Collège
Dunham J0E 1M0
(450) 295-2476
1-877-295-2476
fax (450) 295-1307
www.inns-bb.com/doucesheures
auxdoucesheures@videotron.ca

B&B	
single	$65-95
double	$95-105
Taxes extra VS	
Open: Apr. 1 to Nov. 30	
Number of rooms	**5**
rooms with private bath	5
shared wc	1

10. EASTMAN

☀☀☀☀ F E ⊘ P 〜 ≈ ✕ TA R2

Small details that make up a great whole: a divine setting, a lake in which to swim, with Mont Orford as a backdrop. Gourmet breakfasts served in the solarium, by the fire or on the terrace. Packages: show, ski, business meeting, gift certificate. Home sweet home; reserve the whole house and have dinner too. Bring your own wine. A great place to sin without fear of repentance.

Aut. 10, Exit 106, Eastman, Rte 112 East, 3km past the village.

B&B
GÎTE LES PECCADILLES

Christine and
Jean-Marie Foucault
1029, Route Principale
Eastman J0E 1P0
(450) 297-3551
(514) 482-5347
www.inns-bb.com/lespeccadilles
jmfoucault@videotron.ca

	B&B
single	$55-95
double	$75-95
child	$20

Reduced rates: 1 complementary night after 7 nights consecutive
Open year round

Number of rooms	4
rooms with private bath	1
shared bathrooms	2

11. FARNHAM

☀☀☀ F E ⊘ P 🐾 R.1

This Victorian home was built in 1907 in Farnham, a former Loyalist town located in the heart of Québec's wine region. Bike path, golf course, nature centre. Activities: skydiving school, theatre. Our welcoming, warm house is lovingly decorated; hearty breakfast included.

Aut. 10 East, Exit 55, second stop sign, Rue Yamaska East. Turn left.

LES MATINS DE ROSIE

Lyne Jacques
555, Yamaska est
Farnham J2N 1J4
(450) 293-7331
www.inns-bb.com/matinsderosie
surprises1958@hotmail.com

	B&B
single	$45-65
double	$55-75
child	$10

Taxes extra VS MC
Open: May 1 to Oct. 31 and low season weekends by reservation only

Number of rooms	3
shared bathrooms	1

12. FRELIGHSBURG

☀☀☀ F e ⊘ P ✕ R1.5

Come gather wild fruits or mushrooms, surprise the deer in the orchard or on wooded trails, feed the small animals or simply relax in one of Québec's loveliest villages, at the foot of Mont Pinacle. French specialties. Packages available. **Country-Style Dining p 20. Farm Explorations p 52. Farm Shops p 36.**

Aut. 10, Exit 22, to the end of Aut. 35 South. Left, twd St-Alexandre, twd Bedford. Rte 202, about 7km. Right at Frelighsburg sign. We are 1km past village, on right.

B&B
À LA GIRONDINE

Françoise and François Bardo
104, Route 237 sud
Frelighsburg J0J 1C0
(450) 298-5206
fax (450) 298-5216
www.netc.net/lagirondine
lagirondine@netc.net

	B&B
single	$70
double	$80

Taxes extra VS MC
Open year round

Number of rooms	2
shared bathrooms	1
shared wc	1

13. GOULD

In the heart of Québec's Highlands, in a small village of Scottish origin, three houses offer 11 guest rooms whose character evokes the homeland of the first Highlander pioneers. The woodwork, antique fur-nishings and Scottish-style ambiance and cuisine will transport you to the 19th century. Eat, sleep and live in the Scottish tradition in the former Gaelic capital of the Eastern Townships.

From Montréal, Aut. 10, Exit 143, Rte 112 East. In East Angus, Rtes 214 and 108 East. From the U.S., Rtes 3 and 257 North. From Québec City, Aut. 73 twd Ste-Marie, Rte 173 twd Vallée-Jct. Rte 112 twd Thetford and Weedon, Rte 257 South.

INN
LA RUÉE VERS GOULD

Daniel Audet and
Jacques Cloutier
19, Route 108
Gould, Lingwick J0B 2Z0
tel/fax (819) 877-3446
1-888-305-3526
www.rueegouldrush.com
info@rueegouldrush.com

	B&B	MAP
single	$50-70	$80-95
double	$75-90	$135-150
triple	$100-115	$190-205

Taxes extra VS MC IT
Open: Feb. 1 to Jan. 10

Number of rooms	11
rooms with private bath	3
shared bathrooms	3

---

14. GRANBY

Unique family concept (16 to 24 people) located next to the zoo and Amazoo. This spacious B&B designed for families and groups will simply enchant you. Four large suites with two air-conditioned rooms, private bathroom, refrigerator and TV offer unparal-leled privacy. And let's not forget the hearty break-fasts served at the family table! Close to the zoo; private, air-conditioned suite. We specialize in zoo, cycling and theatre packages. New: Zen ambiance and massage therapy.

From Aut. 10, follow Zoo sign. On Boul. David Bouchard at traffic light, South St-Hubert. 2 stops. Left on Bourget West.

B&B
AUBERGE DU ZOO

Claude Gladu
347, Bourget Ouest
Granby J2G 1E8
(450) 378-6161
1-888-882-5252
fax (450) 378-0470
www.aubergeduzoo.com
info@aubergeduzoo.com

	B&B
single	$60-70
double	$85-90
triple	$110-115
quad.	$125-140
child	$15-20

Taxes extra VS IT

Reduced rates: 20 % Sept. 1 to May 1, 3 nights and more
Open year round

Number of rooms	4
rooms with private bath	4

---

15. GRANBY

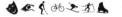

This old-fashioned B&B will provide pleasant moments in a peaceful decor rich in history. Our five stylish rooms are great for catching up with family or friends. Located on the edge of L'Estriade bike path, the house overlooks Lac Boivin. In summer, after a cycling excursion, our spa invites you to relax. In winter, enjoy breakfast near the antique-style wood-burning stove. An old-fashioned piano, a violin and a guitar await for unforgettable evenings.

Aut. 10, Exit 74 twd Granby, at the lights, left on Rue Denison.

B&B
AUX ABORDS

Johanne Roy and
Louis Tétreault
116, Denison est
Granby J2G 4C5
(450) 531-0199
(450) 372-2018
www.auxabords.com
info@auxabords.com

	B&B
single	$55
double	$65
triple	$85-105
quad.	$85-105
child	$10

Taxes extra
Open year round

Number of rooms	5
shared bathrooms	2
shared wc	1

16. GRANBY

☀☀☀ **F** e ⊘ **P** 🏊 🐾 **TA** R.2

Le Campagnard, located only 30m from a bike path, is a warm, simple home set on a 65,000 square-foot property where nature meets the city. Enjoy campfires and an exceptional setting, which includes two ponds, rabbits, chickens and birds. If the Eastern Townships intrigue you, why not take advantage of our affordable bike rentals?

From Montréal, Aut. 10 East, Exit 68. Rte Denison West twd Granby. From Sherbrooke, Aut. 10 West, Exit 74. Rte Pierre-Laporte West twd Granby. At Rte Denison, left after the 3rd light.

B&B
B&B LE CAMPAGNARD

Jean-Claude Houle and
Richard Denis
146, Denison ouest
Granby J2G 4C8
(450) 770-1424
(450) 777-0245
fax (450) 777-1093
http://campagnard.tripod.com
lecampagnard@sympatico.ca

	B&B
single	$50-60
double	$65-75
triple	$95
quad.	$125
child	$15

VS MC
Open year round

Number of rooms	5
shared bathrooms	2

17. GRANBY

☀☀☀ **F E P** 🛶 R5

Chez Marie is the ideal spot for a family vacation, a romantic getaway or a business trip. Nearby, enjoy various activities such as the zoo, Amazoo, Parc de la Yamaska, bike paths, skiing, hiking, theatre, etc., all less than a 10min drive away. The B&B is warmly decorated and offers a relaxing ambiance reminiscent of 1910-1944. We look forward to seeing you.

Aut. 10 Exit 68 twd Granby, Boul. David-Bouchard North, 17.6km.

B&B
CHEZ MARIE B&B

Jean-Marc Légaré
1059, boul. David Bouchard nord
Granby J2G 8C7
(450) 375-2212
(450) 405-5626
fax (450) 375-7775
www.inns-bb.com/chezmarie
jmarclegare@total.net

	B&B
single	$60-80
double	$60-80
triple	$75-85
quad.	$100
child	$15

Taxes extra
Open year round

Number of rooms	3
rooms in basement	2
rooms with private bath	1
shared bathrooms	2

18. GRANBY

☀☀☀☀ **F** E ⊘ **P** 🛶 **TA** R1

Prize for Excellence "Special Favorite" Regional 2000. From the terrace of our bed and breakfast, on Lac Boivin and a short bike ride away from l'Estriade, you can admire stunning sunsets in an enchanting setting. Private living room with fireplace, barbecue in season, skiing, skating, hiking: everything for your comfort and relaxation.

Aut. 10, Exit 74 twd Granby. At the traffic light, left on Rte 112, right on Rue de L'Iris, left on Rue de la Potentille and left on Rue du Nénuphar. By bike at Km 1 on L'Estriade.

B&B
LA MAISON DUCLAS

Ginette Canuel and
Camil Duchesne
213, rue du Nénuphar
Granby J2H 2J9
(450) 360-0641
www.maisonduclas.com
info@maisonduclas.com

	B&B
single	$55
double	$75

Reduced rates: Nov. 1 to May 1
Open year round

Number of rooms	2
rooms in semi-basement	2
rooms with private bath	2

19. GRANBY

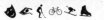

Carole and Michel welcome you to their charming raspberry-coloured house. Let us mapper you in this relaxing setting on Lac Boivin located near a park. Enjoy coffee on the waterfront among flowers and facing the Estriade cycling path. Close to the downtown shops and restaurants. Rooms with air conditionning, heated pool. **See colour photos.**

From Montréal, Aut. 10 East, Exit 74 twd Granby, at the traffic light make a left on Rte 112 West. Right at the 2nd traffic light on Rue de la Gare, right on Drummond.

B&B
UNE FLEUR AU BORD DE L'EAU

Carole Bélanger and
Michel Iannantuono
90, rue Drummond
Granby J2G 2S6
(450) 776-1141
1-888-375-1747
fax (450) 375-0141
www.clubtrs.ca/fleurvtg
fleurvtg@login.net

R.2

B&B	
single	$60-75
double	$65-80

Taxes extra VS MC AM

Reduced rates: Jan. 8 to Apr. 15, Oct. 31 to Dec. 15
Open year round

Number of rooms	4
rooms with private bath	2
shared bathrooms	1

---

20. LAC-BROME, FULFORD

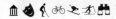

A warm welcome to our Tudor-style house, located between Bromont and Knowlton. Come and stroke our pure-bred Norwegian horses (Fjords). Enjoy a walk on our 26-acre property. You'll find a brook, a woodland, a pool and patios. Golf club and Bromont ski resort 5min away. Western-style horseback riding with guide and group sleigh rides. Snowshoes available on site in winter.

Aut. 10, Exit 78 twd Bromont. Straight ahead, 7km, right at flashing light on Brome road. We are 1km further on your left.

B&B
LE TU-DOR

Ghislaine Lemay and
Jean-Guy Laforce
394, chemin Brome
Lac-Brome J0E 1S0
(450) 534-3947
fax (450) 534-5543
www.inns-bb.com/letu_dor
lemay.laforce@citenet.net

R5

B&B	
single	$65-70
double	$75-80
triple	$110
quad.	$140
child	$15

VS MC

Reduced rates: on long stay
Open year round

Number of rooms	4
rooms with private bath	4

---

21. LAC-MÉGANTIC

Tastefully decorated warm and cosy house, located downtown in a quiet residential neighbourhood near the lake, marina and restaurants. Our breakfasts are also very generous; guests benefit from air conditioning in summer.

From Sherbrooke Rte 161, left at 2nd light, Rue Maisonneuve, right on Rue Dollard. From Québec City or Woburn, cross downtown after railway, right on Rue Villeneuve, left on Dollard.

B&B
LA MAISON BLANCHE

Noreen Kavanagh Legendre
4850, rue Dollard
Lac-Mégantic G6B 1G8
(819) 583-2665
www.inns-bb.com/lamaisonblanche

R4

B&B	
single	$60
double	$60

Reduced rates: after Thanksgiving
Open year round

Number of rooms	2
rooms with private bath	2

22. LAC-MÉGANTIC

★★★ F E 🚭 P ≈ ✕ TA R2

Spacious victorian style country inn on lake Mégantic in a peacefull red pine forest. Cosy rooms, each with their own distinctive décor. An inviting dining-room serving regional fine cuisine with good wines and views on the lake. Comfortable living rooms, fire place and a sunny veranda where time stands still and days are spent pleasurably, reading and resting. Various package are available in all seasons. **See colour photos.**

Aut. 10, Exit 143, Rtes 112 East, 214 East, 108 East and 161 South.

INN
LES VICTORINES DU LAC

Rollande and Louis Cormier
1886, Route 161 Sud
Lac-Mégantic G6B 2S1
(819) 583-6904
1-866-494-6904
fax (819) 583-6906
www.victorines.qc.ca
lesvictorinesdulac@sogetel.net

	B&B	MAP
single	$85-115	$110-140
double	$95-125	$145-175
child	$24	

Taxes extra VS MC AM IT

Reduced rates: Oct. 15 to May 15
Open year round

Number of rooms	15
rooms with private bath	15

🚶 🎿 🚴 🐎 ⛷ 🛷 🐕 🐟

23. LAC-MÉGANTIC

★★★ F E P ✕ TA

Built in 1891 on the lakeshore, the Manoir D'Orsennens was completely restored and expanded. It offers the comfort of a large hotel with the charm of a small inn, well-equiped rooms, excellent cuisine and a unique décor. Near numerous tourist attractions, guests are greeted with a warm welcome and personalized service. You will definitely want to come back! Packages available. 75km from St-George-de-Beauce, 100km from Sherbrooke.

From Montréal or Sherbrooke, Aut. 10, Rtes 143 South, 108 East and 161 South. Cross the town, after the bridge, to the right.

INN
MANOIR D'ORSENNENS

Nathalie Michaud
3502, rue Agnès
Lac-Mégantic G6B 1L3
(819) 583-3515
1-877-583-3515
fax (819) 583-0308
www.inns-bb.com/manoirdorsennens
manoirorsennens@globetrotter.net

	B&B	MAP
single	$90-95	$115-120
double	$108-113	$158-163
triple	$136	$211
quad.	$159	$259

Taxes extra VS MC AM ER IT

Reduced rates: Oct. 15 to June 15
Open year round

Number of rooms	12
rooms with private bath	12
shared wc	2

24. MAGOG

☀☀☀☀ F e 🚭 P ⚓ TA R.1

Looking for a warm ambiance, in a century-old house with period decor, piano, fireplace, dream rooms and whirlpool bath? Then look no further. In the morning, you'll start your day with a lavish, varied breakfast, followed by summer/winter outdoor activities. Packages available—it's all here. Near the lake and downtown, with the bike path right at our doorstep. Heartfelt welcome.

Aut. 10, Exit 118, Rte 141 South twd Magog. At the McDonald's, left on Chemin Hatley. Keep left, 1st house on the headland.

B&B
À AMOUR ET AMITIÉ

Nathalie and Pascal Coulaudoux
600, ch. Hatley Ouest
Magog J1X 3G4
(819) 868-1945
1-888-244-1945
fax (819) 868-4475
www.bbamouretamitie.com
amouretamitie@sympatico.ca

	B&B
single	$60-100
double	$70-110
triple	$115-130
quad.	$135-140
child	$20

Taxes extra VS MC AM

Reduced rates: Oct. 15 to May 31, 3 nights and more and group
Open year round

Number of rooms	5
rooms with private bath	5

25. MAGOG

Experience the peace and quiet of the countryside (not too far from the city) on our wooded, 250-acre property with stunning panoramic view of Mont Orford, Owl's Head, Maine, Vermont, etc. Several walking paths open to snowmobiles and all-terrain vehicles in winter; snowshoeing. Spacious rooms, one detached suite (four to six people) with dining area. Hearty breakfasts and table d'hôte. Homemade bread and jams, organic products from our garden and orchard served on the terrace, next to the pool or by the fire. **Farm Stay p 67.**

From Montréal, Aut. 10, from Québec City, Aut. 20, Aut. 55 South, Exit 29 Ste-Catherine de Hatley twd Magog. Past the Ultramar gas station, left on Rue Nicolas Vieil for 3km.

B&B
À LA COLLINE AUX CHEVAUX

Sylvie Cockenpot
1630, chemin Benoît
Magog J1X 3W2
(819) 843-2401
www.inns-bb.com/collineauxchevaux
info@legite.net

	B&B	MAP
single	$60-90	$95-105
double	$70-110	$130-150
triple	$95-115	$185-205
quad.	$110-140	$235-260
child	$15	$25

Taxes extra

Reduced rates: 10% for group 3 nights and more

Open year round

Number of rooms	3
rooms with private bath	3

26. MAGOG

Whether it's for business or pleasure, for one or several nights, rejuvenate yourself in the tranquility of our warm Queen Anne home and its hundred-year-old pine trees. Four spacious rooms (1 to 4 people) with TV and air conditioning; BBQ, dining area with fridge and microwave. Steps away from downtown, lake and restaurants and near all cultural and outdoor activities. Motorcycle/bicycle garage.

Aut. 10, Exit 118, twd Magog. At the 2nd stop sign, left on McDonald and 2nd street right on Des Pins.

B&B
À LA MAISON DREW

Françoise Guézennec and Michel Meyniel
206, rue des Pins
Magog J1X 2H9
tel/fax (819) 843-8480
1-888-639-9941
www.maisondrew.com
lamaisondrew@sympatico.ca

	B&B
single	$85-105
double	$85-105
triple	$130-135
quad.	$160-165
child	$20

Reduced rates: Nov. 1 to Apr. 30, except holidays and long weekend

Open year round

Number of rooms	4
rooms with private bath	4

27. MAGOG

Winner of the 2001 Regional Prize for Excellence "Achievement" and 2002 "Eastern Townships Tourism Grand Prix." Imagine an attentive innkeeper, with a Gothic Revival-style house on the heritage tour in the heart of the village. We offer four bright rooms with romantic names, healthy meals, a fireplace and piano, and welcome you in a warm atmosphere yearround. Perfect for business meetings, vacations or anniversaries. Available for rent by the month, week or weekend. Welcome! **See colour photos and back cover.**

From Montréal, Aut. 10, Exit 118 twd Magog, 3.2km. Facing church left on St-Patrice and 1st street left Abbott.

B&B
À L'ANCESTRALE B&B

Monique Poirier
200, rue Abbott
Magog J1X 2H5
tel/fax (819) 847-5555
1-888-847-5507
www.ancestrale.qc.ca
infos@ancestrale.qc.ca

	B&B
single	$65-105
double	$75-115
triple	$95-135
quad.	$115-155

Taxes extra VS

Reduced rates: 20% 3 nights, Nov. 1 to May 15 in weekdays except Holidays/School Holidays

Open year round

Number of rooms	4
rooms with private bath	4

28. MAGOG

☀ ☀ ☀ ☀ **F E** 🚫 **P** ⊟ 🐾 **TA R.7**

Our elegant Victorian house, lush garden, warm ambiance and international gourmet breakfasts will charm you! Living rooms, fireplace, solarium, kitchenette. Near majestic lake, restaurants, shops, bike path; 8km from Parc du Mont-Orford, perfect for discovering the charms of the townships. Ski package and more. We lend bikes. Comfort and relaxation guaranteed!

From Montréal or Sherbrooke, Aut. 10, Exit 118 twd Magog. After Magog river, left at flashing light, 3rd house on the right.

B&B
À TOUT VENANT

Maria Foulquier and
Sylvain Cruz
624, rue Bellevue Ouest
Magog J1X 3H4
(819) 868-0419
1-888-611-5577
fax (819) 868-5115
www.atoutvenant.com
atoutvenant@sympatico.ca

	B&B
single	$75-90
double	$80-95
triple	$125
child	$25

Taxes extra

Reduced rates: Nov. 1 to May 31 except holiday and school holidays.
Open year round

Number of rooms	5
rooms with private bath	5

🏛 🔥 ⊟ 🎿 🏃 🚲 ⛷

29. MAGOG

☀ ☀ ☀ ☀ **F E** 🚫 **P** ⊟ 🏊 **TA R.1**

This peaceful century home with old-world charm will win you over. Whatever the season, enjoy some time off in a warm atmosphere and cosy rooms. Savour our delicious breakfasts and take advantage of the pool, garden, fireplace and reading nooks. Gift certificates, anniversaries, business, various packages. Near the lake with mountain view, bike path. In the heart of Magog, 10 min from Orford.

Aut. 10, Exit 115 or 118, 92 Merry South.

B&B
AU MANOIR DE LA RUE MERRY

Sylvie Goulet and Carmel Labbé
92, rue Merry Sud
Magog J1X 3L3
(819) 868-1860
1-800-450-1860
www.manoirmerry.com
labbe@manoirmerry.com

	B&B
single	$70-85
double	$75-90
triple	$110
quad.	$120
child	$0-20

Taxes extra VS MC IT

Reduced rates: mid-Oct. to mid-May or 3rd night except holidays
Open year round

Number of rooms	5
rooms with private bath	5

🔥 🎿 🏃 🚲 ⛷ 🎣 🔭

30. MAGOG

☀ ☀ ☀ ☀ **F E** 🚫 **P** ⊟ **TA R.5**

Regional Prize for Excellence "Special Favorite" 2002. Pamper yourself in our warm, quiet, non-smoking Loyalist home, located near a historic church and all of Magog-Orford's cultural and outdoor activities. Cozy, inviting rooms illuminated by the cardinal points. Delicious five-course breakfast to delight athletes and epicureans. Bike shed. Show/cruise packages. Welcome.

Aut. 10, Exit 118 twd Magog, 3km, Rue Merry North. Before the church, turn left.

B&B
AU VIRAGE

Louise Vachon and Jean Barbès
172, rue Merry Nord
Magog J1X 2E8
(819) 868-5828
1-866-868-5828
fax (819) 868-6798
http://pages.infinit.net/auvirage
barbesjean@sympatico.ca

	B&B
single	$75-90
double	$80-95

Taxes extra VS IT

Reduced rates: Oct. 15 to May 15 except holidays and school holidays
Open year round

Number of rooms	5
rooms with private bath	3
rooms with sink	3
shared bathrooms	1
shared wc	1

⊟ 🎣 🏃 🚲 ⛷ 🔭

31. MAGOG

★★★ F E P 🦌 🐕 ✕ TA R6

Enjoy a change of scenery and breathe in the fresh country air. Savour an unforgettable five-course breakfast by the fireside or a six-course country dinner on our poolside terrace. After a stroll through our flower gardens, to the small farm or the stream, you will have but one desire: to come back! Ulysses Favourite 2000/01. **Country-Style Dining p 21. See colour photos. Ad back cover.**

From Montréal, Aut. 10 East, Exit 115 South-Magog/ St-Benoît-du-Lac, 1.8km. Right on Chemin des Pères twd St-Benoît-du-Lac/Austin, 6.1km. From Québec City, Aut. 20 West, 55 South and 10 West, Exit 115 twd St-Benoît-du-Lac.

INN
AUX JARDINS CHAMPÊTRES

Monique Dubuc and Yvon Plourde
1575, ch. des Pères, R.R. 4
Magog J1X 5R9
(819) 868-0665
1-877-868-0665
fax (819) 868-6744
www.auxjardinschampetres.com
*auxjardinschampetres@
qc.aira.com*

	B&B	MAP
single	$90-110	$130-150
double	$100-120	$184-200
triple	$130-150	$256-276
quad.	$180	$340
child	$30	$50

Taxes extra VS MC IT
Open year round

Number of rooms	6
rooms with private bath	6
shared wc	2

---

32. MAGOG

☀☀☀ F E 🚭 P TA R.1

Escape to the Eastern Townships! This warm 1880 house will delight you with its creature comforts, guaranteed peace and quiet and sublime breakfasts. Take a nap beneath the apple trees or discover the peacefulness of Lake Memphrémagog or, again, the bustle of the Main Street. **See colour photos.**

From Montréal or Sherbrooke, Aut. 10 Exit 118, twd Magog Rte 141, 3km. At traffic light, left on St-Patrice West, then 1st left Rue Abbott.

B&B
LA BELLE ÉCHAPPÉE

Louise Fournier
145, rue Abbott
Magog J1X 2H4
tel/fax (819) 843-8061
1-877-843-8061
www.inns-bb.com/belleechappee
labelleechappee@qc.aira.com

	B&B
single	$45-80
double	$60-100
child	$25

VS MC

Reduced rates: Nov. 1 to June 1
Open year round

Number of rooms	5
rooms with private bath	1
rooms with sink	2
shared bathrooms	2

---

33. MAGOG

☀☀☀☀ F E 🚭 P 🦌 TA R.1

Succomb to the discreet charm of our sunny, century-old home. For one or more nights, you'll love our breakfasts and thoughtfulness. Discover the legendary Lac Memphrémagog and Mont Orford. Depending on the season, after cycling, skiing, golfing, hik-ing or swimming, let us welcome you by the fire or in the garden!

From Montréal or Sherbrooke, Aut. 10, Exit 118 twd Magog. Pass over the Magog river left at the flashing yellow light, twd Ayer's Cliff, keep to the right Rue Bellevue.

B&B
LA MAISON CAMPBELL

Lorraine Lauzier and
Larry Duclos
584, rue Bellevue Ouest
Magog J1X 3H2
(819) 843-9000
1-888-843-7707
www.maisoncampbell.qc.ca
maisoncampbell@sympatico.ca

	B&B
single	$75-85
double	$80-90
child	$20

Taxes extra VS

Reduced rates: Nov. 1 to May 31 except holiday and long week-end.
Open year round

Number of rooms	5
rooms with private bath	5

34. MANSONVILLE

This isolated country spot, away from the city's hustle and bustle, is very comfortable and located on the mountainside, offering a stunning view of Vermont. 10km from the U.S. border. Hiking, cycling, horseback riding, snowshoeing, cross-country and downhill skiing (Owl's Head, Jay Peak, Mont Sutton). Art and Wine routes. Gregorian song on Sundays at the Abbaye de St-Benoît du Lac. Warm ambiance, wildfowl cuisine and various breakfasts. Massage and pool, relaxation guaranteed.

Aut. 10 Exit 106 twd Mansonville 29km, twd Highwater, twd Sutton Chemin de la Vallée Missisquoi 6km. Right on Rue Ruiterbrook, 100m, right.

B&B
LE MAGESTIK

Normand Arsenault
63, chemin Sargent
Mansonville J0E 1X0
(514) 229-9229
fax (514) 879-0706
www.magestik.com
info@magestik.com

B&B	
single	$75-90
double	$90-105
triple	$105-120
child	$20

Taxes extra VS MC
Open year round

Number of rooms	2
rooms with sink	1
shared bathrooms	2

35. NORTH-HATLEY

Century-old house in the heart of North Hatley with magnificent view of the village. Suites with private bathroom; balcony, terrace, telephone, refrigerator. Refined continental breakfast.

From Montréal, Aut. 10 Exit 121, Aut. 55 South Exit 29. Rte 108 East twd North Hatley, left on Chemin Capelton. Next to the Ste-Elizabeth church.

B&B
LE CACHET

Marcel Brassard
3105, chemin Capelton Rte. 108
North Hatley J0B 2C0
(819) 842-4994
1-866-842-4994
fax (819) 820-9977
www.inns-bb.com/lecachet
supersan@abacom.com

B&B	
single	$90-145
double	$90-145
triple	$110-165
child	$0

Taxes extra IT
Open year round

Number of rooms	4
rooms with private bath	4

36. PIKE-RIVER

One hour from Montréal and 10 min from Vermont: on the riverbank, an opulent, flowery B&B invites you for a restful break in a cosy atmosphere. Hearty Swiss breakfast with home-made bread and goods from our farm. Bicycling tours. Near the wildlife reserve, the Musée Missisquoi and the vineyards.

From Montréal, Champlain bridge. Aut. 10 East, Exit 22 twd St-Jean, Rte 35 South then Rte 133 twd St-Pierre-de-Vérone-à-Pike-River. In the curve, left on Chemin des Rivières, 1.5km.

B&B
LA VILLA DES CHÊNES

Noëlle and Rolf Gasser
300, ch. Des Rivières
Pike-River J0J 1P0
(450) 296-8848
fax (450) 296-4990
www.inns-bb.com/villadeschenes

B&B	
single	$50-55
double	$60-75
child	$15

Reduced rates: 10% 3 nights and more
Open: Feb.1 to Nov. 30

Number of rooms	4
rooms in basement	1
rooms with private bath	1
shared bathrooms	2

37. PIKE-RIVER, ST-PIERRE-DE-VÉRONNE ☀☀☀ F E⊘ P X

Located in the heart of farming country. We are a Swiss family that has lived here for 37 years. In our small restaurant we serve Swiss home-cooked meals and produce home-made breads, jams and sauces. Take long quiet walks on the 100 acres of land surrounding our inn. We look forward to meeting you.

From Montréal, Champlain bridge, Aut. 10 East, Exit 22 St-Jean-sur-Richelieu. Aut. 35 South to Rte 133 South (30 min), brown house on left. Or from US, Interstate 89 North twd Philipsburg, then Rte 133 North, about 13km on the right.

INN
AUBERGE LA SUISSE

Dora and Roger Baertschi
119, Route 133
Saint-Pierre-de-Véronne-à-
Pike-River J0J 1P0
(450) 244-5870
fax (450) 244-5181
www.inns-bb.com/lasuisse
*reservations@
aubergelasuisse.com*

B&B	
single	$65-75
double	$75-85
child	$30

Taxes extra VS MC AM IT

Reduced rates: Feb. 1 to Avr. 30
Open: Apr. 1 to Feb. 28

Number of rooms	4
rooms with private bath	4

38. ST-JOACHIM-DE-SHEFFORD ☀☀☀☀ F e⊘ P ≈ R10

On the La Campagnarde bike path, a warm Canadian house with all comforts: cozy beds, TV in every room, central air conditioning, fireplace. Hearty, varied breakfasts with homemade products served in the solarium, with a view of the lake, in a flowery setting. Enjoy walks on our forest trails, swimming or pedal-boating. Bikes at your disposal, or a game of bowls...

Aut. 10, Exit 68, Boul. David-Bouchard North, twd Granby, 4km after Parc de la Yamaska, left on Chemin Ingram.

B&B
LA BELLE AU BOIS DORMANT

Pauline and Marcel Labelle
623, ch. Ingram
Saint-Joachim-de-Shefford
J0E 2G0
(450) 539-4039
fax (450) 539-2296
**www.inns-
bb.com/belleauboisdormant**
belledormant@videotron.ca

B&B	
single	$70-80
double	$75-85

Open: June 1 to Oct. 31

Number of rooms	2
shared bathrooms	1
shared wc	1

39. STE-CATHERINE-DE-HATLEY ☀☀☀☀ F E⊘ P TA R5

Our lovely fieldstone house nestled in a flowery bower, its warm woodwork, the brook and our personalized welcome will charm you. You will then fall under the spell of your suite: a private, spacious floor opening out on magnificent wooded grounds alive with birds and deer. Queen-size bed, fireplace, refrigerator, telephone and other treats will enhance your stay. Welcome!

From Montréal, Aut. 10, Exit 121, Aut. 55 South, Rte 108 East, 7km, Rte 216 East, 2km.

B&B
MAPIROL

Marie-Paule Dessaint
97, chemin Lavallée
Sainte-Catherine-de-Hatley
J0B 1W0
(819) 842-2569
1-877-442-2569
www.mapirol.com
mapirol@mapirol.com

B&B	
single	$100-130
double	$110-140
triple	$170-200
quad.	$185-215

VS MC
Open year round

Number of rooms	1
rooms with private bath	1

40. STANSTEAD

☀ ☀ ☀ **F E P** ⊟ R2.5

Dating from 1940, this residence is situated on one of the only border streets in North America. Everything is done to ensure you have a pleasant stay in our peaceful and relaxed environment. Delicious five-course breakfast are served. Located only 5 min from Parc Weir (swimming and boat launch). Excursions on Lac Memphrémagog are possible and the property links up with a bike path. There's also a museum, opera house, antique shop and much more. See you soon!

From Montréal, Aut. 10 twd Sherbrooke, Exit 121. Aut. 55 twd Stantead. Vermont, Exit 1 Rte 247 twd Stantead (Beebe Plain) 4.5km.

B&B
LA GRENOUILLÈRE
DES TROIS VILLAGES

Francyne and Serge Tougas
25, rue Canusa
Stanstead J0B 3E5
tel/fax (819) 876-5599
www.inns-bb.com/lagrenouillere
stougas@abacom.com

	B&B
single	$60-80
double	$65-85
child	$15

Taxes extra VS MC AM
Open year round

Number of rooms	3
rooms with private bath	1
shared bathrooms	1
shared wc	1

🏛 🚶 🏊 🎿 🚶 🚴 ⛷

---

41. SUTTON

☀ ☀ ☀ ☀ **F E** 🚫 **P** 🏊 🐄 R2

A mountain inn where the clientele (mostly adults) receives a warm reception in a peaceful atmosphere. Nestled high in the mountains, it offers direct access to ski and hiking trails. Its polished character, hearty breakfasts and comfortable, spacious rooms with fireplace and private bathroom, make it a refined, exquisite establishment.

From Montréal, Aut. 10 Exit 68. Rte 139 twd Sutton. Left on Chemin Maple for about 4km: Right on Chemin Boulanger.

B&B
AUBERGE ALTITUDE 2000

Denise and Jacques Lange
484, chemin Boulanger
Sutton J0E 2K0
(450) 538-1011
1-877-797-1011
fax (450) 538-1229
www.aubergealtitude.com
lange@aubergealtitude.com

	B&B
single	$100-135
double	$100-135

Taxes extra VS MC ER IT

Reduced rates: 6 nights and more
Open year round

Number of rooms	5
rooms with private bath	3
shared bathrooms	1
shared wc	1

🍷 🚶 🏊 🚶 🚴 ⛷ 🎿

42. COATICOOK

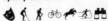

Warm, cosy country house dating from the last century with old-style charm of woodwork and fireplace. Suite or luxury rooms with king- or queen-size beds. Copious breakfast composed of regional products. Nearby golf, hiking and lakes for romantic couple or adventure-friendly family. Farm tour included. **Country-Style Dining p 19. Farm Shops p 35. Farm Explorations p 52.**

From Montréal, Aut. 10 Exit 121, Aut. 55 Exit 21. Rte 141 South, 1km before Barnston. Right at Chemin Madore, left at Chemin Martineau.

COUNTRY HOME
LA FERME MARTINETTE

Lisa Nadeau and
Gérald Martineau
1728, chemin Martineau
Coaticook J1A 2S5
tel/fax (819) 849-7089
1-888-881-4561
www.lafermemartinette.com
martinet@abacom.com

No. houses	1
No. rooms	3
No. people	1-6
WEEK-SUMMER	$480-720
WEEK-WINTER	$480-720
DAY-SUMMER	$75-135
DAY-WINTER	$75-135

Taxes extra VS MC IT
Open year round

---

43. COATICOOK

Located 30min from Mont-Orford, this large, comfortable home is ideal for relaxation and reunions. Near bike and snowmobile paths. Hunting and fishing. On this agricultural site, guests can watch and participate in farm chores, such as feeding and milking cows. Our daughters work on the farm and will help make your visit a most pleasant one. **Country Home on a Farm p 74.**

From Montréal, Aut. 10 East, Exit 121, Aut. 55 South, Exit 21, Rte 141 South to Coaticook. After traffic lights, turn right on Rue Cutting, first farm on your left.

COUNTRY HOME
SÉJOUR NADEAU

Fernand and Gisèle Nadeau
616, chemin Nadeau
Coaticook J1A 2S2
tel/fax (819) 849-3486
(819) 849-9932
**http://membres.lycos.
fr/sejournadeau**
fnadeau@videotron.ca

No. houses	1
No. rooms	3
No. people	15-18
WEEK-SUMMER	$575
WEEK-WINTER	$575
W/E-SUMMER	$375
W/E-WINTER	$375

Open year round

---

44. WOTTON

★ ★ ★

Cosy cottage with old-fashioned charm and magnificent view of the lakes. Activities include pedal-boats, canoeing, snowmobiling, hiking through forests and fields. Cross-country skiing, snowshoeing, golf and swimming close by. 4km from Asbestos.

From Montréal, Aut. 20 East, Exit 147. Rte 116 East twd Danville, Rte 255 South twd Wotton. 4km after crossing Rte 249, left on Route des Lacs, 2km.

COUNTRY HOME
LA MAISON DES LACS

Monique Mercier
28, chemin des Lacs
Wotton J0A 1N0
(819) 346-3575
(819) 573-9478
**www.tourisme-
cantons.qc.ca/maisondeslacs**

No. houses	1
No. rooms	5
No. people	10
WEEK-SUMMER	$600
WEEK-WINTER	$600
W/E-SUMMER	$300
W/E-WINTER	$300

Open year round

AGROTOURISM

Farm Explorations:

🐌 **12** À LA GIRONDINE, Frelighsburg ....*Page 52*

🐌 **42** LA FERME MARTINETTE, Coaticook .... *Page 52*

🐌 **45** LA FERME DU WAPITI, Frelighsburg ....*Page 53*

Farm Stays:

🐌 **4** L'AUBERGE D'ANDROMÈDE, Courcelles ....*Page 67*

🐌 **25** À LA COLLINE AUX CHEVAUX, Magog ....*Page 67*

Country Home on a Farm :

🐌 **43** SÉJOUR NADEAU, Coaticook ....*Page 74*

Farm Shops:

🐌 **12** À LA GIRONDINE, Frelighsburg ....*Page 36*

🐌 **42** LA FERME MARTINETTE, Coaticook..*Page 35*

🐌 **46** DOMAINE DE LA CHEVROTTIÈRE, Dunham ....*Page 35*

🐌 **47** LA CIDRERIE FLEURS DE POMMIERS, Dunham ....*Page 36*

🐌 **48** LE VIGNOBLE LE CEP D'ARGENT, Magog....................................*Page 37*

🐌 **49** LE VIGNOBLE LES CHANTS DE VIGNES, Magog...........................*Page 37*

🐌 **50** DOMAINE FÉLIBRE, Stanstead ....*Page 38*

Country-Style Dining:

🐌 **12** À LA GIRONDINE, Frelighsburg ....*Page 20*

🐌 **31** AUX JARDINS CHAMPÊTRES, Canton-de-Magog............................*Page 21*

🐌 **42** LA FERME MARTINETTE, Coaticook..*Page 19*

🐌 **51** LA CHÈVRERIE DES ACACIAS, Dunham ....*Page 19*

🐌 **52** AU GRÉ DU VENT, Magog ....*Page 20*

CENTRE-DU-QUÉBEC

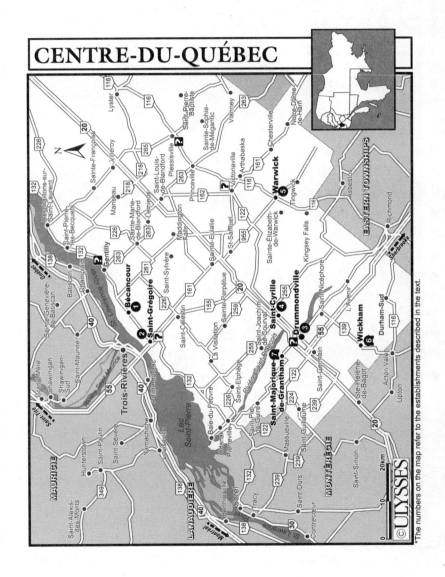

*The numbers on the map refer to the establishments described in the text.

1. BÉCANCOUR

We are renowned for our welcome, our food and our B&B inside a sumptuous Victorian house. We serve: ostrich, buffalo, caribou, venison, duck, rabbit, beef, seafood and perch. Refined local cuisine. Right nearby: canoeing, tennis, horseback riding, snowmobiling, swimming, fishing, tourist attractions. Hablamos español. **See colour photos.**

From Montréal or Québec City, Aut. 40. In Trois-Rivières, cross the Laviolette bridge, Aut. 30, Rte 132 East. Bécancour Exit.

INN
MANOIR BÉCANCOURT

Yvon Beaulieu
3255, Nicolas Perrot
Bécancour G0X 1B0
(819) 294-9068
fax (819) 294-9060
**www.inns-
bb.com/manoirbecancourt**
manoirbecancourt@hotmail.com

	B&B	MAP
single	$40-50	$60-70
double	$55-65	$95-105
child	$15	$35

Taxes extra VS MC

Reduced rates: weekdays
Open year round

Number of rooms	5
shared bathrooms	2
shared wc	5

---

2. BÉCANCOUR, ST-GRÉGOIRE

On the banks of the St. Lawrence River, 10 min from downtown Trois-Rivières, discover the peacefulness of the countryside. Welcome, comfort, pool and terrace await you. Enjoy our gourmet breakfast while taking in the magnificent view of the river. Admire herons, ducks and geese in season. Near museums and Centre de la Biodiversité du Québec.

From Montréal or Québec City, Aut. 40. In Trois-Rivières, cross over the Laviolette bridge, Ste-Angèle Exit. Facing the river, left on Boul. Bécancour West, 1.6km.

B&B
REGARD SUR LE FLEUVE

Rita and André Caya
18440, Gaillardetz (boul. Bécancour)
Saint-Grégoire, Bécancour
G9H 2G5
(819) 233-2360
**www.inns-
bb.com/regard_sur_le_fleuve**

	B&B
single	$45
double	$60

Open year round

Number of rooms	3
rooms with private bath	3

---

3. DRUMMONDVILLE

Prize for Excellence "Special favorite" Provincial 2000. "Experience the house from long ago, where both roses and children grow". "Our small" family (11) welcomes you to its table set with home-made bread and jams, fresh eggs, juice and aromatic coffee. Make yourself at home! Halfway between Montréal and Québec City, between Sherbrooke and Trois-Rivières. **See colour photos.**

Aut. 20, Exit 175 twd Drummondville, Boul. Lemire South, 300m from Aut. 20.

B&B
LE GÎTE DES ROSES

Diane and Denis Lampron
215, boul. Lemire
Drummondville J2C 7X2
(819) 474-4587
fax (819) 474-1500
www.inns-bb.com/gitedesroses
info@rose.ca

	B&B
single	$50-65
double	$65-85
triple	$75-95
quad.	$85-115

Open year round year round except Aug 1 to Aug 20

Number of rooms	4
rooms with private bath	1
shared bathrooms	3

4. DRUMMONDVILLE, ST-CYRILLE

Halfway between Montréal and Québec City, 5km from Drummondville. Amidst vast spaces, trees, flowers, water gardens and waterfall. Non-smoking B&B with fireplace and air conditioning. Healthy homemade breakfasts. 4km from Village d'Antan and Légendes Fantastiques, local festivals, health clinic, cross-country skiing and bike path.

Aut. 20, Exit 185, 2km. At the church, right on Rte 122, continue 1km.

B&B
OASIS

Johanna Putzke Beier
3500, Route 122
Saint-Cyrille-de-Wendover
J1Z 1C3
(819) 397-2917
www.inns-bb.com/oasis

	B&B
single	$35
double	$45-65
child	$10

Reduced rates: 15% Sept. 15 to May 15
Open year round

Number of rooms	3
rooms with private bath	1
rooms with sink	1
shared bathrooms	1

5. WARWICK

Located in the heart of Warwick, our bed and breakfast borders on several km of bike paths and snowmobile trails. Also right nearby: golfing, skiing, summer theatre and various festivals. All our rooms have a private bathroom. Upon waking up, the aroma of breakfast beckons you upstairs. Cyclists, snowmobilers and drivers, our home is your home.

Aut. 20, Exit 210, Rte 122 East, St-Albert, twd Warwick.

B&B
GÎTE LA TOURELLE

Solange Nault
91, rue Saint-Louis
Warwick J0A 1M0
(819) 358-9555
www.inns-bb.com/latourelle

	B&B
single	$45
double	$55
triple	$65
child	$10

Open year round

Number of rooms	5
rooms in basement	5
rooms with private bath	5

6. WICKHAM

A small farm that combines gardens, woodlands and old buildings. Share good times and relaxation in a vast country setting. Spend the night in a cozy bed. Two comfortable rooms in which to sleep, snore and, above all, dream. Dinner by reservation. Taxe include. Many activities nearby. 2km from the "La Campagnarde" bike path. **Farm Stay p 67.**

From Montréal, Aut. 20 East, Exit 157 twd Wickham. About 7km past the village of St-Nazaire twd Wickham, left on Rte 139. Right at the church, 1.8km.

B&B
LA FERME DE LA BERCEUSE

Robin Fortin and Réjean Forget
548, Rang 10
Wickham J0C 1S0
(819) 398-6229
(819) 398-6411
fax (819) 398-6496
www.inns-bb.com/fermedelaberceuse

	B&B	MAP
single	$60	$75
double	$70	$115
child	$12	$20

Taxes extra
Open: May 1 to Oct. 31

Number of rooms	2
shared bathrooms	1
shared wc	1

AGROTOURISM

Farm Stays:

🐚 6   LA FERME DE LA BERCEUSE, Wickham ....*Page 67*

Country-Style Dining:

🐚 7   FLEUR EN BOUCHÉE, Saint-Majorique ....*Page 22*

CHARLEVOIX

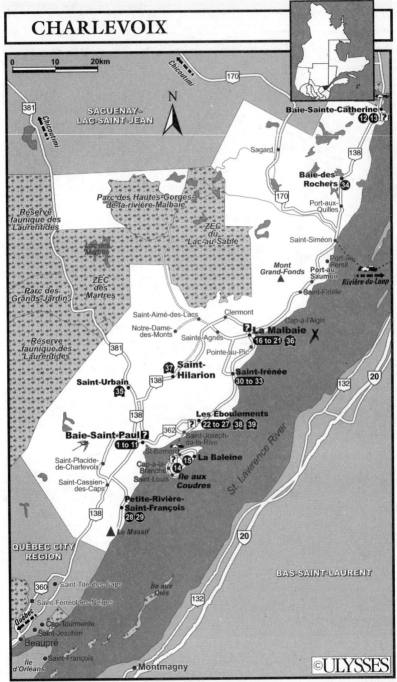

SAGUENAY–
LAC-SAINT-JEAN

Chicoutimi

Baie-Sainte-Catherine
12 13 7

Sagard

Baie-des-
Rochers **34**

Port-aux-
Quilles

Saint-Siméon

Port-au-
Persil

Réserve
faunique des
Laurentides

Parc des Hautes-Gorges-
de-la-rivière-Malbaie

ZEC
du
Lac-au-Sable

Mont
Grand-Fonds

Port-au-
Saumon

Rivière-du-Loup

Lac des
Martres

Saint-Fidèle

Parc des
Grands-Jardins

ZEC
des
Martres

Saint-Aimé-des-Lacs

Clermont

Cap-à-l'Aigle

Réserve
faunique des
Laurentides

Notre-Dame-
des-Monts

Sainte-Agnès

La Malbaie
16 to 21 **36**

Pointe-au-Pic

37 **Saint-
Hilarion**

Saint-Irénée
30 to 33

Saint-Urbain

35

Baie-Saint-Paul 7
1 to 11

Les Éboulements
7 **22 to 27** **38** **39**

Saint-Joseph-
da-la-Rive

St-Bernard

Saint-Placide-
de-Charlevoix

7 **15** **La Baleine**

Cap-à-la-
Branche

14

Saint-Cassien-
des-Caps

Saint-Louis

Île aux
Coudres

St. Lawrence River

**Petite-Rivière-
Saint-François**
28 29

BAS-SAINT-LAURENT

Le Massif

QUÉBEC CITY
REGION

Saint-Tite-des-Caps

Île aux
Oies

Saint-Ferréol-les-Neiges

Québec

Cap-Tourmente

Saint-Joachim

Beaupré

Saint-François

Île
d'Orléans

Montmagny

©ULYSSES

*The numbers on the map refer to the establishments described in the text.

1. BAIE-ST-PAUL

Choose this B&B for its tranquil country atmosphere and its proximity (on foot) to lively Baie-St-Paul. A happy and colourful century-old home with wood-work and lace. Wood-burning oven for chilly morn-ings. Piano, books, music. Rooms and balconies overlooking the countryside, mountains and magical seasons. Large beds, goose duvets. Homemade and local products for breakfast. Available to guests: living room, kitchen, patios, pool, flower gardens. Ideal for long stays. Packages: ski, whale-watching, music.

From Québec City, Rte 138 East, 100km. In Baie-St-Paul, Rte 362 East. At the church, right on Rue Ste-Anne. At the fork, blue house on the right.

B&B
À LA CHOUETTE

Ginette Guérette and
François Rivard
2, rue Leblanc
Baie-Saint-Paul G3Z 1W9
(418) 435-3217
1-888-435-3217
www.inns-bb.com/chouette
chouettephoto@sympatico.ca

 **R.2**

	B&B
single	$80-110
double	$85-120
child	$10

Taxes extra

Reduced rates: Avr. 21 to May 22, Oct. 15 to Dec. 20
Open year round

Number of rooms	5
rooms with private bath	5

---

2. BAIE-ST-PAUL

A unique inn and panorama at the very top of Cap-aux-Corbeaux, a few min from Baie-St-Paul. All rooms have an exceptional view of the river, the Massif and Isle-aux-Coudres. In the summer, breakfast is enjoyed on the terrace while watching boats sail by. Meeting room, art gallery and "table d'hôte" in winter. Available packages include ski, golf, massage, whale-watching and Domaine Forget.

From Québec City, Rte 138 East, 100km. In Baie-St-Paul, Rte 362 East. At the church, Rte 362 twd Les Éboulements, 5km. Right on Rue Cap-aux-Corbeaux, 1km. From La Malbaie, Rte 362 West, left on Rue Cap-aux-Corbeaux.

INN
AUBERGE CAP-AUX-CORBEAUX

Murielle Otis and
Pierre Prud'homme
2, Cap-aux-Corbeaux Sud
Baie-Saint-Paul G3Z 1B1
(418) 435-5676
1-800-595-5676
fax (418) 435-4125
www.cap-aux-corbeaux.com
aucap@charlevoix.net

 **R1**

	B&B	MAP
single	$85-130	$105-150
double	$95-140	$135-180
triple	$115-160	$175-220
quad.	$135-180	$200-260
child	$0-20	$0-30

Taxes extra VS MC IT

Reduced rates: Oct. 16 to Dec. 14 and Apr. 16 to June 14
Open year round

Number of rooms	9
rooms with private bath	9

---

3. BAIE-ST-PAUL

A delightful treasure located 1hr from Québec City and 3.5hrs from Montréal. Escape, passion and temptation await you at our charming, stylish inn. Our restaurant, Le Marion, will take you on a fine-dining adventure, while our health centre, La Cajolerie, offers personalized care. Let us pamper you, guide you and welcome you to our home!

From Québec City, Rte 138 twd Baie St-Paul. At McDonald's, left on Rue St-Paul.

INN
AUBERGE LA GRANDE MAISON

Diane Savard
160, rue St-Jean-Baptiste
Baie-Saint-Paul G3Z 1N3
tel/fax (418) 435-5575
1-800-361-5575
www.grandemaison.com
lagrandemaison@charlevoix.net

	B&B	MAP
single	$60-200	$92-232
double	$70-225	$135-290
triple	$100-170	$167-197
quad.	$120	$250
child	$15	

Taxes extra VS MC AM ER IT

Number of rooms	24
rooms with private bath	24

4. BAIE-ST-PAUL

★★★ F E ⊙ P ⇌ 🐖 ✕ TA

This charming century-old Victorian home is nestled under maple trees in the heart of the village. Fine cuisine composed of local products served as table d'hôte in the evening and for breakfast on the terrace, in the sunny dining room or, in winter, in front of the fireplace. Near art galleries and shops. Available: Le Massif ski package, relaxation, cruise, golf. In summer, MAP (half-board) only. **See colour photos.**

100km from Québec City twd Ste-Anne-de-Beaupré, Rte 138 E. At Baie-St-Paul, Rte 362 E. At church, left on Rue St-Jean-Baptiste. Or from La Malbaie, Rtes 138 or 362 West.

INN
AUBERGE LA MUSE

Evelyne Tremblay and
Robert Arsenault
39, rue Saint-Jean-Baptiste
Baie-Saint-Paul G3Z 1M3
(418) 435-6839
1-800-841-6839
fax (418) 435-6289
www.lamuse.com
lamuse@lamuse.com

	B&B	MAP
single	$80-130	$104-154
double	$90-150	$139-199
triple	$130-150	$204-224
quad.	$170	$269
child	$17	$35

Taxes extra VS MC ER IT

Reduced rates: weekdays Apr. 1 to June 19 and Oct. 13 to Dec. 25

Open year round

Number of rooms	12
rooms with private bath	12

---

5. BAIE-ST-PAUL

☀☀☀ F E ⊙ P ⇌ 🐖 R.5

Welcome to our century-old home, located a few steps from restaurants and the art district. Garden in the woods on the riverside. Our comfortable rooms are warm and well ventilated. Fine breakfast with local and homemade products. Tips for your outdoor excursions. 15min from the Le Massif ski resort.

From Québec City, twd Ste-Anne de Beaupré, Rte 138 East, 100km in Baie St-Paul, Rte 362 East, right at the third light, keep your left at the fork.

B&B
AU BONHOMME SEPT HEURES

Rachel Tremblay and
Benoît Frigon
113, rue Ste-Anne
Baie-Saint-Paul G3Z 1N9
(418) 240-3191
(418) 240-0668
**www.aubonhommeseptheures.
com**

	B&B
single	$60-75
double	$75-90
triple	$90-105
quad.	$120
child	$15

Reduced rates: Oct. 15 to Dec. 1 and Apr. 15 to May 15

Open year round

Number of rooms	3
rooms with private bath	3

---

6. BAIE-ST-PAUL

☀☀☀☀ F e ⊙ P ⇌ TA R.5

Located on one of the most picturesque streets in town, our 100-year-old house, whose garden extends to the Gouffre River, is yours to appreciate. Steps away from good restaurants, art galleries, shops and the exhibition centre. 15 min from "Au Massif de Petite Rivière St-François" ski resort. Hearty breakfasts await.

From Québec City, twd Ste-Anne-de-Beaupré, Rte 138 East, 100km. In Baie-St-Paul, Rte 362 East. At the church, cross the bridge, 1st street on the right.

B&B
AU CLOCHETON

Johanne and Laurette Robin
50, rue Saint-Joseph
Baie-Saint-Paul G3Z 1H7
(418) 435-3393
1-877-435-3393
fax (418) 435-6432
www.inns-bb.com/clocheton

	B&B
single	$60-85
double	$70-100

Taxes extra MC

Open year round

Number of rooms	4
rooms with private bath	2
rooms with sink	2
shared bathrooms	1

7. BAIE-ST-PAUL

☀ ☀ ☀ ☀ F E ⊘ P 🛏 🐾 R3.5

Come discover one of the loveliest places in Charlevoix! Perched on the mountainside, we offer an exceptional view of the St.Lawrence River, in a peaceful environnement... Rooms with panoramic view, private entrance and terrace. Varied, regionally flavoured home-style breakfast. Massif ski package. Located 5 min from downtown. Be sure to check out our Web site!

From Québec City, Rte 138 East. In Baie-St-Paul, Rte 362 East, 3km. At the "Au Perchoir" sign, right on Chemin Cap-aux-Rets. After the cross, 2nd house on the left.

B&B
AU PERCHOIR

Jacinthe Tremblay and
Réjean Thériault
443, Cap-aux-Rets
Baie-Saint-Paul G3Z 1C1
tel/fax (418) 435-6955
1-800-435-6955
www.auperchoir.com
perchoir@charlevoix.net

	B&B
single	$55-110
double	$60-115
triple	$100-135
quad.	$155
child	$10

Taxes extra VS

Reduced rates: Oct. 15 to Dec. 23 and Apr. 15 to May 15

Open year round

Number of rooms	5
rooms with private bath	3
rooms with sink	1
shared bathrooms	1
shared wc	1

🏛 🎿 🏃 🚴 🐎 ⛷ 🎿

8. BAIE-ST-PAUL

★ ★ ★ F e ⊘ P 🛏 R.2

In the heart of tourist activities, away from the hustle and bustle but just steps from art galleries and restaurants, and 15 min from the Massif, our house has retained its charm of yesteryear, with its high ceilings and large balcony. Our rooms are decorated in art-related themes. Queen-size beds. Gourmet breakfast by the fireplace or on the patio in summer. Communal living room. Regional winner of the 2002 Québec Tourism grand prize.

From Québec City, Rte 138 East. In Baie-St-Paul, Rte 362, across from the hospital.

INN
AUX PETITS OISEAUX

Danielle Trussart and
Jacques Roussel
30, boul. Fafard, rte 362
Baie-Saint-Paul G3Z 2J4
tel/fax (418) 435-3888
1-877-435-3888
www.quebecweb.com/oiseaux
trussel@charlevoix.net

	B&B
single	$80-110
double	$80-110
triple	$115-130
child	$15

Taxes extra

Reduced rates: Oct. 15 to Dec. 20, Avr. 15 to June 20 in weekdays except Christmas Holiday and school holidays

Open year round

Number of rooms	7
rooms with private bath	7

🏛 🎿 🏃 🚶 ⛷ 🎿

9. BAIE-ST-PAUL

☀ ☀ ☀ ☀ ☀ F E ⊘ ♿ P 🛏 R.1

Your hosts welcome you to their 1920s home with maritime decor, located on the shore of Rivière-du-Gouffre. Walking distance from galleries, restaurants, museums and activities. Enjoy our quaint wood floors, sumptuous fabrics, antique furnishings, works of art and ancestral maritime pieces. Completely renovated and adapted, our house offers a living room, terrace, private bathroom and balcony, queen-size bed, soundproofing and multimedia access. At breakfast time, the dining room table is set banquet-style, just like on a cruise ship!

In Baie St-Paul, Rte 362, at the church, right on Rue Ste-Anne.

B&B
GÎTE À L'ANCRAGE

Adrien Levasseur
29, rue Ste-Anne
Baie-Saint-Paul G3Z 1N9
tel/fax (418) 240-3264
www.giteancrage.com
ancrage@sympatico.ca

	B&B
single	$85-95
double	$105-115
triple	$125-135

Taxes extra VS MC ER IT

Reduced rates: Oct. 15 to June 15

Open year round

Number of rooms	4
rooms with private bath	4

🏛 🎿 🏃 ⛷ 🎿 🏂

10. BAIE-ST-PAUL

☀☀☀☀ **F E P** 🛏️🐕 TA R4

This 200-year-old house was renowned for its hospitality towards homeless people, and it has kept its shelter charm and vocation. Wake up to the smell of a crackling fire and enjoy a copious breakfast with regional accents. Our home has a lavishly decorated interior. In the rooms, queen-size beds, view of the St. Lawrence River and L'Îsle aux Coudres. Packages and group rates. Near the Massif ski resort. Come visit us!

From Québec City, Rte 138 East. At the tourist info. bureau before Baie-St-Paul, turn right, follow St-Antoine South at left, 500m, 1st street on right.

B&B
GÎTE LE NOBLE QUÊTEUX

Marie Lou Jacques and Claude Marin
8, ch. Côte-du-Quêteux
Baie-Saint-Paul G3Z 2C7
(418) 240-2352
1-866-744-2352
fax (418) 240-2377
**www.charlevoix.
qc.ca/noblequeteux**
noblequeteux@charlevoix.qc.ca

	B&B
single	$65-80
double	$70-85
triple	$85-100
quad.	$100-115

Taxes extra VS MC AM ER
Open year round

Number of rooms	5
rooms with private bath	2
shared bathrooms	2

11. BAIE-ST-PAUL

☀☀☀☀ **F E** 🚭 **P** TA R.2

Come discover a prestigious bed and breakfast in the heart of Baie-St-Paul that combines plush comfort and the elegance of houses of yore, with its many rooms, large windows, woodwork, furniture, colours and objets d'art. Charming rooms, king/queen-size beds, flowery garden and terrace. Lavish breakfast featuring regional products. A 5 min walk from galleries and restaurants; 15 min from the Massif.

From Québec City, Rte 138 East. In Baie-St-Paul, Rte 362 East. At the church, right on Rue Ste-Anne.

B&B
GÎTE LES COLIBRIS

Lise Rousseau and Marc Skinner
80, rue Sainte-Anne
Baie-Saint-Paul G3Z 1P3
(418) 240-2222
1-888-508-4483
www.charlevoix.net/lescolibris
colibris@charlevoix.net

	B&B
single	$69-100
double	$88-118

Taxes extra VS MC

Reduced rates: Oct. 15 to Dec. 15 and Apr. 15 to May 20
Open year round

Number of rooms	5
rooms with private bath	3
rooms with sink	2
shared bathrooms	1
shared wc	1

12. BAIE-STE-CATHERINE

☀☀☀☀ **F e** 🚭 **P** 🛏️ ✗ TA R1

Now swept away by the fury of the waves, now enchanted by the tranquillity of the woods, N.-D. de l'Espace watches over the secret world of whales and our village. Anne-Marie's table d'hôte, regional home cooking. Dogsled, cruise tickets. Prize for Excellence "Special Favorite" Regional 1994-95.

From Québec City, Rte 138 East twd La Malbaie. At bridge, twd Tadoussac. At Baie-Ste-Catherine, watch for blue tourist sign, drive 1km. From Tadoussac, 4km.

B&B
ENTRE MER ET MONTS

Anne-Marie and Réal Savard
476, Route 138
Baie-Sainte-Catherine G0T 1A0
(418) 237-4391
fax (418) 237-4252
**www.fjord-best.com/entre-mer-
et-monts**
*entre-mer-et-monts@
fjord-best.com*

	B&B	MAP
single	$40-45	$63
double	$50-55	$92
triple	$65-75	$128
child	$20	$30

VS MC

Reduced rates: Nov. 1 to May 31
Open year round

Number of rooms	5
rooms in semi-basement	3
rooms with sink	3
shared bathrooms	2
shared wc	1

13. BAIE-STE-CATHERINE

☀☀☀ F P ⟐⟐ TA R.5

Beautifully located in a magnificent bay, near a little church at the heart of a peaceful village, come and immerse yourself in the beautiful countryside. Discover the beauty of the sea. Far from the noise of Rte 138 for peaceful and restful nights. Rooms on the main floor or in the basement. Boat cruise tickets for sale.

From Québec City, Rte 138 East twd Tadoussac. From the Baie-Ste-Catherine "Bienvenue" sign, drive 4km. First road on the left. Watch for the provincial sign on Rte 138.

B&B
GÎTE DU CAPITAINE

Benoît Imbault
343, rue Leclerc
Baie-Sainte-Catherine G0T 1A0
(418) 237-4320
tel/fax (418) 237-4359
www.giteducapitaine.com

	B&B
single	$40
double	$55
triple	$75
quad.	$95
child	$15-20

VS

Open: May 1 to Oct. 31

Number of rooms	5
rooms in basement	2
shared bathrooms	2

14. ISLE-AUX-COUDRES

☀☀☀☀ F e P ⟐ R2

Large, peaceful, beautiful and welcoming house where your hosts Rita and Vincent offer you warm hearts and good food. Steps from the river and near cultural and tourist activities. Let yourself be soothed and pampered by the rhythm of the tides in a unique setting.

From Québec City, Rte 138 East twd Baie-St-Paul. Rte 362 to St-Joseph-de-la-Rive ferry. On the island, left at stop sign, 3km.

B&B
GÎTE LA MAISON BLANCHE

Rita and Vincent Laurin
232, rue Royale Est, C.P. 238
Isle-aux-Coudres G0A 3J0
(418) 438-2883
www.inns-bb.com/maisonblanche

	B&B
single	$50
double	$70

Reduced rates: Oct. 15 to June 15
Open year round

Number of rooms	5
rooms with private bath	1
rooms with sink	4
shared bathrooms	4

15. ISLE-AUX-COUDRES

☀☀☀ F e P ⟐ 🐾 TA R1

Away from the bustle of the city, on an enchanting island. As if time had stopped. Wake up to birds chirping and breakfast on the terrace. Relaxing, large, sunny and flowered living-room.

From Québec City, Rte 138 East twd Baie-St-Paul. Rte 362 to St-Joseph-de-la-Rive ferry. On the island, right at flashing light, 10km. 500 ft after St-Louis church.

B&B
VILLA DU MOULIN

Louise F. Belley
252, chemin des Moulins
Isle-aux-Coudres G0A 1X0
(418) 438-2649
1-888-824-6263
**www.quebecinformation.
com/villa-du-moulin**
villadumoulin@hotmail.com

	B&B
single	$45
double	$60
triple	$75
quad.	$90

Open: Apr. 1 to Oct. 31

Number of rooms	5
shared bathrooms	2

16. LA MALBAIE

★★★ F e ⊘ P ⇌ ✕ TA

This 1875 mansion truly embodies the spirit of Canada. Surrounded by an immense cedar park, it offers a warm ambiance in an old-fashioned decor that is ideal for relaxation. The gourmet in you will be seduced by our chef's preparation of Charlevoix's regional products. Nine of our spacious rooms are located in the old section and 11 are in the modern section, and feature either a fireplace or a king-size bed. Our inn is located near all activities, steps from the St. Lawrence River and the majestic Manoir Richelieu.

From Québec City, Rte 138 East or Rte 362. At La Malbaie/Pointe au Pic, twd Manoir Richelieu/Casino, Chemin des Falaises, right on Rue des Pins.

INN
AUBERGE LES SOURCES INC

Evelyne and André Litzelmann
8, rue des Pins
La Malbaie G5A 2S3
(418) 665-6952
fax (418) 665-3802
www.aubergelessources.com
info@aubergelessources.com

	B&B	MAP
single	$80-115	$109-144
double	$80-115	$138-173
triple	$130	$217
quad.	$150	$266
child	$20	$33

Taxes extra VS MC IT

Reduced rates: Dec. 1 to May 31
Open year round close: Nov. and Apr.

Number of rooms	20
rooms with private bath	20

---

17. LA MALBAIE

☼☼☼ F E P ⇌ ≋ TA R4.5

In the mood to hit the casino? It's only 130 seconds away! How about mountains, lakes and attractions? They are all near our residence, where guests are always warmly greeted in a quiet, enchanting setting. Welcome.

Rtes 138 or 362, by the river, the street before or after traffic light at the shopping centre, turn on Rue Laure-Conan and it's the 3rd house on the right.

B&B
GÎTE E.T. HARVEY

Etudienne Tremblay and
Jacques Harvey
19, rue Laure-Conan
La Malbaie G5A 1H8
(418) 665-2779
fax (418) 665-4650
www.inns-bb.com/et_harvey

	B&B
single	$42
double	$47-58
triple	$60-75
child	$15

Reduced rates: 3 nights and more Oct. 30 to Avr. 30
Open year round

Number of rooms	4
rooms in basement	1
rooms with sink	1
shared bathrooms	1
shared wc	1

---

18. LA MALBAIE

☼☼☼☼ F e ⊘ P ⇌ ≋ TA R.5

Our B&B offers rest and relaxation, with its flowery garden, indoor and outdoor fireplaces, outdoor spa, 2-person therapeutic bath, soundproof rooms, TV, small lounge, front and back balconies with view of the river. Not to mention the delicious breakfasts, from orange crepes to Yvonne's brioches.

2km from the casino. Rte 138 East twd La Malbaie 1st street on your right after the tourist office then left on Rue Laure-Conan. Or Rte 362 twd La Malbaie, 2nd street after shopping centre. Left side.

B&B
LA MAISON DUFOUR-
BOUCHARD

Micheline Dufour
18, rue Laure-Conan
La Malbaie G5A 1H8
(418) 665-4982
fax (418) 665-4945
**www.charlevoix.qc.ca/
maisondufourbouchard**
*maisondufourbouchard@
hotmail.com*

	B&B
single	$45-50
double	$60-65
triple	$80
quad.	$95
child	$15

Open year round

Number of rooms	4
shared bathrooms	2

19. LA MALBAIE

Prize for Excellence "Special Favorite" Regional 2000 and 1995-96. Come enjoy peace and comfort in a warm and cozy Austrian house overlooking the winding St. Lawrence River and away from the main road, designed with you in mind. Private entrance, fireplace, balcony, terraces, flowery gardens and varied breakfasts! In the midst of activities, 5 min from the casino.

Québec City, Rte 138 East twd La Malbaie. Leclerc bridge, Rte 362 West 4.4km, left on Côteau-sur-Mer. From Baie-St-Paul, Rte 362 East twd La Malbaie, Pointe-au-Pic. 2km from Manoir Richelieu golf club, right on Côteau-sur-Mer.

B&B
LA MAISON FRIZZI

Raymonde Vermette
55, rue Côteau-sur-Mer
La Malbaie G5A 3B6
(418) 665-4668
fax (418) 665-1143
www.inns-bb.com/maisonfrizzi

B&B	
single	$65-70
double	$75-80
triple	$95-100
quad.	$115-120
child	$0-15

Taxes extra VS MC

Reduced rates: yes
Open year round

Number of rooms	4
rooms with sink	4
shared bathrooms	2

---

20. LA MALBAIE

This vast, ancestral residence is surrounded with fragrant flower gardens and is located in the heart of Charlevoix, near the river. Our home will charm you with its antique furnishings, works of art and three stone chimneys. Enjoy delectable treats in our dining room, such as homemade terrine; after your meal, enjoy hikes, cruises, horseback riding (in summer) and skiing, ice-skating, dog-sledding and snowmobiling (in winter). Breathe in the fragrances and listen to the sounds of nature's many charms.

From Québec City, Rte 138 La Malbaie, past Leclerc bridge twd Cap-à-l'Aigle, right on Rue St-Raphaël.

B&B
LA MAISON SOUS LES LILAS

Suzanne Rémillard
649, Saint-Raphaël
La Malbaie G5A 2P1
(418) 665-8076
(450) 585-1399
www.inns-bb.com/sousleslilas
*lamaisonsousleslilas@
hotmail.com*

B&B	
single	$60-80
double	$65-85

Open year round

Number of rooms	3
rooms with sink	1
shared bathrooms	1
shared wc	1

---

21. LA MALBAIE

The ancestral Eau Berge house faces the river and welcomes you with its unique decor. The rooms are particulary comfortable and inviting. Choice of healthy breakfast, or otherwise! Come and be refreshed. Close to the casino and other activities. See you soon.

From Québec City, twd Ste-Anne-de-Beaupré, Rte 138 East twd La Malbaie. At the traffic light of the bridge, continue straight. 500m from the shopping centre. On the right across from the "Irving". Or Rte 362 twd Pointe-au-Pic, staight beside the river, on the Boul. du Fleuve, at the "Irving" on the left.

INN
L'EAU BERGE

Claudette Dessureault
315, boul. De Comporté
La Malbaie G5A 2Y6
(418) 665-3003
fax (418) 665-2480
www.quebecweb.com/leauberge

B&B	
single	$65-100
double	$69-110
triple	$90-125
quad.	$145

Taxes extra VS MC
Open: Jan. 20 to Nov. 17

Number of rooms	7
rooms with private bath	2
rooms with sink	1
shared bathrooms	2
shared wc	1

22. LES ÉBOULEMENTS

★★ F E ♿ P 🚍 🐑 R.5

Up in the heights of Les Éboulements, overlooking the St. Lawrence and l'Île aux Coudres and centred among the marvels of Charlevoix, Auberge La Bouclée is a haven of peace for your vacation. Fall in love... An old-fashioned charm that thrills many a heart. For groups, families or sweethearts, young and old, our family welcomes you into its home.

From Baie St-Paul, Rte 362 East twd La Malbaie/Isle-aux-Coudres, about 16km. Right at the flashing light. Left after 500m. Welcome.

INN
AUBERGE LA BOUCLÉE

Ginette and Mario Ouellet
6, Route du Port
Les Éboulements G0A 2M0
(418) 635-2531
1-888-635-2531
www.quebecweb.com/labouclee

	B&B
single	$52
double	$69-89
triple	$104
quad.	$119
child	$0-15

Taxes extra VS MC ER IT

Reduced rates: Oct. 20 to June 20
Open year round

Number of rooms	9
rooms with sink	9
shared bathrooms	4
shared wc	1

---

23. LES ÉBOULEMENTS

☀☀☀ F P ╳ R5

On arriving, you'll fall under the spell of an open view: the St. Lawrence River lazily stretching before your eyes. You'll then climb the stairs leading to our majestic terrace with panoramic view, where you can leisurely enjoy a refreshing drink along with the enchanting setting of L'Île-aux-Coudres.

From Québec City, twd Ste-Anne-de-Beaupré, Rte 138 East twd Baie-St-Paul, about 100km. From Baie-St-Paul, Rte 362 East twd Les Éboulements, 20km. From La Malbaie, Rte 362 West, 25km.

INN
AUBERGE LA PENTE DOUCE

Noëlla Desmeules, Michel
Pilote and Éric Léonard
215, rue Principale
Les Éboulements G0A 2M0
(418) 635-1345
fax (418) 635-1537
www.inns-bb.com/pentedouce

	B&B
single	$55
double	$65
child	$10

Taxes extra VS MC IT
Open: May 1 to Dec. 31

Number of rooms	4
rooms with private bath	1
rooms with sink	3
shared bathrooms	2
shared wc	1

---

24. LES ÉBOULEMENTS

☀☀☀☀ F E ⊘ P 🐑 TA R3

This remarkable home, typical of the Charlevoix region, offers the charms of the country and the nearby river. Our house is almost 200 years old and has preserved its original character and country-style decor, and is located near a farmyard that will take you back to the old days. Several packages available; Swedish massage on-site. An unforgettable stay is guaranteed!

From Québec City, Rte 138 East twd Ste-Anne-de-Beaupré, to Baie-St-Paul about 100km, Rte 362 twd Ile-aux-Coudres/Les Éboulements approximately 10km. To your left, set back.

B&B
GÎTE DE LA BASSE-COUR

Jean-François Larocque
60, Rang St-Marc
Les Éboulements G0A 2M0
(418) 635-1191
fax (418) 635-1199
**www.charlevoix.net/
gitedelabasse-cour**
jfl@charlevoix.net

	B&B
single	$65-75
double	$65-75
triple	$85
quad.	$105

Taxes extra
Open year round

Number of rooms	4
rooms with private bath	2
shared bathrooms	1

25. LES ÉBOULEMENTS

☀☀☀ **F e P** 🐐 **R2**

Bicentenary family home located right in the country. Domestic animals. Children welcome! Central location to discover all of Charlevoix's tourist attractions. Come stay with us for a few days; special rates for three days or more. A smile and a big surprise breakfast await you.

From Québec City, Rte 138. In Baie-St-Paul, at the church, straight ahead twd Les Éboulements, Rte 362 East, about 14km.

B&B
GÎTE DU VACANCIER

Jacqueline Audet
104, Rg St-Joseph (Route 362)
Les Éboulements G0A 2M0
(418) 635-2736
(418) 653-5861
www.inns-bb.com/vacancier

	B&B
single	$45-60
double	$55-75
triple	$70-85
quad.	$75-90
child	$0-15

Reduced rates: 10% Oct. 15 to Dec. 20 and 3 nights and more
Open: June 15 to Dec. 31

Number of rooms	5
rooms with private bath	2
rooms with sink	3
shared bathrooms	2

26. LES ÉBOULEMENTS

☀☀☀ **F e 🚫 P** 🚶 **R2**

Ancestral house facing Île-aux-Coudres. The village's first hotel in 1930. Decor in the style of yesteryear. Relax on the big porch and admire the mountains and the river that runs between the houses. A paradise to discover, amidst the region's tourist attractions. Varied all-you-can-eat breakfast complemented by little treats lovingly prepared by your hosts.

From Québec City, Rte 138 East twd Baie-St-Paul. From Baie-St-Paul, Rte 362 East twd Les Éboulements.

B&B
GÎTE VILLA DES ROSES

Pierrette Simard and
Léonce Tremblay
290, rue Principale, C.P. 28
Les Éboulements G0A 2M0
(418) 635-2733
www.inns-bb.com/villadesroses

	B&B
single	$45
double	$55-60
triple	$75
quad.	$90
child	$0-15

Reduced rates: Oct. 15 to June 15
Open year round

Number of rooms	5
rooms with sink	4
shared bathrooms	2
shared wc	1

27. LES ÉBOULEMENTS

☀☀☀ **F e P TA R1.5**

Nestled between the mountains and the river, this 200-year-old house offers, calm, reverie and peace of mind. Comfortable family-size rooms with private bathrooms, antique furniture, a smiling welcome and the delight of home-made pastries and jams make for a veritable Nid-Chouette, or cute little nest!

From Québec City, twd Ste-Anne-de-Beaupré, Rte 138 East twd Baie-St-Paul, about 100km. From Baie-St-Paul, Rte 362 East twd Les Éboulements, 20km. Or from La Malbaie, Rte 362 West, 25km.

B&B
LE NICHOUETTE

Gilberte Tremblay
216, rue Principale
Les Éboulements G0A 2M0
(418) 635-2458
www.chouette.freeservers.com/
nichouette.html
chouette@charlevoix.net

	B&B
single	$45-50
double	$50-60
triple	$70-80
quad.	$90-100
child	$0-12

VS MC

Reduced rates: May 1 to June 24 and Sept. 1 to Oct. 31
Open: May 1 to Oct. 31

Number of rooms	3
rooms with private bath	3

28. PETITE-RIVIÈRE-ST-FRANÇOIS

★★★ F E ⊘ P ⟷ ✕ TA

With its panoramic view of the river, our home is nestled on the mountain, in the forest. Our rooms offer tranquility, cleanliness and the warm coziness of wood, with comfortable queen and king-size beds. Our meals and breakfasts are inspired from the flavours of the Charlevoix region. Located along the Circuit des Métiers d'Art, the inn also features a shop and wood workshop. Located near the Le Massif ski resort and Baie-St-Paul.

From Québec City, Rte 138 East twd Baie-St-Paul, 90 km. At the Petite-Rivière-St-François sign, right for 4km.

INN
AUBERGE LA CÔTE D'OR

Sylvie Bardou and
Jean-Michel Dirand
348, rue Principale
Petite-Rivière-St-François
G0A 2L0
(418) 632-5520
1-877-632-5520
fax (418) 632-5589
www.quebecweb.com/lacoted'or

	B&B	MAP
single	$75-110	$97-132
double	$95-135	$139-179
triple	$125-165	$191-231

Taxes extra VS MC AM IT
Open year round

Number of rooms	9
rooms with private bath	9

---

29. PETITE-RIVIÈRE-ST-FRANÇOIS

☀☀☀☀ F e ⊘ P R4

In the heart of the wilderness, a B&B located in the mountains, on the heights of Petite-Rivière-St-François. Just 10 min from the Massif ski resort and Baie-St-Paul. Welcoming, comfortable rooms. Enjoy a rejuvenating stay in this haven of peace and savour our homemade breakfasts.

From Québec City, Rte 138 East, 90km. At the Petite-Rivière-St-François sign, right and drive 2.5km. The B&B is on the right, set back from the road.

B&B
GÎTE L'ÉCUREUIL

Viviane De Bock and
Éric Velghe
264, rue Principale
Petite-Rivière-St-François
G0A 2L0
(418) 632-1058
fax (418) 632-1059
www3.sympatico.ca/eric.velghe
eric.velghe@sympatico.ca

	B&B
single	$75
double	$85
child	$20

Reduced rates: 3 nights and more
Open year round

Number of rooms	3
rooms with private bath	3

---

30. ST-IRÉNÉE

★★★ F E ⊘ P ⟷ ✕ TA

This inn offers an exceptional view of the river, both in winter and summer. In the morning, admire the most amazing sunrise. Traditional, charming century-old home, warm and romantic atmosphere, top-quality reception. Our generous meals are exquisite and refined, composed of regional products, international flavours, exotic aromas... a sensation of world travels and childhood memories under your tongue! This heavenly site is yours to discover. July to mid-September, MAP (half-board) only. **Ad start of the guide.**

From Québec City, Rte 138 twd Ste-Anne-de-Beaupré. Rte 138 twd Baie St-Paul then Rte 362, panoramic route twd Les Éboulements/St-Irénée.

INN
AUBERGE DES SABLONS

Brigitte Dubois and
Alain Guillemant
290, chemin les Bains
St-Irénée G0T 1V0
(418) 452-3594
1-800-267-3594
fax (418) 452-3240
www.quebecweb.com/sablons
aubergesablons@hotmail.com

	B&B	MAP
single	$92-165	$147-193
double	$104-190	$194-240

Taxes extra VS MC AM ER IT
Open year round

Number of rooms	14
rooms with private bath	14

31. ST-IRÉNÉE

Regional Prize for Excellence "Special Favorite" 2002. Charlevoix Grand Prize of Tourism 2001. A refined, century-old house, overlooking the river and the beach, where you'll enjoy watching eiders gliding over the St. Lawrence River. Savour our delicious homemade, locally inspired breakfasts in the dining room or on our spacious porch with panoramic view. Relax with the mesmerizing tides and let the melodies of the Domaine Forget, located just steps away, intoxicate you.

From Québec City, Rte 138 East twd Baie-St-Paul, Rte 362 twd St-Irénée, 25km. From La Malbaie, Rte 362 West, 15km.

B&B
L'EIDER MATINAL

Annie-Christine Laliberté and
Stéphane L'Écuyer
310, ch. des Bains
Saint-Irénée G0T 1V0
(418) 452-8259
fax (418) 452-8245
**www3.sympatico.ca/
eider.matinal/**
eider.matinal@sympatico.ca

	B&B
single	$85-120
double	$90-125
child	$20

Taxes extra VS IT

Reduced rates: 3 nights and more
Open year round

Number of rooms	4
rooms with private bath	4

---

32. ST-IRÉNÉE

★★ F E P ✕

Le Rustique stands out from Charlevoix's other bed and breakfasts. Cozily nestled in the heart of St-Irénée, overlooking the river, this beautiful manor house has been welcoming city-dwellers, music-lovers (Domaine Forget concert packages) and seagoing travellers for 10 years. With its warm ambiance, its cuisine and little considerations, this is one of the best places around.

From Québec, Rte 138 twd Baie-St-Paul, 90km, Rte 362 twd St-Irénée 25km, 500m right at the church. From La Malbaie, Rte 362 West, 15km.

INN
LE RUSTIQUE

Diane Lapointe
102, rue Principale
Saint-Irénée G0T 1V0
(418) 452-8250
www.charlevoix.qc.ca/lerustique
lerustique@sympatico.ca

	B&B
single	$45-55
double	$55-75
triple	$75-80
quad.	$85-90

Taxes extra VS MC IT

Reduced rates: May 1 to June 25, Sep. 3 to Oct. 26
Open: May 1 to Oct. 26

Number of rooms	6
shared bathrooms	2
shared wc	3

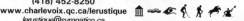

---

33. ST-IRÉNÉE

Between sea and sky, 3km from the Domaine Forget and the Saint-Irénée beach, this lovely blue Canadian house offers a panoramic view of the St. Lawrence River. In a house that combines comfort and conviviality, your hosts invite you to partake of charming, treat-filled breakfasts.

From Québec City, Rte 138 twd Baie-St-Paul, 25km. Rte 362, the Panoramique, twd La Malbaie, 500m past l'Anse-au-Sac.

B&B
LES CHANTERELLES

Michelle Poisson
800, ch. des Bains
Saint-Irénée G0T 1V0
(418) 452-1099
www.gite-chanterelles.com
midoarts@sympatico.ca

	B&B
single	$58
double	$73
triple	$93

Reduced rates: 10% 3 nights and more
Open: May 1 to Oct. 31

Number of rooms	3
shared bathrooms	2

34. ST-SIMÉON, BAIE-DES-ROCHERS

You are invited to stop over in the hamlet of Baie-des-Rochers where warmth, peace and comfort come together. Nature awaits with the river flowing behind the house. The bay is 3km away, as is the network of hiking trails offering staggering panoramic views of the surroundings.

From Québec City, Rte 138 East twd Tadoussac. 15km from St-Siméon at the corner store, sign indicating "Gîte de la Baie", right.

B&B
GÎTE DE LA BAIE

Judith and Maurice Morneau
68, rue de la Chapelle
Baie-des-Rochers, Saint-Siméon
G0T 1X0
(418) 638-2821
www.inns-bb.com/delabaie

	B&B
single	$35
double	$60
triple	$75
quad.	$85
child	$10

Open: June 1 to Oct. 13

Number of rooms	**5**
rooms with private bath	2
shared bathrooms	2

---

35. ST-URBAIN

Winner of the 1999 Regional Excellence award and the Tourist Services award. Open for 24 years. Warm, thoughtful welcome. Located in the heart of Charlevoix, 10min from Parc des Grands-Jardins, Mont du Lac des Cygnes and Baie-St-Paul, 30min from Parc des Hautes-Gorges. Tickets for various activities sold here. On site, salmon river, picnic area (BBQ) and emu farm. Large living room with TV. Wide variety of homemade breakfasts. See you soon! **Farm Stay p 68. Farm Explorations p 55. See colour photos.**

From Québec City, Rte 138 East. 10km past Baie-St-Paul, Rte 381 North, 3km.

B&B
CHEZ GERTRUDE CENTRE
DE L'ÉMEU DE CHARLEVOIX

Gertrude and Raymonde Tremblay
706, Saint-Édouard, (rte 381), C.P. 293
Saint-Urbain G0A 4K0
(418) 639-2205
1-866-639-2205
fax (418) 639-1130
www.gite.gertrude.qc.ca
raymondetremblay@videotron.ca

	B&B
single	$40-50
double	$55-65
triple	$70-80
quad.	$90
child	$15

VS MC AM
Open: May 1 to Oct. 31

Number of rooms	**5**
rooms with sink	5
shared bathrooms	2
shared wc	3

AGROTOURISM

Farm Explorations:

 35   CHEZ GERTRUDE CENTRE DE L'ÉMEU DE CHARLEVOIX, Saint-Urbain ....*Page 55*

🍎 36   LA VALLÉE DES CERVIDÉS, La Malbaie .... *Page 54*

🍎 37   ÉLEVAGE DE LA BUTTE AUX CAILLES, Saint-Hilarion.....................................*Page 54*

Farm Stays:

🍎 35   CHEZ GERTRUDE CENTRE DE L'ÉMEU DE CHARLEVOIX, Saint-Urbain ....*Page 68*

Farm Shops:

🍎 36   LA VALLÉE DES CERVIDÉS, La Malbaie ....*Page 39*

🍎 38   LES FINESSES DE CHARLEVOIX, Les Éboulements.......................................*Page 39*

Country-Style Dining:

🍎 39   LES SAVEURS OUBLIÉES, Les Éboulements...*Page 23*

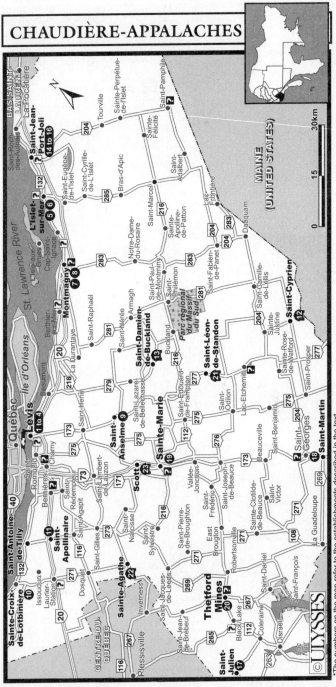

CHAUDIÈRE-APPALACHES

BASSIN ST-LAURENT

La Pocatière
Saint-Roch-des-Aulnaies
Saint-Jean-Port-Joli 14 to 16

Tourville
Sainte-Perpétue-de-l'Islet
Saint-Pamphile

204

Sainte-Félicité

L'Islet 5 6
sur-Mer
L'Islet-aux-Coudres
Saint-Cyrille-de-l'Islet
Saint-Eugène-de-l'Islet
132

285
Bras-d'Apic
Saint-Adalbert

St. Lawrence River
Cap-Saint-Ignace

Montmagny 7 8
283
Notre-Dame-du-Rosaire
Sainte-Apolline-de-Patton
Saint-Marcel
216

Lac-Frontière
Daaquam
204 283
204

Berthier-sud
Saint-Raphaël
281
Sainte-Nérée
Armagh
Saint-Paul-de-Montminy
Saint-Philémon
Saint-Fabien-de-Panet

Saint-Camille-de-Lellis
Saint-Cyprien 12

Île d'Orléans
La Durantaye
20
Beaumont
218
279
Saint-Damien-de-Buckland 13
Buckland
Parc régional du Massif du Sud
281
216
Saint-Léon-de-Standon 21
Saint-Odilon
Sainte-Justine
204
Sainte-Rose-de-Watford
Saint-Prosper
277

Québec
Lévis 1 to 4
Saint-Romuald
Charny
173
Saint-Henri
Saint-Anselme 9
275
Saint-Lazare-de-Bellechasse
Sainte-Marie 19
112
Saint-Édouard-de-Frampton
275
Saint-Odilon
Lac-Etchemin
276
Beauceville
Saint-Benjamin
275
Saint-Georges
Saint-Martin 18

Saint-Antoine-de-Tilly
40
132
Bernières
Charny
275
73
Saint-Agapit
Saint-Lambert-de-Lauzon
171
Scott 23
Saint-Narcisse
Saint-Sylvestre
216
Vallée-Jonction
Saint-Frédéric
173
Saint-Victor
271

Saint-Apollinaire 11
116
Saint-Redempteur
Saint-Gilles
273
Saint-Pierre-de-Broughton
East Broughton
271
Sainte-Clotilde-de-Beauce
Saint-Joseph-de-Beauce
271
108
La Guadeloupe
269

Sainte-Croix-de-Lotbinière 10
Issoudun
Laurier-Station
271
Dosquet
20
116

Sainte-Agathe 22
Inverness
269
Saint-Jacques-de-Leeds
Robertsonville
271
Saint-Daniel
Saint-François
Lac Saint-François

CENTRE-DU-QUÉBEC
116
Plessisville
265
267
Saint-Jean-de-Brébeuf
Thetford Mines 20 2
Black Lake
267
112
Coleraine
Disraëli
263
Lac Noir

Saint-Julien 17

© ULYSSES

MAINE (UNITED STATES)

N

30km
0   15

*The numbers on the map refer to the establishments described in the text.

1. LÉVIS

Regional Prize for Excellence "Special Favorite" 2002. Welcome to this splendid hundred-year-old mansion whose heritage is recognised by the town of Lévis. With three living rooms, a garden and a wooded area at your disposition, enjoy complete privacy. Breakfasts here are a culinary experience that should not be missed! Well-lit parking, motorcycle and bicycle garage. Discover our town and Québec City.

Aut. 20, Exit 325 or Rte 132 or ferry, twd Côte du Passage, Rue St-Georges East.

B&B
AUBERGE DE LA VISITATION

Ginette L'Heureux and
Martin Bergeron
6104, rue Saint-Georges
Lévis G6V 4J8
(418) 837-9619
www.inns-bb.com/visitation
*aubergedelavisitation@
videotron.ca*

☀☀☀☀ F e ⊘ P R.5

	B&B
single	$55
double	$70
triple	$85
quad.	$100

VS MC

Reduced rates: 20 % 3 nights and more
Open: May 1 to Sep. 30, Oct. 1 to Apr. 30, by reservation, except Dec. 24 to Jan. 2.

Number of rooms	4
rooms with sink	4
shared bathrooms	2

🏛 🦪 ⇌ 🎿 🚶 🚲 ⛷

2. LÉVIS

Prize for Excellence "Special Favorite" regional 1998. By the ferry leading to the heart of old Québec City, a traditional bed and breakfast on the most beautiful street in Vieux-Lévis. Superb view of the river and the Château Frontenac. Stained-glass windows, woodwork and high ceilings adorn this stately Victorian house (1890) with period cachet, antiques and modern comfort. Peaceful ambiance and intimacy.

Aut. 20, Exit 325, or Rte 132, or ferry follow indications for "Maison Alponse-Desjardins", from there go down Rue Guénette to Fraser.

B&B
AU GRÉ DU VENT

Michèle Fournier and
Jean L'Heureux
2, rue Fraser
Vieux-Lévis G6V 3R5
(418) 838-9020
1-866-838-9070
fax (418) 838-9074
www.inns-bb.com/greduvent
augreduvent@msn.com

☀☀☀☀☀ F E ⊘ P ≈ 🐑 TA R.2

	B&B
single	$85
double	$95
triple	$120
child	$15

Taxes extra VS MC IT

Reduced rates: Nov. 1 to Mar. 31 except Christmas Holiday
Open year round by reservation Nov. 1 to Apr. 30

Number of rooms	5
rooms with private bath	5

🏛 🦪 ⇌ 👓 🎿 🚶 🚲

3. LÉVIS

A unique B&B with comfortable, stylish rooms: African, Mayan, Indian, English. In a peaceful and warm ambiance, your hosts offer a hearty, homemade breakfast. Lovely, semi-shaded property, flower garden, patio. Visit Vieux-Lévis and its historic houses, restaurants, bistros, chocolate shop. The bike path runs along the St. Lawrence, with Château Frontenac in the background. The ferry, 10min from the B&B will take you to the heart of Vieux-Québec. An unforgettable stay!

From Montréal, Aut. 20 East, Exit 325 North. Right twd Côte du Passage, left at traffic light, 2.7km. From Riv.-du-Loup, Aut. 20 West, Exit 325 North. Côte du Passage, at the light, straight ahead, 2.7km. From the ferry, right on C. du Passage, 700m.

B&B
GÎTE AU VIEUX BAHUT

France Gingras and
Yvon Lamontagne
116, Côte du Passage
Lévis G6V 5S9
(418) 835-9388
www.inns-bb.com/vieuxbahut
auvieuxbahut@globetrotter.net

☀☀☀ F E ⊘ P ⇌ R.1

	B&B
single	$60-70
double	$70-80
child	$15

Taxes extra VS

Reduced rates: 10% Oct. 1 to Apr. 30, 2 nights and more
Open year round

Number of rooms	4
rooms with private bath	2
shared bathrooms	2
shared wc	1

🏛 🦪 ⇌ 🎿 🚶 🚲 ⛷

4. LÉVIS

☀☀☀☀☀ F E ⊘ P ⟵ R.5

La Maison sous L'Orme is an old renovated home in Vieux-Lévis that has a warm character and a large veranda overlooking Québec City. Located in a peaceful area of town, it has a private living room, food service, generous breakfast and queen beds. A 5 min walk from the ferryboat takes you to the heart of Vieux-Québec. Familial suite in the basement, with kitchenette, private entrance, autonomous stay.

Aut. 20, Exit 325 North or Rte 132 or the ferryboat. Follow the signs for the hospital. Before the hospital, Rue Wolfe. 150m, right on St-Félix.

B&B
LA MAISON SOUS L'ORME

Maud and Bruno Chouinard
1, rue Saint-Félix
Lévis G6V 5J1
(418) 833-0247
www.geocities.com/sousorme
sous.orme@qc.aira.com

	B&B
single	$70-80
double	$85-95
triple	$100-110
quad.	$125-135
child	$15

Taxes extra VS MC IT

Open year round

Number of rooms	4
rooms with private bath	4

🏛 🦞 ⟵ 🎿 🚲 ⛷ 🏃 🎣

---

5. L'ISLET-SUR-MER

★★★ F E ⊘ P ⟵ ✕ R1

Near the river, an invitation to relive the history of the Côte-du-Sud in a manor dating from the French regime (1754). Fully renovated, central air conditioning, queen-size beds, TVs. Warm welcome, sunny dining room, hearty breakfast, dinner available, landscaped garden. Packages: Grosse-Île, golf. Activities: ornithology, cycling, theatre, cruise, health spa. Steps away from the Musée Maritime.

100km from Québec City. Aut. 20, Exit 400, Rte 285 North, 2.5km. Rte 132 East, 1km.

INN
AUBERGE LA MARGUERITE

Claire Leblanc and
Louis Boucher
88, des Pionniers Est, rte 132
L'Islet-sur-Mer G0R 2B0
(418) 247-5454
1-877-788-5454
www.aubergelamarguerite.com
lamarguerite@globetrotter.net

	B&B	MAP
single	$64-114	$93-143
double	$78-128	$136-186
triple	$128-152	$215-239
quad.	$156	$272

Taxes extra VS MC IT

Reduced rates: Nov. 1 to May 15
Open year round

Number of rooms	8
rooms with private bath	8
shared wc	1

🏛 🦞 ⟵ 🎿 🚲 ⛷

---

6. L'ISLET-SUR-MER

☀☀☀ F e ⊘ P ⟵ 🛷 TA R.5

A privileged place for relaxing to the sound of the waves. Charming, very comfortable hundred-year-old house specially decorated for you. Dreamy rooms and dining room on the river. Fancy health/delicacy breakfast. Snow geese in the fall, relaxation, photography, fresh air, music and hospitality. **Ad end of this region.**

One hour from Québec City or Rivière-du-Loup, 100km, Aut. 20, Exit L'Islet North, Rte 132 East Chemin des Pionniers East, 5km, or Exit St-Jean-Port-Joli North, Rte 132 West, 10km.

B&B
LES PIEDS DANS L'EAU

Solange Tremblay
549, boul. des Pionniers Est
L'Islet-sur-Mer G0R 2B0
(418) 247-5575
pages.globetrotter.net/seul
seul@globetrotter.net

	B&B
single	$45-50
double	$65-80
triple	$80-100
quad.	$120-140
child	$20

Reduced rates: Nov. 1 to May 1, 3 nights for price of 2
Open year round

Number of rooms	4
rooms in basement	1
rooms with private bath	4
shared wc	1

🏛 🦞 🎿 🐎 ⟵ ⛷ 🔭

7. MONTMAGNY

Special Mention by the jury for "Succes" category 2001. Winner of Blizz'or prize. This small corner of Europe in the middle of old Montmagny will delight you! Enjoy our warm welcome in this cosy, turn-of-the-century home with Victorian-style rooms. Sample the tasty, authentic cuisine in the quiet ambiance of our dining room or stretch out on our sunny terrace. A variety of packages are offered: visiting Grosse-Île, golfing, flying, biking, skiing on a «lunar ground», snowmobiling, relaxation—and much more. **See colour photos.**

Aut. 20 East, Exits 376 or 378 for downtown or the scenic Rte 132. Snowmobilers path 75 and 55.

★★★ F E P ⏤ ✕ TA R.5

INN
AUBERGE LA BELLE ÉPOQUE

Carole Gagné
100, rue Saint-Jean-Baptiste Est
Montmagny G5V 1K3
(418) 248-3373
1-800-490-3373
fax (418) 248-7957
www.epoque.qc.ca
carole@quebectel.com

	B&B	MAP
single	$77-97	$100-120
double	$85-105	$130-150
triple	$105-125	$175-195
quad.	$125-145	$220-240
child	$10	$25

Taxes extra VS MC AM ER IT

Reduced rates: B&B free less than 5 years old
Open year round

Number of rooms	5
rooms with private bath	5

---

8. MONTMAGNY

We would like to share the charm of our beautiful 200-years-old home with you. Furnished with pieces of period furniture, you will enjoy its peaceful, cheery atmosphere. You can either relax on our large landscaped property or visit the activity centre 4 min away. Generous breakfasts served up in a friendly home. A hearty welcome to all.

From Québec City, Aut. 20 East, Exit 376, Chemin des Poiriers, Rte 132 East, 1.1km. At the college twd downtown, Rue de la Fabrique, 0.2km.

☀☀☀ F E ⊘ P ⏤ 🐄 TA R.2

B&B
AUX DEUX MARQUISES

Danielle Proulx
153, rue Saint-Joseph
Montmagny G5V 1H9
(418) 248-2178
www.inns-bb.com/deuxmarquises
les2.marquises@globetrotter.net

	B&B
single	$55-65
double	$65-75

Open: Mar. 1 to Jan. 31

Number of rooms	4
rooms with private bath	1
rooms with sink	1
shared bathrooms	2

---

9. ST-ANSELME

In the heart of Chaudière-Appalaches, on the doorstep of the Beauce, a dreamy spot decorated to ensure comfort, escape relaxation. Soundproofed rooms, boudoirs, livingroom, fireplace, hot tub, etc. Outdoor fireplace, 40' heated pool, patio, terrace, flowery wooded property. Golf, cycling, skiing. Staying at Douces Évasions is energizing, enriching. Welcome! Room with kitchenette, private bathroom and living room in the basement.

20 min from Québec City. Aut. 20, Exit 325 South twd Lac Etchemin, right at the entrance of St-Anselme.

☀☀☀☀ F e ⊘ P ≋ TA R.5

B&B
DOUCES ÉVASIONS

Gabrielle Corriveau and
Gérard Bilodeau
540, Route Bégin, rte 277
Saint-Anselme G0R 2N0
tel/fax (418) 885-9033
(418) 882-6809
www.inns-bb.com/doucesevasions
gabycor@globetrotter.net

	B&B
single	$55
double	$70
child	$15

Reduced rates: 10% 5 nights and more
Open year round

Number of rooms	4
rooms in semi-basement	2
rooms with private bath	1
shared bathrooms	3

10. ST-ANTOINE-DE-TILLY

In the heart of this magnificent ancestral village, next to the church, you'll find the Victorian-style former general store where Desneiges and Philéas Normand left their mark. Three rooms with private bathroom are available for your comfort. Kayaking on the river. Near bike paths and snowmobile trails, Domaine Joly, horseback riding, tennis, cross-country skiing and more.

Aut. 20, Exit 291, Rte 273 North twd St-Antoine-de-Tilly, 8km.

B&B
LA MAISON NORMAND

Diane Bouchard and
Carol Bourdages
3894, Ch. De Tilly, C.P. 181
Saint-Antoine-de-Tilly G0S 2C0
(418) 886-1314
www.inns-bb.com/normand
carolbourdages@hotmail.com

	B&B
single	$70
double	$80
Open year round	
Number of rooms	3
rooms with private bath	3

---

11. ST-APOLLINAIRE

This is an ideal base for visiting Québec City (20min away) and its surroundings, while enjoying our peaceful oasis! From the gourmet breakfast to the gastronomic dinner (by reservation), prepared on our antique wood stove, you will share our bicentennial home, sleigh or skidoo ride or or an outdoor activity (packages available). 5 min from the river (kayak). Near bike paths and skidoo trails, sugar shack, Domaine Joly, golf course...

Aut. 20, Exit 291, Rte 273 North twd St-Antoine-de-Tilly 2.5km, right 1.7km.

B&B
NOTRE CAMPAGNE D'ANTAN

Marie-Claude and Donald
412, rang Bois-Franc Est
Saint-Apollinaire G0S 2E0
(418) 881-3418
fax (418) 881-4393
www.inns-bb.com/notrecampagnedantan

	B&B	MAP
single	$55-70	$70-98
double	$65-80	$95-135
child	$20	$35-48
Open year round		
Number of rooms		3
rooms with private bath		1
shared bathrooms		1

---

12. ST-CYPRIEN

In the heart of a bountiful natural environment, discover an inviting, peaceful oasis. The house dates from 1930 and has been entirely renovated for your comfort. Relaxing therapeutic bath. Get a taste of the country: birds, garden, farm and forest. Packages: our sugar bush secrets or health and energy. Nurse owner. Tasty breakfast with homemade and regional products. Stop time for a getaway or enjoy a pro-longed stay in our lovely area. We are pleased to welcome you! **Farm Stay p 68.**

From Québec City, Aut. 20 East, Exit 325, twd Lac-Etchemin, Rte 277 South up to Rte 204 East. At Ste-Justine, right to St-Cyprien.

B&B
LE JARDIN DES MÉSANGES

Hélène Couture and
Roger Provost
482, Route Fortier
Saint-Cyprien, Barré G0R 1B0
tel/fax (418) 383-5777
www.public.sogetel.net/jardindes mesanges
mesanges@sogetel.net

	B&B	MAP
single	$45	$57
double	$60	$84
triple	$75	$111
quad.	$90	$138
child	$5-10	$15-20
Taxes extra		
Reduced rates: 10% 3 nights and more		
Open year round		
Number of rooms		4
shared bathrooms		3

13. ST-DAMIEN-DE-BUCKLAND

☀☀☀ **F** **E** ⊘ **P** 🐾 ✕ **R7**

Welcome nature lovers and children! Located at 15 min from the ski resort and regional Massif du Sud Park, and along the regional bike route, we offer two communicating bedrooms, with a bathroom that will provide you comfort and intimacy. After your escapades, join us at our table to share a supper prepared with organic products grown on our farm (on reservation). English, Français, Deutsch, Nederlands, Español. **Farm Stay p 68.**

Aut. 20, Exit 337, Rte 279 South twd St-Damien, 3.5km past the village of St-Damien, left twd Armagh, 3.5km.

B&B
CASSIS ET MÉLISSE

Aagje Denys and
Frédéric Raulier
212, rang de la Pointe-Lévis
Saint-Damien-de-Buckland
G0R 2Y0
(418) 789-3137
www.inns-
bb.com/cassisetmelisse
adenys@globetrotter.net

	B&B	MAP
single	$40	$50
double	$55	$75
triple	$70	$100
quad.	$85	$125
child	$5-15	$15-25

Taxes extra

Open year round

Number of rooms	1
rooms with private bath	1

---

14. ST-JEAN-PORT-JOLI

☀☀☀ **F** **E** **P** **TA** **R.1**

Authentic 200-year-old Canadian home located in the heart of the sculpture capital of Québec and by the St. Lawrence River. In our house it is our pleasure to receive you as a friend. Year round package for maple grove visits and tastings. **Ad end of this region. See colour photos.**

From Montréal or Québec, Aut. 20 East, Exit 414, right, twd Rte 132. At Rte 132 right, 0.5km. Large white house with red roof, 100m past the church.

B&B
AU BOISÉ JOLI

Michelle Bélanger and
Hermann Jalbert
41, rue de Gaspé Est
Saint-Jean-Port-Joli G0R 3G0
tel/fax (418) 598-6774
www.auboisejoli.com
auboise@globetrotter.qc.ca

	B&B
single	$50-55
double	$55-60
triple	$75
child	$15

Taxes extra VS MC

Reduced rates: Sep. 7 to June 15
Open year round

Number of rooms	5
shared bathrooms	3
shared wc	1

---

15. ST-JEAN-PORT-JOLI

☀☀☀ **F** **e** ⊘ **P** **R.5**

A large, century-old house with unique cachet located in the heart of the village. Spacious, carefully fitted-out rooms decorated with a respect for tradition. Generous breakfast enhanced by homemade and local products. Near restaurants, shops and services. Living room with fireplace, lounge and bike shed. Room for four available.

From Québec City, Aut. 20 East, Exit 414, twd Rte 132 East, right, 0.5km from the church.

B&B
GÎTE DE LA BELLE ÉPOQUE

Jeannine Caron
63, de Gaspé Est
Saint-Jean-Port-Joli G0R 3G0
(418) 598-9905
www.inns-
bb.com/gite_belle_epoque
labelleepoque@hotmail.com

	B&B
single	$50-60
double	$55-65
triple	$75
quad.	$85
child	$10

VS

Reduced rates: Sept. 15 to June 15
Open year round

Number of rooms	5
rooms with private bath	1
rooms with sink	4
shared bathrooms	1
shared wc	1

16. ST-JEAN-PORT-JOLI

Regional Prize for Excellence "Special Favorite" 2001. Located in the village, a lovely Victorian home of yesteryear set back from the main road. Large plot of land by the river, next to the marina. A peaceful place in an intimate setting. Charming rooms and a lavish breakfast will enhance your stay. Welcome to our home. **Ad end of this region. See colour photos.**

From Montréal or Québec City, Aut. 20 East, right on Exit 414 twd Rte 132. Left on Rte 132 West, 0.4km, right on Rue de l'Ermitage.

B&B
LA MAISON DE L'ERMITAGE

Johanne Grenier and
Adrien Gagnon
56, rue de L'Ermitage
Saint-Jean-Port-Joli G0R 3G0
(418) 598-7553
fax (418) 598-7667
**www.bonjourquebec.com/
info/ermitage**
ermitage@globetrotter.net

B&B	
single	$55-75
double	$65-85
triple	$85-105
quad.	$125
child	$15-20

Taxes extra VS MC

Reduced rates: Sep. 1 to June 13
Open year round

Number of rooms	5
rooms with private bath	1
rooms with sink	3
shared bathrooms	2

---

17. ST-JULIEN

Prize for Excellence "Special Favorite" Regional 2000 and 1996-97. Nature-lovers, hikers, cyclists and skiers, our cedar-shingled B&B in the Appalaches awaits you. Enjoy peace and quiet, views, "armchair bird-watching" and walks. After a good dinner (available on request), set the world to rights on the terrace or by the fireplace. Various packages. Treat yourself! O' P'tits Oignons, a B&B apart!

From Montréal, Aut. 20, Exit 228. From Québec City, Exit 253 twd Thetford-Mines. After the bypass to Bernierville/St-Ferdinand, Rte 216 West twd St-Julien. Right before the village.

B&B
O' P'TITS OIGNONS

Brigitte and Gérard Marti
917, chemin Gosford, route 216
Saint-Julien G0N 1B0
tel/fax (418) 423-2512
www.minfo.net/ptits-oignons/
bgmarti@megantic.net

	B&B	MAP
single	$50-60	$67-77
double	$55-65	$89-99

Reduced rates: 10% 3 nights and more, special rates for 6 nights and more
Open year round

Number of rooms	3
rooms with private bath	1
shared bathrooms	1
shared wc	1

---

18. ST-MARTIN

Built in 1916, La Maison Martin is a large family home with a view of the Chaudière river. Its period charm intact, it offers three rooms, an additional small living room upstairs, 2 magnificent dining rooms and a meeting space that doubles as a tearoom. Enjoy a stay here, in a place with a personal touch that combines the charm of the past and modern comfort. Central climatisation. The four-course breakfast is your hostess's secret.

From Québec City, Aut. 73 South twd St-Georges and Rte 204 South twd St-Martin/Lac Mégantic. From Montréal, Aut. 10. From Sherbrooke, Rte 108 and Rte 269 twd St-Martin.

B&B
LA MAISON MARTIN

Violette Bolduc and
Serge Thibault
116, 1re Avenue
Saint-Martin G0M 1B0
(418) 382-3482
fax (418) 382-3484
www.inns-bb.com/maisonmartin
st12@globetrotter.net

B&B	
single	$45
double	$60

VS
Open year round

Number of rooms	3
shared bathrooms	1
shared wc	1

19. STE-MARIE

☀☀☀☀ **F** **e** ⊗ **P**

Nominated for the 2000 Perseïdes award, this bed and breakfast offers a panoramic view of downtown. In a warm, relaxing and comfortable ambiance, ski, golf and cycling enthusiasts will love the intimacy of our dining room where a hearty, varied breakfast is served. You can also enjoy a fully equipped kitchen for a more independent stay. Air conditioning refreshes our guests before they hit the road for Québec City or Maine.

From Québec City, Aut. 73 South, Exit 91, Rte Carter, 4th street on the right, Taschereau-Sud.

B&B
NIAPISCA

Lise Dufour and Réjean Lavoie
487, boul. Taschereau-Sud
Sainte-Marie G6E 3H6
(418) 387-4656
fax (418) 386-1819
www.niapisca.ca.tc
niapisca@hotmail.com

B&B	
single	$60-70
double	$70-80
triple	$90-100

VS MC

Reduced rates: 10% 3 nights and more, Nov. 1 to Dec. 15 and Jan. 15 to Apr. 1
Open year round

Number of rooms	3
rooms with private bath	3

20. THETFORD-MINES

☀☀☀☀ **F** **E** **P** 🐐 ✕

Relaxation, quiet and rest await you here. A warm welcome, tasteful decor and gourmet dining will provide you with pleasurable moments. An enchanting, pine-shaded site, a reading nook in the pavilion and a moment of relaxation in the spa or sauna will enhance your stay. See you soon!

From Montréal, Aut. 20, Exit 228 twd Thetford Mines. Rte 112, at the Dunkin Donuts, Rte 267 South (Rue St-Alphonse), 3km. Right on Rue Mooney South, 2.9km.

INN
AUBERGE LA BONNE MINE

Dany Tremblay and
Laurent Théberge
1425, Mooney Sud
Thetford-Mines G6G 2J4
(418) 338-2056
fax (418) 338-8462
labonnemine.ca.tc
bonnemine@qc.aira.com

B&B	
single	$55-60
double	$60-80

Taxes extra VS MC AM IT
Open year round

Number of rooms	4
rooms with private bath	3
shared bathrooms	1
shared wc	2

AGROTOURISM

Farm Explorations:

🌳 **21** JARDINS DES TOURTEREAUX DE LA FERME LA COLOMBE, Saint-Léon-de-Standon ....*Page 56*

🌳 **22** FERME PÉDAGOGIQUE MARICHEL, Sainte-Agathe-de-Lotbinière ....*Page 56*

Farm Stays:

🌳 **12** LE JARDIN DES MÉSANGES, Saint-Cyprien, Barré..*Page 68*

🌳 **13** CASSIS ET MÉLISSE, Saint-Damien-de-Buckland...*Page 68*

Farm Shops:

🌳 **23** LA CACHE À MAXIME, Scott ....*Page 40*

Country-Style Dining:

🌳 **21** FERME LA COLOMBE, Saint-Léon-de-Standon ....*Page 24*

SAINT-JEAN-PORT-JOLI

Érablière Marc-A. Deschênes

483, 2e rang Ouest, Saint-Jean-Port-Joli
Tel. : (418) 598-6606 Tel. & Fax : (418) 598-6517

- Authentic maple grove
- Guided tour by the producer, all year round
- You will have the opportunity to taste their maple syrup and different kinds of maple products and even bring some back home.

By staying in one of the following Bed & Breakfasts, get a 50 % discount on the visit at « l'Érablière ».

AU BOISÉ JOLI	LA MAISON DE L'ERMITAGE	LES PIEDS DANS L'EAU
SAINT-JEAN-PORT-JOLI	SAINT-JEAN-PORT-JOLI	L'ISLET-SUR-MER
TEL. : (418) 598-6774	TEL. : (418) 598-7553	TEL. : (418) 247-5575

See the descriptions on the Bed & Breakfasts in the prior pages of the guide.

For an unforgettable experience, choose from our selection of accommodations and agrotourism activities...

www.inns-bb.com
(Secure online booking service)

www.agricotours.qc.ca

Click here!

CÔTE-NORD

©ULYSSES

Gulf of
St. Lawrence

ÎLES DE LA
MADELEINE

0   50   100km

*The numbers on the map refer to the establishments described in the text.

1. BAIE-COMEAU, POINTE-LEBEL

Calm, cosy and comfortable B&B to discover. Warm family welcome. Nature lovers will cherish the grandeur and beauty of our beach, where the St.Lawrence River meets the Manicouagan; swimming, walks and pool await you. Lavish home-made breakfast. Package deals upon reservation, from November to May.

From Québec City, Rte 138 East twd Baie-Comeau. 7.5km after Chute-aux-Outardes right at the traffic light, 14km twd Pointe-Lebel.

B&B
AU PETIT BONHEUR

Carmen Poitras and
Mario Lévesque
1099, rue Granier
Pointe-Lebel G0H 1N0
(418) 589-6476
(418) 589-1294
fax (418) 295-3419
www.inns-bb.com/petitbonheur
mario.levesque@clarica.com

B&B	
single	$40-50
double	$45-55
triple	$65
quad.	$75
child	$10

Open year round

Number of rooms	4
rooms in basement	4
shared bathrooms	2
shared wc	1

---

2. BAIE-TRINITÉ

Old lighthouse: rooms upstairs. 2nd bathroom outside. Also, 7 cottages with bathrooms, by the sea, some of which are log houses. Breakfast service in the main house. Whale-, seal- and gannet-watching. Museum, excursion and fine-cuisine restaurant on site, from mid-June to late August. **Ad end of this region.**

From Québec City or from the Matane-Godbout ferry, Rte 138 East, right at the entrance to Pointe-des-Monts, 11km.

INN
LE GÎTE DU PHARE
DE POINTE-DES-MONTS

Jean-Louis Frenette
Route du Vieux Phare
Baie-Trinité G0H 1A0
(418) 939-2332
(418) 589-8408
www.pointe-des-monts.com
*pointe-des-monts@
globetrotter.net*

B&B	
single	$41-56
double	$50-65
triple	$64-74
quad.	$110

Taxes extra VS MC IT
Open: June 15 to Sep. 30

Number of rooms	12
rooms with private bath	8
shared bathrooms	1
shared wc	1

---

3. BERGERONNES

This rustic inn, located in the heart of the village, features a small rear terrace with gorgeous view of the valleys. Whale-watching tours, sea kayaking, bike path, whale-watching lookout. Rooms in the Inn or the pavilion. 2 rooms with kitchenette and 3 rooms with shared kitchenette. Evening buffet includes buffalo lasagne, caribou and stag stew and seafood "béchamel". Packages available. Taxes and services not included.

24km from Tadoussac on Rte 138 East. 500m from the tourist office.

INN
LA BERGERONNETTE

Anne Roberge and Daniel Brochu
65, rue Principale, C.P. 134
Bergeronnes G0T 1G0
(418) 232-6642
1-877-232-6605
fax (418) 232-1285
www.bergeronnette.com
info@bergeronnette.com

	B&B	MAP
single	$45	$64
double	$57	$95
triple	$70	$130
child	$15	$35

Taxes extra VS MC IT

Reduced rates: 10% Oct. 1 to May 31
Open: May 1 to Oct. 31

Number of rooms	7
rooms with sink	7
shared bathrooms	5
shared wc	1

4. BERGERONNES

Regional Prize for Excellence "Special Favorite" 2001. Rock and chat on Petite Baleine's green veranda. The sloping hills unfold in front. Ducks and locals chat on Côte-à-Bouleau hill. One river flows by, then another and another. A smile invites you in. A spirit flows from room to room, breathing the perfumes of yesterday. A piano. A catalogne in bed inspires dreams. Sun beams dance across the crystal jam pots as if this were a ball, with Cinderella on the throne. Chicoutai charms our morning table! **See colour photos.**

Near the church.

B&B
LA P'TITE BALEINE

Geneviève Ross
50, rue Principale
Bergeronnes GOT 1G0
(418) 232-6756
(418) 232-2000
fax (418) 232-2001
www.inns-bb.com/baleine
nross@notarius.net

☀ ☀ ☀ **F e P** R.1

	B&B
single	$50
double	$60
triple	$80
child	$20

Open year round

Number of rooms	5
rooms with sink	2
shared bathrooms	2
shared wc	2

5. COLOMBIER

Winner of the Silver National Prize of Grands Prix du Tourisme Québécois 2002. Private beach, showered in the salty waters of the St-Lawrence River. A walk by the rocks on the shore will seduce nature lovers. Comfortable new rooms of superior quality. Suite with front and back balconies. Rooms with private entrance. French, Spanish and English spoken. Family package.

From Québec City, Rte 138 East, 300km. From Tadoussac, 100km. From Forestville, 27km. From the ferry Matane-Baie-Comeau, Rte 138 West, 70km.

B&B
GÎTE ANSE-AU-SABLE

Noëlla Thibault and
Jocelyn Gagnon
104, Anse-au-Sable
Colombier GOH 1P0
(418) 565-3047
(418) 587-3050
fax (418) 587-4808
www.anseausable.com
ntibo@quebectel.com

☀ ☀ ☀ ☀ **F e P TA R25**

	B&B
single	$65-100
double	$75-125
triple	$150
child	$10

VS

Open year round Apr. 1 to Oct. 15. Oct. 15 to Apr. 15 by reservation.

Number of rooms	3
rooms with private bath	1
shared bathrooms	1

6. LES ESCOUMINS

"A stop along the way to discovering the Côte-Nord..." Good beds, good cooking (meals with reservation). Personalized service whether you prefer to relax or explore: the sea, the river or the forest. Whales, salmon and trout are plentiful. Wonderful places for scuba-diving, snowmobiling. The inn is a cosy stop between the river and forest.

From Tadoussac, Rte 138 East, 40km. From Baie-Comeau, Rte 138 West 150km. 2km from the Les Escoumins-Trois-Pistoles ferry.

INN
AUBERGE DE LA BAIE

Esther Gagné
267, Route 138, C.P. 818
Les Escoumins G0T 1K0
(418) 233-2010
fax (418) 233-3378
www.aubergedelabaie.com
*aubergedelabaie@
globetrotter.net*

★ ★ **F E P X TA R.5**

	B&B
single	$55-65
double	$65-95
triple	$110
quad.	$125
child	$0-5

Taxes extra VS MC AM ER

Reduced rates: Oct. 15 to June 15
Open year round

Number of rooms	12
rooms with private bath	12

7. SACRÉ-COEUR

Share in our family ambiance. "4-seasons" activities and packages. Québec cuisine also served to our customers staying in our country homes. No charge: visit or care of animals, sugar shack, tennis, pool, hiking trails, game park. Info and reservation service. Visit our web page. **Farm Stay p 69. Country Home p 142. Ad end of region Côte-Nord and Saguenay-Lac-St-Jean. Ad start of the guide.**

From Tadoussac, twd Chicoutimi, 17km from the intersection of Rtes 138 and 172, and 6km from Sacré-Coeur.

**B&B
FERME 5 ÉTOILES**

Stéphanie and Claude Deschênes
465, Route 172 Nord
Sacré-Coeur G0T 1Y0
(418) 236-4833
1-877-236-4551
fax (418) 236-4551
www.ferme5etoiles.com
info@ferme5etoiles.com

F E P 〰 ≋ ✕ TA R1

	B&B	MAP
single	$40	$55
double	$50	$88
triple	$60	$111
child	$10	$29

Taxes extra VS MC AM IT
Open year round

Number of rooms	4
rooms with sink	2
shared bathrooms	2
shared wc	1

---

8. STE-ANNE-DE-PORTNEUF

Prize for Excellence "Special Favorite" Regional 2000 and Prov. 94-95.
A warm welcome;
Dreamy rooms;
A well-earned sleep;
A generous breakfast;
Fresh fruits and vegetables;
Tides to behold;
A beach for strolling;
Birds to observe;
An enchanted forest;
Endless trails;
Friendship assured.
Tickets for boat cruises.

From Québec City, Rte 138 East, 288km and 84km from Tadoussac. Or from Matane/Baie Comeau ferry, Rte 138 West, 135km. From Les Escoumins, 33km. From Forestville, 17km.

**B&B
GÎTE LA NICHÉE**

Camille and Joachim Tremblay
46, rue Principale, route 138
Sainte-Anne-de-Portneuf
G0T 1P0
(418) 238-2825
1-888-966-2825
fax (418) 238-5513
www.iquebec.com/lanichee

☀☀☀ F ⊘ P 〰 TA R.1

	B&B
single	$40
double	$50
triple	$65
child	$10

VS

Reduced rates: Nov. 1 to Apr. 30
Open year round

Number of rooms	5
rooms with sink	5
shared bathrooms	2
shared wc	1

---

9. STE-ANNE-DE-PORTNEUF

Regional Prize for Excellence "Special Favorite" 2002. Going to Germina's is like visiting your grandmother. Crepes, jams and giggling fits await you here. Stroll along the sandbank, see the birds, marina, blue whales and a century-old house with a past tinged by the movie and general-store era. Welcome to a region as big as the wind, sea and forest.

From Québec City, Rte 138 East, 288km. Three houses from the church. 84km from Tadoussac. Ferries: Escoumins, 33km, Forestville, 17km, Baie-Comeau, 135km, Godbout, 189km, Havre, 505km.

**B&B
LA MAISON FLEURIE**

Germina and Thérèse Fournier
193, Route 138, C.P. 40
Sainte-Anne-de-Portneuf
G0T 1P0
(418) 238-2153
fax (418) 238-2793
www.fjord-best.com/portneuf/fournier.htm
lamaisonfleurie@hotmail.com

☀☀ F e P 〰 R2

	B&B
single	$40
double	$50
child	$10

Open year round

Number of rooms	3
shared bathrooms	2

10. TADOUSSAC

Côte-Nord Excellence Prize 1999. At the top of the village, tasteful, romantic, soundproof rooms with breathtaking view of the St.Lawrence River, fjord, lake, flower garden, private balcony, queen-size beds. Luxurious suite, therapeutic bath, king-size bed, air conditioned, TV. Ideal for couple. Hospitality. Copious, varied breakfasts. Bear/whale-watching, fjord, seaplane tickets.

From the ferry, Rte 138, 1km. Halfway up the hill, at the roadsign, left on Rue des Forgerons, then Rue de la Montagne and Rue Bellevue.

B&B
LA MAISON HARVEY-LESSARD

Sabine Lessard and Luc Harvey
16, rue Bellevue
Tadoussac G0T 2A0
(418) 235-4802
(418) 827-5505
fax (418) 827-6926
www.harveylessard.com

☀☀☀☀ **F E** 🚫 **P** 🛏 **R.5**

B&B	
single	$85-90
double	$89-95
suite	145
child	$20

Reduced rates: June 23 to June 30 and Oct. 1 to Oct. 31
Open: June 23 to Oct. 31

Number of rooms	4
rooms with private bath	4
shared wc	1

11. TADOUSSAC

We are happy to welcome you to our home. Seen from Tadoussac, the Saguenay is breathtaking. Cruises with whale watching. Bus service 1km away. Welcome to our home.

From Québec City, Rte 138 East to the ferry across the Saguenay. Once off the ferry, take the 1st road on the right.

B&B
MAISON FORTIER

Madeleine B. Fortier
176, rue des Pionniers
Tadoussac G0T 2A0
(418) 235-4215
fax (418) 235-1029
www.inns-bb.com/maisonfortier

☀☀☀ **F P R.1**

B&B	
single	$42
double	$52
triple	$67
child	$10-15

Taxes extra VS
Open: Mar. 1 to Dec. 1

Number of rooms	5
rooms with sink	5
shared bathrooms	3
shared wc	1

12. TADOUSSAC

Cosy, comfortable hundred-year-old house with view of the Saguenay, on the shores of the lake, in the heart of the village of Tadoussac. 5 rooms with private bathrooms. Rooms with private baths also available in the annex the "Suites de l'Anse". Buffet breakfast served in the Maison Gauthier or in your room. Some rooms are ideal for families. Exceptional off-season rates. **Maison Hovington p 141.**

From Québec City, Rte 138 East to the Saguenay ferry at Baie Ste-Catherine. Once off the ferry, 250m on your left. Fax Tadoussac (418) 235-4897.

INN
MAISON GAUTHIER ET LES SUITES DE L'ANSE

Lise and Paulin Hovington
159, rue du Bateau-Passeur
Tadoussac G0T 2A0
(418) 235-4525
(450) 671-4656
fax (450) 671-7586
www.maisongauthier.com

★★ **F E P** 🛏 **TA R.4**

B&B	
single	$65-75
double	$70-85
triple	$100-105
quad.	$120-125
child	$20

Taxes extra VS MC IT

Reduced rates: Sept. 1 to June 24
Open: May 1 to Oct. 31

Number of rooms	12
rooms with private bath	12

13. TADOUSSAC

Located on one of the world's most beautiful bays, our century-old house offers comfortable, warm-coloured rooms with double or queen-size beds and private bathrooms; some also have a view of the sea. Varied, lavish, homemade breakfast. Tadoussac-born Paul and his spouse Lise will acquaint you with Tadoussac and the region. Good advice on activities and tickets available on site. **Maison Gauthier p 140. See colour photos.**

From Québec City, Rte 138 East twd Baie-Ste-Catherine. After getting off the ferry, take the 1st street on your right, Rue des Pionniers. Fax Tadoussac (418) 235-4897.

B&B
MAISON HOVINGTON

Lise and Paulin Hovington
285, rue des Pionniers
Tadoussac G0T 2A0
(450) 671-4656
(418) 235-4466
fax (450) 671-7586
**www.charlevoix.qc.ca/maisonhov
ington**

B&B	
single	$70-85
double	$75-100
triple	$100-120
quad.	$130-140
child	$20

Taxes extra VS MC IT

Reduced rates: Sept. 1 to June 15
Open: May 1 to Oct. 31

Number of rooms	5
rooms with private bath	5

Gift certificate

Inns and Bed & Breakfasts

For a gift that's sure to please,
offer a delightful getaway...

INNS AND BED & BREAKFASTS

Information : 1-877-869-9728

14. SACRÉ-COEUR

F E P 〰 ≋ ✕ TA R1 M5

Share our family ambiance, our 700 acres of farm and forest, access to the fjord, our choice of activities and accommodations with bedding, kitchen and amenities, t.v. and services free of charge. Near Tadoussac and Sainte-Rose-du-Nord. Visit our web page. **Farm Stay p 69. B&B p 139. Ad end of region Côte-Nord and Saguenay-Lac-St-Jean. Ad start of the guide.**

From Tadoussac, twd Chicoutimi, 17km from the intersection of Rtes 138 and 172, and 6km from the Sacré-Coeur church. From Chicoutimi-Nord, Rte 172 South to the right, 60m before the rest area.

COUNTRY HOMES
FERME 5 ÉTOILES

Stéphanie and Claude Deschênes
465, Route 172 Nord
Sacré-Coeur G0T 1Y0
(418) 236-4833
1-877-236-4551
fax (418) 236-4551
www.ferme5etoiles.com
info@ferme5etoiles.com

No. houses	10
No. rooms	1-3
No. people	2-8
DAY-SUMMER	$59-110
DAY-WINTER	$49-110

Taxes extra VS MC AM IT
Open year round

AGROTOURISM

Farm Stays:

🐾 7   FERME 5 ÉTOILES, Sacré-Coeur ....*Page 69*

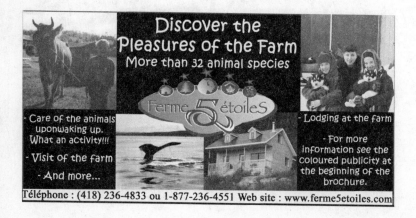

Discover the Pleasures of the Farm
More than 32 animal species

Ferme 5 étoiles

- Care of the animals upon waking up. What an activity!!!
- Visit of the farm
- And more...

- Lodging at the farm
- For more information see the coloured publicity at the beginning of the brochure.

Téléphone : (418) 236-4833 ou 1-877-236-4551 Web site : www.ferme5etoiles.com

GASPÉSIE

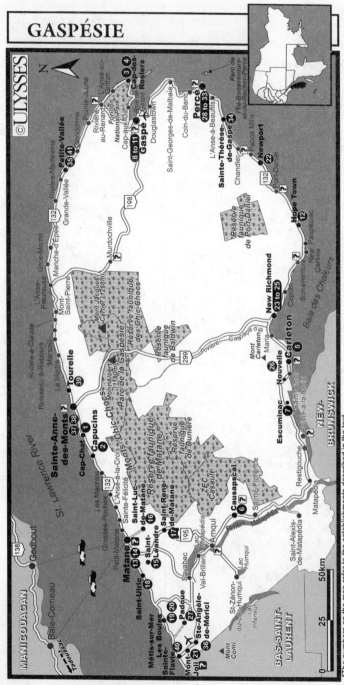

© ULYSSES

1. CAP-CHAT

Come join us to the sound of the waves and crying gulls. From our beach, see the whales disappear over the still horizon. At sunset, close your eyes and feel the very soul of Gaspé. Visit the 76-windmill park, the largest vertical-axis windmill and Parc de la Gaspésie. Our 11th year of welcoming guests. Dinner: seafood gratin, by reservation only.

From Québec City, Aut. 20 East, Rte 132 East twd Cap-Chat. At West entrance, 3km from the windmill, and 2km from the Centre d'Interprétation du Vent et de la Mer.

B&B
AUBERGE AU CRÉPUSCULE

Monette Dion and Jean Ouellet
239, rue Notre-Dame Ouest,
route 132
Cap-Chat GOJ 1E0
tel/fax **(418) 786-5751**
www.aucrepuscule.com
jeanou@globetrotter.net

	B&B
single	$45
double	$60-65
triple	$80
quad.	$100
child	$15

VS MC IT
Open: May 15 to Oct. 15

Number of rooms	**5**
rooms in basement	2
rooms with private bath	1
rooms with sink	2
shared bathrooms	3

2. CAP-CHAT, CAPUCINS

Between the Reford Gardens and Forillon National Park, (or Parc de la Gaspésie), the former general store has become an inn made of wood. We are located right on the riverside, off Route 132. Come breathe in the sea air, savour our fresh fish and sea-food, admire magnificent sunsets and be rocked to sleep by the waves. Come and stay a while, a few days even... you'll never want to leave!

From Québec City, Aut. 20 East, Rte 132 East twd Capucins. Follow signs for the Centre d'Interprétation, left on Rue du Village.

INN
AUBERGE DE LA
BAIE-DES-CAPUCINS

Sylvain Legris and
Bertrand Cloutier
274, rue du Village
Capucins, Cap-Chat GOJ 1H0
(418) 786-2749
1-877-600-2749
**http://pages.globetrotter.
net/capucins**
capucins@globetrotter.net

	B&B	MAP
single	$75	$105
double	$85	$140

Taxes extra VS MC IT
Open year round by reservation
Sep. 15 to June 23

Number of rooms	**2**
rooms with private bath	2

3. CAP-DES-ROSIERS, FORILLON

Friendly, welcoming B&B near Forillon Park, with its enchanting landscape and animal life. Visit the tallest lighthouse in the country and go on one of our cruises (whale, seal and bird watching). While savouring a copious breakfast, you'll be dazzled by a magnificent view of the sea. Welcome to our home.

From Québec City, Aut. 20 East and Rte 132 East twd Cap-des-Rosiers. From Gaspé, Rte 132 twd Cap-des-Rosiers, 3km from the entrance to the North part of Forillon Park.

B&B
AUX PÉTALES DE ROSE

Alvine Lebrun
1184, boul. Cap-des-Rosiers
Cap-des-Rosiers GOE 1E0
(418) 892-5031
www.inns-bb.com/petalesderose

	B&B
single	$40
double	$55
triple	$70
quad.	$80
child	$10

Reduced rates: May 1 to June 1,
Sep. 15 to Oct. 31
Open: May 1 to Oct. 31

Number of rooms	**5**
rooms in basement	2
shared bathrooms	2

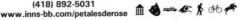

4. CAP-DES-ROSIERS, FORILLON

Two min from Forillon National Park, our seaside B&B is the place for those who long for a little peace and quiet. In our solarium with breathtaking sea views, enjoy our succulent, homemade mega-breakfasts with rich black coffee. Our rooms are cosy and comfortable. Numerous activities await: marine birds and mammals, cruises, kayaking, summer theatre. Less than 2km from the lighthouse. Welcome!

From Québec, Aut. 20 East and Rte 132 East twd Cap-des-Rosiers.

B&B
GÎTE LA MAISON ROSE

Danielle Slonina
1182, boul. Cap-des-Rosiers,
Route 132 Est
Cap-des-Rosiers G4X 6H1
(418) 892-5602
(450) 666-0303
fax (450) 666-9749
www.inns-bb.com/maisonrose
gitelamaisonrose@videotron.ca

☀☀☀ F e ⊘ Ⓟ R1

B&B	
single	$50-60
double	$55-65
triple	$70-80
quad.	$85-95
child	$5-15

Open: July 1 to Sep. 4

Number of rooms	3
rooms with private bath	2
rooms with sink	1
shared bathrooms	1

5. CARLETON

Two Acadians welcome you to their granite Canadian-style house. Spacious rooms, country decor. Large veranda with view of Mont St-Joseph, a few km from the B&B. Children welcome. Near playground, beach, hiking trails, bird-watching tower. 25km from Parc de Miguasha.

From Québec City, Aut. 20 East, Rte 132 East. At the entrance to Carleton, next to "Optique Chaleurs". Entrance on Rue des Érables, 1st house on right. From Percé, 3km from the church, next to Motel.

B&B
GÎTE LES LEBLANC

Jocelyne and Rosaire LeBlanc
346, boul. Perron, C.P. 143
Carleton G0C 1J0
(418) 364-7601
(418) 364-3208
fax (418) 364-6333
www.inns-bb.com/leblanc
lesleblanc@globetrotter.net

☀☀☀ F E ⊘ Ⓟ ⊨ TA R1

B&B	
single	$45
double	$55
triple	$65
quad.	$75
child	$10

VS MC

Open: May 1 to Oct. 31

Number of rooms	4
rooms with sink	2
shared bathrooms	2

6. CAUSAPSCAL

B&B right in the heart of the village of Causapscal. Come relax in a setting typical of the Matapédia valley; it's just like being in a Swiss village. Enjoy a view of the Rivière Matapédia, where you'll see fishermen trying to catch salmon. Just the place for a pleasant stay!

Rte 132 West, Rue d'Anjou 1st street on the right after the traffic light, left on Rue Belzile. Or Rte 132 East, Rue d'Anjou, by the "caisse populaire", left on Rue Belzile.

B&B
LE GÎTE DE LA VALLÉE

Gilberte Barriault
71, rue Belzile
Causapscal G0J 1J0
(418) 756-5226
(418) 756-3072
www.inns-bb.com/vallee

☀☀☀ F Ⓟ R.2

B&B	
single	$35
double	$50
child	$10

Reduced rates: Nov. 1 to Avr. 30
Open: Jan. 16 to Dec. 14

Number of rooms	3
shared bathrooms	1
shared wc	1

7. ESCUMINAC, MIGUASHA

F E 🚭 P 🛶 🏊 🐾 TA R10

Wanta-Qo-Ti, an experience that worthy of its name : "serenity". Come and discover our enchanting site framed by the red cliffs of Miguasha and the bay of Chaleur. Converted fishing shed conceived with taste and space. Foresee two nights to fully experience that which we share with you. We are 2km from the Miguasha Park, directly on the water, a little away from everything.

Either in Nouvelle or Escuminac, leave Route 132 and make your way twd the Parc de Miguasha. We are 2km from the Park.

INN
AUBERGE WANTA-QO-TI

Bruce Wafer
77, chemin Pointe-Fleurant
Escuminac G0C 1N0
tel/fax (418) 788-5686
www.inns-bb.com/wanta_qo_ti
bwafer@globetrotter.net

	B&B
single	$40-52
double	$60-75
triple	$75-90
quad.	$90-105
child	$0-12

MC IT

Reduced rates: Sep. 15 to Jan. 15 and Mar. 15 to June 15

Open year round

Number of rooms	7
rooms with private bath	5
shared bathrooms	2

8. GASPÉ

☀☀☀☀ F E 🚭 P 🛶 🏊 R.2

On entering the Gîte Historique l'Émerillon, you'll discover the history of the Gaspésie. Located 30 min from the Forillon National Park and 45 min from Percé, this bed and breakfast stands in the heart of the Gaspé, overlooking the magnificent bay. Just steps away from restaurants, services and activities: museum, walks, swimming. Each of the four rooms has its own history and charm. As for breakfast, it will introduce you to local and homemade products.

In Percé, left at the 2nd light. From Forillon park, right at 1st light and left at 2nd light.

B&B
GÎTE HISTORIQUE L'ÉMERILLON

Caroline Leclerc and
Olivier Nolleau
192, rue de la Reine
Gaspé G4X 1T8
(418) 368-3063
fax (418) 368-3263
www.multimania.com/emerillon
gaspeg@globetrotter.net

	B&B
single	$60-80
double	$60-80
triple	$70-100
quad.	$115
child	$15

VS

Open year round

Number of rooms	4
rooms with private bath	1
shared bathrooms	1

9. GASPÉ

☀☀☀ F E 🚭 P 🛶 🐾 TA R1

Family home (3 generations). Built in 1922 with period furniture. Honeys lodged, survivors from torpedoed merchant marine ships sunk off the Gaspe during World War 39-45. Enjoy a cocktail on the large porch facing the bay while admiring the superb sunset. Next to the marina. Gaspesian breakfast. Picnic on the grounds.

From Percé, right at flashing light after the Gaspé tourist office. From Forillon, left at Gaspé bridge, left at flashing light. From Murdochville, right at the bridge, left at flashing light.

B&B
GÎTE HONEYS

Françoise Lambert Kruse and
Harold Kruse
4, rue de la Marina
Gaspé G4X 3B1
tel/fax (418) 368-3294
www.inns-bb.com/honeys
honeys@cgocable.ca

	B&B
single	$50-55
double	$55-60
triple	$75
child	$15

VS

Open: May 1 to Oct. 31

Number of rooms	5
rooms with private wc	2
shared bathrooms	2

10. GASPÉ

Located near Forillon National Park. A 5 min walk from all services, this Canadian-style house will please you with its hosts' welcome and its cleanliness, comfort and tranquillity. Documentation and information on our beautiful region's attractions. Five-course, copious breakfast. Washer, dryer and kitchenette available in high season, motorcycle/bicycle garage. See you soon!

Rte 132 or 198 to Gaspé. Rue Jacques-Cartier or Rue de la Reine to the cathedral, where Rue Mgr Leblanc begins opposite the steeple.

B&B
GÎTE LA CANADIENNE

Lorraine Philibert and Georges Dorion
201, rue Mgr. Leblanc
Gaspé G4X 1S3
(418) 368-3806
fax (418) 368-8167
www.inns-bb.com/lacanadienne
lacanadienne@globetrotter.net

	B&B
single	$50-65
double	$60-80
triple	$75-95
Open year round	
Number of rooms	5
rooms in semi-basement	3
rooms with private bath	5

11. GASPÉ

Across from the town of Gaspé, discover a lovely, welcoming period house, with its carved staircase, panoramic view and rich history. Come sample delicious cuisine where seafood holds pride of place. Fresh lobster from the fish tank, terrace, fireplace.

Rte 132 to Gaspé. Located on Boul. York East or Rte 198, across from the town, on the bay, near the tourist office.

INN
L'ANCÊTRE DE GASPÉ

Diane Lauzon and Ronald Chevalier
55, boul. York Est
Gaspé G4X 2L1
(418) 368-4358
fax (418) 368-4054
www.aubergeancetre.com
ancetre.gaspe@globetrotter.net

	B&B
single	$65-80
double	$65-80
triple	$80
quad.	$95
child	$15
Taxes extra VS MC AM ER IT	
Open: May 1 to Nov. 30	
Number of rooms	4
rooms with private bath	2
shared bathrooms	1
shared wc	2

12. HOPE TOWN, PASPÉBIAC

Regional Prize for Excellence "Special Favorite" 2002 and 2001. Prize for Excellence "Special Favorite" Provincial and Regional 1995-96. A dream stay by the sea awaits you in a quiet village located halfway between Rocher Percé and the Matapédia valley. Your visit here will be full of surprises. A trail of larches lined with wild berries leads to the salmon river. Awaken your taste buds with a dinner (lobster in season), by reservation only.

From Québec City, Aut. 20 East, Rte 132 East twd Hopetown. From Percé, Rte 132 West twd Hopetown, 4km West of the village of St-Godefroi, on the right.

B&B
LA CLÉ DES CHAMPS

Bernard Gauthier
254, Route 132
Hope Town, Paspébiac G0C 2K0
tel/fax (418) 752-3113
1-800-693-3113
www.simarts.com/lacle.html
lacle@globetrotter.net

	B&B
single	$48
double	$58
child	$18
Open year round	
Number of rooms	3
rooms with sink	1
shared bathrooms	1
shared wc	1

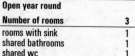

13. MATANE

★★★ F e ⊘ P ━ TA R1

Former site of the Fraser seigneury, where the Rivière Matane joins the St.Lawrence River. Near downtown, ancestral house, woodlands, balcony and swings. Participate in a treasure hunt that ends with a welcoming cocktail by the fireplace. Window lace; resplendent with Raymonde and Guy's warm, affable welcome. Gaspésie tourism grand prize for hospitality 1999. 3 stars.

From Québec City, Aut. 20 East, Rte 132 East. In Matane, Av. du Phare, after "Tim Horton's", right on Rue Druillette, at no. 148. Reception and parking 621 Rue St-Jérôme.

INN
AUBERGE LA SEIGNEURIE

Raymonde and Guy Fortin
621, rue Saint-Jérôme
Matane G4W 3M9
(418) 562-0021
1-877-783-4466
fax (418) 562-4455
aubergelaseigneurie.com
info@aubergelaseigneurie.com

	B&B
single	$60-90
double	$60-90
triple	$75-105
quad.	$90-120
child	$15

Taxes extra VS MC IT

Reduced rates: Sep. 15 to June 15
Open year round

Number of rooms	9
rooms with private bath	7
rooms with sink	2
rooms with bath and sink	1
shared bathrooms	2
shared wc	1

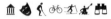

14. MATANE

☀☀☀ F e ⊘ P ━ 🐾 R.25

Located in Matane, near the downtown area, facing the enchanting islands of the Matane river and the migration corridor. Le Gîte des Îles and its owner, Maryse, welcome you with the warmth and friendliness that is characteristic of the region's inhabitants. This ancestral home decorated with care features three cozy rooms and beautiful bathroom. Not to mention the hearty breakfast that awaits you to begin your day!

From Québec City, Aut. 20, Rte 132 East. In Matane, right on Rte 195 twd Amqui. Left at the second Exit, next to the bridge, at the "Bienvenue centre-ville" sign, left for 1.7km.

B&B
GÎTE DES ÎLES

Maryse Caron and
Bernard Ouellet
29, Desjardins
Matane G4W 2Y5
(418) 562-6688
(418) 566-5964
www.inns-bb.com/gitedesiles

	B&B
single	$45
double	$55
triple	$70
child	$10

Reduced rates: $10 less per room low season end of Sept. to May 25
Open year round

Number of rooms	3
rooms with sink	1
shared bathrooms	1
shared wc	2

15. MATANE, ST-LÉANDRE

☀☀☀☀ F e ⊘ P ≈ 🐾 TA R14

Winner of the 2000 Regional prize for excellence "Special Favourite." 15min from Matane, an enchanting site in the tranquil countryside. Charming aeolian mountain village 15 min from Matane. Fine home with old-manor-style ancestral decor. In homage to Nelligan, poetry in the rooms, romance by the fire, singing around the old piano. Refinement, cheery mornings, gourmet food. 100 acres of land, forest walks, swimming in the falls, natural spa. Golden retriever, affectionate kittens. Nearby: windmills, deer park, salmon-migration path, moose observation, Reford Gardens. Regional winner of the "Tourist Services" Grand Prix.

Rte 132 twd Matane. In St-Ulric, South twd St-Léandre. Follow the signs.

B&B
LE JARDIN DE GIVRE

Ginette and Gérald Tremblay
3263, Route du Peintre
Saint-Léandre-de-Matane
G0J 2V0
tel/fax (418) 737-4411
1-800-359-9133
www.inns-bb.com/jardindegivre
*jardin de-givre@
globetrotter.net*

	B&B
single	$45-55
double	$65-75
triple	$85-95
quad.	$95
child	$10-15

Taxes extra VS
Open year round

Number of rooms	5
rooms with private bath	2
shared bathrooms	1
shared wc	1

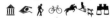

16. MATANE, ST-LUC

☀☀☀ **F E ⊘ P** ⛵ **TA** R7

Regional Prize for Excellence "Special Favorite" 2002. Gaspésie Excellence Prize 1997-98. At 200m in altitude, away from Rte 132, 5 min from Matane. View over the St. Lawrence River and the region.Therapeutic bath, hearty breakfast, European coffee, near salmon pass, Matane/Baie-Comeau/Godbout ferry. Winter sports, visit the beaver pond, 8km, maple grove, 20km and Moose Park, 28km.

In Matane, opposite Jean Coutu, Av. Jacques-Cartier to light, left on Av. St-Rédempteur, continue about 7km. Blue "Gîte Le Panorama 1km" signpost, continue 100m, left on Ch. Lebel, 700m.

B&B
LE PANORAMA

Marie-Jeanne and Hector Fortin
23, chemin Lebel
Saint-Luc-de-Matane G0J 2X0
tel/fax (418) 562-1100
1-800-473-3919
www.chez.com/gitepanorama
gitepanorama@globetrotter.net

	B&B
single	$40
double	$55-60
triple	$80
quad.	$90

VS	
Open year round	
Number of rooms	**4**
rooms in semi-basement	2
shared bathrooms	2

17. MATANE, ST-RENÉ

☀☀ **F e P** ✕ **TA** R10

A B&B renovated in the old-fashioned style, on the road that once led to the village of St-Nil, founded by our ancestors during the economic crisis of 1930. It died out in the 1970s, along with 12 other communities in Gaspésie backcountry. Enjoy several outdoor activities while living in harmony with nature. Stay in the den of the settler who left his mark at the summits of these mountains. Dinner by reservation only. Your hosts await you. **Farm Stay p 69.**

From Matane, twd Rte 195 South. At the St-René church, 5.5km. Left on Route du 10e and 11e, 6.2km.

B&B
GÎTE DES SOMMETS

Marie-Hélène Mercier and
Louis-Philippe Bédard
161, Route 10e et 11e Rang
Saint-René-de-Matane G0J 3E0
(418) 224-3497
www.inns-bb.com/sommets

	B&B	MAP
single	$35	$45
double	$50	$70
triple	$75	$105
child	$15	$20

Open year round	
Number of rooms	**3**
shared bathrooms	2

18. MATANE, ST-ULRIC

☀☀☀ **F e P** **TA** R5

In Matane, see fishers at work, stock up on shrimp and visit the salmon run. In St-Ulric, take in the river's fresh air, watch superb sunsets and windmill aeolian, unique in Canada. Savour home-made jams, admire our magnificent vegetables and flower gardens, both different every year (winner of many prizes). Rooms with sinks. Welcome all.

From Montréal, Aut. 20 East, Rte 132 East. 45km East of Ste-Flavie and 18km West of Matane. From Gaspé, Rte 132 North. From Matane, 18km on Rte 132.

B&B
CHEZ NICOLE

Nicole and René Dubé
3371, Route 132
Saint-Ulric-de-Matane G0J 3H0
tel/fax (418) 737-4896
www.inns-bb.com/nicole

	B&B
single	$40
double	$50-55
triple	$65
quad.	$80
child	$10

Open: May 1 to Oct. 31	
Number of rooms	**3**
rooms with sink	3
shared bathrooms	1
shared wc	1

19. MÉTIS-SUR-MER, LES BOULES

★ ★ F e P

Jardins de Métis packages and golf. Nature and wide-open spaces. Easy access, away from Rte 132. Enjoy breathtaking views of the river, one of the most beautiful seascapes around, long walks and a gastronomic experience that reflects both sea and land. European ambiance recreated by Raynald, a former Breton bookseller, and Marie, who has returned to her native Gaspésie. Sleep to the sound of gentle waves. Enjoy absolute peace, surrounded by the sea.

At the entrance to Gaspésie, 10km past the Jardins de Métis, left on Rte de Métis-sur-Mer, 5km along the river.

INN
AUBERGE DU GRAND FLEUVE

Marie-José Fradette and Raynald Pay
47, rue Principale, C.P. 99
Les Boules, Métis-sur-Mer
G0J 1S0
tel/fax **(418) 936-3332**
**www.aubergedugrandfleuve.
qc.ca**

	B&B	MAP
single	$82	$145-175
double	$85-105	$155-185
triple	$105-125	$205-235
quad.	$125-145	$255-285
child	$15	

Taxes extra VS MC IT
Open: Apr. 15 to Oct. 15

Number of rooms	13
rooms with private bath	13
shared wc	2

---

20. MÉTIS-SUR-MER, LES BOULES

★ ★ F E P  TA

Open year round and located near the Jardins de Métis and Métis-sur-Mer, the inn is licensed and offers fine dining. Choose the beauty of nature and the peacefulness of the countryside. Sugar shack, farm animals, winter sports bogey. Warm reception and lavish breakfasts, home made jam and european coffee. Meet the innkeeper and enjoy activities and tales beside the fireplace.

Between Rimouski and Matane, following Rte 132, 10km from Jardins de Métis, after blue tourist sign, inland via Rte McNider, 4km, turn on 5ᵉ Rang.

INN
L'AUBERGE
UNE FERME EN GASPÉSIE

Pierre Dufort
1175, 5ᵉ Rang
Les Boules, Métis-sur-Mer
G0J 1S0
(418) 936-3544
1-877-936-3544
fax (418) 936-3199
www.aubergegaspesie.com
*fermeengaspesie@
globetrotter.net*

	B&B
single	$45
double	$70
triple	$80
quad.	$90
child	$10

Taxes extra VS MC
Open year round

Number of rooms	6
shared bathrooms	3

---

21. MONT-JOLI

☀ ☀ ☀ F e ⊘ P  TA R2

Our house, located on a plateau 2km from Mont-Joli and 7km from Ste-Flavie, offers a magnificent view of the river. Just a few min from the Jardins de Métis, the Atlantic Salmon Interpretation Centre and good restaurants. Lodging in winter with skiing right nearby. We'll be waiting with a hearty breakfast and traditional accordion music.

From Québec City, Aut. 20 East, Rte 132 East. 2km from Mont-Joli. Or from the Vallée de la Matapédia, before Mont-Joli, 5 min from the shopping centre.

B&B
GÎTE BELLEVUE

Nicole and Émilien Cimon
2332, Route 132
Mont-Joli G5H 3N6
(418) 775-2402
1-888-551-2402
www.inns-bb.com/bellevue

	B&B
single	$45
double	$50-55
triple	$75
quad.	$85
child	$15

Reduced rates: Sep. 15 to May 31
Open year round

Number of rooms	3
shared bathrooms	2

22. NEWPORT

A place to discover! The former estate of a wealthy merchant stretches along the most beautiful beach in the area. Old-world charm, enchanting setting and cosy comfort. Located between Percé and Bonaventure. Enjoy fresh sea and land delights. Your stay will be a memory to cherish!

From Ste-Flavie, Rte 132 East twd Newport. 1.5km East of the church, house facing the islets.

B&B
AUBERGE LES DEUX ÎLOTS

Guylaine and André Lambert
207, Route 132, C.P. 223
Newport G0C 2A0
(418) 777-2801
1-888-404-2801
fax (418) 777-4719
www.inns-bb.com/lesdeuxilots
*aubergelesdeuxilots@
globetrotter.net*

	B&B	MAP
single	$50-60	$75-85
double	$65-75	$115-125
triple	$90	$165
quad.	$100	$200
child	$5-10	$15-25

Taxes extra VS

Reduced rates: Sep. 1 to July 15
Open year round

Number of rooms	5
rooms with private bath	2
shared bathrooms	2
shared wc	1

23. NEW RICHMOND

Ancestral house surrounded by flowers, nestled in a peaceful spot in the heart of Baie des Chaleurs. Your cheerful, friendly hostess serves up lavish breakfasts. Enjoy a stroll on the footpath, located a few min away, where you can admire a paradise of birds, including eagles, kingfishers and others.

From Québec City, Aut. 20 East, Rte 132 twd New Richmond. At the 3rd flashing light, right on Chemin St-Edgar, 1.7km, left on Av. Leblanc, 150m. From Percé, Rte 132 West, at the 1st flashing light, left on Chemin St-Edgar, 1.7km, then left on Av. Leblanc.

B&B
GÎTE DE LA MAISON LEVESQUE

Vyola A. Levesque
180, avenue Leblanc
New Richmond G0C 2B0
(418) 392-5267
1-888-405-5267
fax (418) 392-6948
**www.gitedelamaisonlevesque.
qc.ca**
*maison.levesque@
globetrotter.net*

	B&B
single	$35-45
double	$50-60
triple	$65-75
child	$5-10

Open year round

Number of rooms	3
shared bathrooms	2

24. NEW RICHMOND

Amidst beautiful white birch on the Baie-des-Chaleurs, our cottage awaits you with a warm welcome. Wooded paths, access to the beach and peaceful surroundings are yours to enjoy.

From Québec City, Aut. 20 East, Rte 132 East twd New Richmond. At the intersection of Rte 299, right, 3.5km to Rue de la Plage and right. From Percé 1st Exit twd New Richmond, left 7km, left on Rue de la Plage.

B&B
GÎTE LES BOULEAUX

Patricia Fallu and
Charles Gauthier
142, rue de la Plage
New Richmond G0C 2B0
(418) 392-4111
fax (418) 392-6048
www.inns-bb.com/bouleaux
*gitelesbouleaux@
globetrotter.net*

	B&B
single	$40-50
double	$55-65
triple	$70-80
quad.	$90
child	$10-15

VS
Open year round

Number of rooms	4
rooms in basement	2
rooms with sink	3
shared bathrooms	2

25. NEW RICHMOND

☀ ☀ ☀ ☀ **F** E ⊘ **P** ⇌ ⚡ TA **R.5**

Experience the atmosphere of a cosy Victorian and its exceptional view of Baie-des-Chaleurs. A large veranda facing the sea and the mountains. Spacious and comfortable rooms. The seashore and beach are right nearby! Quiet surroundings, away from route 132.

From Québec City, Aut. 20 East, Rte 132 East twd New Richmond. At the intersection of Rte 299, right, 5km to Boul. Perron. Or from Percé, once in New Richmond, left on Boul. Perron.

B&B
L'ÉTOILE DE MER

Diane Bourdages and
Jacques Veillette
256, boul. Perron Ouest
New Richmond G0C 2B0
(418) 392-4248
www.inns-bb.com/etoiledemer
etoilebb@globetrotter.net

	B&B
single	$60-75
double	$60-75
triple	$85
child	$15

Taxes extra VS

Open year round Sep. 15 to June 15 by reservation

Number of rooms	4
rooms with private bath	3
shared bathrooms	1

---

26. NOUVELLE

☀ ☀ ☀ **F** e ⊘ **P** ⇌ **R1**

Located in Baie des Chaleurs, this village presbytery (1897) offers five personalized rooms. Come stay in one of our large rooms. Warm yet discreet reception. Exquisite breakfast with a touch of home, in keeping with the house. You'll appreciate the comfort and tranquility of our home. Set back from Route 132, 5min from Parc National de Miguasha, a world heritage site, and 15 min from Carleton.

Rte 132 East or West, in the village centre, set back from Rte 132, next to the church.

B&B
À L'ABRI DU CLOCHER

Sylvie Landry and
Sylvain Savoie
5, rue de l'Église
Nouvelle G0C 2E0
(418) 794-2580
www.inns-bb.com/labriduclocher
alabriduclocher@
globetrotter.net

	B&B
single	$50-65
double	$60-75
triple	$80
quad.	$100
child	$10

VS

Open: June 1 to Oct. 15

Number of rooms	5
rooms with private bath	2
rooms with sink	1
rooms with private wc	1
shared bathrooms	2

---

27. PADOUE

☀ ☀ ☀ **F** e **P** ⇌ ✕ TA **R14**

Situated in the backcountry between the sea and the mountain near the Matapédia River (15 min from Rte 132), Gîte la Villa du Vieux Clocher used to be a presbytery (1910). It's now furnished with period furniture and filled with good humour and conviviality. A variety of activities await. Exquisite Gaspesian breakfasts! Cozy, personalized rooms in a remarkable decor. Discover our village... it's worth the detour! Ideal spot to relax and meditate. 15min from the Reford Gardens, Route des Arts, sea, golf, horse-back riding, etc. The old-fashioned pavilion allows for independent family stays.

From Québec City, Aut. 20 East, Rte 132 East. In front of Jardins de Métis, take the Rte 234 twd St-Octave-de-Métis and Padoue.

B&B
GÎTE LA VILLA DU VIEUX CLOCHER

Marjolaine Fournier
179, rue Beaulieu
Padoue G0J 1X0
(418) 775-9654
1-877-598-2907
fax (418) 775-8965
www.inns-
bb.com/villaduvieuxclocher
fourniermarjolaine@hotmail.com

	B&B
single	$45-60
double	$55-75
child	$15

VS

Reduced rates: 20% Oct. 1 to May 31 3 nights and more
Open year round

Number of rooms	5
rooms with private bath	1
shared bathrooms	3

28. PERCÉ

We are located in the centre of the village, behind the church. Everything is very quiet, especially at night. Spacious solarium, large rooms, home-made breakfasts. Here you will be able to park the car, relax and go for a walk. Everything is within reach: Île Bonaventure, Percé rock, mountains, restaurants, boutiques. We are from Percé, live hear yearound and can help you plan your activities.

Rte 132 East to the village of Percé. Rue du Cap Barré to the last house.

B&B
À L'ABRI DU VENT

Ginette Gagné and
Michel Méthot
44, Cap Barré
Percé G0C 2L0
tel/fax (418) 782-2739
1-866-782-2739
www.inns-bb.com/labriduvent

	B&B
single	$45
double	$55
triple	$70
child	$15

VS

Reduced rates: $10/room May 15 to July 1 and Sept. 1 to Oct. 15
Open: May 15 to Oct. 15

Number of rooms	5
rooms in basement	2
rooms with sink	4
shared bathrooms	2

29. PERCÉ

A lovely old house located in the heart of Percé, steps away from the famous Rocher Percé. We offer you the calm and comfort our maritime-themed rooms, as well as savoury, homemade dishes prepared by your charming hostess. We are originally from this region so we can give you plenty of tips and information to make your stay a most pleasant one. Free parking, near all the services. Ask for our great excursion package. We also offer guided tours.

From Québec City, Aut. 20 East, Rte 132 East twd Percé. Near the Palais de Justice, Rue St-Michel.

B&B
À LA RÊVASSE

Brenda Cain and
William Lambert
16, rue Saint-Michel, C.P. 281
Percé G0C 2L0
(418) 782-2102
1-866-782-2102
fax (418) 782-2890
membres.lycos.
fr/revasse/revasse.html
revasse@globetrotter.net

	B&B
single	$45-55
double	$55-65
triple	$75-80
quad.	$85-95
child	$15

Taxes extra VS

Reduced rates: Sept. 1 to June 20
Open year round

Number of rooms	5
rooms in basement	1
rooms with private bath	1
rooms with sink	3
shared bathrooms	2

30. PERCÉ

A love story in a stylish 18th-century home. Historic domain in the heart of Percé, right on the sea. Pauline Vaillancourt and Jean-François Guité offer comfortable stays in a dreamy decor. Enjoy meals on the veranda, facing Rocher Percé. Departures for Parc National du Rocher Percé and Île Bonaventure a few steps away. Take advantage of discounts offered during Indian-summer celebrations. The inn and its restaurant are listed in the best travel guides: Michelin, Ulysses and others. New in 2003, an exclusive package for salmon-fishing enthusiasts.

Rte 132, in the village centre, by the sea, look for the large black sign.

INN
AUBERGE AU PIRATE 1775

Pauline Vaillancourt
169, Route 132
Percé G0C 2L0
(418) 782-5055
fax (418) 782-5680
www.inns-bb.com/pirate1775
getty@globetrotter.net

	B&B
single	$90-150
double	$90-150
triple	$175
quad.	$200
child	$25

Taxes extra VS MC AM ER IT

Reduced rates: 25% 3 nights and more, rates for 1 or 2 people
Open: June 1 to Oct. 10

Number of rooms	5
rooms with private bath	3
rooms with sink	2
shared bathrooms	1
shared wc	1

31. PERCÉ

☀☀☀ **F E P** 🚌 🐾 **TA R2**

Lucille and her 12-year-old son Victor invite you to their traditional family home situated just outside the affluent downtown of Percé. The setting exudes calm and tranquility, and this vast landscaped property has a beautiful view of the sea. Simplicity, info, advice and generous breakfasts made from local products await you!

From Gaspé, Rte 132 West twd Percé. Only 3.1km from Percé Tourist information. From Carleton, Rte 132 East twd Percé. It's 12.6km from the Cap d'Espoir caisse populaire.

B&B
GÎTE CHEZ DESPARD

Lucille Despard
468, Route 132 Ouest
Percé G0C 2L0
(418) 782-5446
www.inns-bb.com/despard
*lucilledespard@
globetrotter.net*

B&B	
single	$35-45
double	$45-55
triple	$65
quad.	$75
child	$10

Reduced rates: Sep. 1 to May 31
Open year round

Number of rooms	4
shared bathrooms	2

32. PERCÉ

☀☀☀ **F e P** 🚗 **TA R2**

Located west of Percé, Nicole and Adelard's house is a haven of peace with a splendid view of the sea and a relaxing patio area. Spacious rooms, bathroom with whirlpool bath, where everything is in place to ensure your well-being. Lavish breakfasts made of homemade products. Fiddle entertainment provided by grandma in the evening. We are told: "Your welcome makes us feel right at home".

2km West of the Percé tourist office.

B&B
GÎTE DU CAP BLANC

Nicole Laflamme and
Adélard Dorion
442, Route 132 Ouest, C.P. 221
Percé G0C 2L0
(418) 782-2555
fax (418) 782-2662
**www.iquebec.com/
giteducapblanc**
ndorion@globetrotter.qc.ca

B&B	
single	$50
double	$55-75
triple	$90
quad.	$105
child	$5-15

VS

Reduced rates: Oct. 15 to May 15
Open year round

Number of rooms	5
rooms with private bath	2
rooms with sink	2
shared bathrooms	1

33. PERCÉ

☀☀☀ **F E 🚭 P** 🍴 **R.25**

The century old, historic presbytery of Percé is now a Bed & Breakfast. With a parish ambiance, tranquil situation, yet only a step away from downtown, singular view of Percé Rock, gracious hospitality, generous home style breakfast, and trilingual service,"Le Presbytère" welcomes the apportunity to assist guests in enjoying their stay with us.

From Rte 132 in the center of Percé, opposite the wharf, take Rue de l'Église, to the last house on your left.

B&B
LE PRESBYTÈRE

Michel Boudreau
47, rue de l'Église, C.P. 178
Percé G0C 2L0
(418) 782-5557
tel/fax (418) 782-5587
www.perce-gite.com
percegite@yahoo.ca

B&B	
single	$49-69
double	$59-79
triple	$69-99
quad.	$79-109
child	$5-10

VS MC

Open: June 15 to Oct. 15

Number of rooms	5
rooms with sink	2
shared bathrooms	3

34. PERCÉ, STE-THÉRÈSE

※ ※ ※ **F e P** 🐑 **TA** R1.5

Enjoy a stay in this picturesque fishing village. Upon entering our B&B, you will be greeted by an old fisherman carved into the door by a St-Jean-Port-Joli artist. Comfortable, well-decorated rooms. Lavish breakfasts in a spacious, Bahutier-style dining room next to the sunny-coloured kitchen. Stay 2 nights and get a free picnick. Patio, B.B.Q. available.

15 min from Percé, Rte 132 West. In Ste-Thérèse, halfway between the dock and the church. At the windmill, opposite the Bria restaurant.

B&B
GÎTE DU MOULIN À VENT

Janine Desbois
247, Route 132, C.P. 10
Sainte-Thérèse-de-Gaspé
G0C 3B0
(418) 385-4922
tel/fax (418) 385-3103
www.inns-bb.com/moulinavent

	B&B
single	$35
double	$50-60
child	$10

Open: June 1 to Sep. 30

Number of rooms	4
shared bathrooms	2

---

35. PETITE-VALLÉE

★ ★ **F e P** 🛶 🏊 ✕ **TA** R5

On a long headland, set back from Route 132 and one hour (70km) from Forillon Park, our centenary house opens its doors to offer you a family welcome and traditional cuisine, featuring fish and seafood. Glassed-in dining-room with superb sea view. Dinner and theatre or concert packages available. **Country Home p 159. Ad start of the guide.**

From Québec, Aut. 20 East, Rte 132 East twd Petite-Vallée. At the entrance to the village, take the 1st street on the left, Longue-Pointe. At the fork, stay left.

INN
LA MAISON LEBREUX

Denise Lebreux
2, rue Longue-Pointe
Petite-Vallée G0E 1Y0
(418) 393-2662
1-866-393-2662
fax (418) 393-3105
www.lamaisonlebreux.com
*lamaisonlebreux@
globetrotter.net*

	B&B	MAP
single	$40-45	$55-65
double	$50-60	$80-100
triple	$70	$115-130
quad.	$80	$140-160
child	$7-10	$15-20

Taxes extra VS MC IT
Open year round

Number of rooms	8
rooms with sink	4
shared bathrooms	3

---

36. STE-ANGÈLE-DE-MÉRICI

※ ※ ※ **F E P** 🏊 **TA** R.3

14km from St-Flavie and the St. Lawrence River, in the heart of the village of Ste-Angèle, nature centre of the Métissienne region. In-ground pool; cozy, comfortable rooms; hearty breakfast any time. 10 to 20km from Mont Comi, Jardins de Métis, salmon fishing, canoe and kayak descent, on the Métis river 300m, Ste-Luce beach, De La Pointe golf course, Mont-Joli airport. Rimouski: 48km. Free stay for children under 6 years old.

Aut. 20 and Rte 132 East. In Ste-Flavie, twd Mont-Joli.

B&B
LA GUIMONTIÈRE

Jeanne-Mance Guimont
515, av. Bernard Lévesque
Sainte-Angèle-de-Mérici
G0J 2H0
(418) 775-5542
(418) 725-9135
www.inns-bb.com/guimontiere

	B&B
single	$40
double	$55
triple	$75
quad.	$100
child	$10

Reduced rates: 20 % 3 nights and more, Sept. 1 to June 30
Open year round

Number of rooms	5
shared bathrooms	2

37. STE-ANNE-DES-MONTS

☀☀☀ **F** e **P** 🛏 TA R1

Why Ste-Anne-des-Monts? Well, of course to discover the magnificent Parc de la Gaspésie, Mont Albert and Mont Jacques Cartier. Golf, Explorama, and a warm welcome from the locals. 10% reductions for stays of three days or more. Rooms in the basement have a separate entrance.

From Québec City, Aut. 20 East, Rte 132 East twd Ste-Anne-des-Monts. Left before the bridge. At the stop sign left on 1st Av.

B&B
CHEZ MARTHE-ANGÈLE

Marthe-Angèle Lepage
268, 1ʳᵉ Avenue Ouest
Sainte-Anne-des-Monts G4V 1E5
tel/fax (418) 763-2692
www.inns-bb.com/marthe_angele

B&B	
single	$45
double	$60-65
triple	$75
quad.	$85
child	$10-15

Reduced rates: 10% 3 nights and more

Open year round

Number of rooms	5
rooms in basement	3
rooms with sink	3
shared bathrooms	3

---

38. STE-ANNE-DES-MONTS

☀☀☀ **F** **E** **P** 🛶 R.3

This tranquil, old-style home faces the fishing port and is near services, shopping centre and public transportation. Located at the entrance to Parc de la Gaspésie, between the sea and mountains, we offer a friendly atmosphere, comfortable rooms, living room and large parking lot. English and German spoken, excursions nearby, observation of moose, beavers and deer. Large enough for comfort but small enough for privacy!

From Québec City, Rte 132 East, Exit Rue de l'Église, 300m to the right of the church, facing the fishing port.

B&B
GÎTE L'ESTRAN

Monelle Pelletier
43, 1ᵉ Avenue Est
Sainte-Anne-des-Monts G4V 1A2
(418) 763-3261
(418) 763-2330
www.inns-bb.com/estran

B&B	
single	$40
double	$55
child	$20

Open year round

Number of rooms	3
rooms with sink	2
shared bathrooms	2

---

39. STE-ANNE-DES-MONTS, TOURELLE

☀☀☀☀ **F** **E** **P** 🛶 R.5

At the heart of the Gaspé peninsula, outdoor terrace from which to admire marine mammals, superb sunsets and fishing village. Discover Parc de la Gaspésie, Mont-Albert, Mont Jacques-Cartier, Explorama, walking by the river. Two rooms with private bathrooms. Copious gaspesian breakfast. We have been welcoming guests to our seaside home for nine years. Use the toll free number for reservation only.

From Québec City, Aut. 20 East, Rte 132 East twd Tourelle. From the rest area, 0.2km, left.

B&B
AU COURANT DE LA MER

Bibiane Miville and
Rino Cloutier
3, rue du Fleuve
Sainte-Anne-des-Monts G4V 2Y7
tel/fax (418) 763-5440
1-800-230-6709
www.iquebec.com/au-courant-de-la-mer
aucourantdelamer@iquebec.com

B&B	
single	$52-62
double	$62-72
triple	$82
quad.	$97
child	$15

VS

Open: Mar. 1 to Oct. 31

Number of rooms	5
rooms in basement	1
rooms with private bath	2
shared bathrooms	2
shared wc	1

40. STE-FLAVIE

Magnificent site, facing the majestic St. Lawrence River. Vast landscaped grounds. Small covered bridge across the river to the falls and the lake, where you can feed the trout. Welcome to snowmobilers; warm reception, memorable decor, lavish breakfasts. Jardins de Métis, 5km; art centre, 0.7km; snowmobiling, 1.5km. Family-size room available.

From Québec City, Aut. 20 East, Rte 132 East twd Ste-Flavie. Continue to 571 Route de la Mer.

B&B
AUX CHUTES

Jocelyn Bélisle
571, Route de la Mer
Sainte-Flavie G0J 2L0
(418) 775-9432
1-877-801-2676
fax (418) 775-5747
www.inns-bb.com/chutes

	B&B
single	$50-68
double	$60-75
triple	$75-90
quad.	$90-105
child	$15

VS MC

Reduced rates: 10% 3 nights and more for Oct. 15 to Apr. 15
Open year round

Number of rooms	5
rooms with sink	3
shared bathrooms	2
shared wc	1

AUBERGE DE LA BARONNIE DE PORTNEUF, Portneuf, région de Québec

AUBERGE LA SOLAILLERIE, Saint-André, Kamouraska, Bas-Saint-Laurent

AUBERGE DE L'EIDER, Sainte-Luce-sur-Mer, Bas-Saint-Laurent

UNE FLEUR AU BORD DE L'EAU, Granby, Cantons-de-l'Est

LES VICTORINES DU LAC, Lac Mégantic, Cantons-de-l'Est

Prix Excellence 2001 Agricotours

LES GRANDS PRIX DU TOURISME QUÉBÉCOIS 2002

À L'ANCESTRALE, Magog, Cantons-de-l'Est

www.auxjardinschampetres.com

AUX JARDINS CHAMPÊTRES, Magog, Cantons-de-l'Est

LA BELLE ÉCHAPPÉE, Magog, Cantons-de-l'Est

MANOIR BÉCANCOURT, Bécancour, Centre-du-Québec

LE GÎTE DES ROSES, Drummondville, Centre-du-Québec

AUBERGE LA MUSE, Baie-Saint-Paul, Charlevoix

CHEZ GERTRUDE CENTRE DE L'ÉMEU DE CHARLEVOIX, Saint-Urbain, Charlevoix

AUBERGE LA BELLE ÉPOQUE, Montmagny, Chaudière-Appalaches

AU BOISÉ JOLI, Saint-Jean-Port-Joli, Chaudière-Appalaches

LA MAISON DE L'ERMITAGE, Saint-Jean-Port-Joli, Chaudière-Appalaches

LA P'TITE BALEINE, Bergeronnes, Côte-Nord

MAISON HOVINGTON, Tadoussac, Côte-Nord

AUBERGE

Du Vieux Moulin

200, Chemin du Vieux Moulin
Sainte-Émélie-de-L'Énergie
Québec, Canada J0K 2K0

Téléphone sans frais
1-866-884-0211

www.auberge-lanaudiere.com
info@auberge-lanaudiere.com

LAURÉAT RÉGIONAL
LES GRANDS
PRIX
DU TOURISME
QUÉBÉCOIS
2002
Québec

AGRICOTOURS
2002
PRIX EXCELLENCE
RÉGIONAL
COUP DE CŒUR DU PUBLIC

AUBERGE DU VIEUX-MOULIN, Sainte-Émilie-de-l'Énergie, Lanaudière

LE GÎTE SAINT-MICHEL, Saint-Michel-des-Saints, Lanaudière

AUBERGE « CHEZ IGNACE », Lac Nominingue, Laurentides

Auberge
Villa Bellerive
LAC-NOMININGUE

AUBERGE VILLA BELLERIVE, Lac Nominingue, Laurentides

LA BELLE AU BOIS DORMANT, Mont-Tremblant, Laurentides

L'AUBERGE À LA CROISÉE DES CHEMINS, Mont-Tremblant, La Conception, Laurentides

GÎTE ET COUVERT LA MARIE-CHAMPAGNE, Mont-Tremblant, Lac Supérieur, Laurentides

La maison de l'Enclos

LA MAISON DE L'ENCLOS, Maison de campagne, Rosemère, Laurentides

AUBERGE ROCHE DES BRISES, Saint-Joseph-du-Lac, Laurentides

AUBERGE LAC DU PIN ROUGE, Saint-Hippolyte, Laurentides

AUBERGE DE LA GARE, Sainte-Adèle, Laurentides

Le St-Venant
www.st-venant.com

AUBERGE LE SAINT-VENANT, Sainte-Agathe-des-Monts, Laurentides

Gîte Aux Champs des Elfes

Nouveau Gîte
http://www.gitedeselfes.com

GÎTE AUX CHAMPS DES ELFES, Sainte-Agathe-des-Monts Nord, Laurentides

B&B L'Ancestral

ANCESTRAL B&B, Sainte-Agathe-des-Monts, Laurentides

Chez Grand-mère Zoizeaux

LAURÉAT NATIONAL
OR
LES GRANDS
PRIX
DU TOURISME
QUÉBÉCOIS
2002
Québec

www.zoizeaux.com

CHEZ GRAND-MÈRE ZOIZEAUX, Sainte-Lucie-des-Laurentides, Laurentides

NOTRE MAISON SUR LA RIVIÈRE, Laval, Saint-François, Laval

AUBERGE ET RESTAURANT

Edelweiss

l'Edelweiss

AUBERGE EDELWEISS, Val-David, Laurentides

LAURÉAT RÉGIONAL

Hébergement
6 à 49 chambres

★ ★ ★ ★ ★

Les Grands
Prix
du tourisme
québécois

2 0 0 0

Québec

PRIX D'EXCELLENCE
AGRICOTOURS
ACCUEIL 1999

LES JARDINS DE LA GARE, Val-Morin, Laurentides

AUBERGE LE MONTAGNARD, Saint-Rock-de-Mékinac, Mauricie

MAISON ÉMERY JACOB, Saint-Tite, Mauricie

L'air du Temps

AUBERGE L'AIR DU TEMPS, Chambly, Montérégie

LA MAISON DUCHARME , Chambly, Montérégie

AUBERGE LA JARNIGOINE, Chambly, Richelieu, Montérégie

LA TEMPLERIE, Huntingdon, Montérégie

LES ÉLEVAGES RUBAN BLEU, Saint-Isidore-de-Laprairie, Montérégie

LA RABOUILLÈRE, Saint-Valérien, Montérégie

PIERRE ET DOMINIQUE, Carré Saint-Louis, Montréal, région de Montréal

Au Gîte Olympique B&B

www.gomontrealgo.com
1-888-254-5423

2752

AU GÎTE OLYMPIQUE, Montréal, région de Montréal

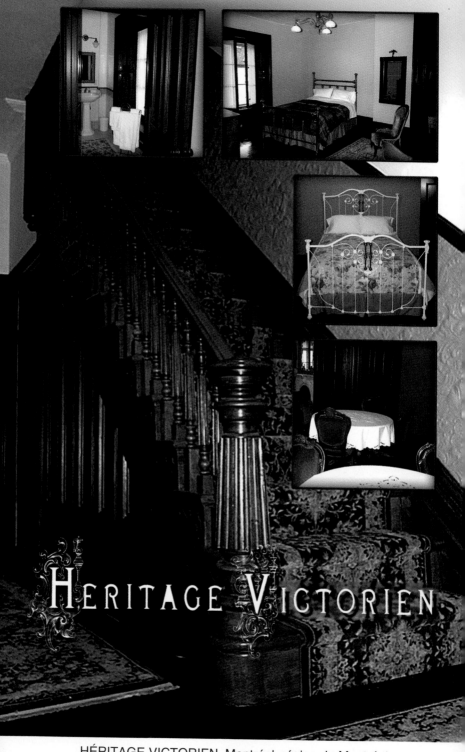

HÉRITAGE VICTORIEN, Montréal, région de Montréal

FERME DE BELLECHASSE, Gatineau, Outaouais

LES JARDINS DE VINOY, Vinoy, Chénéville, Outaouais

AUBERGE CHEMIN DU ROY, Deschambault, région de Québec

www.goeliche.ca

AUBERGE LA GOÉLICHE, Sainte-Pétronille, Île-d'Orléans, région de Québec

CHALETS-VILLAGE MONT-SAINTE-ANNE, Mont-Sainte-Anne, Saint-Ferréol, région de Québec

B&B MAISON LESAGE, Québec, région de Québec

CHÂTEAU DES TOURELLES, Québec, région de Québec

GÎTE DU PARC, Québec, région de Québec

Château du Faubourg

du style Second Empire Napoléon III

Ville de Québec

www.lechateaudufaubourg.com

LE CHÂTEAU DU FAUBOURG, Québec, région de Québec

LA MAISON ANCESTRALE THOMASSIN, Québec, Beauport, région de Québec

B&B LES CORNICHES, Québec, Sillery, région de Québec

AUBERGE DE LA FERME ST-ADOLPHE, Stoneham, Saint-Adolphe, région de Québec

AUBERGE PRESBYTÈRE MONT LAC VERT, Hébertville, Saguenay-Lac-Saint-Jean

Certificats-cadeaux

Gîtes et Auberges du Passant[MC]

*Pour son plus grand plaisir,
offrez-lui une douce évasion...*

Montage photo réalisé à l'Auberge l'Air du Temps, Chambly, Montérégie (Photo : Sandra Fabris) Conception Spin design

ACCRÉDITÉ PAR
AGRICOTOURS
QUALITÉ ❖ CONFORT

GÎTES ET AUBERGES DU PASSANT[MC]
Marque déposée par
Fédération des Agricotours du Québec

Information: 1-877-869-9728

41. PETITE-VALLÉE

★★ **F** **e** **P** 〰 ≈ ✕ **TA** **R5** **M1**

On the coast, magnificent fully equipped chalets offer you the rest you want. You will go to sleep and wake up to the sound of the waves and watch the sun set or rise over the sea. This is what awaits you here! Domestic animals are accepted for an additional fee. **Inns p 156. Ad start of the guide.**

From Québec, Aut. 20 East, Rte 132 East twd Petite-Vallée. At the entrance to the village, 1st street on the left, Longue Pointe. At the fork, stay left.

COUNTRY HOMES
LA MAISON LEBREUX

Denise Lebreux
2, Longue-Pointe
Petite-Vallée GOE 1Y0
1-866-393-2662
fax (418) 393-3105
www.lamaisonlebreux.com
*lamaisonlebreux@
globetrotter.net*

No. houses	4
No. rooms	2
No. people	4-6
WEEK-SUMMER	$600-665
WEEK-WINTER	$475-550
DAY-SUMMER	$90-100
DAY-WINTER	$80-90

Taxes extra VS MC IT

Reduced rates: Sep. 16 to May 16
Open year round

🏛 🦞 🐚 🚶 ⚓ 🎿 🐟 ➡

AGROTOURISM

Farm Stays:

🐚 **17**   GÎTE DES SOMMETS, Saint-René-de-Matane .... *Page 69*

ÎLES DE LA MADELEINE

Réserve écologique
de l'île Brion

La Grosse Île

Grosse-Île

Réserve nationale
de faune de la
Pointe-de-l'Est

Havre de la
Grande-Entrée

199

Gulf of
St. Lawrence

Grande-Entrée

Île de la
Grande Entrée

199

Île aux Loups

Pointe-aux-Loups

Dune-du-Sud

Île du Cap
aux Meules

Île du Havre
aux Maisons

Fatima

Havre-
aux-Maisons

199

Les Caps

Gulf of
St. Lawrence

Cap-aux-
Meules

?

L'Étang-
du-Nord

1

La Vernière

Anse aux
Étangs

L'île-d'Entrée

Baie de
Plaisance

Ile d'Entrée

199

Baie du
Havre aux
Basques

Dune de
Sandy Hook

Île du
Havre Aubert

La Grave

Havre-Aubert

L'Étang-
des-Caps

L'Anse-à-
la-Cabane

Bassin

Souris (P.E.I.)

Montréal

0   5   10 km

©ULYSSES

*The numbers on the map refer to the establishments described in the text.

1. ÉTANG-DU-NORD

Looking for a little corner of paradise? You'll find it here. Guests will appreciate the peaceful, beautiful beaches and magnificent sunsets at our seaside establishment. After a good night's sleep, chit-chat with Rosaline over a good breakfast loaded with lot of little treats. Our welcome is so warm that you are bound to want to come back.

From the ferry, Rte 199 West, 6km, head twd Fatima and take Chemin les Caps, 2km. We await you.

B&B
HÉBERGEMENT ROSALINE

Rosaline and Roméo Vigneault
1359, Chemin les Caps,
C.P 1309
Étang-du-Nord GOB 1E0
(418) 986-2824
www.inns-bb.com/rosaline

	B&B
single	$40
double	$60
child	$10
Open year round	
Number of rooms	2
shared bathrooms	2

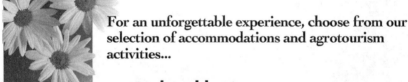

LANAUDIÈRE

0   10   20km

N

Réservoir
Taureau

Réserve
faunique
Mastigouche

Saint-Michel-
des-Saints 7

131

Saint-Zénon

MAURICIE

Parc du
Mont-Tremblant

Lac des Îles

Saint-Alexis-
des-Monts

125

Saint-Donat 5 6

Lac
Ouareau

Lac
Archambault

Lavigne

Sainte-Émélie-
de-l'Énergie 8

Saint-Damien-
de-Brandon

347

Lac
Maskinongé

349

Saint-
Didace

Saint-Gabriel-
de-Brandon

Saint-Côme

131

Notre-Dame-
de-la-Merci

343

St-Jean-
de-Matha

347

125

3
Saint-Alphonse-
Rodriguez

337

Sainte-
Mélanie

131

Saint-Félix-
de-Valois

345

Entrelacs

337   343

348

Sainte-
Élizabeth

347

Chertsey

Saint-Ambroise-
de-Kildare 4

343

Saint-Charles-
Borromée

Berthierville

158

St-Ignace-
de-Loyola

Sainte-Marguerite-
du-Lac-Masson

117

Rawdon
11 12 13

341

346

346

Joliette
2 1 2

Sorel

335

125

Saint-Liguori

158

Saint-Paul

132

Sainte-Julienne

346

Saint-Jacques

343   31

40

Lanoraie

335   337   125

L'Épiphanie

138

Saint-Gérard-
de-Majella

Lavaltrie

LAURENTIDES
(LAURENTIANS)

Saint-Esprit

Laurentides

Saint-Roch-
de-l'Achigan

339

125

L'Assomption 10

138

Saint-Sulpice

Contrecœur

15

337

La Plaine

25

Mascouche

640

Verchères

30

Saint-Jérôme

335

337

Repentigny

158

15

Mirabel

Terrebonne 9

117   640

640

132   30

Laval   25   Montréal

MONTÉRÉGIE

© ULYSSES

*The numbers on the map refer to the establishments described in the text.

1. JOLIETTE

☀☀☀ **F** e **P** 🛏 🐂 TA R.5

Prize for Excellence "Special Favorite" Regional 1997-98. Enjoy comfort, human warmth, breakfast, the terrace, flowery garden and the soul of this hundred-year-old house. Located near downtown, the amphitheatre, art museum, golf courses, bike paths, skating rink or boating on the river. Bikes available.

From Montréal or Québec city, Aut. 40, Exit 122 twd Joliette. In Joliette, left on Rue Salaberry, facing the tourist office, to Boul Base-de-Roc, left.

B&B
GÎTE AUX P'TITS OISEAUX

Céline Coutu
722, boul. Base-de-Roc
Joliette J6E 5P7
(450) 752-1401
fax (450) 759-8852
www.inns-bb.com/giteauxptitsoiseaux

	B&B
single	$50-60
double	$60-75
triple	$90
quad.	$100
child	$15

VS MC

Reduced rates: 7 nights and more

Open year round

Number of rooms	3
rooms in basement	1
rooms with private bath	1
shared bathrooms	1

🏛 🦃 🚶 🎿 🚲

2. JOLIETTE

F e **P** 🚫 🏊 R2

Rest and relaxation await you at our friendly, down-to-earth B&B, where you will enjoy a scrumptious breakfast. Take a walk in our enchanting garden or huddle around a bonfire. Numerous activities nearby: music, golf (0.5km), bike path, amphitheatre (2km), Joliette (5km), art museum (6km). Indoor pool open May-Sep. Skating rink in winter. Visit to the greenhouses and guided tours of Joliette ($).

Aut. 40, Exit 122, Aut. 31 Exit 7 twd St-Paul, 1st street on your right, 2.4km.

B&B
LA PETITE MONET

Francine and Claude Coulombe
3306, boul. Base-de-Roc
Joliette J6E 3Z1
tel/fax (450) 759-5798
www.inns-bb.com/monet

	B&B
single	$60
double	$70
child	$25

Open year round

Number of rooms	3
rooms in semi-basement	2
rooms with private bath	1
shared bathrooms	1

🏛 👁 🚶 🎿 🚲 🛷 ⛸

3. ST-ALPHONSE-RODRIGUEZ

☀☀☀ **F** E 🚫 **P** 🐂 R2.5

In an exceptional setting, overlooking Lac Pierre, this "Swiss chalet" transports you to heaven! A marvellous place for relaxation, offering a warm welcome, delicious hearty breakfast, fireplace and communal kitchen. 500m from the beach. Nearby: hiking, skiing, snowmobiling, golfing, horseback riding, music, theatre.

From Montréal, Aut. 40 East, Exit 122 twd Joliette, Rte 343 North. In St-Alphonse, right at Lac Pierre, left on N.-Dame, past the church, take Chemin Lac Pierre North, 2km, Rue Promontoire.

B&B
LA PETITE CHARTREUSE

Christiane Merle
55, rue Promontoire
Saint-Alphonse-Rodriguez
J0K 1W0
(450) 883-3961
1-866-464-5315
www.petitechartreuse.com
info@petitechartreuse.com

	B&B
single	$55-75
double	$70-90
triple	$80-100
quad.	$90-110

Reduced rates: Nov., Apr. and May

Open year round

Number of rooms	3
rooms with sink	1
shared bathrooms	2

🚶 🏇 🛷 🎿

4. ST-AMBROISE-DE-KILDARE

A row school restored for your comfort and intimacy. Private, self-catering bungalow, equipped kitchen, fireplace, terrace, heated in-ground pool. Just 15 min from Festival Lanaudière, L'Assomption River skating rink, Route des Artisans, agrotourism, Parc des Chutes. Discover our family farm. Lovers, friends, families, we await you with infectious enthusiasm.

From Montréal, Aut. 40 East, Exit 122, Aut. 31 North. Rte 158 West, 1km, at 1st traffic light, right on Rue St-Pierre, about 1.5km twd St-Ambroise. Left on Boul. Manseau, right on Rte 343 North (Rue Beaudry), twd St-Ambroise, 15km. At traffic light, left on Rang 5, 2km past the church.

B&B
BERGERIE DES NEIGES

Desneiges Pepin and Pierre Juillet
1401, Rang 5 (Principale)
Saint-Ambroise-de-Kildare
J0K 1C0
(450) 756-8395
www.bergeriedesneiges.com
info@bergeriedesneiges.com

	B&B
single	$70
double	$80
child	$20

Taxes extra VS
Open year round

Number of rooms	5
rooms with private bath	5

5. ST-DONAT

Charm, warmth and comfort await you at this Canadian house right on Lac Archambault, across from the village and a 5 min walk via Parc des Pionniers. Private beach, fishing dock, pedal boat, canoe and bike supplied. Motor-boat rental. Mont-Tremblant Park: 12km away; Mont-Garceau: 3km away; snowmobile trail: 50m away; a few metres from cross-country ski trail; golf course: 4km away.

From Montréal, Aut. 25 North or 15 North, Exit 89 twd St-Donat, left on Av. du Lac, right on Chemin Bilodeau, right on Chemin La Marguerite.

B&B
AU PETIT CHÂTEAU DU LAC

Johanne Bertrand
59, chemin la Marguerite
Saint-Donat J0T 2C0
(819) 424-4768
www.inns-bb.com/chateaudulac
petitchateau@st-donat.com

	B&B
single	$65-75
double	$70-95
child	$15-20

VS
Open: Dec. 1 to Mar. 31 and from May 15 to Oct. 15

Number of rooms	4
rooms with private bath	2
shared bathrooms	1
shared wc	1

6. ST-DONAT

Steps away from Mt-Garceau, 10km from Mont-Tremblant park, our lakeside bed and breakfast offers one room with queen-size bed, sofa bed and TV, and a suite with living room, private bathroom, fireplace, TV and fridge. On site: swimming, pedal-boat, exterior fireplace. Small families welcome.

From Montréal, Aut. 25, Rte 125 North twd St-Donat or Aut. 15 North, Exit 89, Rte 329 North twd St-Donat. At the flashing light, Rte 125 North. At the traffic light in the centre of the village, right on Rue Allard, 2km. At the end, left, 1km.

B&B
LA MAISON SUR LE LAC

Line and Denis Boivin
103, chemin Lac Blanc
Saint-Donat J0T 2C0
(819) 424-5057
fax (819) 424-1795
www.st-donat.com/maison

	B&B
single	$50-60
double	$60-70
triple	$80-90
quad.	$100-110
child	$0-20

VS MC
Reduced rates: 7th night free
Open year round

Number of rooms	2
rooms with private bath	1
shared bathrooms	1

7. ST-MICHEL-DES-SAINTS

	B&B
single	$55-65
double	$75-85
triple	$105
child	$10-15

VS

Open year round

Number of rooms	5
shared bathrooms	3

Excellence Prize "Achivement" 2002. Regional Prize for Excellence "Special Favorite" 2001. Crowning the summit of Mont-Roberval, this big country house with chapel was once the home of the founder of Saint-Michel-des-Saints. Several lounges, fireplace, piano, sumptuous period decor, panorama over magnificent Lac Toro, forest trails, swimming pool, river and waterfall... A haven of peace near activities. **See colour photos.**

2 hours from Montréal, Aut. 40, Exit 122, Aut. 31 twd Joliette and Rte 131 North. In Saint-Michel-des-Saints, left at bowling alley on Rue Provost and right on Rue Laforest to the end.

B&B
LE GÎTE SAINT-MICHEL

Robert Burelle and
Michel Des Jardins
1090, rue Laforest
Saint-Michel-des-Saints
J0K 3B0
(450) 833-6008
www.gitesaintmichel.qc.ca
memo@gitesaintmichel.qc.ca

---

8. STE-ÉMÉLIE-DE-L'ÉNERGIE

	B&B	**MAP**
single	$85	$115-200
double	$115	$160-220
triple	$130	$195
quad.	$145	$230
child	$5	$15

Taxes extra VS MC IT

Open year round

Number of rooms	18
rooms with private bath	18

Regional Prize for Excellence "Special Favorite" 2002. A log house on a private lakeside property by the Noire river, with activities and equipment included in our prices. The chef-owner offers gourmet fare of game, steak and seafood. A snowmobiling resort with an indoor Jacuzzi and sauna. Hiking trails with panoramic views, observation of bears and deer in season. **See colour photos.**

From Montréal, Aut. 40, Exit 122, Aut. 31 twd Joliette and Rte 131 North. In Ste-Émélie, right at the flashing light, 11.3km twd St-Zénon.

INN
AUBERGE DU VIEUX MOULIN

Sylvie and Yves Marcoux
200, ch. du Vieux Moulin
Sainte-Émélie-de-l'Énergie
J0K 2K0
(450) 884-0211
1-866-884-0211
fax (450) 884-0702
www.aubvieuxmoulin.com
info@aubvieuxmoulin.com

---

9. TERREBONNE

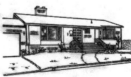

	B&B
single	$50
double	$60-65
triple	$75
child	$10

Open year round

Number of rooms	2
rooms with sink	2
shared bathrooms	1
shared wc	2

Set in vast woodlands, our large house awaits lovers of cultural activities, music, history, genealogy and ornithology, who enjoy the company of country folk. We are a few min walking distance from old Terrebonne, Île des Moulins and public transportation. Quiet, restful place.

Aut. 440 or 640 to Aut. 25, Exit 22 Boul des Seigneurs, right at 1st street, on St-Michel, East of Chemin Gascon (Moody).

B&B
LE MARCHAND DE SABLE

Paule and Jacques Tremblay
658, rue Saint-Michel
Terrebonne J6W 3K2
(450) 964-6016
fax (450) 471-7127
www.inns-bb.com/marchanddesable
lemarchanddesable@videotron.ca

AGROTOURISM

Farm Explorations:

🐚 **10**   ÉRABLIÈRE DES PATRIOTES, L'Assomption..*Page 57*

🐚 **11**   ARCHE DE NOÉ, Rawdon..*Page 57*

Farm Shops:

🐚 **12**   FERME GUY RIVEST, Rawdon..*Page 41*

🐚 **13**   LES SUCRERIES DES AÏEUX, Rawdon ....*Page 41*

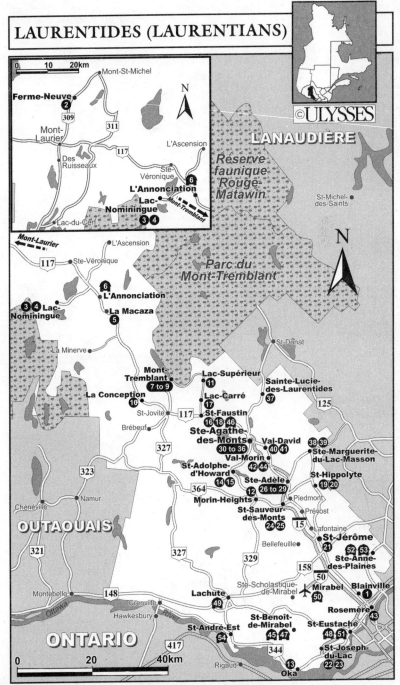

LAURENTIDES (LAURENTIANS)

©ULYSSES

LANAUDIÈRE

Réserve faunique Rouge-Matawin

Parc du Mont-Tremblant

Mont-St-Michel

Ferme-Neuve **2**
309
311
Mont-Laurier
Des Ruisseaux
117
L'Ascension
Ste-Véronique
L'Annonciation
Lac-Nominingue **3 4**
Lac-du-Cerf
Mont-Tremblant

0 10 20km
N

Mont-Laurier
117
L'Ascension
Ste-Véronique
6 L'Annonciation
3 4 Lac-Nominingue
La Macaza **5**
La Minerve

St-Michel-des-Saints

N

St-Donat

Mont-Tremblant **7 to 9**
La Conception **10**
St-Jovite
117
Brébeuf
327

Lac-Supérieur **11**
Lac-Carré **17**
St-Faustin
16 18 46
Ste-Agathe-des-Monts **30 to 36**
Val-Morin
St-Adolphe-d'Howard
14 15
364
Morin-Heights
327

Sainte-Lucie-des-Laurentides **37**
125
Val-David **38 39**
40 41 Ste-Marguerite-du-Lac-Masson
42 44
Ste-Adèle **26 to 29**
12
St-Hippolyte
19 20
Piedmont
Prévost
15
Lafontaine
Bellefeuille

OUTAOUAIS
323
321
Chénéville
Namur

St-Sauveur-des-Monts **24 25**
329
158
50

St-Jérôme
21
Ste-Anne-des-Plaines **52 53**
Blainville
1
Rosemère **43**

Montebello
148
Grenville
Hawkesbury
Ottawa River

ONTARIO
417
20 40km
0

Lachute
49
St-André-Est **54**
344
Rigaud

Ste-Scholastique-de-Mirabel
Mirabel **50**
St-Benoit-de-Mirabel **45 47**
St-Eustache **48 51**
Oka **13**
St-Joseph-du-Lac **22 23**

*The numbers on the map refer to the establishments described in the text.

168. LAURENTIDES

1. BLAINVILLE

15 min from Mirabel, to fight the inconveniences of jet lag, we offer you the comfort and quietness of our home. At the foot of the Laurentides and 30 min from Montréal, it is a pleasant stop for cyclists. Biking, skiing and walking trails nearby.

From Mirabel, Aut. 15 South, Exit 31 twd St-Janvier. Right Rte 117, 3km. Right Rue Notre-Dame, left Rue J. Desrosiers. From Montréal, Aut. 15 North, Exit 25. Left Rte 117, 3km, left 98th Av.

B&B
LE GÎTE DU LYS

Francine Beauchemin
1237, rue Jacques-Desrosiers
Blainville J7C 3B2
tel/fax (450) 437-4948
www.inns-bb.com/lys
gitedulys@videotron.ca

B&B	
single	$40
double	$50-55
child	$10

Open year round

Number of rooms	2
rooms in basement	2
shared bathrooms	1

2. FERME-NEUVE

A quiet, cozy house with tremendous charm, artistic woodwork and full of windows. A picture-postcard landscape, 106 acres of fields, forest and a little river. Delicious, lavish cuisine. 20 min from the beaches of the Baskatong Reservoir, the devil's mountain and the Windigo Falls.

From Montréal, Aut. 15 North, then Rte 117. In Mont-Laurier, 309 North. In Ferme-Neuve, past the church, left at the ball park, left on Montée Gravel, 8km.

INN
AUBERGE AU BOIS
D'MON COEUR

Louison Morin
183, rang 4, montée Gravel
Ferme-Neuve J0W 1C0
(819) 587-3383
(819) 623-7143
www.inns-bb.com/boisdmoncoeur

	B&B	MAP
single	$50	$70-80
double	$65	$95-125
triple	$75	$135-165
quad.	$85	$145-185
child	$5	$15

Open year round

Number of rooms	4
shared bathrooms	2

3. LAC-NOMININGUE

We offer cycling, snowmobiling and nature packages so that you may share in our passion for this beautiful region. Regionally renowned cuisine. The rooms with therapeutic bath and the on-terrace spa will enchant you. Réal Pelletier (La Presse): "It's good, beautiful and warm. What more could you ask for from an inn!" Grand Prix du Tourisme 1999 and 2001. **See colour photos.**

From Montréal, Aut. 15 North, Rte 117. Past L'Annonciation, at flashing light, Rte 321 South, 8.8km. Right on Chemin des Tilleuls, 200m. By bike, Km 141.5 on the P'tit Train du Nord bike path.

INN
AUBERGE CHEZ IGNACE

Yolande Louis and
Ignace Denutte
1455, ch. des Tilleuls
Lac-Nominingue J0W 1R0
(819) 278-0689
1-877-278-0677
fax (819) 278-0751
www.ignace.qc.ca
info@ignace.qc.ca

	B&B	MAP
single	$60-75	$70-95
double	$75-90	$120-150
triple	$110	$175-195
child	$10	$20

Taxes extra VS MC AM IT

Reduced rates: 10% 3 nights and more, Mar. 15 to May 15, Oct. 15 to Dec. 15

Open year round

Number of rooms	5
rooms with private bath	5

4. LAC-NOMININGUE

Located on the shores of Lac Nominingue and the Linear Park, Auberge Villa Bellerive is a renovated historic inn that is popular with cyclists and snowmobilists. Enjoy a coffee on the pier or in the dining room, which serves delectable six-course dinner. A terrace garden and a heated spa will delight you, even in winter, and the variety of our rooms will fulfill all of your desires. Discover our fine cuisine and cordial welcome. **See colour photos.**

Aut. 15 and 117 North. After L'Annonciation, at the flashing light, 321 South, 9km.km 142 Le P'tit Train du Nord bike path.

INN
AUBERGE VILLA BELLERIVE

Cécile L'Heureux and
Yvon Massé
1596, ch. des Tilleuls
Lac-Nominingue J0W 1R0
1-800-786-3802
(819) 278-3802
fax (819) 278-0483
www.villabellerive.com
villabellerive@hotmail.com

	B&B	MAP
single	$60	$75-85
double	$75-125	$118-168
triple	$90-100	$165-195
quad.	$95-110	$200-240
child	$15	

Taxes extra VS MC AM IT

Reduced rates: Mar. 15 to May 15, Oct. 15 to Dec. 15

Open year round

Number of rooms	12
rooms with private bath	12

5. LA MACAZA

We offer two luxurious rooms with private living room, bathroom and entrance. Terraces with view and access to the beach. Free canoeing and paddle-boating. Smoke-free environment. Your stay will allow you to savour precious moments of relaxation in an enchanting decor beneath the trees. Mont-Tremblant airport less than 1km away. "Juliette adored our little Alexis. We really appreciated our hosts Dominique and André; their simplicity, kindness and warm reception. And your breakfasts are so fresh and hearty!"

Aut. 15 North, then 117 twd l'Annonciation, right at the traffic lights, twd rte 122 Lac Chaud for 12km.

B&B
GÎTE DU TEMPS QUI PASSE

André Cadieux
122 Lac Chaud
La Macaza J0T 1R0
(819) 275-5840
www.zebeline.com/gite
andre.cadieux@sympatico.ca

	B&B
single	$65
double	$80
triple	$100
child	$10

Reduced rates: 20% 4 nights and more

Open year round

Number of rooms	2
rooms with private bath	2

6. L'ANNONCIATION

We cleared this patch of mountainside land so that our small herd could graze and we could set up house comfortably. Former teachers, your hosts are genuine, unpretentious people who enjoy sharing the happiness of living with their guests according to old-fashioned values. A warm welcome awaits you. **Country-Style Dining p 25. Farm Stay p 69.**

From Montréal, Aut. 15 North and Rte 117 twd L'Annonciation, 4.3km past the hospital, and left on Chemin Laliberté. First house on the right.

B&B
LA CLAIRIÈRE DE LA CÔTE

Monique Lanthier and
Yves Bégin
16, chemin Laliberté
L'Annonciation J0T 1T0
(819) 275-2877
www.inns-bb.com/clairieredelacote

	B&B	MAP
single	$35-50	$65
double	$50-65	$90
child	$15	$20-25

Open: Dec. 1 to Mar. 31, May 1 to Oct. 31

Number of rooms	4
rooms in basement	3
rooms with private bath	1
shared bathrooms	1
shared wc	2

7. MONT-TREMBLANT

Get away from it all in our B&B that offers very modern comfort in the style of yore. You'll be amazed by our exquisite breakfasts, overflowing with fresh fruit. Just steps away from a vast choice of activities. Located 8km from Mont Tremblant and Mont Blanc. Linear park 500m away (cycling, snowmobiling), cross-country skiing. Our motto: to welcome you back.

From Montréal, Aut. 15 and 117 North. Right at the 1st Exit twd St-Jovite, 100m. Right at the 1st intersection, Montée Kavanaugh, 1.8km.

☀☀☀☀ F E 🚭 P ⇌ ≋ ✕ TA R2

B&B
GÎTE LA TREMBLANTE

France Renault
1315, montée Kavanagh
Mont-Tremblant J8E 2P3
(819) 425-5959
1-877-425-5959
fax (819) 425-9404
**www.mt-tremblant.
com/tremblante**
tremblante@mt-tremblant.com

	B&B
single	$55-65
double	$65-75
triple	$90
child	$15

Taxes extra VS MC AM ER

Reduced rates: low season

Open year round

Number of rooms	4
rooms with private bath	4

---

8. MONT-TREMBLANT

Two min away from the village, experience another Mont-Tremblant. Welcome to Isabelle and Didier's spacious log home, with sumptuous living room with chimney and five rooms, each with private bathroom. Enjoy the view and the antique decor while savouring a personalized breakfast and all of nature's charms. **See colour photos.**

From Montréal, Aut. 15 North, 117 North, right at the lights, Montée Ryan twd Mont-Tremblant 6km, left at the lights twd Village Tremblant, left twd Labelle/La Conception. 2km, left on Chemin des Bois Francs.

☀☀☀☀ F e 🚭 P R2.5

B&B
LA BELLE AU BOIS DORMANT

Didier Jougler
108, chemin des-Bois-Franc
Mont-Tremblant J8E 1L6
(819) 425-1331
fax (819) 429-5519
www.belleauboisdormant.com
agri@belleauboisdormant.com

	B&B
single	$70-109
double	$85-119
triple	$110-144
child	$25

Taxes extra VS MC IT

Reduced rates: Oct. Nov. Apr. May and June

Open year round

Number of rooms	5
rooms with private bath	5

---

9. MONT-TREMBLANT

Situated 500m from the Linear Park "Le P'tit Train du Nord" and 10 min from Mont-Tremblant, Le Second Souffle is a Canadian-style home in the hilly St-Jovite region. Sports, cultural and gastronomic activities are a stone's throw from the B&B. There are five rooms, each with their own private bathroom and unique décor. Unforgettable breakfasts served in a laid-back, friendly ambiance.

From Montréal, Aut. 15 and Rte 117 North. At St-Jovite, Rue Ouimet and then immediately turn on Rue Kavanagh, 500m.

☀☀☀☀ F E 🚭 P ⇌ TA R.5

B&B
LE SECOND SOUFFLE

Monique and Jean-Marie Leduc
815, montée Kavanagh
Mont-Tremblant J8E 2P2
tel/fax (819) 429-6166
www.inns-bb.com/secondsouffle
second.souffle@sympatico.ca

	B&B
single	$70
double	$80
triple	$100
child	$15

Taxes extra VS MC AM

Reduced rates: Nov. 1 to Dec. 15 and Apr. 1 to June 1

Open year round

Number of rooms	5
rooms with private bath	5

10. MONT-TREMBLANT, LA CONCEPTION ★★★ F E ⊗ P 〜≋ ✕ TA R6

Located on the shores of the Rouge river, a few min from the "Le P'tit Train du Nord" bike path and the ski slopes of Mont Tremblant. Cozy, comfortable rooms. Breakfast included in the price of our rooms. We serve dinner. SAQ liquor permit. **See colour photos.**

From Montréal, Aut. 15 North, Rte 117 North. 6.5km past the Montée Ryan traffic light. La Conception Exit, at the stop sign, straight ahead, 6.5km. Left at the stop sign, 1km.

INN
L'AUBERGE À LA CROISÉE
DES CHEMINS

Odile Malépart and
Claude Lapointe
4273, chemin des Tulipes
La Conception J0T 1M0
(819) 686-5289
1-888-686-5289
fax (819) 686-9205
www.alacroiseedeschemins.com
croiseedeschemins@hotmail.com

	B&B
single	$80-100
double	$100-110
triple	$120-155
child	$15

Taxes extra VS AM IT

Reduced rates: Oct. 1 to Dec. 15, Apr. 16 to May 14
Open year round

Number of rooms	9
rooms with private bath	7
shared bathrooms	1
shared wc	2

---

11. MONT-TREMBLANT, LAC-SUPÉRIEUR ☀☀☀ F E P 〜≋🐑 TA R2.5

At the entrance to Mont-Tremblant park, and the northern mountain, a magnificent Canadian house embraced by nature. Linear park 2.5km away. Skiing and cycling, swimming pool. Snowmobile package. Pool, terrace, relaxation by the fireplace. Dinner by reservation. Enjoy family breakfasts and the joy de vivre of your hosts. Family-size suite with kitchenette for an independent stay. **See colour photos.**

From Montréal, Aut. 15 North, Rte 117 North, St-Faustin/Lac-Carré Exit. Right at the stop sign, 2.3km, follow signs for Mt-Tremblant park, 2.5km along chemin Lac-Supérieur.

B&B
GÎTE ET COUVERT
LA MARIE-CHAMPAGNE

Micheline Massé and
Gérald Gagnon
654, chemin Lac-Supérieur
Lac-Supérieur J0T 1J0
(819) 688-3780
fax (819) 688-3758
www.mariechampagne.ca
lamariechampagne@qc.aira.com

	B&B
single	$65
double	$75
triple	$90
quad.	$110
child	$15

VS AM

Reduced rates: 20% 3 nights and more
Open year round

Number of rooms	4
rooms with private bath	4

---

12. MORIN-HEIGHTS ☀☀☀ ⊟ F E ⊗ P 〜🐑 TA R3

Come and relax in a charming ancestral house located between Saint-Sauveur-des-Monts and Morin-Heights. Just min from sports and cultural activities as well as shops. You will be captivated by both our warm welcome and delicious, lavish breakfasts. Let yourself be pampered in a dream setting.

From Montréal, Aut. 15 North, Exit 60, Rte 364 West. Right on Chemin de Christieville twd Legault, straight ahead.

B&B
AUX BERGES
DE LA RIVIÈRE SIMON

Louise LeBlanc and
Pierre-Yves Bouchard
54, rue Legault
Morin-Heights J0R 1H0
(450) 226-1110
1-877-525-1110
www.aubergedelariviere.com
info@aubergedelariviere.com

	B&B
single	$53-100
double	$61-100

Taxes extra VS MC

Reduced rates: 10 % 3 nights and more or Mar. 15 to May 15 and Oct. 15 to Dec. 15
Open year round

Number of rooms	5
rooms with private bath	2
rooms with sink	2
shared bathrooms	1
shared wc	1

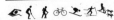

13. OKA

☀☀☀ **F e ⊘ P ⊷ 🐾 TA R.3**

In the charming village of Oka, just steps away from the ferry, Lac des Deux-Montagnes, small shops, the bike path, the park and its superb beach, we welcome you as you are yearound in the spirit of friendship. Exquisite, delicious breakfasts. Comfort and relaxation guaranteed.

From Montréal, Aut. 15 North or 13 North, Exit 640 to the end, Rte 344 West, about 10km twd Oka. From Mirabel, Aut. 15 South, Aut. 640 to the end, Rte 344 West...

B&B
LE ZIBOU

Guylaine Gérault and
Éric Lebailly
119, rue des Cèdres
Oka J0N 1E0
tel/fax (450) 479-6407
www.inns-bb.com/zibou
zibou@videotron.ca

	B&B
single	$45
double	$60-75
triple	$75
child	$0-15

Taxes extra

Reduced rates: 10% Nov. 1 to Mar. 31

Open year round

Number of rooms	3
shared bathrooms	1
shared wc	1

🔥 ⊷ 🐾 🎿 🚴 ⛷ 🔭

14. ST-ADOLPHE-D'HOWARD

☀☀☀☀ **F E ⊘ P ⊷ TA R4**

Prize for Excellence "Special Favorite" Regional 2000. A white, stone-built turreted house on the lake, surrounded by mountains. Come in and luxuriate in the peace and quiet. Cozy rooms for the laziest of nights. Near the fire: books, games, soft couch. As for breakfast? Wow! Aube Douce: "a charming place".

From Montréal, Aut. 15 North, Exit 60, Rte 364 West to Rte 329 North, 10km, left on Montée Lac Louise, 1.5km, right on Gais Lurons, left at the 1st stop sign.

B&B
AUBE DOUCE

Michèle Ménard and
Gilles Meilleur
22, chemin de la Québécoise
Saint-Adolphe-d'Howard J0T 2B0
(819) 327-5048
1-877-527-5851
fax (819) 327-5254
www.inns-bb.com/aubedouce
aubedouce@hotmail.com

	B&B
single	$55-80
double	$65-90
triple	$85-110
child	$5-20

Open year round

Number of rooms	4
rooms with private bath	4

🔥 🐾 🎿 🚴 ⛷

15. ST-ADOLPHE-D'HOWARD

☀☀☀☀ **F E ⊘ P ⊷ R2**

Located 8km from Sainte-Agathe facing Lac Saint-Joseph, come experience some of the greatest pleasures in life. Meticulously decorated rooms, private bathrooms, living room with balcony and view of the lake. Sumptuous breakfast served in the spacious dinning-room. A great place to rejuvenate yourself and practice aquatic and winter sports. Welcome to our friendly home.

From Montréal, Aut. 15, Exit 60 Rte 364 twd Morin-Heights, Rte 329 twd Saint-Adolphe, 3km after the town.

B&B
CHEZ BÉCASSINE

Nicole Sénécal and Maurice Roy
2875, chemin du Village
Saint-Adolphe-d'Howard J0T 2B0
(819) 327-5029
1-888-822-5029
www.chez.com/chezbecassine
chezbecassine@hotmail.com

	B&B
single	$70-85
double	$80-105
child	$10-20

Taxes extra VS MC IT

Open year round

Number of rooms	4
rooms with private bath	4
shared wc	1

🔥 🐾 🎿 ⛷

16. ST-FAUSTIN, LAC-CARRÉ

★★★ F E ⊘ P ⇌ 🐾 ✕ TA R1.5

Authentic victorian ancestral house (1890). Located in front of Mont-Blanc, proximity of Mont-Tremblant (tourists complex and Park). Few minutes form bike path. Martine and Paul will be happy to welcome you in their house with rooms fulfilling your needs in comfort and quietness. You will appreciate the fine quality of the meals entirely prepared in our kitchen.

From Montréal, Aut. 15 North, Rte 117 right at Mont-Blanc and follow "Maison des Arts".

INN
LA BONNE ADRESSE

Martine Bourdon and
Paul Pichet
1196, rue de la Pisciculture
Saint-Faustin-Lac-Carré
J0T 1J3
(819) 688-6422
1-877-688-6422
fax (819) 688-5052
www.bonneadresse.ca
info@bonneadresse.ca

	B&B	MAP
single	$60-100	$86-129
double	$75-125	$128-184
triple	$120-150	$200-238
quad.	$145-185	$250-300
child	$15-20	$30-35

Taxes extra VS MC IT

Open year round

Number of rooms	7
rooms with private bath	4
shared bathrooms	1

17. ST-FAUSTIN, LAC-CARRÉ

☀☀☀ F E P ⇌ 🐾 ✕ TA R1

Honorary mention, Grand Prix du Tourisme 2001, finalist, regional "Coup de coeur" 2001 award. 10km from St-Jovite and 18km from Mont Tremblant, our octogenarian house is a haven of peace for nature-lovers. Just 50m from the linear park, cycling, snowmobiling; 1km from Mont Blanc. Relax on the beach by the lake, the terrace or by the fireplace on arrival. Complimentary pre-dinner drinks: homemade wine and beer. Memorable, famous breakfast. Dinner by reservation. Gift certificates and packages available.

From Montréal, Aut. 15 and Rte 117 North. 18km after Ste-Agathe. Lac-Carré Exit. At 1st stop sign, right, 1.5km, right on Rue de la Gare.

B&B
LE GÎTE DE LA GARE

Johanne Mathon
362, rue de La Gare
Saint-Faustin-Lac-Carré
J0T 1J1
tel/fax (819) 688-6091
1-888-550-6091
www.inns-bb.com/gitedelagare

	B&B	MAP
single	$55-65	$80-90
double	$65-75	$115-125
child	$15	

VS MC AM IT

Reduced rates: 10% May 1 to June 15 and Nov. 1 to Dec. 15 and corporate rates

Open year round

Number of rooms	5
shared bathrooms	2

18. ST-FAUSTIN, LAC-CARRÉ

☀☀☀ F E ⊘ P 🐾 TA R1

Enjoy a pleasant, relaxed welcome in a recently renovated, century-old house. Ideal location, facing Mont Blanc and 15 min from Mont Tremblant. Near the "P'tit Train du Nord" bike path and the entrance to the "La Diable" sector of Mont Tremblant. Discounts on ski tickets. Rooms with queen-size bed and duvet, one family unit, hearty breakfast. Numerous outdoor activities both day and night for night owls!

From Montréal, Aut. 15 North, Rte 117 North, St-Faustin Exit, left at 2nd stop sign.

B&B
L'ENTREMONT

Manon and David Bruchez
1119, rue de la Pisciculture
Saint-Faustin-Lac-Carré
J0T 1J3
(819) 688-6662
1-888-928-6662
www.entremont.net
info@entremont.net

	B&B
single	$55-65
double	$65-115
triple	$85-135
quad.	$105-155
child	$10

Taxes extra VS MC AM

Open year round

Number of rooms	5
rooms with private bath	1
shared bathrooms	2

19. ST-HIPPOLYTE

Facing the lake, admire the beauty of the sun painting its canvas! Peaceful lake, private beach, free watercraft. No motorboats allowed. 15 min from St-Sauveur, bike path and other activities. 4-course dinner, lavish, high-quality cuisine. Satisfaction guaranteed. Liquor license. Discover edible flowers in our gardens. 1st prize for "Village Fleuris". Unique view on the lake and the mountains with their reddish autumn hues. Out of Montréal use the toll free phone number. **See colour photos.**

Aut. 15 North, Exit 45 twd St-Hippolyte, left at 1st light, 16km to Rte 333 North. Left at the church, 4km, keep to the right, inn is 300m further.

INN
AUBERGE LAC DU PIN ROUGE

Nicole Bouffard and
Yvan Trottier
81, chemin Lac-du-Pin-Rouge
Saint-Hippolyte J8A 3J3
(450) 563-2790
1-800-427-0840
**aubergelacdupinrouge.
tripod.com/quebec.html**
*aubergelacdupinrouge@
bellnet.ca*

★★ F E P ⚓ ✕ TA R4

	B&B	MAP
single	$55-80	$84-108
double	$70-95	$129-151
triple	$93-124	$175-208
child	$20	

Taxes extra VS MC

Reduced rates: $40, 2 nights and more MAP double occupancy and B&B 3 nights and more, 10%
Open: Upon reservation May 16 to Oct. 13

Number of rooms	8
rooms with private bath	4
rooms with sink	4
shared bathrooms	2
shared wc	3

20. ST-HIPPOLYTE

A quiet place at 45 min of Montréal. Terrace with panoramic view. Water garden with water fall. Fire place in living room. Shared kitchenette. Welcoming bedrooms decorated with good taste. King size beds or twin beds. Swimming in the lake, free pedal boats rides. At 6km from linear park "Le p'tit Train du Nord".

From Mtl, Aut. 15 North, Exit 45, twd St-Hippolyte, Rte 333 North, 9,3 km, at left Ch. du Lac Écho, 50m, at right, rue Desjardins, 1 km, at right 88th Av., at left at the stop.

B&B
L'ÉVEIL SUR LE LAC

Huguette Péloquin and
René St-Vincent
214, 92ᵉ Avenue
Saint-Hippolyte J8A 1V1
(514) 865-9485
1-888-224-9716
www.eveilsurlelac.cjb.net
eveil@aei.ca

☀☀☀ F e ⊘ P ⚓ ⚓ TA R2

	B&B
single	$55-65
double	$65-75

VS MC

Reduced rates: Oct. 16 to May 31, 10% 3 nights and more
Open year round

Number of rooms	4
shared bathrooms	2

21. ST-JÉRÔME

10 min from Mirabel airport and 30 min from Dorval, generous and considerate hospitality à la québécoise. Nice ambiance, room conditioned, gourmet breakfast. Gérard, a history professor, is proud to tell you about his Québec! Located at 100m from the bicycle path "Le P'tit train du Nord".

Aut. 15 North, Exit 43 East twd downtown. After the bridge, right on Rue Labelle. At the light, left on Rue du Palais, after 2 other light, left on Rue Melançon, B&B is 200m on your left.

B&B
L'ÉTAPE CHEZ MARIE-THÉRÈSE
ET GÉRARD LEMAY

Marie-Thérèse and Gérard Lemay
430, rue Melançon
Saint-Jérôme J7Z 4K4
(450) 438-1043
www.inns-bb.com/letape

☀☀☀ F E ⊘ ⚓ 🦌 TA R.3

	B&B
single	$50
double	$60
triple	$90
child	$10-15

Reduced rates: 5 nights and more
Open year round

Number of rooms	3
shared bathrooms	2
shared wc	1

22. ST-JOSEPH-DU-LAC

Like a nest overhanging mountains and apple trees, at the foot of the vineyards, this is a unique place that combines a winery and award-winning wines, only steps away from a singular gastronomic experience with a French twist. And after reception, what could be better than sipping port by the fire before retiring for the night? **See colour photos.**

25 min from Montréal, Aut. 13 or 15 North, Aut. 640 West, Exit 2, left on chemin Principal, 4.7km.

INN
AUBERGE ROCHE DES BRISES

Gina Pratt and Bryan Harvey
2006, rue Principale
Saint-Joseph-du-Lac J0N 1M0
(450) 472-2722
(450) 472-8756
fax (450) 473-5878
www.rochedesbrises.com
info@rochedesbrises.com

	B&B	MAP
double	$130-155	$210-260

Taxes extra VS MC IT

Reduced rates: 10% Feb. to Apr.
Open year round

Number of rooms	5
rooms with private bath	5

23. ST-JOSEPH-DU-LAC

Surrounded by a forest, gardens and apple trees, our bed and breakfast welcomes you to share good times and gourmet breakfasts. Quiet, invigorating, comfortable stay in rooms with panoramic views and private bathrooms. Pool, hiking on 30 acres and cycling (12ha). Located 5 min from Parc d'Oka (package) and Oka ferry (Aut. 401 or 417), 15 min from Mirabel and 35 min from Dorval.

From Montréal, Aut. 13 or 15 North, 640 West twd Oka, Exit 2, St-Joseph-du-Lac, turn left, 4km past the church.

B&B
GÎTE DES JARDINS
DE LA MONTAGNE

Jocelyne Dion and
Richard Gravel
2371, ch. Principal
Saint-Joseph-du-Lac J0N 1M0
(450) 623-0574
1-866-623-0574
fax (514) 856-2595
pages.infinit.net/jardinsm
jardinsm@videotron.ca

	B&B
single	$45-60
double	$55-65
triple	$70-85
child	$10

Reduced rates: 5 nights and more
Open year round

Number of rooms	3
rooms with private bath	3

24. ST-SAUVEUR-DES-MONTS

Winner of the Grand Prix du Tourisme Laurentides: welcome and customer service 1997. Facing ski hills, 2km from town. Enchanting decor, tranquillity, attention and discretion. Heated pool, central air conditioning, flowered terrace, 2 rooms with fireplaces, including one semi-basement suite. Many recreational/tourist activities nearby. But above all, relaxation, comfort and a warm welcome. Gourmet breakfast.

From Montréal, Aut. 15 North left at Exit 60, at Rte 364 West turn right, 3rd set of light, left on Rue Principale, 2km.

INN
AUBERGE SOUS L'ÉDREDON

Mia Van Otterdijk
777, rue Principale
Saint-Sauveur-des-Monts
J0R 1R2
tel/fax (450) 227-3131
www.inns-bb.com/aubergesousledredon
mia@aubergesousledredon.com

	B&B
single	$64-104
double	$79-119
triple	$94-134
child	$10-15

Taxes extra VS MC
Open year round

Number of rooms	7
rooms in semi-basement	1
rooms with private bath	5
shared bathrooms	1

25. ST-SAUVEUR-DES-MONTS

In the heart of the village, next to the shops and restaurants, a lovely wooden house with splendid view of the Mont Saint-Sauveur's ski runs. 4 charming rooms, equipped with AC an TV cable. From the small cozy nest...to the suite with balcony and double jacuzzi. Terraces, private swimming pool and beautiful garden. Relax and enjoy our wonderful living-room with a real log fire, anytime of the day. A delicious «home made» breakfast served at your discretion...for a smooth and relaxed wake-up! Activities : ski, dog sledding, skidoo, golf, quad, bicycle, horseback riding, water park, theatre...

From Montréal, Aut. 15 North, left at Exit 60, right on Rte 364 West, at the 2nd light, right on Rue de la Gare, left on Rue Principale, 0.4km.

B&B
LES BONHEURS DE SOPHIE

Sophie D'Hugues
342, rue Principale
Saint-Sauveur-des-Monts
J0R 1R0
(450) 227-6116
1-877-227-6116
fax (450) 227-6171
www.lesbonheursdesophie.com
*lesbonheursdesophie@
qc.aira.com*

B&B	
single	$75-140
double	$85-160
triple	$105-185
quad.	$130-210
suite	$160-210
child	$10-20

Taxes extra VS MC AM

Reduced rates: week days Apr., May, Sep., Nov., 3 nights and more except summer and holidays
Open year round

Number of rooms	4
rooms with private bath	2
shared bathrooms	1
shared wc	1

26. STE-ADÈLE

Provincial and Regional Prize for Excellence "Special Favorite" 2002. Regional and provincial winner of the 2002 "People's Special Favourite" award. Winner of the "Nuit Adeloise 2002" award. Century-old inn with rich history located along the P'tit Train du Nord bike path; cross-country skiing in winter. European furnishings. Antiques and meticulous decor. Refined breakfast, homemade goods. Two sitting rooms, fireplace, pool table, games, TV, library, terrace for sampling Belgian and microbrewed beers. Excellent restaurants nearby, renowned summer playhouses. Welcome to our home, where you will discover the charms and character of yesteryear. **See colour photos.**

From Montréal, Aut. 15 North, Exit 69, 370 East 4km.

B&B
AUBERGE DE LA GARE

Geneviève Ostrowski and
Michel Gossiaux
1694, ch. P.-Péladeau, C.P. 2587
Sainte-Adèle J8B 1Z5
(450) 228-3140
1-888-825-4273
fax (450) 228-1089
www.aubergedelagare.com
gossiauxm@qc.aira.com

	B&B	MAP
single	$57-67	$77-87
double	$65-75	$105-115

Taxes extra VS MC AM ER IT

Open: close on monday except holidays May 1 to Oct. 31.

Number of rooms	5
rooms with sink	5
shared bathrooms	3
shared wc	2

27. STE-ADÈLE

Large and majestic, this authentic Victorian house offers you the pleasure of staying in one of the beautiful homes of yesteryear. Period cachet, gourmet breakfasts, country fare, huge fireplace, extensive woodlands. Located by the linear park, near winter and summer activities. Exclusive use of the inn available for conferences, weddings and anniversaries. Dinner by reservation, groups only.

Aut. 15 North, Exit 67. At the light, right on Rue St-Joseph, right on Rue Rolland and right on Rue St-Jean. Next to the church.

INN
AUBERGE LE CLOS ROLLAND

Sylvie Garcia
1200, rue Saint-Jean
Sainte-Adèle J8B 1E6
(450) 229-2797
1-888-409-2797
fax (450) 229-2791
www.leclosrolland.ca
aubergeclosrolland@qc.aira.com

B&B	
single	$75-119
double	$85-129
triple	$95-139
quad.	$105-149
child	$0-10

Taxes extra VS MC IT

Reduced rates: 10% Apr. to June, Nov. weekdays and 3 nights and more
Open year round

Number of rooms	9
rooms with private bath	6
shared bathrooms	1
shared wc	1

28. STE-ADÈLE

Up high on the mountainside, peaceful setting near the lake, beach, Chanteclerc ski resort and restaurants. Air-conditioned B&B with European cachet, private balconies, VIP suites and splendid views! Stone chimneys, living room, large sauna, indoor spa...even snow baths. Learn a little Swiss German at breakfast!

From Montréal, Aut. 15 North. Exit 67, Rte 117, Boul. Ste-Adèle, left at the 4th light at Rue Morin, 0.3km, left Rue Ouimet, 0.2km. 4th house on your left at the end of the street.

B&B
GÎTE/AUBERGE
LA GIROUETTE DES GLOOR

Sylviane and Reinhard Gloor
941, rue Ouimet
Sainte-Adèle J8B 2R3
tel/fax (450) 229-6433
1-800-301-6433
www.lagirouette.com
la.girouette@securenet.net

	B&B
single	$55-90
double	$65-110
triple	$105-135
quad.	$120-160
child	$0-15

Taxes extra VS MC IT

Reduced rates: Apr., May and Nov.
Open year round

Number of rooms	**5**
rooms with private bath	5

---

29. STE-ADÈLE

Let yourself be amazed by this Swiss chalet and its treasures: antiques, stone fireplace, cozy rooms and an unforgettable breakfast. Offering a panoramic view of the Laurentian Mountains, facing the water slides and an interprovincial snowmobile trail (packages available), just steps away from downtown and its summer theatres, and 30 min from Mont Tremblant. Dinner available by reservation.

Aut. 15 North, Exit 67, left at the village Exit.

B&B
GÎTE DES AMÉRIQUES

Laurence and Claude Albert
1724, boul. Sainte-Adèle
Sainte-Adèle J8B 2N5
tel/fax (450) 229-9042
www.inns-bb.com/ameriques
amerique@citenet.net

	B&B
single	$40-55
double	$55-65
triple	$80
quad.	$95
child	$0-15

MC

Reduced rates: 10% 3 nights and more
Open year round

Number of rooms	**3**
rooms with sink	2
shared bathrooms	2

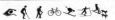

---

30. STE-AGATHE-DES-MONTS

This ancestral, New England-style home will transport you to paradise thanks to its private beach on the shore of wonderful Lac des Sables, an outdoor pool and two-acre property. Four spacious, luxurious rooms in a rich European decor with private bathroom. You'll feel like the only guest as soon as you walk in the door! Our breakfast room will amaze you thanks to its superb view of the lake and private terrace. Winter and summer sports nearby (P'tit Train du Nord path). Steps away from downtown. Restaurant packages. Massage therapist on site, by reservation. Spa nearby. **See colour photos.**

From Montréal, Aut. 15 North, Exit 83. Left at the stop sign, 2km. Right at the stop sign (Rte 329), 1,000m. L'Ancestral is on your left, as soon as you pass the lake.

B&B
ANCESTRAL B&B

Brygitte Lupien
147, St-Venant
Ste-Agathe-des-Monts J8C 2Z7
tel/fax (819) 323-3856
1-888-838-3856
www.lancestral.com
reservation@lancestral.com

	B&B
single	$100-125
double	$115-140
triple	$165-190
child	$50

Taxes extra VS MC AM IT

Reduced rates: 15% Apr. and Nov., 5% 3 nights and more
Open year round

Number of rooms	**4**
rooms with private bath	4

31. STE-AGATHE-DES-MONTS

★★★ F E P ➞➞≋ R.1

Right on the shore of Lac des Sables with 5 luxurious thematic rooms including double therapeutic bath, chimney, balcony, sound system, air conditioning, private bathroom and breakfast served in the privacy of your own room. Canoes, pedal-boats and bikes included! On site massage. Snowmobiling and winter sports nearby. 1hr from Montréal, 35 min from Tremblant. Free massages: look for the "promotion" page on our Web site. **Ad end of the guide.**

From Montréal, Aut. 15 North, Exit 86. Rte 117 North, 3rd light, left on Rue Principale, left on Rue Ste-Lucie and left on Rue Larocque

INN
AUBERGE AUX NUITS DE RÊVE

Carol McCann
14, rue Larocque Ouest
Sainte-Agathe-des-Monts
J8C 1A2
tel/fax (819) 326-5042
1-888-326-5042
www.reve.ca
auberge@reve.ca

	B&B
single	$139-149
double	$139-149

Taxes extra VS MC

Reduced rates: Sun. to Thurs., Mar. 16 to May 15, Oct. 14 to Dec. 19, Jan. 13 to Feb. 6
Open year round

Number of rooms	5
rooms with private bath	5

32. STE-AGATHE-DES-MONTS

★★★ F E P TA R1

Special Mention «Our beautiful Inns of yesteryear» success 1999. Imagine a beautiful 100-year-old house where comfort is a living tradition. A fire burning in the hearth, Swedish massages. The colours of the changing seasons. The peaceful contentment of gathering twilight. 1 hour from Montréal, 35 min from Tremblant: 12 rms, including 8 with fireplace and whirlpool bath. **Ad end of the guide.**

From Montréal, Aut. 15 North. Exit 86. Rte 117 North, at 5th light left on Rue Préfontaine, right on Chemin Tour-du-Lac.

INN
AUBERGE DE LA TOUR DU LAC

Jean-Léo Legault
173, ch. Tour-du-Lac
Sainte-Agathe-des-Monts
J8C 1B7
1-800-622-1735
(819) 326-4202
fax (819) 326-0341
www.delatour.qc.ca

	B&B
single	$73-103
double	$88-118
child	$15

Taxes extra VS MC AM ER IT

Reduced rates: Apr. and Nov.
Open year round

Number of rooms	12
rooms with private bath	12

33. STE-AGATHE-DES-MONTS

★★★ F E P ➞🐕 TA R2

Between lake and mountains, our inn offers nine rooms that were designed with care for unique style and character. Our establishment overlooks the Laurentians, offering a soothing panorama from the majestic Lac-des-Sables to the forest of Mont Sainte-Agathe. We are a few steps away from the village and many activities. Thanks to our refined, sublime breakfasts, warm and comfortable atmosphere and quality service, the Auberge has earned a three-star rating. **See colour photos.**

From Montréal, Aut. 15 North, Exit 83, left at the stop sign, 2km along Rte 329 South. Right at the stop sign, 500m along Rte 329 North, left on private road.

INN
AUBERGE LE SAINT-VENANT

Kety Kostovski and
Benoît Meyer
234, rue Saint-Venant
Sainte-Agathe-des-Monts
J8C 2Z7
1-800-697-7937
(819) 326-7937
fax (819) 326-4848
www.st-venant.com
info@st-venant.com

	B&B
single	$80-130
double	$90-140

Taxes extra VS MC AM

Reduced rates: 20% Apr. and Nov., 10% Jan.6 to Mar. 31
Open year round

Number of rooms	9
rooms with private bath	9

34. STE-AGATHE-DES-MONTS

☀☀☀☀ F E 🚫 P 🚣 🐷 R2

Regional Prize for Excellence "Special Favorite" 2001. Situated in the heart of a picturesque, quaint little village, Au Nid D'Hirondelles was built pieces on pieces. The Canadian-style decor with two fireplaces creates the atmosphere of a bygone era. In harmony with Mother Nature, we celebrate her changing seasons. After a night of restful sleep, you will be served a copious breakfast. Located between Mont-Tremblant and St-Sauveur, it's the ideal spot for sports enthusiasts and nature lovers.

From Montréal, Aut. 15 North to the end, 1km. Right on Chemin Mt-Castor, 1.5km.

B&B
AU NID D'HIRONDELLES

Suzanne and Michel Grêve
1235, rue des Hirondelles,
Mont Castor
Sainte-Agathe-des-Monts
J8C 2Z8
(819) 326-5413
1-888-826-5413
fax (819) 326-3839
www.nidhirondelles.qc.ca
gite@nidhirondelles.qc.ca

	B&B	MAP
single	$80-100	$100-120
double	$80-100	$120-140

Taxes extra VS MC
Open year round

Number of rooms	5
rooms with private bath	5

🛶 🎣 🎿 🚴 🛷 🎿

---

35. STE-AGATHE-NORD

☀☀☀ F e P 🐷 R4

Surrounded by trees and flowers on a magnificent site, our warm, antique-style home, decorated with care, will enchant you. The woodwork and soft music will brighten your stay. For your comfort, the B&B features three unique rooms with a delicate, romantic and warm ambiance. Three bathrooms, two fireplaces and a wonderful view of Lac Daoust. This is the ideal spot for hikes in the woods and for admiring the beautiful Laurentian landscape. In the morning, your hosts offer a delicious breakfast, a savoury treat before heading out. **See colour photos.**

From Montréal, Aut. 15 North. At the end of the highway, junction with Rte 117, first road to the left, Chemin Renaud, 0.5km left, Chemin Daoust.

B&B
GÎTE AUX CHAMPS DES ELFES

Louise Coté and
Richard Lussier
4420, Ch. Daoust
Ste-Agathe-des-Monts J8C 2Z8
(819) 321-0797
fax (819) 321-0934
www.gitedeselfes.com
info@gitedeselfes.com

	B&B
single	$80-100
double	$90-110
child	$10

Taxes extra

Reduced rates: 3rd night free
Open year round

Number of rooms	3
rooms in basement	2
rooms with private bath	1
shared bathrooms	1
shared wc	1

🛶 🎣 🎿 🚴 🐎 🎿

---

36. STE-AGATHE-NORD

★★ F E P 🚣 🐷 TA R5

This manor was built in 1902 for the Count d'Ivry, and we added an artist's touch to its beautiful original woodwork and stone fireplaces. The aroma of our espresso and homemade waffles will brighten your mornings. 1km from the P'tit Train du Nord path. Golf and ski packages. Whatever the season, nature and its inhabitants will enhance your stay.

From Montréal, Aut. 15 North. When the highway ends and joins Rte 117, 1st street on your left, Chemin Renaud.

INN
MANOIR D'IVRY B&B

Isabelle Taverna, Daniel Potvin,
Isabelle Giroux, Pascal Potvin
3800, chemin Renaud
Sainte-Agathe-Nord J8C 2Z8
(819) 321-0858
www.manoirdivry.com
manoirdivry@ste-agathe.net

	B&B
single	$50-55
double	$60-65

Taxes extra VS

Reduced rates: price for group, $5 off/night, 3 nights and more
Open year round

Number of rooms	9
shared bathrooms	3
shared wc	1

🛶 🎣 🎿 🚴 🚣 🎿

37. STE-LUCIE-DES-LAURENTIDES

☀☀☀ **F E P** ⛷ ✕ TA R12

National winner of the 2002 Gold "Grand Prix du Tourisme." An oasis of peace and nature, with bird sanctuary and fox den. Located on a mountain top, we offer four luxurious rooms, including a suite with sunroom, one with kitchenette and one with private balcony. Our famous breakfast with choice of dishes (pancakes, French toast, omelets, eggs Benedict, eggs with maple syrup, buckwheat cakes, etc.) and five-course candlelight dinner will win you over! Whirlpool on the terrace. **See colour photos.**

Aut. 15 North, Exit 89 twd St-Donat, travel 19km right for l'Interval, 3km right, 2nd house.

B&B
CHEZ GRAND-MÈRE ZOIZEAUX

Carole Daneau
3496, 10ième rue
Ste-Lucie-des-Laurentides
J0T 1V0
tel/fax (819) 326-8565
www.zoizeaux.com
grandmere@zoizeaux.com

	B&B	MAP
single	$60-80	$100-120
double	$70-95	$150-175
triple	$105-130	$225-250

VS MC

Reduced rates: 3 nights on weekdays except July-August

Open year round

Number of rooms	4
rooms in basement	1
rooms with private bath	2
rooms with sink	2
shared bathrooms	1

---

38. STE-MARGUERITE-DU-LAC-MASSON

☀☀☀ **F e P** ⛵ ⛷ 🐾 ✕

In a restful environment of forests and lakes, discover a spacious house, a warm interior with fireplace and the artist/host's water colours. Enjoy breakfast on the lakeside terrace and in the evening, savour traditional Belgian dishes in our restaurant. Also to be enjoyed are cycling, hiking, cross-country skiing, ice-skating, snowmobiling... 1hr from Montréal.

Aut. 15 North, Exit 69, Rte 370 East, 8km. At the "Les 2 Roses" seniors' home, left on Chemin Guénette, 4.5km.

INN
AUBERGE AU PHIL DE L'EAU

Marie-Noëlle Brassine and
Bruno Leclerre
150, chemin Guénette
Sainte-Marguerite-du-Lac-Masson J0T 1L0
(450) 228-1882
fax (450) 228-8271
www.auphildeleau.com
aubergeauphildeleau@yahoo.com

	B&B	MAP
single	$55-70	$76-98
double	$65-80	$107-136
triple	$85-90	$148-174
quad.	$105	$189-217
child	$0-15	

Taxes extra VS MC IT

Reduced rates: Mar. 15 to Apr. 30 weekdays in november

Open year round

Number of rooms	5
rooms with private bath	1
shared bathrooms	2
shared wc	2

---

39. STE-MARGUERITE-DU-LAC-MASSON

☀☀☀ **F E** 🚭 **P** 🐾 R2

"The tranquillity of the forest, the beautiful setting, the sun-lit house, the warmth of two hearths, such warm-hearted people, an extra-special breakfast. The place had it all." Here you will find the contentment of a pleasant, informal home. Near St-Sauveur and Ste-Adèle, between Montréal and Mont Tremblant. 2km from the "Bistrot Champlain".

From Montréal, Aut. 15 North, Exit 69. Rte 370, 10.5km. After the cemetery and Sommet Vert, left on Lupin. Left on Rue Des Rapides, to the end of the street.

B&B
GÎTE DU LIÈVRE

Thérèse Chouinard and
Daniel Fraser
34, rue Du Lièvre
Sainte-Marguerite-du-Lac-Masson J0T 1L0
(450) 228-1877
(514) 983-6662
pages.citenet.net/users/ctmx0131
gite_du_lievre@citenet.net

	B&B
single	$60
double	$65
triple	$80
quad.	$95

Open year round

Number of rooms	3
rooms with private bath	1
shared bathrooms	1

40. VAL-DAVID

★★★ **F** e **P** 〰 ✐ ✕ **R.5**

Come discover our charming little inn, located deep in the country, in an exceptional wooded area by the river. Cozy and gastronomic comfort await you here. On site, which is sure of success, canoeing or cycling adventure, or relaxation by the pool. Package for every season. Be on the lookout, our visitors such as the beaver and the moose can surprise you! Welcome to a world apart!

Aut. 15 North, Exit 76, Rte 117 North. After the Val David light, right on chemin de L'Île.

INN
AUBERGE CHARME DES ALPES

Béatrice and Laurent Loine
1459, rue Merette, ch. de L'Île
Val-David J0T 2N0
(819) 322-3434
(819) 323-0099
fax (819) 322-5478
www.aubergecharmedesalpes.com
info@aubergecharmedesalpes.com

	B&B	MAP
single	$75-95	$95-115
double	$85-145	$125-185
triple	$105-165	$165-225
quad.	$135-185	$215-265
child	$0	$5-15

Taxes extra VS MC IT

Reduced rates: 3 nights and more
Open year round

Number of rooms	12
rooms with private bath	12
shared wc	1

41. VAL-DAVID

★★★ **F P** ✐ ✕ **R1**

On the mountainside, discover an inn with Austrian charm and a warm, romantic ambiance. Large rooms with whirlpool and fireplace. Reputable cuisine. Pool, outdoor spa, cycling, cross-country skiing, various sports and cultural activities nearby. Olivier, the owner/chef, and his spouse Nathalie will welcome you with open arms. **See colour photos.**

Aut. 15 North, Exit 76 twd Val-David, Rte 117 North. At the 2nd light, right on Rue de l'Église, 2.8km.

INN
AUBERGE EDELWEISS

Nathalie Chenier and
Olivier Sadones
3050 ch. Doncaster
Val-David J0T 2N0
(819) 322-7800
1-866-355-7800
fax (819) 322-1550
www.ar-edelweiss.com
info@ar-edelweiss.com

	B&B	MAP
single	$80-120	$108-148
double	$100-140	$156-196
triple	$130-170	$214-254
child	$12	$24

Taxes extra VS MC AM IT

Reduced rates: Special package week-end
Open year round

Number of rooms	14
rooms with private bath	14

42. VAL-MORIN

★★ **F** E ⊘ **P** ✐ 🐑 ✕ **TA** **R1**

Recipient of the Laurentians tourism grand prize 2000 and Prize for Excellence "Special Favorite" Regional 1999. Former general store and post office. A heritage gem. A privileged site by the linear park and Lac Raymond. Free pedal-boating, canoeing and cycling. Relax on the large lakeside porches. Enjoy our 5-course breakfast and a memorable stay. Gift certificate. **See colour photos.**

From Montréal, Aut. 15 North, Exit 76. Rte 117 North, 0.5km, right on Curé-Corbeil to the end. Rght on Rue Morin, 0.5km. Left at 1st stop sign, to the end.

INN
LES JARDINS DE LA GARE

Françoise and Alain
1790, 7ᵉ Avenue
Val-Morin J0T 2R0
tel/fax (819) 322-5559
1-888-322-4273
pages.infinit.net/racetr/jardin.html

	B&B	MAP
single	$65-90	$90-115
double	$85-115	$130-160

Taxes extra VS MC IT

Reduced rates: Apr. 1 to May 1
Open year round

Number of rooms	8
rooms with private bath	3
rooms with sink	2
shared bathrooms	2
shared wc	1

43. ROSEMÈRE

F E P ... **TA** **R.1 M.3**

Century house of the French-Canadian sculptor Louis-Philippe Hébert. This magnificient home has all the modern comforts. For business meetings or family get-togethers, it can accommodate 8 people. Reflecting of our recent past, it invites you to its peaceful surroundings on the banks of the 1000 Islands River. 20 min from Montréal, 5 min from Laval. **See colour photos.**

Aut. 15 North, Exit 19. Right at stop sign, left at 1st light, 1.5km on Grande-Côte. Right on Boul. Labelle, 0.5km. Right, reception at 125 Boul. Labelle (Hôtel Le Rivage).

COUNTRY HOMES
LA MAISON DE L'ENCLOS

Christianne and
Pierre Verville
463, Île Bélair Ouest
Rosemère J7A 2G9
(450) 437-2171
1-888-437-2171
fax (450) 437-3005
www.inns-
bb.com/maisondelenclos

No. houses	2
No. rooms	1-4
No. people	2-8
WEEK-SUMMER	$1043-2450
WEEK-WINTER	$1043-2450
W/E-SUMMER	$300-700
W/E-WINTER	$300-700
DAY-SUMMER	$150-350
DAY-WINTER	$150-350

Taxes extra VS MC AM ER IT
Open year round

44. VAL-MORIN

★★★★★ **F E ⊘ P** ... **TA** **R2 M6**

An upscale chalet on a lake off-limits to power boats, 1hr North of Montréal and 40 min South of Tremblant. In summer, enjoy canoeing or dive into the lake's pure water. In winter, relax around the central fireplace after a day of skiing. Enjoy life with family and friends or a retreat with your colleagues in a rejuvenating environment. Wooded grounds, beach, three rooms with private bathroom. Specials for long stays.

Aut. 15 North, Exit 76, Rte 117 North. Follow signs for Far Hills ski resort. After Far Hills, straight ahead, 1.7km. Keep right on Chemin du Lac Lasalle twd cul-de-sac.

COUNTRY HOME
NID D'AMOUR

Lise and Camil
6455, chemin du Lac Lasalle
Val-Morin J0T 2R0
tel/fax 1-888-432-1643
www.nidamour.qc.ca
nidamour@hotmail.com

No. houses	1
No. rooms	2-3
No. people	4-8
WEEK-SUMMER	$1000-1800
WEEK-WINTER	$1000-1800
W/E-SUMMER	$300-500
W/E-WINTER	$300-500

Open year round by reservation.

AGROTOURISM

Farm Explorations:

🔔 **45**   INTERMIEL, Saint-Benoît, Mirabel .... *Page 58*

🔔 **46**   FERME DE LA BUTTE MAGIQUE, Saint-Faustin-Lac-Carré .... *Page 58*

Farm Stays:

🔔 **6**   LA CLAIRIÈRE DE LA CÔTE, L'Annonciation .... *Page 169*

Farm Shops:

🔔 **47**   AU GIBIER DU ROI, Saint-Benoît, Mirabel .... *Page 42*

🔔 **48**   VIGNOBLE DE LA RIVIÈRE DU CHÊNE, Saint-Eustache .... *Page 42*

Country-Style Dining:

🔔 **6**   LA CLAIRIÈRE DE LA CÔTE, L'Annonciation .... *Page 25*

🔔 **47**   AU GIBIER DU ROI, Saint-Benoît, Mirabel .... *Page 26*

🔔 **49**   AU PIED DE LA CHUTE, Lachute .... *Page 25*

🔔 **50**   LES RONDINS, Mirabel .... *Page 26*

🔔 **51**   LE RÉGALIN, Saint-Eustache .... *Page 27*

🔔 **52**   BASILIC ET ROMARIN, Sainte-Anne-des-Plaines .... *Page 28*

🔔 **53**   LA CONCLUSION, Sainte-Anne-des-Plaines .... *Page 28*

🔔 **54**   LA FERME DE CATHERINE, St-André-d'Argenteuil .... *Page 27*

LAVAL

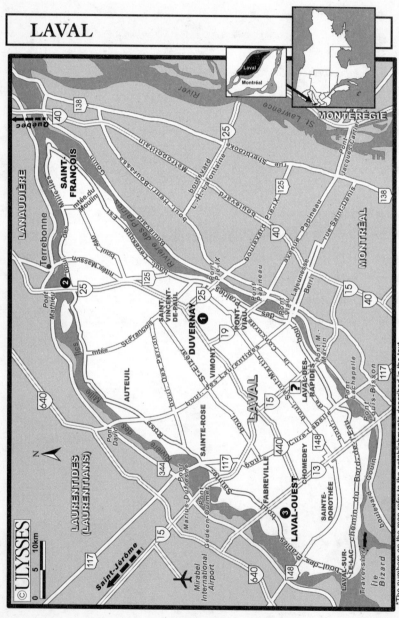

*The numbers on the map refer to the establishments described in the text.

1. LAVAL, PONT-VIAU

For tourists and business people, near the metro, the Cosmodôme and the Laval convention centre, with the park and bike path leading straight to the old port right at our doorstep. Our rooms include a magnificent suite with private bathroom and whirlpool bath. Our breakfasts are a pleasure to savour, whether inside or in a secluded garden with a pond. Free parking.

Aut. 15, Exit 7, left on .Boul. Cartier to the end, left on St-Hubert and right on Boul. Lévesque.

B&B
GÎTE DU MARIGOT

Chantal Lachapelle
128, boul. Lévesque Est
Pont-Viau, Laval H7G 1C2
(450) 668-0311
fax (450) 668-5624
www.gitedumarigot.com
gitedumarigot@sympatico.ca

B&B	
single	$50-70
double	$65-80
triple	$80-95

Taxes extra VS
Open year round

Number of rooms	4
rooms with private bath	2
rooms with sink	2
shared bathrooms	1

---

2. LAVAL, ST-FRANÇOIS

Special Mention Excellence "Achievement" 2002. Regional winner at the 2002 Québec Tourism Grand Prix. Facing Île-des-Moulins, Notre Maison sur la Rivière is sheltered by ash trees and watched over by herons. The babbling river, and nearby arts and culinary pleasures will entice you to visit our stone house, which has a fireplace and relaxing atmosphere. Air conditioned for your comfort. Our breakfasts are full of pleasant surprises. You will want to make this your first visit of many. **See colour photos.**

From Montréal, Boul. Pie IX, Rte 25, Exit 20, right Boul. des Milles-Îles, 1st stop sign, left on Rue Guglia, 1st street right Dessureaux.

B&B
NOTRE MAISON SUR LA RIVIÈRE

Viviane Charbonneau and
Serge Gaudreau
6125, rue Dessureaux
Saint-François, Laval H7B 1B1
(450) 666-4095
fax (450) 666-6383
**www3.sympatico.
ca/viviane.serge**
viviane.serge@sympatico.ca

B&B	
single	$65-70
double	$75-85

Taxes extra VS

Reduced rates: corporate rates
Open year round

Number of rooms	2
rooms with sink	2
shared bathrooms	1
shared wc	1

3. LAVAL, FABREVILLE

★ ★ ★ F e ⊘ P ⬳ TA R1 M.4

Large, furnished studio with microwave oven, coffee maker, cable TV, VCR, alarm clock, etc. Heated outdoor pool. Private parking. Landscaped backyard. Fax service. Reduced rate for 1 month or more ($45/day) and for 3 months or more ($35/day). Located less than 8 min from expressways 13 and 15. Whether for business or pleasure, enjoy quiet, cosy and comfortable accommodations. Looking forward to seeing you.

Aut. 13, Boul. Dagenais West Exit to 1st Av.

CITY HOME
POUR UN INSTANT

Lyne Léonard
780, 1ᵉ avenue
Fabreville, Laval H7R 4H2
(514) 708-2058
(450) 627-2058
fax (450) 627-0909
**www.inns-
bb.com/pour_un_instant**
pouruninstant@videotron.ca

No. houses	1
No. rooms	1
No. people	1-3
WEEK-SUMMER	$385
WEEK-WINTER	$245
W/E-SUMMER	$120
W/E-WINTER	$120
DAY-SUMMER	$60
DAY-WINTER	60

VS

Reduced rates: for one month and more
Open year round

MAURICIE

©ULYSSES

La Tuque **?**

Carignan

Lac Wawagamac

155

Rivière-aux-Rats

Grande-Anse

Lac Mékinac

Réserve faunique du Saint-Maurice

155

Saint-Joseph-de-Mékinac

Lac-aux-Sables 6

Notre-Dame-des-Anges

QUÉBEC CITY REGION

Rivière-Matawin

Saint-Roch-de-Mékinac
10

Sainte-Thècle

153

Saint-Ubalde

354

La Mauricie National Park

155 **159**

11 **Saint-Tite**
?

Saint-Adelphe

363

Réserve faunique Mastigouche

Grandes-Piles
2

Hérouxville
4 **5**

159

9

Saint-Stanislas

Sainte-Anne-de-la-Pérade
12 **?**

Lotbinière

138

132

Saint-Mathieu

? **Grand-Mère**
3

Ste-Geneviève-de-Batiscan

Deschaillons

226

Shawinigan

Shawinigan-Sud 16 17

14 15

359

Batiscan
1

Saint-Pierre-les-Becquets

351

155

Saint-Prosper-de-Champlain

Champlain

40

132

Sainte-Françoise

218

265

Saint-Paulin

55 Saint-Louis-de-France

26

Cap-de-la-Madeleine

St. Lawrence

Manseau

20

153

Sainte-Marthe-du-Cap
13

Trois-Rivières

18 to 20 **25** **?**

Bécancour

Sainte-Marie-de-Blandford

263

350

Saint-Sévère

LANAUDIÈRE

Pointe-du-Lac
21 to 23

155

Nicolet

55

261

Saint-Louis-de-Blandford

Louiseville **?**
7 **8** **24** **40**

138

Lac Saint-Pierre

132

CENTRE-DU-QUÉBEC

Saint-Wenceslas

Princeville

162

Baie-du-Febvre

161

Sainte-Eulalie

116

Berthierville
St-Ignace-de-Loyola

Pierreville

226

Sainte-Perpétue

155

20

Victoriaville

138

Sorel
Tracy

132

Saint-Elphège

259

255

122

161

N

0   10   20km

*The numbers on the map refer to the establishments described in the text.

1. BASTICAN

☀☀☀ **F** e ⊘ **P** R.5

Surrounded by silver maples, apple trees and a vast property on Rivière Batiscan, near the St. Lawrence River, this old-fashioned home offers an art and antique shop, a tearoom, intimate concerts, warmth and hearty breakfasts, a treat for the eyes and palate. Welcome to Chemin du Roy! By car, bicycle or boat. Warm reception, unforgettable stay.

From Montréal or Québec City, Rte 138 (Chemin du Roy) via Aut. 40, Exit 229 right, then left at the junction for 2km. Past the steel bridge, left for 300 metres.

B&B
LE GÎTE AU BOIS DORMANT

Ginette Lajoie
1521, rue Principale
Batiscan G0X 1A0
tel/fax (418) 362-3182
www.inns-
bb.com/giteauboisdormant

	B&B
single	$50
double	$60-65
child	$10
VS	

Open year round

Number of rooms	3
shared bathrooms	1
shared wc	1

🏛 🚤 🎿 🚶 🚴 🏊 🎿 🏃 🏂

2. GRANDES-PILES

☀☀☀ **F** E ⊘ **P** 🌊 **TA** R.1

Relive the region's history and enjoy a clear view of the St-Maurice River at our warm, ancestral B&B. Comfort, human warmth, patios, rooms with TV, delicious breakfasts, suggestions for activities, itineraries, guide service. 15 min from the national park. Four-seasons packages: meals, cruise, snowmobiling. Observation of black bears, moose, red-headed vulture. Hablamos español! **Auberge du Trappeur p 190. See ad inside the front cover.**

Halfway between Québec City and Montréal, Aut. 40, Aut. 55 North and Rte 155 North twd La Tuque/Lac-St-Jean. In the village, left at Garage Crevier.

B&B
À LA CAPITAINERIE
DU PASSANT

Anie Desaulniers
740, 3ᵉ Avenue
Grandes-Piles G0X 1H0
(819) 533-1234
1-877-213-1234
fax (819) 532-1301
www.bonjourmauricie.com
info@bonjourmauricie.com

	B&B
single	$60-85
double	$60-85
triple	$85-95
quad.	$100-110
child	$15
VS	

Reduced rates: Nov. and Apr., 2 nights and more
Open year round

Number of rooms	3
rooms with private bath	2
shared bathrooms	2

🚤 🌊 🚶 🚴 🎿 🏃 🏂

3. GRAND-MÈRE

☀☀☀ **F** e ⊘ **P** 🚍 🐎 **TA** R1

Encounter a page of history in our large, century-old house. Cosy rooms, shared or private bathroom. A large porch invites you to relax or chat with fellow guests, while a hearty breakfast complemented by homemade treats is served in the warm ambiance of the dining room. Guests also benefit from the advice of a tourist "guide." Canoe and bike at your disposal.

From Québec City, Aut. 40 West, Exit 220 twd Grand-Mère. From Montréal, Aut. 40 East, 55 North, Exit 223, 5ᵉ Av., 3km. Circle the park on your left, 1st street on your left 3ᵉ Av.

B&B
GÎTE L'ANCESTRAL

Monique Rossignol and
Jacques Brouillard
70, 3ᵉ Avenue
Grand-Mère G9T 2T3
(819) 538-7797
1-888-538-7797
www.inns-bb.com/l_ancestral
gite.l.ancestral@qc.aira.com

	B&B
single	$45-55
double	$60-70
triple	$60-75
child	$0-15

Open year round

Number of rooms	4
rooms with private bath	1
shared bathrooms	2

🍁 🚍 🚶 🚴 🐎 🏃

4. HÉROUXVILLE

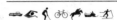

A B&B designed for young and old alike. Share in the simplicity and joie de vivre of our family enterprise in a farming environment. Let yourself be charmed by the special language of animals in a country setting, and rediscover human warmth and well-deserved rest and relaxation. Air-conditioned house and outdoor pool. Several tourist attractions nearby. **Farm Stay p 69.**

From Montréal or Québec City, Aut. 40. In Trois-Rivières, Aut. 55 North. At the end of Aut. 55, Exit Rte 153 North. In Hérouxville, cross the railway, 2km.

B&B
ACCUEIL LES SEMAILLES

Christine Naud and
Nicolas Dion
1460, rang Saint-Pierre
Hérouxville G0X 1J0
(418) 365-5190
www.inns-bb.com/semailles
christine_nicolas@hotmail.com

	B&B	MAP
single	$45	$55
double	$55	$75
child	$12	$18
Open year round		
Number of rooms		4
shared bathrooms		2

5. HÉROUXVILLE

Next to Parc de la Mauricie, a Québec house amidst flowers, lush gardens and stretches of water. A home away from home, with woodwork and cozy, attractively decorated rooms. Warm family atmosphere, very Québécois breakfasts. Reasonably priced "winter packages" (tax included) such as snowmobiling, ice fishing, dogsledding, snowshoeing and hockey. Indoor/ outdoor fireplace. Welcoming you is a pleasure.

Aut. 20 or 40, Aut. 55 North via Trois-Rivières. At the end of Aut. 55, Exit Rte 153 North. In Hérouxville, at the light, street next to the church.

B&B
MAISON TRUDEL

Nicole Jubinville and
Yves Trudel
543, rue Goulet
Hérouxville G0X 1J0
(418) 365-7624
fax (418) 365-7041
www.maison-trudel.qc.ca
maison-trudel-qc@sympatico.ca

	B&B
single	$40
double	$55
triple	$85
child	$15
VS	
Open year round	
Number of rooms	4
shared bathrooms	3

6. LAC-AUX-SABLES

In the Québec countryside, discover the Auberge Marcil, an ancestral home that was converted into an inn. Warm welcome assured. A graduate of the Institut du Tourisme et de l'Hôtellerie du Québec, Normand will make you forget all your worries as you savour his culinary delights and, especially, his pastries. On the second floor, four rooms and two shared bathrooms ensure our clients' comfort.

From Montréal, Aut. 40 East twd Trois-Rivières, 55 North twd Shawinigan. 153 North twd St-Tite, follow directions to Lac-Aux-Sables. From Québec City, Aut. 40 West, Exit 254, 363 North to Lac-aux-Sables.

B&B
AUBERGE MARCIL

Normand Marcil and Daniel Côté
930, Principale
Lac-aux-Sables G0X 1M0
(418) 336-2534
1-877-636-2534
www.aubergemarcil.com
info@aubergemarcil.com

	B&B
single	$30
double	$52
triple	$69
child	$17
Taxes extra	
Reduced rates: 1 night free for 5 nights reservation	
Open year round	
Number of rooms	4
shared bathrooms	2
shared wc	1

7. LOUISEVILLE

Built in 1858, the Victorian-era La Maison de l'Ancêtre has retained its architectural charms of yesteryear. Conveniently located 1km from downtown, it offers guests a tasteful decor with quality furnishings in a peaceful oasis. Lavish breakfast complemented by homemade goods. Your hosts' warm, heart-felt welcome awaits.

From Montréal, Aut. 40, Exit 166. Rte 138 East, 3.5km. Rte 349, Rue Notre-Dame North, 1km. From Québec City, Aut. 40, Exit 174. Rte 138 West, 4.9km, Rte 349, Rue Notre-Dame North, 1km.

B&B
LA MAISON DE L'ANCÊTRE

Julienne Leblanc
491, Notre-Dame Nord
Louiseville J5V 1X9
(819) 228-8195
www.inns-bb.com/ancetre

	B&B
single	$45-55
double	$50-60
triple	$65-75
Open year round	
Number of rooms	3
shared bathrooms	2

8. LOUISEVILLE

Comfortable, peaceful Victorian farmhouse (1880). A romantic trip back in time. Quality and harmony, it has been called "a corner of paradise" (La Presse). 10km from Ste-Ursule waterfalls, Lac St-Pierre. 6 years old, 6 prizes for excellence. **Country-Style Dining p 29. Country Home p 196.**

From Montréal or Québec City, Aut. 40, Exit 166. Rte 138 East, 2.4km to Rte 348 West. Left twd St-Ursule, 1.5km, 1st road on the right.

B&B
LE GÎTE DE LA SEIGNEURIE

Michel Gilbert
480, chemin du Golf
Louiseville J5V 2L4
(819) 228-8224
fax (819) 228-5576
www.agricotours.qc.ca/
anglais/gitedelaseigneurie
m.gilbert@infoteck.qc.ca

	B&B	MAP
single	$45-85	$65-105
double	$60-110	$100-150
triple	$90	$150
quad.	$105	$185
child	$15	$25
Taxes extra		
Open year round		
Number of rooms		5
rooms with private bath		1
shared bathrooms		2

9. ST-MATHIEU-DU-PARC

Welcome to this hospitable inn located 500 metres from Mauricie National Park! Welcoming hosts; quaint, cozy rooms; delicious breakfasts. Our kitchen specializes in game: moose, deer, quail, salmon, etc. Fireplace, Aboriginal-art shop, outdoor Greek amphitheatre! Observation: black bears, moose, beavers. Four-season packages offered on the Web, including snowmobile, snowshoeing, dog-sledding, canoe, kayak, cycling, etc. Hablamos español. 1h30 from Québec City and Montréal. **La Capitainerie du Passant p 188. See ad inside the front cover.**

90 min away from Québec City and Montréal. From Montréal, Aut. 40 East, Aut. 55 North, Exit 217, Rte 351 North. Follow directions to Parc Récréoforestier St-Mathieu.

B&B
AUBERGE DU TRAPPEUR

Mario Therrien
150, chemin St-François
St-Mathieu-du-Parc G0X 1N0
(819) 532-2600
1-866-356-2600
fax (819) 532-1301
www.bonjourmauricie.com
info@bonjourmauricie.com

	B&B	MAP
single	$65-90	$90-115
double	$65-90	$115-140
triple	$80-105	$155-180
quad.	$95-120	$195-220
child	$15	$40
Taxes extra VS MC IT		
Reduced rates: Nov. and Apr. 2 nights and more		
Open year round		
Number of rooms		5
rooms with private bath		3
shared bathrooms		2
shared wc		2

10. ST-ROCK-DE-MEKINAC

★ ★ ★ F E P 🛶 🐾 ✕ TA R10

Auberge Le Montagnard will make your dreams of staying in a real Canadian cabin come true, and with comfort to boot! Listed as the most beautiful log inn in Québec, its magical setting will seduce you. Our magnificent rooms overlook the Manigance rapids on the beautiful Saint-Maurice river. The best feature, however, is the dining room: the fine detail in the large central chimney will catch your eye. **See colour photos.**

From Montréal, Aut. 40 East, Aut. 55 North and Rte 155 North twd La Tuque, Km 39.

INN
AUBERGE LE MONTAGNARD

Edgar Borloz
3462, Route 155 (Km 39)
St-Rock-de-Mekinac G0X 2E0
(819) 646-5555
1-877-646-5550
fax (819) 646-5595
www.aubergelemontagnard.ca
info@aubergelemontagnard.ca

	B&B	MAP
single		$80
double	$92	$150
child		$40

Taxes extra VS MC IT
Open year round

Number of rooms	13
rooms in basement	2
rooms with private bath	8
shared bathrooms	2

🔥 🛶 👁 ⛷ 🐕 🔭

---

11. ST-TITE

☀ ☀ ☀ ☀ F e 🚭 P 🛶 🦌 R.4

Prize for Excellence "Special Favorite" Regional 1999. In St-Tite, a town with western cachet, discover our wooden Victorian house (1907) renowned for its warm welcome, cozy decor and lavish breakfasts. Nearby: Parc de la Mauricie, Village du Bûcheron, Cité de l'Énergie, maple grove, seaplane, dogsled. Swimming pool on site. Lucie and Réal welcome you. **See colour photos.**

From Québec City or Montréal, Aut. 40. In Trois-Rivières, Aut. 55 North, Exit Rte 153 North. In St-Tite, 500m left of the "caisse populaire".

B&B
AU GÎTE MAISON
EMERY JACOB

Lucie Verret and
Réal Trépanier
211, rue Notre-Dame
Saint-Tite G0X 3H0
(418) 365-5532
1-877-600-5532
fax (418) 365-3957
www.maisonemeryjacob.qc.ca
emeryjac@globetrotter.net

	B&B
single	$45
double	$60

VS
Open year round

Number of rooms	2
shared bathrooms	2
shared wc	1

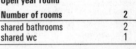

---

12. STE-ANNE-DE-LA-PÉRADE

☀ ☀ ☀ ☀ F e P 🛶 🦌 🐾 ✕ TA

Regional Prize for Excellence "Special Favorite" 2002. Finalist for the 2000 "People's Favourite" award; winner of the 2001 "People's Favourite" award. Finalist at the Gala des Radissons; first prize in 2001. Regional winner at the 2002 Québec Tourism Grand Prix. An ancestral house where time has stopped. Stay in a historic monu-ment-residence-museum and furnishings (circa 1702), part of the heritage route. Formal garden-gazebo-spa (year round), solarium. Enhance your stay with a fishing excursion ("poisson des chenaux"), 2km away. Festin du Terroir (evening); packages available.

On the Chemin du Roy, Rte 138, 2hrs from Montréal, 1hr from Québec City, via Aut. 40, Exit 236, 2km East of the church.

INN
À L'ARRÊT DU TEMPS

Serge Gervais and René Poitras
965, boul. de Lanaudière,
Chemin du Roy
Sainte-Anne-de-la-Pérade
G0X 2J0
tel/fax (418) 325-3590
www.laperade.
qc.ca/arretdutemps
arretdutemps@globetrotter.net

	B&B	MAP
single	$45-95	$63-113
double	$60-110	$96-146
triple	$75-125	$129-179
quad.	$140	$212
child	$15	

Taxes extra VS MC AM ER IT

Reduced rates: 3 nights and more
Open year round

Number of rooms	4
rooms with private bath	1
rooms with sink	4
shared bathrooms	2
shared wc	2

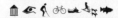

13. STE-MARTHE-DU-CAP

☀☀☀ F e ⊘ P ≋ ✕ R3

Shaded by the most beautiful maples in Québec, this beautiful farmhouse reveals a history lived by a family that is modest yet rich in personality. Plain on the outside but warm within. A patio perfect for conversation; in the back: BBQ, tables and swings for picnics between friends, summer kitchen for an extended breakfast, farm tours, stroll on the trail that inspired Félix Leclerc. Access to the river, bike path, golf, snowmobile trail and more. See you soon!

From Montréal, Aut. 40, Exit 205, twd Ste-Marthe, Rte 138. From Québec City, Exit 220 twd Champlain, right.

B&B
LA MAISON DES LECLERC

Georgie and Michel Leclerc
2821, Notre-Dame
Sainte-Marthe-du-Cap G8V 1Y8
(819) 379-5946
(819) 374-8441
www.inns-bb.com/leclerc
maisondesleclerc@videotron.ca

	B&B
single	$50
double	$65
child	$10

Reduced rates: 10% 2 nights and more

Open year round

Number of rooms	4
rooms with sink	1
shared bathrooms	2

---

14. SHAWINIGAN

☀☀☀☀ F E P 🛏 🐾 R2

Gîte du Manoir Kane is steps away from the Cité de l'Énergie and the downtown area, on the most beautiful street in Shawinigan. This Tudor mansion will enchant you with its decor, charm and peaceful atmosphere. Enjoy delicious breakfasts in a historical setting. Your hosts, Céline and Guy.

From Québec City or Montréal, Aut. 40 twd Trois-Rivières, Aut. 55 North twd Shawinigan, right at Exit 211. Right at the first light, first street to your right before the viaduct.

B&B
GÎTE DU MANOIR KANE

Céline and Guy Bilodeau
1162 des Érables
Shawinigan G9N 1B2
(819) 537-8931
www.inns-bb.com/manoirkane
manoirkane@caramail.com

	B&B
single	$55-60
double	$60-70

Reduced rates: Oct. 15 to May 31 except holidays

Open year round

Number of rooms	2
shared bathrooms	1
shared wc	1

---

15. SHAWINIGAN

☀☀☀☀ F e ⊘ P 🦌 R1

Upon encountering this lovely Victorian house, you will be delighted by its reserved charm, comfort and breakfasts, not to mention your hosts' warm welcome. A stone's throw from downtown, near Cité de l'Énergie and the bike path, 20 min from La Mauricie National Park.

Halfway between Québec City and Montréal, Aut. 40, Aut. 55 North, Exit 211 twd Shawinigan. At 1st light, right on Rue de la Station. After the viaduct, right. Pass over the viaduct and head twd Hemlock.

B&B
LA MAISON SOUS LES ARBRES

Denise Olivier and
Robert Tessier
1002, av. Hemlock
Shawinigan G9N 1S7
(819) 537-6413
www.maisonsouslesarbres.com
robert.tessier@sh.cgocable.ca

	B&B
single	$60-90
double	$60-90
triple	$75-105
quad.	$90-120

Reduced rates: 15 % Oct. 15 to May 31

Open year round

Number of rooms	3
shared bathrooms	2
shared wc	1

16. SHAWINIGAN-SUD

☀☀☀ **F E ⊘ P** R.5

In the heart of town and next to "La Cité de L'Énergie", a bicycle path, nearby and several activities, we are reserving you a warm welcome and a special breakfast. It will be a pleasure to accommodate you!

From Trois-Rivières, Aut. 55 North, Exit 211 twd Shawinigan-Sud, after Cité de L'Énergie, 1st light, left, 109ᵉ Rue, continue twd right for 110ᵉ Rue.

B&B
LE GÎTE DU SUD

Simone Forest and
Claude Pruneau
630, 110ᵉ Rue
Shawinigan-Sud G9P 2R5
(819) 536-0109
www.gitedusud.com
simoneforest@sympatico.ca

	B&B
single	$40
double	$50
child	$10

Reduced rates: 20% Sept. 15 to Nov. 1
Open: June 1 to Nov. 1

Number of rooms	3
shared bathrooms	2

17. SHAWINIGAN-SUD

☀☀☀ **F E P** ~~ 🐾 TA R1

Regional Prize for Excellence "Special Favorite" 2001 and 2001 Grand Prix Tourisme. Pamper yourself at the cosy refuge of two artists, and retire to apartments that were born of a dream. Discover Cité de l'Énergie and the national park. Private living room with fireplace, bathrooms with shower or whirlpool, pool, breakfast on the terrace. All that's missing... is you.

Aut. 55 North, Exit 211, twd Shawinigan-Sud. After Cité de l'Énergie, 1st Exit on your right, Boul. Capitaine Veilleux, 2km, left on Rue Lacoursière (119ᵉ Rue). 2nd stop, right on Rue Adrienne-Choquette. Right on Rue Albert-Dufresne.

B&B
LES P'TITS POMMIERS

Michelle Fortin and
Jean-Louis Gagnon
2295, rue Albert-Dufresne
Shawinigan-Sud G9P 4Y6
(819) 537-0158
1-877-537-0158
fax (819) 537-4839
www.inns-bb.com/pommiers
pommiers@yahoo.com

	B&B
single	$45
double	$55
child	$10

VS
Open year round

Number of rooms	3
rooms in semi-basement	3
shared bathrooms	2

18. TROIS-RIVIÈRES

☀☀☀☀ **F E ⊘ P ✗** TA

Our beautiful Victorian inn is nestled in the centre of town, on the way into historic Trois-Rivières, on a secluded, shady street. Rich oak woodwork, bevelled doors, gilding and lovely moulding, handed down from the old aristocracy. The elegant dining room, with its lustrous chandelier, lacework and old lamps is open to the public. Parking and air conditioning.

Aut. 40 Exit Trois-Rivières downtown. To Notre-Dame. Left on Rue Radisson.

INN
AUBERGE DU BOURG

Jean-Marc Beaudoin
172, rue Radisson
Trois-Rivières G9A 2C3
(819) 373-2265
(819) 379-9198
www.inns-bb.com/bourg

	B&B	MAP
single	$50-70	$65-85
double	$60-80	$90-110

Taxes extra VS MC AM IT
Open year round

Number of rooms	4
rooms with private bath	2
rooms with sink	2
shared bathrooms	1
shared wc	2

19. TROIS-RIVIÈRES

☀ ☀ ☀ **F** e ⊘ **P** ⟷ **TA** R.3

Family property! Grandpa Beau would be proud, his house welcomes so many people! Spacious, attractively decorated home whose attic rooms bring back wonderful childhood memories. You'll enjoy a generous breakfast complemented with garden-fresh vegetables. Near all tourist attractions and the university.

From Québec City, Aut. 40 West, Exit 199, to downtown, right on Rue Ste-Marguerite, 2km. From Montréal, Aut. 40, Exit 199. At 2nd light, left on Rue Ste-Marguerite, 2km.

B&B
CHEZ GRAND'PAPA BEAU

Carmen and Yvon Beaudry
3305, rue Sainte-Marguerite
Trois-Rivières G8Z 1X1
(819) 693-0385
www3.sympatico.ca/grandpapabeau/gite
grandpapabeau@sympatico.ca

	B&B
single	$45-55
double	$55-65
triple	$75
quad.	$95

VS

Open year round

Number of rooms	4
shared bathrooms	2

🏛 ⟷ 👁 🎿 🚴 🏃

20. TROIS-RIVIÈRES

☀ ☀ ☀ ☀ **F** **E** **P** ⟷ **TA** R.1

This beautiful home, located on the shore of the St. Lawrence River, offers comfort, tranquillity, safety, air conditioning, parks, gardens and a large pool... not to mention great ambiance and decor. La Presse described it as "the Mercedes of B&B." Renowned and appreciated for its reception and gourmet breakfast. Good place for get-togethers with family or friends. One French guide commented: "In short, an excellent place for the price". More information in the "Downtown Apartment" section. **City Home p 196.**

From Aut. 55, Exit 181, Rue Notre-Dame, left Rte 138 East, about 1km. At McDonald's, right on Rue Garceau. Right on Rue Notre-Dame.

B&B
GÎTE SAINT-LAURENT

Yolande and René Bronsard
4551, rue Notre-Dame
Trois-Rivières Ouest G9A 4Z4
tel/fax (819) 378-3533
1-866-866-3533
www.iquebec.com/bbsaintlaurent
rene.bronsard@sympatico.ca

	B&B
single	$50-60
double	$65-75
triple	$90-105
quad.	$105-120

Taxes extra VS

Reduced rates: Nov. 1 to Apr. 30
Open year round

Number of rooms	5
rooms with private bath	1
rooms with sink	5
shared bathrooms	2
shared wc	3

⟷ 👁 🎿 🚴 🛷 🐟

21. TROIS-RIVIÈRES, POINTE-DU-LAC

★ ★ ★ 🍽 **F** e **P** ⟷ 🐕 ✕ **TA**

Let us share a corner of paradise on the St. Lawrence River! You will appreciate the beauty and peacefulness of this Lac St-Pierre bay yearound. Energised by home-style, gourmet French cuisine, tackle our local nature-based activities, enjoy well-deserved, pleasurable idleness by the pool or productive work in the meeting room. The phone number 866 is tool free.

From Montréal, Aut. 40 East, Exit 187, Rte 138 East, 7km. From Québec City, Aut. 40 West and 55 South, Notre-Dame Exit, Rte 138 West, 5km.

INN
AUBERGE BAIE-JOLIE

Françoise and Jean-Marie Roux
709, rue Notre-Dame, route 138
Pointe-du-Lac G0X 1Z0
(819) 377-2226
1-866-302-2226
fax (819) 377-4221
www.baie-jolie.com
auberge@baie-jolie.com

	B&B	MAP
single	$55-65	$75-85
double	$75-85	$115-125
triple	$95-105	$155-165
quad.	$115	$195
child	$15	$25

Taxes extra VS MC IT

Reduced rates: special low season
Open year round

Number of rooms	11
rooms with private bath	11

⟷ 🎿 🏃 🚴 🛷 🔭 🐟

22. TROIS-RIVIÈRES, POINTE-DU-LAC

☀ ☀ ☀ **F E P** ⇌ **TA** **R.3**

An oasis of peace on the shore of the St. Lawrence River and Lac St-Pierre, 9km from Vieux Trois-Rivières and its port. Vast, shaded park ideal for relaxation. Large, beautiful rooms, private baths, view of the river. Chalet-style studio, fully equipped with large terrace. Hearty breakfast made to order. Organised tours yearound. "French fine dining" restaurant, golf package. Discounts for long stays. Tips for discovering this magnificent region. Free Internet access. Welcome to our home.

From Montréal, Aut. 40 East, Exit 187. Rte 138 East, 7km. From Mirabel, Aut. 15 South, 640 East, 40 East... From Québec City, Aut. 40 West and 55 South, Exit 181, Rte 138 West, 5.5km.

B&B
GÎTE BAIE-JOLIE

Barbara and Jacques Piccinelli
711, rue Notre-Dame, route 138
Pointe-du-Lac G0X 1Z0
tel/fax **(819) 377-3056**
1-877-271-4341
www.baie-jolie.com
gite@baie-jolie.com

	B&B
single	$45-50
double	$65-80
triple	$85-105
quad.	$100-125
child	$12

VS

Reduced rates: Oct. 31 to Apr. 15 and long stay
Open: Dec.1 to Oct. 31

Number of rooms	3
rooms with private bath	3

23. TROIS-RIVIÈRES, POINTE-DU-LAC

☀ ☀ ☀ ☀ **F** e ⊘ **P** ⇌ **R2**

Prize for Excellence "Special Favorite" Regional 2000 and 1997-98. This B&B in the country side is just 10 min from Trois-Rivières. Enjoy calm, rest, a warm welcome and unforgettable gourmet breakfasts in our secluded Canadian house. Enchanting decor, flowery gardens, living room, air conditioning, fireplace, therapeutic bath, indoor pool, yearound. Inexpensive dream stay.

From Montréal, Aut. 40 East, Exit 187. Rte 138 East, 7km, left on Rue des Saules (at the end). From Québec City, Aut. 40 West, Aut. 55 South, Notre-Dame Exit, Rte 138 West, 5km. Right on Rue des Saules.

B&B
SOLEIL LEVANT

Léonie Lavoie and Yves Pilon
300, av. des Saules
Pointe-du-Lac G0X 1Z0
tel/fax **(819) 377-1571**
1-877-876-5345
www.inns-bb.com/soleillevant
gitesoleillevant@qc.aira.com

	B&B
single	$50-55
double	$60-70
child	$15

Reduced rates: 2 nights and more Nov. 1 to May 1
Open year round

Number of rooms	3
shared bathrooms	2

24. LOUISEVILLE

F e P ⊷ TA R1 M1.5

Heritage home located on a farm surrounded by large gardens of yesteryear. Take advantage of the gardens and tend your own! Ideal place to get into gardening or learn more. Gardening library. All-season guided excursions: hiking, canoeing, fishing, biking, snowshoeing, dogsledding... Ste-Ursule waterfalls, Lac St-Pierre. **B&B p 190. Country-Style Dining p 29.**

From Montréal or Québec City, Aut. 40, Exit 166, Rte 138 East, 2.4km, Rte 348 West. Left twd Ste-Ursule, 1.5km, 1st road on the right.

COUNTRY HOME
LA MAISON DU JARDINIER

Michel Gilbert
480, chemin du Golf
Louiseville J5V 2L4
(819) 228-8224
fax (819) 228-5576
www.agricotours.qc.ca/ anglais/gitedelaseigneurie
m.gilbert@infoteck.qc.ca

No. houses	1
No. rooms	3
No. people	4
WEEK-SUMMER	$400
WEEK-WINTER	$400
DAY-WINTER	100

Taxes extra
Open year round

25. TROIS-RIVIÈRES

F E P ⊷ ≋ TA R.1 M.1

This lovely loft near the pool is found on the most beautiful site in Trois-Rivières West. Generous continental breakfast; several discount coupons for outdoor activities, restaurants and tourist attractions. Vieux Trois-Rivières is 5min away, the university 7min, restaurants 1min, shops and movie theatre 2min, Mauricie National Park 45min. (See Gîte Saint-Laurent since the loft is part of the B&B.) Look for our packages on our Web site. **B&B p 194.**

Aut. 55, Exit 181, Rue Notre-Dame. Left on Rte 138 East for about 1km. At McDonald's, right on Rue Garceau, right on Rue Notre-Dame.

B&B
APPARTEMENT DU
CENTRE-VILLE

Yolande and René Bronsard
4551, rue Notre-Dame
Trois-Rivières Ouest G9A 4Z4
tel/fax (819) 378-3533
1-866-866-3533
www.iquebec.com/bbsaint-laurent
rene.bronsard@sympatico.ca

No. houses	1
No. rooms	1
No. people	1-5
WEEK-SUMMER	$525-840
WEEK-WINTER	$420-595
W/E-SUMMER	$225-360
W/E-WINTER	$180-300
DAY-SUMMER	$75-130
DAY-WINTER	$60-100

Taxes extra VS
Open year round

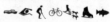

AGROTOURISM

Farm Stays:

🛖 4   ACCUEIL LES SEMAILLES, Hérouxville...*Page 69*

Farm Shops:

🛖 26   FERME LA BISONNIÈRE, St-Prosper-de-Champlain...*Page 43*

Country-Style Dining:

🛖 8   LA TABLE DE LA SEIGNEURIE, Louiseville ....*Page 29*

Hand *in* hand
with nature...

Tourisme
mauricie
www.icimauricie.com
1 800 567-7603

La Mauricie,
one **region**
a **thousand passions**!

MONTÉRÉGIE

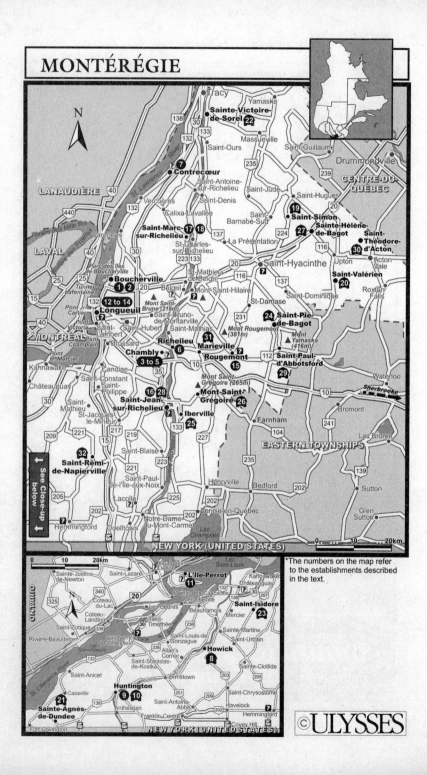

Tracy
Yamaska
Sainte-Victoire-de-Sorel **22**
138 30
133
132
Massueville
Saint-Ours
Saint-Guillaume
235
Drummondville
239
7 Contrecœur
Saint-Antoine-sur-Richelieu
Saint-Jude
Saint-Hugues
CENTRE-DU-QUÉBEC
LANAUDIÈRE 40
Verchères
132
Saint-Denis
20
Calixa-Lavallée
Saint-Barnabé-Sud
19 Saint-Simon
224 **27**
Sainte-Hélène-de-Bagot
Saint-Théodore-d'Acton
Saint-Marc-sur-Richelieu **17 18**
137
La Présentation
116
30
Acton Vale
St-Charles-sur-Richelieu
223 133
St-Mathieu-de-Beloeil
Saint-Hyacinthe
Upton
Saint-Valérien **20**
LAVAL
Rivière des Mille Îles
Rivière des Prairies
Varennes
40
30
Boucherville **1 2**
Beloeil
20
116
137
Saint-Dominique
Roxton Falls
25
Parc des Îles de Boucherville
Mont-Saint-Hilaire
12 to 14
Mont Saint-Bruno (218m)
St-Damase
231
24 Saint-Pie-de-Bagot
15
Tunnel Lafontaine
Pont J.-Cartier
132
Longueuil
Saint-Bruno-de-Montarville
Mont Rougemont (381m)
Mont Yamaska (416m)
40
Pont Victoria
Saint-Lambert
Saint-Hubert
Saint-Mathias
MONTRÉAL
Pont Champlain
Brossard
Richelieu **6**
31
Marieville
112
Saint-Paul-d'Abbotsford
Pont H.-Mercier
Candiac
Chambly
3 to 5
35
Rougemont
15
29
Kahnawake
Saint-Constant
Saint-Philippe
10
Mont Saint-Grégoire (265m)
Waterloo
Sherbrooke
Châteauguay
Saint-Mathieu
16 28
Mont-Saint-Grégoire **26**
10
Bromont
St-Jacques-le-Mineur
Saint-Jean-sur-Richelieu
Iberville
Farnham
241
Lac Brome
209 221
217 219
25
EASTERN TOWNSHIPS
15
Saint-Blaise
133
227
104
235
Sutton
32
Saint-Rémi-de-Napierville
221
Saint-Paul-de-l'Île-aux-Noix
139
205
202
Lacolle
225
Henryville
Bedford
202
Glen Sutton
See Close-up below
Hemmingford
Odelltown
Notre-Dame-du-Mont-Carmel
202
Venise-en-Québec
Lac Champlain
NEW YORK (UNITED STATES)
0   10   20km

0   10   20km
ONTARIO
Sainte-Justine-de-Newton
Saint-Lazare
Vaudreuil-Dorion
Lac Saint-Louis
L'Île-Perrot
11
Kahnawake
Châteauguay
340
325
Coteau-du-Lac
20
Pointe-des-Cascades
Melocheville
132
138
207
30
Saint-Isidore **23**
Coteau-Landing
Les Cèdres
Beauharnois
Mercier
Saint-Zotique
338
Saint-Timothée
236
Sainte-Martine
Rivière-Beaudette
30
Salaberry-de-Valleyfield
Canal
Saint-Louis-de-Gonzague
Saint-Urbain
236
Allan's Corner
Howick **8**
Saint-Anicet
Saint-Stanislas-de-Kostka
203
Sainte-Clotilde
Rivière
Ormstown
205
Huntington **9 10**
Saint-Antoine-Abbé
209
Saint-Chrysostome
21
Cazaville
138
Anthelstan
Saint-Antoine-Abbé
202
Havelock
Sainte-Agnès-de-Dundee
Franklin Centre
Hemmingford
Fort Covington
Covey Hill
NEW YORK (UNITED STATES)

*The numbers on the map refer to the establishments described in the text.

ⒸULYSSES

1. BOUCHERVILLE

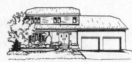 **F E ⊘ P** 🏊 ⛵ **TA R1**

Located 15 min from Montréal, near services. Quiet area facing a bike path. Large, air-conditioned rooms with private bathrooms and TV. In the summer, you can enjoy a lavish breakfast by the pool on our superb covered terrace. Large parking lot. Warm welcome from your hosts Johanne and Michel yearound. Welcome. See you soon.

From Montréal, L.-H. Lafontaine tunnel. Aut. 20, Exit 92, left on Boul. Mortagne, 3km. From Québec City, Aut. 20, Exit 92, Boul. Mortagne East, 3km.

B&B
LA BOUCHERVILLOISE

Johanne and Michel Leverne
605, boul. de Mortagne
Boucherville J4B 5E4
tel/fax (450) 449-6237
(514) 817-1579
pages.infinit.net/boucherv
bouchervilloise@videotron.ca

	B&B
single	$50-60
double	$65-75
child	$0-15

VS

Open year round

Number of rooms	3
rooms with private bath	3

🏊 🏃 🚶 🚴 🏇 ⛷ 🎿

---

2. BOUCHERVILLE

 **F E ⊘ P** 🏊 ⛵ 🦌 **TA R.5**

A welcoming house located 15 min from Montreal's attractions, with three inviting rooms, varied gourmet breakfasts, outdoor swimming pool and terrace, living room with TV, music, reading. Air conditioning. Bike paths. Public transportation. metro. Parking. See you soon!

From Montréal, L.-H. Lafontaine tunnel, Aut. 20, Exit 90, twd Rte 132 East-Varennes, Exit 17. At the stop sign, right on Rue Marie-Victorin, 1st left on Rue Fréchette, 1st left on Rue Jean-Talon, 2nd right on Denis-Véronneau.

B&B
SONNEZ LES MATINES

Ginette Poirier
217, rue Denis-Véronneau
Boucherville J4B 8L7
(450) 655-1112
fax (450) 655-3306
www.sonnezlesmatines.com
info@sonnezlesmatines.com

	B&B
single	$45-55
double	$60-70
triple	$85
quad.	$100
child	$10

VS MC

Open year round

Number of rooms	3
shared bathrooms	2
shared wc	1

🏛 🚶 🏃 🚶 🚴 🎿 🔭

---

3. CHAMBLY

 **F E ⊘ P** 🏊 ⛵ **TA R.2**

In Vieux-Chambly, just steps away from tourist attractions, our B&B blends modern comfort with old-world charm, with a collection of antiques, spacious air-conditioned rooms, private bathrooms and therapeutic bath. Delicious breakfast served on the terrace or in the dining room. Relax to soft music in our yearound spa. Massotherapy/body-care packages available.

Aut. 10, Exit 22 or Rte 112 or 223. Follow signs twd Fort-Chambly.

B&B
À LA CLAIRE FONTAINE

Isabelle Frenette and
Gilles Landry
2130, av. Bourgogne
Chambly J3L 1Z7
(450) 447-7940
http://pages.infinit.net/alaclair
alaclairefontaine@videotron.ca

	B&B
single	$50-65
double	$70-90
child	$20

Taxes extra VS MC IT

Reduced rates: 20 % 3 nights and more Oct. 1 to Apr. 1
Open year round

Number of rooms	4
rooms with private bath	2
shared bathrooms	1

🍁 🚶 🚴 🏇 ⛷ ⛳ ⛸

4. CHAMBLY

☀☀☀☀ **F e ⊘ P** TA R.2

Recipient of the Lauréat Grand Prix du Tourisme Montérégie 2000 and the provincial "Réussite" award of excellence 1999. Located 20 min from Montréal, 1914 Victorian house with old-fashioned woodwork, fireplace, French doors and mouldings. Lounge by the water, where relaxation and escape are guaranteed; the change of scenery and magical setting will make for an unforgettable stay. Breakfast on the veranda, offering a breathtaking view of the mountains and water merging in the distance. Our sunsets are unmatched! Boat dock, air conditioning. By reservation in low season. **See colour photos and front cover.**

From Montréal, Aut. 10, Exit 22, Boul. Fréchette to the end. Follow the signs. Next to St-Joseph's church.

B&B
AUBERGE L'AIR DU TEMPS

Lucie Chrétien and
Daniel Desgagné
124, rue Martel
Chambly J3L 1V3
(450) 658-1642
1-888-658-1642
fax (450) 658-2830
www.airdutemps.qc.ca
hote@airdutemps.qc.ca

	B&B
single	$70
double	$79-89
triple	$114
quad.	$139

Taxes extra VS AM
Open year round close Nov. 20 to Dec. 20 and Mar. 15 to Apr. 15

Number of rooms	5
rooms with private bath	5

5. CHAMBLY

☀☀☀☀☀ **F E P** 🛶 〰 R.2

This old Fort Chambly officer's residence, transformed into a luxurious manor, offers a panoramic view, a superb ambiance and exceptional comfort. Make it a base to visit Montréal (20 min) and the Valley of Forts, and let yourself be serenaded by the songs of the rapids or the flames of the 3 fireplaces. Spacious rooms with TV and modem access. Air conditioned rooms. Gastronomic breakfast. Free access to our outdoor tennis club. Rated 3 diamonds by the AAA (CAA). Air conditioned rooms. **See colour photos.**

Aut. 10, Exit 22, or Rte 112 or Rte 223. Follow the signs twd Fort Chambly. The Maison Ducharme is next to the guardhouse.

B&B
LA MAISON DUCHARME

Danielle Deland and
Edouard Bonaldo
10, rue de Richelieu
Chambly J3L 2B9
(450) 447-1220
1-888-387-1220
fax (450) 447-1018
www.maisonducharme.ca
maisonducharme@videotron.ca

	B&B
single	$95-120
double	$115-140
triple	$140-165
child	$25

Taxes extra VS MC AM

Reduced rates: Oct. 13 to Apr. 30
Open year round

Number of rooms	4
rooms with private bath	4

6. CHAMBLY, RICHELIEU

☀☀☀☀ **F e ⊘ P** 〰 ✕ R3

Located on the banks of the Richelieu river, in a Victorian house, the La Jarnigoine inn offers guests the peacefulness of the countryside, just a few km from Montréal. In the evening, take advantage of our refined table d'hôte featuring local products and traditional French cuisine. By reservation only. **See colour photos.**

Aut. 10, Exit 29, Rte 133 twd Richelieu, left on Rte 112 and left at the 1st street. Or Aut. 20, Exit 113, Rte 133, right on Rte 112 and left at the 1st street.

INN
AUBERGE LA JARNIGOINE

Sébastien Bélair and
Roger René Villeneuve
1156, 1re Rue
Richelieu J3L 3W8
(450) 658-8031
(514) 573-0689
www.lajarnigoine.com
jarnigoi@dsuper.net

	B&B
single	$60-80
double	$80-120

Taxes extra VS MC IT
Open year round

Number of rooms	3
rooms with private bath	1
shared bathrooms	1

7. CONTRECOEUR

 F E Ⓢ P 🚤 R.1

Are you looking for an escape from the hectic pace of life today? Do you want to have a great time and be pampered? Then succumb to the allure of our charming B&B, which offers a friendly and cosy ambiance, and a kitchen full of exciting flavours. Imagine listening to music by candlelight, lounging in a hammock, relaxing in a pool, reading in a garden, going on a pedal-boat trip to some islands, or cycling on a country road. Let all your worries trickle off you like water off a duck's back.

From Montréal, Aut. 20 and 30 East, Exit 158, Rte 132 East, 1.6km.

B&B
LES MALARDS

Hélène Delisle
4741, rue Marie-Victorin
Contrecoeur J0L 1C0
(450) 587-5581
(514) 953-2307
www.inns-bb.com/malards
les.malards@enter-net.com

B&B	
single	$55-70
double	$80-105
triple	$125
quad.	$145

VS MC

Reduced rates: Nov. 1 to May 31
Open year round

Number of rooms	4
rooms with private bath	1
rooms with sink	2
shared bathrooms	2

---

8. HOWICK

 f E Ⓢ P 🚤 🐑 R3

Welcome to our 150 acres fifth generation dairy farm. Enjoy feeding cows and small animals during milking. Take a hay ride, sit by the campfire, stroll the spacious lawn and view the many flower gardens or relax by the inground pool. Quiet area for cycling. A delicious breakfast of home-made specialties. Smoke free B&B. **Farm Stay p 70.**

From Montréal, Mercier Bridge, Aut. 138 West to Rte 203 South. Right twd Howick, cross the Bridge, make two left turns on Rue Lambton. Take English River Road 2km.

B&B
HAZELBRAE FARM

Gloria and John Peddie
1650, English River Road
Howick J0S 1G0
(450) 825-2390
www.inns-bb.com/hazelbraefarm

	B&B	MAP
single	$35	$40
double	$60	$80
child	$10	$15

Open year round

Number of rooms	3
rooms with private bath	1
shared bathrooms	2
shared wc	1

---

9. HUNTINGDON

★ ★ ★ F E P ✕ R.2

Located in the heart of the Chateauguay valley, in the Suroît region, this Georgian style farm house was built in 1835. Guests are welcomed all year in our Country Inn and are charmed by the atmosphere of the old days and the comfort of their private suites. Fine dining can be enjoyed in the field stone barn, which was renovated into a restaurant know as "The Ruins". Activities close by.

From Montréal, Rte 138 West twd Huntingdon, 1km after the village of Huntingdon.

INN
AUBERGE HÉRITAGE
COUNTRY INN

Markus Ritter
2678, Route 138 Ouest
Huntingdon J0S 1H0
tel/fax (450) 264-3123
www.heritageinn.qc.ca
mail@heritageinn.qc.ca

	B&B
single	$59
double	$69
child	$15

Taxes extra VS MC IT
Open year round

Number of rooms	14
rooms with private bath	14

10. HUNTINGDON

F e ⊘ P ⟋

Provincial Prize for Excellence, "Special Favorite", Country-Style Dining 2002. Our ancestral home awaits you. Overnight stays must be combined with our country-dining experience; we offer guests exclusive access to the site for utmost peace and well-being. **Country-Style Dining p 30. See colour photos.**

From Montréal, Rte 138 West twd Huntingdon. 9km past the Ormstown stop, right on Chemin Seigneurial, travel 4.7km, left on Chemin de la Templerie, 350m to the stop sign, New Erin, 1km.

B&B
DOMAINE DE LA TEMPLERIE

Denise Asselin, Roland and François Guillon
312, chemin New Erin
Godmanchester (Huntingdon)
J0S 1H0
tel/fax (450) 264-9405
www.agricotours.qc.ca/ anglais/templerie

	B&B
single	$40-45
double	$45-50
Taxes extra	
Open year round	
Number of rooms	3
shared bathrooms	1
shared wc	1

11. L'ÎLE-PERROT

F E P ⟋ 🐾 R4

Situated on Lac Deux-Montagnes in the middle of the wilderness, our B&B offers a beautiful view facing the north: Oka, the L'Îsle aux Tourtes bridge and some small colourful islands. It also offers peace and tranquillity with a large landscaped property and some magnificent places to relax by the water's edge.

Aut. 20 West, right at the 1st light when you arrive on Île Perrot, after the train track, 1.6km. Right on Roy. Last house by the water.

B&B
GÎTE DE L'ÎLE

Nicole Frappier
10, rue Roy
L'Île-Perrot J7V 8W3
tel/fax (514) 425-0965
(514) 592-2248
www.inns-bb.com/gitedelile

	B&B
single	$60
double	$75
Open year round	
Number of rooms	2
shared bathrooms	2

12. LONGUEUIL

☀☀☀ F E ⊘ P TA R.1

On the South Shore, 10 min from downtown Montréal, near the metro in the heart of Vieux Longueuil. This welcoming home on a quiet street is conducive to relaxation in a warm atmosphere. Come as you are and enjoy its charming rooms and a hearty breakfast. Air conditioning, gas fireplace in the living room.

From Montréal, Jacques-Cartier bridge, keep left, Rte 132. From Aut. 20, Exit 8, right on Rue St-Charles, right on Quinn at the Esso, 100m. Ste-Élizabeth, on the left.

B&B
À LA BRUNANTE

Louise Bélisle
480, rue Sainte-Élisabeth
Longueuil J4H 1K4
(450) 442-7691
www.inns-bb.com/brunante
guy.marion@sympatico.ca

	B&B
single	$50-60
double	$60-75
triple	$75
child	$20
Open year round	
Number of rooms	2
rooms with sink	1
shared bathrooms	2

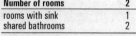

13. LONGUEUIL

Upscale B&B surrounded by restaurants located in the heart of Vieux-Longueil and a few min from Montréal, the metro and the river shuttle. Romantic, air-conditioned rooms with private bathroom and entrance. Let yourself be charmed by our flowery garden and waterfall in the middle of an oasis. Your hosts live upstairs to better respect your privacy. See you soon!

From Montréal, Jacques-Cartier Bridge, St-Charles Exit. Behind city hall.

B&B
À L'OASIS DU
VIEUX-LONGUEUIL

Ginette and Luc Desbiens
316, rue de Longueuil
Longueuil J4H 1H4
(450) 670-9839
pages.infinit.net/loasis
luc.ginette@videotron.ca

	B&B
single	$60-75
double	$65-80

VS MC AM

Reduced rates: long stay and business people
Open year round

Number of rooms	3
rooms with private bath	3

---

14. LONGUEUIL

Enjoy a poetic ambiance in a warm, century home in the heart of Vieux Longueuil. Beautifully decorated, air-conditioned rooms. Exquisite breakfasts hosted by Loulou and served on the terrace in summer and by the fire in winter. Near bike paths and downtown Montréal by metro or ferry. Excellent quality/price ratio. Looking forward to meeting you!

From Montréal, Jacques-Cartier Bridge, keep left, Exit Rte 132 or Aut. 20 immediately right, Exit Rue St-Charles. From Rte 132, Exit 8. Rue St-Charles and right on Rue St-Jean. Located behind Longueuil city hall.

B&B
LE REFUGE DU POÈTE

Louise Vézina
320, rue de Longueuil
Longueuil J4H 1H4
(450) 442-3688
fax (450) 442-4782
www.inns-bb.com/refugedupoete

	B&B
single	$50-60
double	$60-70
triple	$70-80
quad.	$90
child	$10

VS

Reduced rates: $5 night, 5 nights and more
Open year round

Number of rooms	3
rooms with private bath	1
rooms with sink	1
shared bathrooms	1

---

15. ROUGEMONT

Located next to the summer theatre, this country house offers warmth, quiet, comfort and serenity in a unique setting. Breakfast in the solarium with a view of the flower and water gardens. Near local tourist activities: three golf courses, bike path, theatre, etc. "A stopping place in apple country". On-site massage service.

Aut. 20, Exit 115, Rte 229 South twd St-Jean-Baptiste, 1km past the village, left on Rougemont-bound Rte 229. Or Aut. 10, Exit 37 twd Marieville, right on Rte 112 twd Rougemont, on Rte 229 South, at the end, left on Rang de la Montagne.

B&B
UN TEMPS D'ARRÊT

Denise Landry and
Jacques Collette
350, rang de la Montagne
Rougemont J0L 1M0
(450) 469-2323
fax (450) 469-3615
www.untempsdarret.com
untempsdarret@hotmail.com

	B&B
single	$75-95
double	$80-100

Open year round

Number of rooms	3
rooms with private bath	1
shared bathrooms	1

16. ST-JEAN-SUR-RICHELIEU

45min from Montréal. Nothing is more wonderful than falling asleep in a country home with welcoming hosts and tranquil ambiance. In the morning, your hostess will lovingly prepare a delicious homemade breakfast. Pool, lovely path, pond, flowers and birdsong await. Welcome to our home!

Aut. 10, Exit 22, Aut. 35 twd St-Jean-Sur-Richelieu, Exit Pierre-Caisse straight ahead, 2nd light left on Grand Bernier to Des Carrières (Rte 219), right for 1.5km, left on Petit Bernier for 2km.

B&B
AUX CHANTS D'OISEAUX

Lisette Vallée
310, Petit Bernier
St-Jean-sur-Richelieu J3B 6Y8
(450) 346-4118
**www.inns-
bb.com/chantsdoiseaux**

	B&B
single	$50
double	$60
child	$10

Taxes extra
Open: Nov. 15 to Sep 15

Number of rooms	1
shared bathrooms	1

---

17. ST-MARC-SUR-RICHELIEU

A beautiful, Victorian-style century-old house that was by turns the village hotel and the deputy house. The three large, very comfortable rooms offer a view of the magnificent Richelieu River. A warm welcome and very lavish breakfasts await you here. Less than 30 min from Montréal and close to many gourmet restaurants, golf courses and excursions to the villages of the Vallée du Richelieu on the chemin des Patriotes. Boat ride by request. Looking forward to receiving you.

Aut. 20, Exit 112, Rte 223 North.

B&B
AUX RÊVES D'ANTAN

Cécile and André Bergeron
595, rue Richelieu
Saint-Marc-sur-Richelieu
JOL 2E0
(450) 584-3461
pages.infinit.net/antan
bandre@videotron.ca

	B&B
single	$55
double	$65
triple	$80
quad.	$95

Reduced rates: 20% 4 nights and more
Open year round

Number of rooms	3
shared bathrooms	2

---

18. ST-MARC-SUR-RICHELIEU

Regional Prize for Excellence "Special Favorite" 2002 and provincial finalist 2002. Less than 30 min from Montréal, the enchantment begins by following the Richelieu River and the small country roads, continues in the theatres, restaurants and art galleries, and ends in the warm ambiance of our home. We offer guests three spacious rooms with private bathrooms and a delicious three-course breakfast. Take advantage of our theatre packages at the L'Escale showboat, facing the inn. You'll be back...

Aut. 20, Exit 112 follow Rte 223 North.

B&B
LE VIREVENT

Johanne Jeannotte
511, rue Richelieu
Saint-Marc-sur-Richelieu
JOL 2E0
(450) 584-3618
virevent.com
info@virevent.com

	B&B
single	$60
double	$70-75
triple	$90-95
quad.	$110-115

VS
Open year round

Number of rooms	3
rooms with private bath	3

19. ST-SIMON

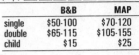

Welcome to our renovated, high-end ancestral home with original ceilings, in the countryside, near our maple grove, traditional sugar shack and stable. We will serve you a hearty breakfast of local products in the country-style sunroom with wood-burning oven. Watch the horses while relaxing near the pond, visit our mini-farm after a trek to the maple grove and enjoy a dip in the in-ground pool before taking a break in the rocking chair, on the veranda. We look forward to welcoming you. Claude and Diane **Farm Stay p 70.**

Aut. 20 Exit 143, right at the stop sign for 2km. At the stop sign, left on 4ᵉ Rang, 0.5km.

B&B
GÎTE À CLAUDIA

Diane Chamberland
923, 4ᵉ Rang ouest
St-Simon J0H 1Y0
(450) 798-2758
(514) 953-0673
www.domaine-st-simon.qc.ca
gite@domaine-st-simon.qc.ca

	B&B	MAP
single	$50-100	$70-120
double	$65-115	$105-155
child	$15	$25

VS MC

Reduced rates: 25% 2 nights and more B&B only
Open year round

Number of rooms	3
rooms in basement	1
rooms with private bath	1
shared bathrooms	1

---

20. ST-VALÉRIEN

Provincial Excellence Prize "Success" 2001 agrotourism. La Rabouillère, a farm with a difference at the border of the Montérégie and the Eastern Townships. Possibility of dining (reservations required), pool, whirlpool, play area. Near summer theatres, bike path, zoo, downhill skiing. Treat yourself to a change of scenery in a warm, rustic and soothing setting. Visit our Web site for package info. **Country-Style Dining p 31. Farm Explorations p 60. Farm Stay p 70. See colour photos.**

From Montréal, Aut. 20 East Exit 141 twd St-Valérien 20km. In the village, 1st flashing light, straight ahead 3km. At the 2nd flashing light, right 1.3km. From Québec City, Aut. 20 West Exit 143 twd St-Valérien...

B&B
LA RABOUILLÈRE

Pierre Pilon, Denise Bellemare and Jérémie Pilon
1073, rang de l'Égypte
Saint-Valérien J0H 2B0
(450) 793-4998
fax (450) 793-2529
www.rabouillere.com
info@rabouillere.com

	B&B	MAP
single	$55-75	$80-100
double	$70-90	$120-140
child	$20	$30-45

Taxes extra VS IT

Reduced rates: 10% 3 nights and more
Open year round

Number of rooms	4
rooms in basement	1
shared bathrooms	2

---

21. STE-AGNÈS-DE-DUNDEE

Peaceful country setting, flowery gardens, spacious house with colonnades and balconies reminiscent of Louisiana. 15km from Dundee border to New York, 5km from Lac St-François National Wildlife Reserve and Droulers (prehistoric Iroquois village) archaeological site. Bicycles on loan, golf courses, lake, water skiing, snowmobiling. Lunch or dinner table d'hôte by reservation. Looking forward to your visit. **Farm Stay p 70.**

Rte 132 from Valleyfield twd Cazaville, left on Montée Cazaville and right on Chemin Ridge.

B&B
LE GÎTE CHEZ MIMI

Émilienne Marlier
5891, chemin Ridge
Ste-Agnès-de-Dundee J0S 1L0
(450) 264-4115
1-877-264-4115
www.inns-bb.com/mimi

	B&B	MAP
single	$45	$55
double	$55	$90
triple	$65	
quad.	$80	
child	$10	$25

Taxes extra VS MC

Open year round

Number of rooms	3
rooms with sink	2
shared bathrooms	1

22. STE-VICTOIRE-DE-SOREL

Situated in the lovely Montérégie region, our B&B is an oasis of tranquillity and nature. We are members of the regional tourism association. Breathe in the fresh country air our home has to offer; whether you enjoy our flowery gardens, blueberry grove, maple grove or small animals, peace and quiet will reign. **Farm Stay p 71.**

Aut. 20 Exit 113, Rte 133 North twd Ste-Victoire de Sorel. Aut. 30, Rte 133 South and Rte 239 South in Ste-Victoire.

B&B
GÎTE À LA FERME DU RANG

	B&B
single	$30
double	$50
child	$20
Open year round	
Number of rooms	1
rooms with private bath	1

Claire Champigny
63, Rang St-Pierre
Ste-Victoire-de-Sorel J0G 1T0
(450) 782-2967
(450) 743-7899
fax (450) 782-3215
www.inns-bb.com/fermedurang
clau@loginnovation.com

AGROTOURISM

Farm Explorations:

🌳 **20**   LA RABOUILLÈRE, Saint-Valérien...*Page 60*

🌳 **23**   LES ÉLEVAGES RUBAN BLEU, Saint-Isidore-de-Laprairie ....*Page 59*

🌳 **24**   FERME JEAN DUCHESNE, Saint-Pie ....*Page 59*

Farm Stays:

🌳 **8**   HAZELBRAE FARM, Howick ....*Page 70*

🌳 **19**   GÎTE À CLAUDIA, Saint-Simon ....*Page 70*

🌳 **20**   LA RABOUILLÈRE, Saint-Valérien ....*Page 70*

🌳 **21**   LE GÎTE CHEZ MIMI, Sainte-Agnès-de-Dundee................................*Page 70*

🌳 **22**   GÎTE À LA FERME DU RANG, Sainte-Victoire-de-Sorel.......................*Page 71*

Farm Shops:

🌳 **23**   LES ÉLEVAGES RUBAN BLEU, Saint-Isidore-de-Laprairie ....*Page 45*

🌳 **25**   VIGNOBLE DIETRICH-JOOSS, Iberville ....*Page 44*

🌳 **26**   CLOS DE LA MONTAGNE, Mont-Saint-Grégoire ....*Page 44*

🌳 **27**   ÉRABLIÈRE L'AUTRE VERSAN, Sainte-Hélène.................................*Page 47*

🌳 **28**   FROMAGERIE AU GRÉ DES CHAMPS, Saint-Jean-sur-Richelieu ....*Page 45*

🌳 **29**   VIGNOBLE ARTISANS DU TERROIR, Saint-Paul-d'Abbotsford ....*Page 46*

🌳 **30**   VERGER CIDRERIE LARIVIÈRE, Saint-Théodore-d'Acton....................*Page 46*

Country-Style Dining:

🌳 **10**   DOMAINE DE LA TEMPLERIE, Godmanchester (Huntingdon)..............*Page 30*

🌳 **20**   LA RABOUILLÈRE, Saint-Valérien...*Page 31*

🌳 **31**   L'AUTRUCHE DORÉE, Marieville...*Page 30*

🌳 **32**   FERME KOSA, Saint-Rémi-de-Napierville...*Page 31*

MONTRÉAL REGION

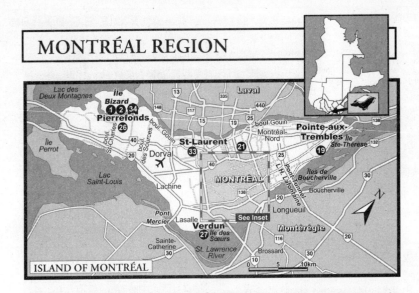

Lac des
Deux Montagnes
Île
Bizard ① ② ③④
Pierrefonds
Laval
13
148
117
335
440
boul.Gouin
15
19
25
Montréal-
Nord
Pointe-aux-
Trembles
Île
Ste-Thérèse
132
138
Île
Perrot
40
St-Laurent
33
21
25
19
Dorval
40
Îles de
Boucherville
30
Lac
Saint-Louis
MONTRÉAL
138
Boucherville
Lachine
20
Longueuil
N
Pont
Mercier
Lasalle
See Inset
Verdun
27
Île des
Sœurs
Montérégie
20
Sainte-
Catherine
30
St. Lawrence
River
116
Brossard
30
ISLAND OF MONTRÉAL
0 10
5
10km

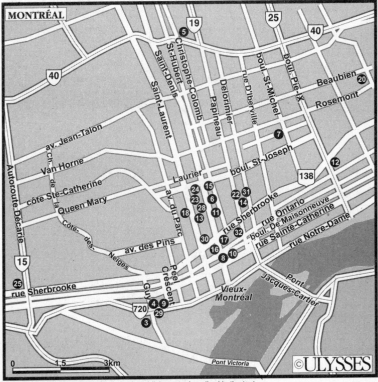

MONTRÉAL

40
19
25
40
5
Christophe-Colomb
Saint-Hubert
Saint-Denis
Saint-Laurent
boul.St-Michel
boul.Pie-IX
Beaubien
20
Delorimier
Papineau
rue D'Iberville
Rosemont
av. Jean-Talon
7
Van Horne
côte Ste-Catherine
Laurier
boul.St-Joseph
12
Queen Mary
av. du Parc
Côte- des-
Neiges
24 15
23 6
18 28
13
22 31
14
11
rue Sherbrooke
rue Ontario
138
boul. De Maisonneuve
av. des Pins
30
17 32
rue Sainte-Catherine
rue Notre-Dame
16
8 10
Pont
Jacques-Cartier
Autoroute Décarie
15
25
rue Sherbrooke
Peel
Crescent
Guy
Vieux-
Montréal
720
4 9
29
3
Pont Victoria
© ULYSSES

*The numbers on the map refer to the establishments described in the text.

1. L'ÎLE-BIZARD

☀ ☀ F E ⊘ P 🚌 🐾 R4

Situated on a peaceful, rustic island, Gîte Île Bizard is a modern and comfortable B&B with two spacious bedrooms. Vibrating bed in one room, and whirlpool in the other. Breakfasts on the terrace. Come for a visit! It won't be your last!

From Montréal, Aut. 20 or Aut. 40 West, Exit Boul. St-Jean North. Left on Boul. Pierrefonds, right on Jacques Bizard (bridge). Left at 1st light on Rue Cherrier, right on Rue de L'Église, to the end of the street, at "Le Bizard" stop, left. From Mirabel, Aut. 15 South and 40 West...

B&B
GÎTE ÎLE BIZARD

Osithe Paulin
1993, rue Bord-du-Lac
L'Île-Bizard H9E 1P9
(514) 620-0766
fax (514) 620-2384
www.inns-bb.com/ilebizard
osithepaulin@videotron.ca

	B&B
single	$60
double	$70
triple	$90
quad.	$110
child	$10

Open year round

Number of rooms	2
rooms in semi-basement	1
rooms with private bath	1
shared bathrooms	1

🏛 🚶 🎿 🚴 ⛷ 🏇

2. L'ÎLE-BIZARD

☀ ☀ ☀ ☀ F E ⊘ P 🚤 🏊 TA R3

Our enchanting site and immense century-old residence on the shore of Lac des Deux Montagnes offers peace and quiet, 20min from Dorval and 30min from Old Montréal. After a day of skiing, you will love lounging by the fireplace. In summer, after a hike in Parc Nature de l'Île Bizard, enjoy a swim in our private pool. Finally, treat yourself to the healthy, hearty breakfasts that have made us famous!

From Aut. 40, Exit 52 Boul. St-Jean North, left on Boul. Gouin, right on Rue Jacques Bizard. After the bridge, left on Rue Cherrier, right on Rue de l'Église to the end. Left on Bord du Lac for 1.6km.

B&B
LE QUAI DU RÊVE

Françoise Paillassard
1765, Bord du lac
L'Île-Bizard H9E 1A2
(514) 626-7357
(514) 815-3604
www.inns-bb.com/quaidureve
lequaidureve@hotmail.com

	B&B
single	$70-100
double	$80-125
triple	$100-145
child	$15

VS

Reduced rates: Oct. 1 to Nov. 30
Open year round

Number of rooms	4
rooms with private bath	1
shared bathrooms	1
shared wc	1

👁 🚶 🎿 🚴 🏇 ⛷ 🏇

3. MONTRÉAL

☀ ☀ ☀ ☀ F e P R.1

Historic Victorian house with a private garden facing a cosy park. 3 min walk from metro, 5 min drive from downtown and Old Montréal. Outdoor market and many antique dealers in the area. Free private parking and easy access from highway. Bicycles available. Full breakfast. Shared or private bathrooms.

Atwater Exit on Ville-Marie expressway (720). Take St-Antoine (one way) until you meet Rue Agnès, left. From Champlain bridge, Exit Atwater. Straight on Atwater after the tunnel, twd St-Antoine...

B&B
À BONHEUR D'OCCASION

Francine Maurice
846, rue Agnès
Montréal H4C 2P8
tel/fax (514) 935-5898
www.inns-bb.com/bonheurdoccasion

	B&B
single	$65-95
double	$80-115
triple	$105
child	$10

Taxes extra

Reduced rates: long stay
Open year round

Number of rooms	5
rooms with private bath	2
shared bathrooms	2

🏛 🍴 🚤 👁 🎿 🚶 🚴

4. MONTRÉAL

A first-rate location right downtown, next to the Bell Centre; two blocks from the corner of Ste-Catherine and Crescent streets, across from a metro station. House with superior comfort, in a room or suite with fireplace and/or Jacuzzi. Whether in business class or on a romantic escapade, you'll enjoy a memorable, uniquely charming stay. Free parking. **La Maison d'à Coté p 210. App.Bon Matins p 217. Photo back of the map on start of guide.**

Ville-Marie Aut. 720 East, Rue Guy Exit. At 1st light, right on René-Lévesque, 2nd light, right on Rue Guy, 1st street, left after Hotel Days Inn. Lucien-L'Allier metro station.

**B&B
À BON MATIN**

Les Frères Côté
1393, av. Argyle
Montréal H3G 1V5
(514) 931-9167
1-800-588-5280
fax (514) 931-1621
www.bonsmatins.com

B&B	
single	$99-149
double	$99-149
triple	$119-169
quad.	$139-189
child	$10

Taxes extra VS MC AM ER IT

Reduced rates: 10 % 7 nights and more

Open year round

Number of rooms	5
rooms with private bath	5

---

5. MONTRÉAL

Located in a residential neighbourhood, on a quiet street, we offer a warm welcome, family atmosphere and copious breakfast. Free parking, flowered terrace with pool, T.V. in room. Near services (0.1km), buses, Crémazie metro, highways, bicycle path and olympic pool (0.8km).

Easy access from Dorval and Mirabel airports. From Dorval, Rte 520 East twd Aut. 40 East, Exit 73, Rue Christophe-Colomb North, 1km. Rue Legendre, right, 0.2km to Av. André-Grasset, left. First street right. From Mirabel, Aut. 15 South twd 40 East, Exit 73...

**B&B
À LA BELLE VIE**

Lorraine and
M. Camille Grondin
1408, rue Jacques Lemaistre
Montréal H2M 2C1
(514) 381-5778
fax (514) 381-3966
www.inns-bb.com/bellevie
alabellevie@hotmail.com

B&B	
single	$50-55
double	$65-75

Open: Feb. 1 to Nov. 30

Number of rooms	2
rooms with sink	1
shared bathrooms	1

---

6. MONTRÉAL

This century-old home has preserved its old-fashioned charm and is located on one of the most beautiful streets of the Plateau Mont-Royal district. Enjoy a fabulous stay, steps away from the best restaurants, shops and cultural events. Spacious, comfy rooms; hearty and varied breakfasts served in a large dining room with original plasterwork, mouldings and chandelier. Discover the friendly side of Montréal! Near Mont-Royal metro.

From the west, Aut. 20, Exit 6 (Berri), left at the second light, Rue St-Hubert. From the east, Aut. 20, past the Jacques-Cartier bridge, left on Rue Sherbrooke, right on Rue St-Hubert.

**B&B
À LA BONNE HEURE**

Catherine Charron
4425, rue St-Hubert
Montréal H2J 2X1
(514) 529-0179
fax (514) 529-1079
www.alabonneheure.ca
info@alabonneheure.ca

B&B	
single	$60-70
double	$80
triple	$95
child	$15

Reduced rates: long stay

Open year round

Number of rooms	5
shared bathrooms	2
shared wc	1

7. MONTRÉAL

"Wow!" exclaim our guests, so amazed are they by the eclectic decor, creature comforts (luxurious bathroom, TV, VCR, air conditioning), the charm of Tout'e Petite small poodle and the ribaldry and graciousness of Daniel. Located near the Botanical Gardens, Olympic Park and Biodome, in a safe, quiet neighbourhood that harbours real restaurant gems.

Aut. 40 East and West, Exit 75, Boul. St-Michel South, 3.5km, right on Rue Masson and right on 10ᵉ Av.

B&B
À LA CARTE B & B

Daniel Labrosse
5477, 10ᵉ Avenue
Montréal H1Y 2G9
(514) 593-4005
1-877-388-4005
fax (514) 593-9997
www.alacartebnb.com
dlabrosse@alacartebnb.com

B&B	
single	$80-100
double	$105-120
triple	$145
quad.	$170

Taxes extra VS MC AM

Reduced rates: 10 % / 1 night, 15 % / 3 nights, Nov. 1 to Apr. 30
Open year round

Number of rooms	2
rooms with private bath	2

---

8. MONTRÉAL

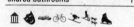

The next best thing to home. Steps from Berri-UQAM metro, bus terminal, old port, museums, restaurants. Ancestral home, roof-top terrace, huge rooms, living room, good breakfasts. Low-season: extended-stay rates. See you soon...

From the terminus, walk one street to the East. By metro, Berri-UQAM, Exit Place Dupuis. By car, Aut. Ville-Marie (720), Berri Exit, right on Ontario, right on St-André, right on de Maisonneuve, right on St-Christophe.

B&B
À L'ADRESSE DU CENTRE-VILLE

Nathalie Messier and Robert Groleau
1673, rue Saint-Christophe
Montréal H2L 3W7
(514) 528-9516
fax (514) 528-2746
www.inns-bb.com/adresseducentre_ville
adresvil@dsuper.net

B&B	
single	$65-115
double	$85-130
triple	$105-145

Taxes extra VS MC AM ER IT

Reduced rates: Nov. 1 to Mar. 31 for long stay
Open year round

Number of rooms	5
rooms with private bath	2
shared bathrooms	1

---

9. MONTRÉAL

Right downtown, next to the Bell Centre. Ideal location, two blocks from the corner of Ste-Catherine and Crescent streets, facing the metro station. Very comfortable apartment and townhouse with fireplace and whirlpool. For a business trip or a romantic escapade, enjoy an unforgettable stay with unique charm. Free parking. **À Bon Matin p 209. App. Bon Matins p 217. Photo back of the map on start of guide.**

Autoroute Ville-Marie (720 East), Exit Guy. Right at the first light (René-Lévesque), right at the second light (Guy south), left at the first street (Argyle) past the Days Inn hotel. Lucien-L'Allier metro.

B&B
À LA MAISON D'À CÔTÉ

Les Frères Côté
1393, av. Argyle
Montréal H3G 1V5
(514) 931-3466
1-800-587-3340
fax (514) 931-1621
www.bonsmatins.com

B&B	
single	$99-179
double	$99-179
triple	$119-199
quad.	$139-219
child	$10

Taxes extra VS MC AM ER IT
Open year round

Number of rooms	5
rooms with private bath	5

10. MONTRÉAL

FER.5

At the Berri-UQAM metro, in the heart of downtown Montréal and local activities, enjoy the quiet comfort of a warm house fully renovated for your convenience: spacious, soundproof rooms, kitchenette available and separate eating area for your personal use. Gracious welcome and lively, lavish breakfasts.

Berri-UQAM metro, Place Dupuis Exit. From the airport, Aut. Ville-Marie (720), Berri North Exit, right on Rue Ontario, right on Rue St-André, right on De Maisonneuve and right on St-Christophe.

B&B
AU GÎT'ANN

Anne and Nicolas Messier
1806, rue Saint-Christophe
Montréal H2L 3W8
(514) 523-4494
www.inns-bb.com/gitann
augite@cam.org

B&B	
single	$65-115
double	$75-115
triple	$110-130
quad.	$150

Taxes extra

Reduced rates: Jan. 15 to Apr. 1
Open year round

Number of rooms	**3**
rooms with private bath	1
shared bathrooms	1

---

11. MONTRÉAL

FE🚭🐾R.2

Located in the Plateau Mont-Royal district, 2min from the metro and good restaurants, we welcome you to Le Rayon Vert, a quiet and comfortable century-old residence. Whether you wish to visit the city or take in a show, we will be happy to share all kinds of information on the must-see attractions and events taking place in Montréal. Healthy breakfast; air conditioning; private garden; on-site bicycle rental.

Mont-Royal metro. Aut. 720, Exit Berri/St-Laurent, Rue Berri to Rue St-Hubert, left. Aut. 40, Exit St-Denis South, left on Rue Roy, left on Rue St-Hubert.

B&B
AU GÎTE LE RAYON VERT

Diane Bouchard
4373, rue St-Hubert
Montréal H2J 2X1
(514) 524-6774
(514) 825-6774
www.lerayonvert.ca
touroule@yahoo.fr

B&B	
single	$65-70
double	$78-80

Reduced rates: 3 nights and more
Open year round

Number of rooms	**3**
rooms with sink	1
shared bathrooms	2

---

12. MONTRÉAL

FE🖐P🐾TAR.2

A name, a place! Gîte means B & B and Olympique, because we are located across the street from the Olympic Park, the Biodome & Botanical Garden : Great location! 77 strides away from Pie-IX metro station. We offer rooms with private bathroom, color tv, A/C. Experience a stay at our B & B ; it will be companionable. Meet Denis, the owner, a real montrealer and Sasha (miniature Schnauzer) our «Public relation director». Montreal's finalist for the best B & B at the « Grand Prize of Tourism 2002 » **See colour photos.**

From U.S.: Rte 87/Rte 15 or Rte 89/91/93, Rte 10. Both 10 & 15 end up to Rte 132 East; Jacques-Cartier Bridge (keep the left lane) 3rd light, turn right on Sherbrooke St, 3 miles, turn right on Pie-IX. From Dorval Airport : 520 East, 40 East, Exit 76 (Pie-IX Boul. South). From downtown : Sherbrooke St to Pie-IX (right).

B&B
AU GÎTE OLYMPIQUE

Denis Boulianne
2752, boul. Pie-IX
Montréal H1V 2E9
(514) 254-5423
1-888-254-5423
fax (514) 254-4753
www.gomontrealgo.com
info@gomontrealgo.com

B&B	
single	$85-105
double	$105-125

Taxes extra VS MC AM ER

Reduced rates: Nov. to Apr. except holidays
Open year round

Number of rooms	**5**
rooms in semi-basement	3
rooms with private bath	5

13. MONTRÉAL

Victorian house with age-old woodwork on a quiet street facing Square St-Louis. Ten min. walking distance from downtown and Old Montréal, in the heart of the Latin Quarter. Lavish breakfasts and warm welcome.

From Dorval, Aut. 20 and Rte 720 East, Boul. St-Laurent North Exit. After 1km, right on Av. Des Pins, right on Laval. Sherbrooke metro station, Rigaud St Exit.

B&B
AUX PORTES DE LA NUIT

Olivia Durand
3496, av. Laval
Montréal H2X 3C8
(514) 848-0833
fax (514) 848-9023
www.inns-bb.com/portesdelanuit
auxportesdelanuit@videotron.ca

B&B	
single	$75-105
double	$85-115
triple	$110-140
quad.	$155-165
child	$15

Taxes extra
Open year round

Number of rooms	**5**
rooms with private bath	**5**

---

14. MONTRÉAL

A little piece of paradise... On the menu: enchantment, rest and relax. A very colourful, singular bed and breakfast! Charming, intimate ambiance. Will you sleep in the Mango, the Mexicaine or the Sunny? Memorable, healthy breakfast. Massotherapy package. Near Parc Lafontaine, in the Plateau, the second-best neighbourhood in Montréal. Easy parking. On a quiet street. A nice stay. **City Home p 218.**

Voyageur terminus, 3 min by taxi. From Sherbrooke metro, Bus 24 East, Rue Papineau, North.

B&B
AZUR

Caroline Misserey
1892, rue Gauthier
Montréal H2K 1A3
(514) 529-6364
fax (514) 529-0860
www.bbazur.com
reservations@bbazur.com

B&B	
single	$55-75
double	$70-95
triple	$110
quad.	$130

Open: Apr. 1 to Jan. 1

Number of rooms	**3**
shared bathrooms	**1**

---

15. MONTRÉAL

We are located on a quiet, tree-lined street, right by a lively avenue that is great for strolling and close to the metro to explore the city. La Cinquième Saison offers an atmosphere where time seems to stand still so that you can fully enjoy a comfortable stay and savour hearty breakfasts. Winner of the 2000 regional "Special Favourite" Award of Excellence.

From the Jacques-Cartier bridge, Rue De Lorimier. Left on Rue Sherbrooke, right on Rue Émile-Duployé, left on Rue Rachel, right on Rue Boyer. From Mont-Royal metro, right at the Exit. Right on Rue Boyer.

B&B
GÎTE LA CINQUIÈME SAISON

Jean-Yves Goupil
4396, rue Boyer
Montréal H2J 3E1
(514) 522-6439
fax (514) 522-6192
www.cinquiemesaison.net
cinquieme.saison@sympatico.ca

B&B	
single	$60
double	$80

Taxes extra VS MC IT
Open year round

Number of rooms	**4**
shared bathrooms	**1**
shared wc	**1**
shared showers	**1**

16. MONTRÉAL

Our historic 1870 home will allow you to relive the splendour of the Victorian era, revealed in its woodwork, majestic staircase and antique furnishings. Large, air-conditioned rooms, queen-size beds, electronic access cards. We are located in downtown Montréal, one block from the popular Rue St-Denis, near Rue Ste-Catherine and Old Montréal. Visit us on the Web! **See colour photos.**

Berri-UQAM metro, Exit St-Denis. From the airport, Ville-Marie Autoroute (Aut. 720 East). Exit Berri North, left on Boul. de Maisonneuve, right on Rue Sanguinet, right on Rue Ontario.

B&B
HÉRITAGE VICTORIEN

Denis Beaulac and
Alberto Serracin
311, Ontario est
Montréal H2X 1H7
(514) 845-7932
1-877-845-7932
fax (514) 845-0809
www.heritagevictorien.com
info@heritagevictorien.com

	B&B
single	$109-119
double	$119-129
triple	$129-139
quad.	$139-149
child	$10

Taxes extra
Open year round

Number of rooms	3
rooms with private bath	3

---

17. MONTRÉAL

A few min from the Old Montréal market, St-Denis and Ste-Catherine, the yellow house right in the midst of Montréal's cultural, social and tourist activities. This ancestral house's unique character and tranquillity will add to your stay. Good advice on activities, restaurants, entertainment.

Aut. 20, Rte 132, Jacques-Cartier bridge twd Rue Sherbrooke, left on Ontario, 1.2km, right on St-Hubert.

B&B
LA MAISON JAUNE

Sylvain Binette and
François Legault
2017, rue Saint-Hubert
Montréal H2L 3Z6
(514) 524-8851
fax (514) 521-7352
www.maisonjaune.com

	B&B
single	$60
double	$80-85

Taxes extra VS MC IT

Reduced rates: Nov. 1 to Apr. 30 for long stay
Open year round

Number of rooms	5
shared bathrooms	2
shared wc	2

---

18. MONTRÉAL

Beautiful Victorian home in the Plateau Mont-Royal district, steps away from downtown, festivals, restaurants, museums and shops. Historical setting, comfort and privacy, refined breakfast, casual atmosphere in a soothing decor. Your hosts are young, friendly and respectful of their guests' privacy.

From Mirabel or Toronto, Aut. 40 East, Exit St-Denis. 6km. Right on Des Pins, right on Laval. From Québec City, Aut. 20, Rte 132, Jacques-Cartier bridge, left on Sherbrooke, right on St-Denis, left on Des Pins, right on Laval.

B&B
L'ATOME

Dominique Collin and
Jacques Chelidonis
3767, avenue Laval
Montréal H2W 2H8
(514) 844-3857
www.bblatome.com
bblatome2000@yahoo.com

	B&B
single	$75
double	$95
triple	$120

Taxes extra VS MC

Reduced rates: 10% Nov. 1 to Mar. 31 except Christmas holidays
Open year round

Number of rooms	3
shared bathrooms	2

19. MONTRÉAL

Prize for Excellence "Special Favorite" Regional 1996-97. Located by the St. Lawrence River, 25 min from downtown, this century-old house will charm you with its large garden, flowers and in-ground swimming pool. Breakfast on the terrace. The country right in the city. Private parking. Children wel-come. After 10 years, we still welcome our guests like royalty.

From Dorval, Rte 520 East Aut. 40 East Exit 87, Tricentenaire to Notre-Dame, right, 200m. From Mirabel, Aut. 15 South 40 East Exit 87... From Aut. 20, Lafontaine tunnel, 1st Exit, twd East. Drive South, Notre-Dame, twd East.

B&B
LA VICTORIENNE

Aimée and Julien Roy
12560, rue Notre-Dame Est
Montréal H1B 2Z1
(514) 645-8328
fax (514) 645-1633
www.inns-bb.com/victorienne

☀ ☀ ☀ F E ⊘ P ⌇ TA R1

B&B	
single	$40
double	$60
triple	$75

Open: May 1 to Oct. 15

Number of rooms	3
rooms with sink	1
shared bathrooms	2

---

20. MONTRÉAL

This is the place for comfort and a warm welcome at a low price. Close to the Olympic tower, L'Assomption metro and 10 min from the botanical garden. Breakfasts are made with fresh, quality ingredients and you can have as much as you like. Pool, bikes available, free laundry.

From Mirabel Aut. 40 East, Boul. Lacordaire South Exit. Drive down to Boul. Rosemont and right, continue to Rue Lemay, right on 2nd street, From Dorval, Aut. 520 East to Aut. 40 East...

B&B
LE 6400 COUETTE ET CAFÉ
BED & BREAKFAST

Lise and Jean-Pierre Durand
6400, rue Lemay
Montréal H1T 2L5
(514) 259-6400
www.inns-bb.com/6400

☀ ☀ ☀ F E ⊘ ⌇ R1

B&B	
single	$50-55
double	$65-70

Reduced rates: Nov. 1 to Apr. 30
Open year round

Number of rooms	2
shared bathrooms	1

---

21. MONTRÉAL

Our large, sunny room, comfortable beds, private entrance, parking and healthy breakfasts await you. Refrigerator, microwave, etc., are also available in the adjoining room. We are near one of the most beautiful parks in the area, in a quiet district where you will find many services and restaurants, a few pedal strokes from the green route.

From Dorval, Aut. 520 East, Aut. 40 East, Exit 73 Av. Papineau North. From Mirabel, Aut. 15 South, 440 East, 19 South, Av. Papineau South. We are 0.6km East of Av. Papineau, via Prieur two blocks South of Boul. Gouin.

B&B
LE CLOS DES ÉPINETTES

Diane Teolis and Léo Lavergne
10358, rue Parthenais, app. 1
Montréal H2B 2L7
(514) 382-0737
www.inns-bb.com/closdesepinettes
*leclosdesepinettes@
sympatico.ca*

☀ ☀ ☀ F E ⊘ P TA R.2

B&B	
single	$75
double	$85
triple	$105
quad.	$115
child	$5-10

Reduced rates: long stay
Open year round

Number of rooms	1
rooms in semi-basement	1
rooms with private bath	1

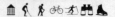

22. MONTRÉAL

A charming spot near downtown Montréal, Le Zèbre is housed in a superb Victorian house on the edge of Parc Lafontaine, close to the Sherbrooke and Mont-Royal metro stations. Steps away from shops and restaurants, Avenue Mont-Royal and Rue St-Denis. Stylish rooms, fireplace, woodwork, piano. Our refined breakfasts will please one and all!

From Mirabel or Toronto, Aut. 40 East, St-Denis Exit, 6km. Right on Des Pins, right on Laval. From Québec City, Aut. 20, Rte 132, J.-Cartier bridge, left on Sherbrooke, right on St-Denis, left on Des Pins, right on Laval.

B&B
LE ZÈBRE

Alain Boulanger and
Jérôme Delville
1125 rue Rachel est
Montréal H3J 2J6
(514) 844-9868
www.bblezebre.com
info@bblezebre.com

B&B	
single	$75-145
double	$101-164
triple	$121-184

Taxes extra VS MC
Open year round

Number of rooms	5
rooms with private bath	3
shared bathrooms	1

23. MONTRÉAL

We are located in the downtown area, facing the famous Carré Saint-Louis! Everything (or almost) is within walking distance: restaurants, shops, museums, universities, metro, festivals, etc. In the morning, we will serve you a gourmet organic breakfast, a great start to a day of exploring! **See colour photos.**

From Dorval, Aut. 20 East, then Aut. 720 East, Boul. St-Laurent North Exit, 1km, then right on Av. des Pins, right on Av. Laval, left on St-Louis square. Or Sherbrooke metro station, Rigaud Exit.

B&B
PIERRE ET DOMINIQUE

Dominique Bousquet and
Pierre Bilodeau
271, Carré Saint-Louis
Montréal H2X 1A3
(514) 286-0307
www.pierdom.qc.ca
pierdom@sympatico.ca

B&B	
single	$50-85
double	$80-100
triple	$130
quad.	$160
child	$30

Open year round

Number of rooms	3
rooms with sink	2
shared bathrooms	1

24. MONTRÉAL

In the heart of the Latin Quarter (restaurants-nightclubs-theatres-boutiques). Easy parking. Garden, hammocks. Quiet, safe street. 2 min from metro. Near the bike path, international events: Jazz Festival, Just For Laughs, World Film Festival. 6-person suite. Superb lovers' suite. Family or group rooms (2 to 6 people).

Airports: Voyageur bus terminus, metro Mont-Royal. By Car: twd downtown. Berri is parallel to St-Denis (2 streets to the East). 4272 Berri is between Mont-Royal and Rachel.

B&B
SHÉZELLES

Lucie Dextras and
Lyne St-Amand
4272, rue Berri
Montréal H2J 2P8
(514) 849-8694
www.inns-bb.com/shezelles
shez.masq@sympatico.ca

B&B	
single	$45-115
double	$70-140
triple	$85-165
quad.	$150-180

Reduced rates: 10 % 7 consecutive nights and more on low season. Children under 5 free
Open year round

Number of rooms	4
rooms with private bath	1
shared bathrooms	1

25. MONTRÉAL, NOTRE-DAME-DE-GRÂCE

Regional Prize for Excellence "Special Favorite" 2001. Pretty Victorian House located in the heart of the Monkland village in N.D.G. close to the restaurants and boutiques. 15 min from Dorval airport via Aut. 20 or 40. Convenient access to downtown attractions by Metro (Villa Maria station). Our rooms are comfortable and well-furnished. Hingston House is filled with warmth.

From Dorval airport, Côte-de-Liesse East and Décarie South, Aut. 15, Exit Sherbrooke West turn right, right on Hingston.

B&B
MAISON HINGSTON 4335

Hélène Groulx
4335, rue Hingston
Montréal H4A 2J8
(514) 484-3396
fax (514) 369-0263
www.inns-bb.com/hingston
maisonhingston@hotmail.com

	B&B
single	$75
double	$85

Open year round Apr. 15 to Oct. 31

Number of rooms	2
shared bathrooms	1

---

26. PIERREFONDS

Regional Prize for Excellence "Special Favorite" 2002. Air-conditioned, renovated ranch house in west-end Montréal, close to Dorval Airport, accessible from downtown via Rtes 40 & 20. Free off-the-street parking. Cozy bedrooms, spacious meeting-rooms, piano, fireplaces, screened veranda, well-kept grounds pesticide free, naturally. Home-maid healthy & hearty breakfast like our grandmothers used to serve. Families welcomed. A restful place to return to.

Fom Dorval Airport, Aut. 20 West, 7km, until Boul Saint-Jean, Exit 50 North, proceed on St-Jean for 7km, then left on Boul Pierrefonds, 1.4km, left at Rue Paiement.

B&B
GÎTE MAISON JACQUES

Micheline and Fernand Jacques
4444, rue Paiement
Pierrefonds H9H 2S7
(514) 696-2450
fax (514) 696-2564
www.maisonjacques.qc.ca
gite.maison.jacques@qc.aira.com

	B&B
single	$53-61
double	$73-82
triple	$94-103
quad.	$116
child	$5-12

VS MC AM

Reduced rates: 7% seniors and 4 nights and more

Open: Mar. 11 to Nov. 21

Number of rooms	3
rooms in basement	1
rooms with private bath	3

---

27. VERDUN

Sunny and peaceful with private entrance and parking just 10 min from downtown (museums, festivals). Close to beautiful park along St.Lawrence River banks (baking, hiking, rafting). Quick access to airports and regional activities via Hwys. Discount on 4 nights and more.

From Dorval, Aut. 20 East, Aut. 15 South. From the South, Champlain Bridge to Aut. 15 North, Exit La Verendry, left at 4th light on Woodland, right on Champlain, straight ahead on Beurling, right on Rolland.

B&B
PACANE ET POTIRON
CAFÉ COUETTE

Nathalie Ménard and
Jean-Pierre Bernier
1430, av. Rolland
Verdun H4H 2G6
(514) 769-8315
www.inns-bb.com/pacaneetpotiron
pacaneetpotiron@hotmail.com

	B&B
single	$55-60
double	$75-80
child	$15

VS

Reduced rates: Oct. 15 to Dec. 10 and Jan. 15 to Apr. 15, long stay

Open year round

Number of rooms	2
shared bathrooms	1

28. MONTRÉAL

★★★ F E ☒ M.05

In the heart of Plateau Mont-Royal, on the friendly Saint-Denis street, 17 rooms-studios all with air conditioning, micro-kitchen, complete bathroom and lots of efficiencies : colour TV, high-speed Internet, telephone with message waiting indicator, coffee maker, microwave, hair dryer, etc. Large balconies, shady backyard, private terraces and...croissants at your door every morning! **Ad start of guide.**

From Dorval or Mirabel, Aut. 40 East, Exit 71, service road for 1.3 km, right on Saint-Denis . By 40 West : Exit 73, service road for 1.3 km, left on Saint-Denis. Jacques-Cartier bridge : De Lorimier av., left on Sherbrooke, at 1.4 km, left on Saint-Denis.

CITY HOMES
ANNE MA SŒUR ANNE

Hélène Duval
4119, St-Denis
Montréal H2W 2M7
(514) 281-3187
fax (514) 281-1601
www.annemasoeuranne.com
infos@annemasoeuranne.com

No. houses	15
No. people	1-4
WEEK-SUMMER	$530-1250
WEEK-WINTER	$530-1250
W/E-SUMMER	$170-370
W/E-WINTER	$170-370
DAY-SUMMER	$85-185
DAY-WINTER	$85-185

Taxes extra VS MC AM IT

Reduced rates: Nov. 1 to Apr. 30
Open year round

29. MONTRÉAL

★★★ F E 🚳 P TA R.1

Right downtown, next to the Bell Centre. Ideal location, two blocks from the corner of Ste-Catherine and Crescent streets, facing the metro station. Very comfortable apartment and townhouse with fireplace and whirlpool. For a business trip or a romantic escapade, enjoy an unforgettable stay with unique charm. Free parking. **À Bon Matin p 209. À la maison d'à Côté p 210. Photo back of the map on start of guide.**

Autoroute Ville-Marie (720 East), Exit Guy. Right at the first light (René-Lévesque), right at the second light (Guy south), left at the first street (Argyle) past the Days Inn hotel. Lucien-L'Allier metro.

CITY HOMES
APPARTEMENTS LES
BONS MATINS

Les Frères Côté
1393, av. Argyle
Montréal H3G 1V5
(514) 931-9167
1-800-588-5280
fax (514) 931-1621
www.bonsmatins.com

No. houses	4
No. rooms	1-2
No. people	2-6
WEEK-SUMMER	$1125-1425
WEEK-WINTER	$1000-1250
W/E-SUMMER	$325-410
W/E-WINTER	$290-359

Taxes extra VS MC AM ER IT
Open year round

30. MONTRÉAL

★★★ F E ≋ 🐕 TA R.5 M.5

Beautifully furnished apartments in a prime, central location! Fully equipped kitchen. Daily, weekly or monthly rentals. Balcony, television, radio, telephone, pool and air conditioning. Great view of the city. Near festivals, Palais des Congrès, shopping centre, universities and hospitals. Parking. Great value for your dollar.

Metro Place-des-Arts, Jeanne-Mance Exit, bus #80, get off at the 2nd bus stop, walk right. By car, situated downtown four streets West of Boul. St-Laurent and 1st street North of Sherbrooke between Milton and Prince-Arthur.

CITY HOMES
APPARTEMENTS TOURISTIQUES
DU CENTRE-VILLE

Bruno Bernard
3463, rue Sainte-Famille, Office 008
Montréal H2X 2K7
(514) 845-0431
fax (514) 845-0262
www3.sympatico.ca/app
app@sympatico.ca

No. houses	12
No. rooms	studio - 1
No. people	1-4
WEEK-SUMMER	$525-750
WEEK-WINTER	$525-750
W/E-SUMMER	$180-300
W/E-WINTER	$180-300
DAY-SUMMER	$95-150
DAY-WINTER	$85-150
COÛT-ACTIVITÉ	$150-

Taxes extra VS MC AM

Reduced rates: Oct. 21 to June 1
Open year round

31. MONTRÉAL

F E ⊘ TA R.3 M.5

Looking for a lovely, completely equipped apartment in downtown Montréal? You've come to the right place! For your comfort, we offer warmly decorated apartments steps away from cafés, restaurants and shops. For your convenience: silk linen, king-size orthopedic beds, private phone, TV, stereo, DVD, computer and Internet access, iron, hair dryer, washer/dryer, equipped kitchen with microwave. Welcome to business travellers and families! Daily, weekly or monthly stays; reserve online or contact us. **B&B p 212.**

Sherbrooke metro.

CITY HOMES
AZUR RESIDENCES
DE TOURISME

Caroline Misserey and
Genya St-Arnaud
1892, rue Gauthier
Montréal H2K 1A3
(514) 529-6364
www.bbazur.com
reservations@bbazur.com

No. houses	2
No. rooms	3
No. people	2-8
WEEK-SUMMER	$945-1400
WEEK-WINTER	$945-1400
DAY-SUMMER	$160-220
DAY-WINTER	$160-220

Reduced rates: 10% Oct. 15 to Apr. 1
Open year round

32. MONTRÉAL

F E ⊘ R.5 M1

Évasion Montréal offers you the chance to enjoy a stay in the very heart of Montréal. Located on a quiet street, near downtown services, this fully equipped, open-plan apartment comes with all modern conveniences. Explore Old Montréal, discover Rue Saint-Denis, attend the Canadian Grand Prix as well as festivals.

From Dorval, Aut. 720, Exit 7, De Lorimier North, left on Sherbrooke, left on Bordeaux.

CITY HOME
ÉVASION MONTRÉAL

Robert Schloesser
2266, de Bordeaux
Correspondance :
545, 33ᵉ avenue
Montréal H1A 5E3
(514) 498-2404
(514) 891-2895
www.inns-bb.com/evasion-montreal
evasion-montreal@sympatico.ca

No. houses	1
No. rooms	1
No. people	1-4
WEEK-SUMMER	$600-800
WEEK-WINTER	$450-650
W/E-SUMMER	$200-300
W/E-WINTER	$175-275
DAY-SUMMER	$125-175
DAY-WINTER	$115-165

Taxes extra
Open year round

33. ST-LAURENT

★ ★ F E ⊘ P ⇆ TA R.3 M.3

Lovely 3½ with living room, kitchen, bathroom. Spacious, quiet, fully equipped, bedding, dishes, iron, hairdryer, etc. Telephone (private line), cable TV, VCR, sound system, microwave. Residential area near Marcel-Laurin park, Raymond Bourque arena, malls and restaurants. 5 min from Côte-Vertu Metro, 15 min from downtown Montréal, 10 min from Dorval airport. Access to garden, laundry (washer and dryer). Private entrance, parking. Personalised reception.

Aut. 40, Exit 67, Marcel Laurin North, about 1.5km. Left on Lucien Thimens. At stop sign, left on Boul. Alexis-Nihon, right on Rue Hufford and left on Rue Sigouin.

CITY HOME
STUDIO MARHABA

Assia and Ammar Sassi
2265, rue Sigouin
Saint-Laurent H4R 1L6
(514) 335-7931
fax (514) 335-2177
www.inns-bb.com/studiomarhaba
studiomarhaba@videotron.ca

No. houses	1
No. rooms	1
No. people	1-3
WEEK-SUMMER	$400-600
WEEK-WINTER	$300-400
DAY-SUMMER	$70-110
DAY-WINTER	$50-90

Reduced rates: Nov. 1 to Apr. 30
Open year round

AGROTOURISM

Farm Explorations:

🐾 *34*   CORPORATION D-TROIS-PIERRES/FERME ÉCOLOGIQUE, Pierrefonds .... *Page 61*

For an unforgettable experience, choose from our selection of accommodations and agrotourism activities...

www.inns-bb.com
(Secure online booking service)

www.agricotours.qc.ca

Click here!

Gift certificate

Inns and Bed & Breakfasts

For a gift that's sure to please,
offer a delightful getaway...

INNS AND BED & BREAKFASTS

Information : 1-877-869-9728

OUTAOUAIS

Lac des Écorces
Le Domaine

117

Réserve faunique La Vérendrye

ZEC Bras-Coupé-Désert

Réservoir Baskatong

ZEC Pontiac

Grand-Remous 🅿

117

Mont-Laurier

Lac-des-Écorces

117

311

309

Maniwaki 🅿

Kiamika

Lac-des-Îles

L'Annonciation

Messines

Lac Blue Sea

Blue Sea

Réserve faunique de Papineau-Labelle

Gracefield

Lac des Trente-et-Un-Milles

Lac Gagnon

Wright 🅿

Kazabazua

Lac Poisson Blanc

Duhamel

Lac-des-Plages

Rivière Coulonge

301

Lac Sainte-Marie

Val-des-Bois

Lac Simon

Lac Simone ⑪ Vinoy ⑰ 323

Fort-Coulonge

Denholm

Notre-Dame-de-la-Salette

Lac Viceroi

Ripon

Île-du-Grand-Calumet 🅿

105

307

309

317 321

Montréal →

Saint-André-Avellin

366

Wakefield 🅿

Saint-Sixte

⑲

⑮ Montebello 🅿 ⑫

148

Lac La Pêche

Gatineau Park

Lac Meech

307

366

Plaisance

🅿

⑬ Papineauville

Shawville

17

Fort-du-Portage 🅿

Pontiac

Luskville ⑭ Chelsea

Val-des-Monts

⑯

148

Rivière

Ottawa

ONTARIO

Breckenridge

⑤ 🅿

Hull 🅿

④⑤⑱

Gatineau

ONTARIO

6 to 10

Aylmer ①②🅿

★ Ottawa 🅿

417

©ULYSSES

*The numbers on the map refer to the establishments described in the text.

1. AYLMER

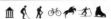

R1.5

New, artistically decorated house located in an enchanting sector 7min from Ottawa/Hull. Patio, wooded area, air conditioning, rest area. Near tourist attractions: bike paths, golf, casino, Parc de la Gatineau, museums. Free parking. Hearty breakfast. Living room with fireplace, piano, TV. Stunning river view all year long. Stylish rooms. Warm reception. We speak French, English and Spanish.

Aut. 417, Exit Island Park Drive, past Champlain bridge, left on Boul. Lucerne, 3rd street right, Félix Leclerc. Or Rte 148 West twd Aylmer, left on Rue Vanier, left on Rue Lucerne, 1st street left Félix Leclerc.

B&B
LA RIVIÈRE AU BOIS DORMANT

Robert Dionne
64, Félix Leclerc
Aylmer J9H 6Y2
(819) 775-3556
1-866-335-3556
www.riviereaubois.ca
info@riviereaubois.ca

B&B	
single	$55-65
double	$60-70
child	$15

Taxes extra VS MC IT

Reduced rates: 15% 3 nights and more
Open year round

Number of rooms	3
shared bathrooms	1
shared wc	1

---

2. AYLMER

R1

Winner of the Provincial Excellence Award in 96-97. Located on the north shore of the Outaouais river, a few minutes away from Parliament Hill and the majestic Parc Gatineau. Aylmer is renowned for its beautiful golf courses and panoramic bike paths. "Your passion for welcoming guests was evident, as outstanding as it was friendly. Simply wonderful."

From Montréal, Aut. 417 to Ottawa, Exit 123 Island Park Drive, twd Champlain bridge. Past the bridge, left at the second light, 2km, Aut. 50 twd Hull, Exit Montcalm, left, twd Boul. Taché, right twd Aylmer. 1km past the Château Cartier hotel.

B&B
L'ESCAPADE B&B

Lise and Rhéal Charron
912, chemin d'Aylmer
Aylmer J9H 5T8
(819) 772-2388
fax (819) 772-4354
www.inns-bb.com/lescapade
escapade@mondenet.com

B&B	
single	$60-65
double	$75-80
child	$10

VS

Reduced rates: 10% 7 nights and more
Open year round

Number of rooms	3
rooms with sink	2
shared bathrooms	1
shared wc	1

---

3. AYLMER, BRECKENRIDGE

R1

Our split-level home offers you comfort, tranquillity and a warm welcome. Take the time to enjoy nature in the magnificent woods bordering the Outaouais River. 20 min to the Parliament and Ottawa's other tourist attractions. Bicycle storage available. Generous breakfast.

From Montréal, Aut. 417, in Ottawa Exit 123 (Island Park Drive) follow Island park, cross Champlain bridge to chemin Aylmer left. At the Aylmer city Hall, right on Rue Eardley, 5km. Left on Terry Fox twd the river, right on Cedarvale.

B&B
MAISON BON REPOS

Denyse and Guy Bergeron
37, rue Cedarvale
Aylmer J0X 2G0
(819) 682-1498
**www3.sympatico.ca/
tranquilitydenise.bergeron2**
denise.bergeron2@sympatico.ca

B&B	
single	$45-55
double	$55-65

Open year round

Number of rooms	3
rooms with private bath	2
shared bathrooms	1

4. GATINEAU

A very comfortable bed and breakfast with large rooms and country charm, 12 min from downtown Ottawa/Hull, casino, museum, bike path and golfing. Hearty breakfast near the fireplace or on the covered terrace. **Farm Stay p 71. See colour photos.**

From Montréal, Aut. 40 twd Ottawa, Aut. 417, Mann Exit, King Edward twd Hull, Aut. 50 East, Paiement North Exit, 1.5km and left on Rue Bellechasse. Or Rte 148, Aut. 50 to Masson, Paiement North Exit, left on Bellechasse.

B&B
FERME DE BELLECHASSE

Jacques Sauvé
115, ch. De Bellechasse
Gatineau J8T 4Y6
(819) 568-3375
(819) 775-7549
www.inns-bb.com/fermedebellechasse
sauvej@videotron.ca

☀☀☀ F E ⊘ P ⇔R5

	B&B
single	$50-75
double	$65-90
triple	$80-105
quad.	$95-120
child	$15

Open year round

Number of rooms	5
rooms in basement	1
rooms with private bath	2
shared bathrooms	1
shared wc	1

---

5. GATINEAU

Warm and peaceful B&B; breakfast in gazebo, inground swimming pool, resting areas. On a hill, view on Gatineau, Hull and Ottawa; 15 min from parliament, casino, Musée des Civilisations, bike baths, Gatineau park and golf course. Tourist information available on site.

From Aut. 417, Exit Nicholas twd Hull, Aut. 50 East, Exit Maloney, left on Main, left on Magnus, right on Craik. From Montréal, Rte 148, right on Main, etc. From Maniwaki, Aut. 5 South, Aut. 50 East...

B&B
LA MAISON SUR LA COLLINE

Josée and Jean-Pierre Allain
520, rue Craik
Gatineau J8P 5N7
(819) 663-3185
1-866-663-3185
fax (819) 663-7108
www.inns-bb.com/maisonsurlacolline
allain@magma.ca

☀☀☀ F E P 🐐R2

	B&B
single	$60-65
double	$70-75
child	$15

VS MC
Open year round

Number of rooms	3
rooms with private wc	1
shared bathrooms	2

---

6. HULL

Walking distance from downtown Hull, downtown Ottawa and several museums. Au 55 Taché is located near bike paths, golf courses and Parc de la Gatineau. Warm welcome, personalized service and succulent breakfasts await you. Peaceful home, air-conditioned rooms, in-ground pool for hot summer days and fireplace for cold winter nights.

Aut. 417, Exit Mann et King Edward twd Hull, Cartier McDonald bridge, keep your right, Exit Boul. Maisonneuve, Rue Laurier becomes Boul. Alexandre Taché, or Rte 148/Aut. 50, left on Rue Montcalm, right on Boul. Alexandre-Taché.

B&B
AU 55 TACHÉ

Francine Martin and
Bruno Girard
55, boul. Alexandre Taché
Hull J8Y 3L4
(819) 772-1454
fax (819) 772-1461
www3.sympatico.ca/le55tache
le55tache@sympatico.ca

☀☀☀ F E ⊘ P ⛵R.5

	B&B
single	$70-80
double	$80-90
child	$15

VS MC
Open year round

Number of rooms	3
rooms with private bath	1
shared bathrooms	1

7. HULL

An invitation to relax in a calm spot, near Gatineau Park, bike paths and walking trails. Country charm in the city. Warm welcome. Comfortable rooms, central air conditioning and delicious breakfasts. Living room with fireplace, piano and TV. A few min from Ottawa, the casino and museums. Make yourself at home.

From Queensway, Mann Exit twd Hull and Aut. 5 North, Mont-Bleu Exit. Right on Boul. Mont-Bleu, on the hill go left. Take Rue des Bouleaux, turn into des Ormes. From Montréal, Rte 148, Aut. 5 North... Mann Exit.

B&B
AU PIGNON SUR LE PARC

Fernande Béchard-Brazeau
63, rue des Ormes
Hull J8Y 6K6
(819) 777-5559
fax (819) 777-0597
www.inns-bb.com/pignonsurleparc
aupignonsurleparc@sympatico.ca

B&B	
single	$55
double	$65
triple	$85
quad.	$100
child	$10-15

Open year round

Number of rooms	3
rooms in basement	1
shared bathrooms	2

---

8. HULL

Regional Prize for Excellence "Special Favorite" 2001. Comfort and tranquillity just min from Ottawa (museums) and the casino: 2 min from Parc de la Gatineau, bike paths. Attentive service. Finely decorated, air-conditioned house with living room, fireplace. Breakfast on the terrace, by magnificent woodlands and a golf course. Bike shed. Welcome!

Aut. 417, Mann Exit, then King Edward twd Hull, Aut. 5 North, Exit 8, right on Hautes-Plaines, left Rue du Contrefort, right on Du Versant. From Montréal, Rte 148 West. In Hull, Aut. 5 North...

B&B
AU VERSANT
DE LA MONTAGNE

Ghyslaine Vézina
19, rue du Versant
Hull J8Z 2T8
(819) 776-3760
fax (819) 776-2453
www.inns-bb.com/versantdelamontagne
auversant@sympatico.ca

B&B	
single	$50-55
double	$65-70
triple	$90-95
child	$10-15

VS

Open year round

Number of rooms	3
rooms in semi-basement	1
shared bathrooms	2

---

9. HULL

Modern home with three air-conditioned rooms, as well as a suite for four to eight people. For your convenience: heated pool, two fireplaces, free Internet access. Your hostess is friendly and communicative and serves hearty breakfasts on the terrace. The attractions are less than 5min from the B&B: Casino du Lac Leamy, Parc de la Gatineau, Hull-Chelsea-Wakefield steam train and Museum of Civilization. Bikes available for free. Hablamos espanol.

Aut. 417, Exit Mann et King Edward twd Hull, Aut. 5 North, Exit 3 Casino, left at the light, right at the fourth street, Rue Richer, left on Rue Lessard.

B&B
GÎTE FANNY ET MAXIME

Nicole Dubé
31, rue Lessard
Hull J8Y 1M6
(819) 777-1960
http://pages.infinit.net/stefani
nickdube@videotron.ca

B&B	
single	$60-75
double	$70-95
triple	$85-110
quad.	$90-120
suite	$140-200
child	$15

VS MC

Reduced rates: 10% Oct. 1 to Mar. 31

Open year round

Number of rooms	4
rooms in basement	1
rooms with private bath	2
shared bathrooms	1

10. HULL

☀☀☀ F E Ⓔ Ⓢ P 🐾 R4

Located by Gatineau Park, a few min from downtown Hull and Ottawa. Welcome to our home with modern/classical decor and family ambiance. You will enjoy comfort, quiet and lavish breakfasts as well as a host of tourist activities: museums, outdoors, etc. See you soon! Families welcome.

From Ottawa or Rte 148, via Montréal, Aut. 5 North, St-Raymond Exit twd Rte 148 West, right on Ch. Pink, left on Rue des Peupliers, left on Rue Atmosphère, right on Rue Astrolabe.

B&B
MANOIR DES CÈDRES

Linda Coton St-Pierre
5, rue de L'Astrolabe #1
Hull J9A 2W1
(819) 778-7276
(819) 743-7277
fax (819) 778-6502
www.inns-bb.com/manoirdescedres
patrice_st-pierre@sympatico.ca

B&B	
single	$65
double	$75
triple	$80-90
quad.	$100-110
child	$10

Reduced rates: 10 % long stay
Open year round

Number of rooms	2
rooms in basement	2
shared bathrooms	1

11. LAC-SIMON, CHÉNÉVILLE

☀☀☀ F E Ⓔ Ⓢ P 🏊 TA R3

Want to get away from it all? Then come enjoy a rejuvenating stay in a picturesque setting with a magnificent view of the lake and mountains. Landscaped property and private, fine-sand beach. Our rooms and lavish breakfasts will seduce you. Various attractions all year long. Pedestrian and cross-country skiing paths, dog-sled rides nearby. Ravage de Chevreuils de Duhamel, 15km and Parc Oméga, 30km.

From Montréal, Rte 148 West or from Ottawa, Rte 148 East twd Papineauville and Rte 321 North. In Chénéville, Rte 315 West, 1.3km, right on Ch. Tour-du-Lac, 1.5km, left on Ch. Marcelais.

B&B
DOMAINE AUX CROCOLLINES

Thérèse Croteau and
Franz Collinge
642, chemin Marcelais
Lac-Simon, Chénéville J0V 1E0
tel/fax (819) 428-9262
www.inns-bb.com/crocollines
crocollines@infonet.ca

B&B	
single	$48
double	$68
triple	$83

Open year round

Number of rooms	2
rooms with sink	2
shared bathrooms	1
shared wc	1

12. MONTEBELLO

☀☀☀☀ F E Ⓔ Ⓢ P 🏊 TA R1

Spacious rooms, simple inspired breakfasts, a grand living room with the warmth and comfort of home. Eminant house at only 3km from the Château Montebello, the Manoir Papineau and Parc Omega. A place to stop and unwind! In-ground pool, canoeing, paddle-boat; ice skating, tobogganing and exciting winter strolls in snowshoes. In the heart of nature, it is a heaven of peace and quiet. Enjoy the luxuries of a spa with an on-sight professionnal massage therapist and personal body care services. One day is not enough!

From Montréal, Aut. 40 West, twd Ottawa-Hull, exit Hawkesbury, Rte 148 West, 1km before Montebello. From Ottawa-Hull, Aut. 50 and Rte 148 East to Montebello, 1km est of the village.

B&B
JARDINS DE RÊVES

Michelle Lachance
1190, Côte-du-Front
Montebello J0V 1L0
(819) 423-1188
fax (819) 423-2084
www.jardinsdereves.com
jardinsdereves@sympatico.ca

B&B	
single	$75
double	$85-150
child	$20

Taxes extra VS MC IT

Reduced rates: Sept. 10 to May 31, sun to thurs: 20% 3 nights and more except Christmas holidays
Open year round

Number of rooms	5
rooms with private bath	5

13. PAPINEAUVILLE, MONTEBELLO

☀☀☀☀ **F E P** 〰 R.1

Our 150-year-old house will charm you. Peaceful environement. Just 5km from Chateau Montebello, 65km from Hull/Ottawa. Home-made jams, outdoor pool. Nearby you will find: golf, horseback riding, rafting, cross-country skiing, ice-fishing. Golf packages available. Member CAA.

Halfway between Montréal and Hull-Ottawa by Rte 148. From Montréal twd Papineauville, right on Rue Joseph Lucien Malo at the corner with the Ultramar garage.

B&B
À L'ORÉE DU MOULIN

Suzanne Lacasse
170, rue Joseph Lucien Malo
Papineauville, Montebello
J0V 1R0
tel/fax **(819) 427-8534**
www.aloreedumoulin.qc.ca
moulin.lacasse@sympatico.ca

B&B	
single	$60
double	$80
triple	$110
child	$30

VS
Open year round

Number of rooms	4
shared bathrooms	2

🏛 🦫 🎣 🚴 🏇 🥾 🐟 🛶

---

14. PONTIAC, LUSKVILLE

☀☀☀ **F E 🚭 P** 🐾 R2

Winner of the Grand Prix du Tourisme Québécois, Outaouais 2000 and the 1998 regional "Special Favorite" Award of Excellence. Located 25 min from Ottawa, next to Gatineau Park. Spend an evening by the fire in a log house. Reiki, reflexology, canoes, guided canoe excursions, antique forge, canoe-building workshop, hiking, snowshoeing, backcountry skiing, wildlife observation (deer, bears), two-person paragliding with qualified instructor.

From Hull, Aut. 5 North, Exit Boul. St-Raymond, Chemin de la Montagne North, 17km, right on Chemin Crégheur.

B&B
AU CHARME DE LA MONTAGNE

Thérèse André and
Armand Ducharme
368, chemin Crégheur
Pontiac, Luskville J0X 2G0
(819) 455-9158
fax (819) 455-2706
www.aucharmedelamontagne.ca
*aucharmedelamontagne@
videotron.ca*

B&B	
single	$50-60
double	$60-70
child	$15

VS
Open year round

Number of rooms	3
rooms with sink	3
shared bathrooms	2

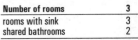

🦫 🎣 🚶 🚴 🏇 ⛷ 🎿

---

15. ST-ANDRÉ-AVELLIN

☀☀☀☀ **F E P** TA R.1

Hundred-year-old house on the heritage tour in the historic heart of the village. Victorian period furniture. 4 cosy romantic rooms. Solarium. Restaurants, shops, attractions and services close by. The charm and simplicity of days gone by... Friendly welcome.

From Montréal, Rte 148 West or from Ottawa-Hull Aut. 50 and Rte 148 East twd Papineauville. Rte 321 North, 12km. In St-André-Avellin, left in front of the church, grey-stone house on the left.

B&B
L'ANCESTRALE

Diane Cardinal
19, rue Saint-André
Saint-André-Avellin J0V 1W0
(819) 983-3232
fax (819) 983-3466
www.inns-bb.com/ancestrale

B&B	
single	$50
double	$65
child	$10

Taxes extra VS MC IT
Open year round

Number of rooms	5
rooms in basement	1
rooms with private bath	2
shared bathrooms	1
shared wc	2

🦫 🎣 🚶 🚴 🏊 🎿

16. VAL-DES-MONTS

☀☀☀ **F** e ⊗ **P** ⮲ R2

Country B&B near lakes, forests and wide expanses, 25km from Hull-Ottawa. Nearby: fish breeding, saphouse, skidoo trails (rentals available) and cross-country skiing, cycling paths, Laflèche cave. On site: bee-keeping, pool, recreation canoes.

From Montréal, Rte 148 West or from Ottawa/Hull, Aut. 50 twd Montréal, Exit Boul. Lorrain, 10.5km on Rte 366 North, left on Rue École, at the dépanneur, 1km, right on Prud'homme.

B&B
AUX PETITS OISEAUX

Gaétane and Laurent Rousseau
6, rue Prud'homme
Val-des-Monts J8N 7C2
(819) 671-2513
www.cyberus.ca/~rousseau/gite
rousseau@cyberus.ca

	B&B
single	$50-55
double	$60-65
child	$10
Open year round	
Number of rooms	**3**
rooms with sink	1
shared bathrooms	2

17. VINOY, CHÉNÉVILLE

☀☀☀ **F** **E** **P** ⭲ ✕ TA

Special mention from the jury "Success" 2000. In a stream-laced wooded valley, retreat where period decor revives old memories while creating new ones. A farmyard enchants children, cosy corners invite lovers' whispers, nature's bounty nurtures the camaraderie of old friends. Taste each season at its peak. Prize for Excellence "Special Favorite" 1995-96. **Farm Stay p 71. See colour photos.**

From Montréal, Rte 148 West From Ottawa/Hull, Aut. 50, Rte 148 East twd Papineauville. North on Rte 321. 12km from St-André-Avellin, right on Montée Vinoy, 5km.

INN
LES JARDINS DE VINOY

Suzanne Benoit and
André Chagnon
497, montée Vinoy Ouest
Vinoy, Chénéville J0V 1E0
(819) 428-3774
fax (819) 428-1877
www.jardinsdevinoy.qc.ca
a.chagnon@infonet.ca

	B&B	MAP
single	$50-65	$69-84
double	$65-80	$103-118
triple	$75-90	$132-147
quad.	$85-100	$161-176
child	$10	$19

Taxes extra VS MC

Reduced rates: Sep. 6 to June 22
Open year round

Number of rooms	**5**
rooms with private bath	1
shared bathrooms	2
shared wc	1

AGROTOURISM

Farm Stays:

🍎 **4** FERME DE BELLECHASSE, Gatineau...*Page 71*

🍎 **17** LES JARDINS DE VINOY, Vinoy, Chénéville ....*Page 71*

Country-Style Dining:

🍎 **18** LE POMMIER D'ARGENT, Gatineau ....*Page 32*

🍎 **19** FERME CAVALIER, Saint-Sixte ....*Page 32*

QUÉBEC CITY REGION

© ULYSSES

Saint-Ferréol-les-Neiges 26 27 31
Parc du Mont-Sainte-Anne 30
Cap-Tournente 6 79
Sainte-Anne-de-Beaupré 75
Château-Richer 7 to 10 82 84
Sainte-Famille 23
Île d'Orléans 18 to 22 85
Saint-Jean 12 to 15
Saint-Pierre
Saint-Laurent 16 17 83
Sainte-Pétronille 24 25
Saint-Adolphe 78
Boischatel 1 to 3
Beauport
Québec City See Close-up of Q.U.C.
Sillery
Sainte-Foy
Wendake
Lac-Delage
Charlesbourg
Cap-Rouge
Shannon 77
Saint-Gabriel-de-Valcartier 72
Station écotouristique de Duchesnay
Saint-Raymond 73 74
Sainte-Catherine-de-la-Jacques-Cartier 76
Neuville 29 28 30
Saint-Alban 70
Saint-Casimir 71
Portneuf 4 5
Cap-Santé
Deschambault 2 11

CHAUDIÈRE-APPALACHES

N

Québec Urban Community 6km

LÉVIS
BEAUPORT 54 to 58 440
See Close-up of Downtown
WENDAKE 69
QUÉBEC
VANIER
SAINTE-FOY 45 63 to 66
SILLERY 67 68
CAP-ROUGE 59 to 61

Downtown Québec City
VANIER
VIEUX-QUÉBEC
33 to 36 37 to 41 42 43 46 50 51 53
44 47 48 52 49

* The numbers on the map refer to the establishments described in the text.

1. BOISCHATEL

Large Canadian house in the heart of all the attractions in the Québec City area. 300m from the Montmorency falls, opposite Île d'Orléans. 10 min from Old Québec City. Fax and Internet service on site. Copious and varied breakfast. Whale excursion reservations. Free parking.

From Montréal, Aut. 20 East or Aut. 40 East twd Ste-Anne-de-Beaupré. Left at Côte-de-l'Église, Boischatel Exit, 1.6km after Chutes Montmorency at 1st traffic light. Head up the hill, Côte de l'Église, left on Av. Royale, 0.6km.

B&B
AU GÎTE DE LA CHUTE

Claire and Jean-Guy Bédard
5143, avenue Royale
Boischatel G0A 1H0
(418) 822-3789
fax (418) 822-2344
**www.quebecweb.com/
gitedelachute**
5143gite@clic.net

	B&B
single	$55
double	$65
child	$15

VS

Reduced rates: 3 nights or more
Open year round

Number of rooms	5
rooms in basement	3
shared bathrooms	2
shared wc	1

---

2. BOISCHATEL

10 min from Québec City, "Le Refuge du Voyageur" offers an exceptional view of the city, the St. Lawrence River, l'Île-d'Orléans and it's bridge. Rustic decor. 2 spacious family-size suite with kitchenette, private entrance and balcony.

From Québec City, Aut. Dufferin-Montmorency East, Boischatel Exit Côte de l'église, to Av. Royale, right.

B&B
LE REFUGE DU VOYAGEUR

Raynald Vézina
5516, avenue Royale
Boischatel G0A 1H0
(418) 822-2589
www.inns-bb.com/voyageur

	B&B
single	$60
double	$60
triple	$80
quad.	$100
child	$0-15

Open year round

Number of rooms	2
rooms with private bath	2

---

3. BOISCHATEL

Our new, old-fashioned-style home is filled with objects gathered during our trips throughout the years; each room and bathroom features a lovely, unique decor. You'll be intrigued by their originality! Discover Maïna the Aboriginal, Lucas the sports fan, Rozi the artist, Mélanie the traveller and Elliot the captain. The splendid view of the St. Lawrence River and Île d'Orléans is conducive to calm and relaxation, and the hearty, refined breakfast is served before an authentic wood-burning stove dating from 1910. 10min from downtown and 20min from Mont-Saint-Anne via Aut. 40 East, and 1km from the Montmorency falls, Manoir and summer playhouse. We look forward to welcoming you warmly.

From Québec City, Aut. Dufferin-Montmorency East, Exit Boischatel, Côte de l'Église, right on Avenue Royale.

B&B
LE ROYAL CHAMPÊTRE

Denise Caron
5494, avenue Royale
Boischatel G0A 1H0
(418) 822-3500
(418) 951-6953
fax (418) 822-1800
www.leroyalchampetre.com
gite.royalbb@bellnet.ca

	B&B
single	$85
double	$90-130
triple	$110-130
child	$20

VS IT

Open year round

Number of rooms	5
rooms with private bath	5

4. CAP-SANTÉ

Experience the colours of Québec and the warmth of Provence at our B&B located in the heart of a new district, near the St. Lawrence River and the Route Verte bike path. Peace and quiet assured. Hearty breakfast, homemade jams. Flower garden, in-ground heated pool and, if you're in the mood, a folk song, a legend, a bit of history with "Nicolas le jardinier," his guitar and harmonicas. Why not?

From Québec City or Montréal, Aut. 40, Exit 269. Rte 358, travel 1.7km south to Rte 138 (Chemin du Roy). Turn right and continue 0.3km to Rue du Roy. Right for 0.3km to Rue Gauthier. Turn right and continue 0.3km.

B&B
GÎTE NICOLAS LE JARDINIER

Marcel La Chance and
Giselle Rouillon
70, Gauthier
Cap-Santé G0A 1L0
(418) 285-3239
(418) 999-2456
fax (418) 285-0124
www.gitenicolaslejardinier.com
marlach@oricom.ca

B&B	
single	$50-60
double	$60-70
triple	$87

Open year round

Number of rooms	3
rooms in basement	1
rooms with private bath	1
rooms with sink	2
shared bathrooms	1

5. CAP-SANTÉ

Near the river, in the heart of a romantic village with bygone charm, a century-old house with period furnishings offers you a rendez-vous with history. In harmony with nature, our garden inspires tranquillity. The unique welcome and ambiance will delight you immediately on arrival.

From Québec City, Aut. 40 West, Exit 269, right, 2km. Right on Rte 138, 1km. At flashing light, left on Vieux Chemin. Or from Montréal, Aut. 40 East, Exit 269, turn left...

B&B
LA MAISON DE MLLE BERNARD

Michelle Buteau
56, Le Vieux Chemin, C.P. 268
Cap-Santé G0A 1L0
(418) 285-3149
www.inns-bb.com/bernard
mberna@globetrotter.net

B&B	
single	$50-68
double	$69-79
child	$15

VS MC AM ER
Open: Jan. 3 to Dec. 22

Number of rooms	4
rooms with private bath	1
shared bathrooms	1

6. CAP-TOURMENTE, MONT-STE-ANNE

In the heart of Cap-Tourmente, 12 min from Mont Ste-Anne (view of the slopes), house with 5 rooms with private bathrooms. Familial room with fireplace. Breakfast in the owners residence (right next to the B&B). On site: outdoor pool, hiking or cross-country skiing to the falls and the sugar shack. **Country Home p 254.**

From Québec City, Henri IV Aut. North, twd 40 East, Ste-Anne-de-Beaupré, Rte 138 East, twd St-Joachim, Cap-Tourmente.

B&B
GÎTE DE L'OIE DES NEIGES

Gisèle Perron
390, ch. du Cap-Tourmente
Saint-Joachim G0A 3X0
(418) 827-5153
tel/fax (418) 827-2246
www.inns-bb.com/oiedesneiges
oiedesneiges@hotmail.com

B&B	
single	$75-85
double	$85-90
triple	$115
quad.	$145
child	$15

VS
Open year round

Number of rooms	5
rooms with private bath	5

7. CHÂTEAU-RICHER

Between Mont Ste-Anne and Québec City, in the heart of the Beaupré region, treat yourself to an incomparable stay at our home, along with delicious meals from the Baker restaurant. You will find all the charm of a country home. Rooms in the Inn or the pavilion.

East of Québec City, Rte 138 East. To Ste-Anne-de-Beaupré. 18.5km from the Montmorency falls. Watch for "Baker" on the roof of the restaurant.

INN
AUBERGE BAKER

Gaston Cloutier
8790, avenue Royale
Château-Richer G0A 1N0
(418) 824-4478
1-866-824-4478
fax (418) 824-4412
www.auberge-baker.qc.ca
gcloutier@auberge-baker.qc.ca

★★★ F E ⊘ P X TA

	B&B	MAP
single	$55-110	$87-142
double	$60-115	$124-179
triple	$80-135	$205-231
quad.	$95-150	$248-278
child	$10	$26

Taxes extra VS MC AM ER IT

Reduced rates: Apr. 21 to June 19, Oct. 13 to Dec. 18

Open year round

Number of rooms	7
rooms with private bath	7

8. CHÂTEAU-RICHER

The warm welcome of a small inn, an ancestral house restored to its original style, only 15 min from the centre of Québec City, facing Île d'Orléans, and 20 min from Mont-Ste-Anne. Hablamos español.

Rte 138 East twd Ste-Anne-de-Beaupré, after the Île d'Orléans bridge, left on Rte du Petit-Pré, right on Av. Royale, 9km after Chutes Montmorency.

INN
AUBERGE DU PETIT-PRÉ

Ginette Dion and Yvon Boyer
7126, avenue Royale
Château-Richer G0A 1N0
(418) 824-3852
www.inns-bb.com/petit_pre

F E P X TA R2

	B&B
single	$75
double	$80
triple	$100
quad.	$120
child	$15

Taxes extra VS MC AM IT

Open year round

Number of rooms	4
rooms with private bath	4
shared wc	1

9. CHÂTEAU-RICHER

15 min from Old Québec City and 10 min from Mont-Ste-Anne, stay in a magnificent Victorian house (1868). Hearty home-made breakfast with exceptional view of the river and Île d'Orléans. Large lounge with fireplace. Exquisite, cosy, traditionally furnished rooms. Dinner by reservation. Delicious French cuisine. We speak German.

From Québec City, Rte 138 East, 15km past the Île d'Orléans bridge. In Château-Richer, left at the traffic light on Rue Dick, right on Av. Royale, left on Côte Ste-Achillée, 100 feet, left on Rue Pichette.

INN
AUBERGE LE PETIT SÉJOUR

Pascal, Steffan, Christiane and Anne-Marie
394, rue Pichette
Château-Richer G0A 1N0
(418) 824-3654
fax (418) 824-9356
www.petitsejour.com
petitsejour@globetrotter.net

☀☀☀☀ F E ⊘ P X TA

	B&B	MAP
single	$60-95	$94-129
double	$70-95	$138-163
triple	$105-115	$207-217
quad.	$135	$271

Taxes extra VS MC

Reduced rates: 5% 3 nights and more

Open year round

Number of rooms	5
rooms with private bath	5
shared wc	1

10. CHÂTEAU-RICHER

At the gates of Charlevoix, a welcoming house whose most beautiful room is outside. Enjoy a rowboat or pedal-boat ride among our magnificent, large white swans. Come take advantage of the superb grounds with swimming pool. **Country Home Direction Mont Ste-Anne p 254.**

From Québec City, Rte 138 East or Boul. Ste-Anne. On the right, behind the Motel Roland.

B&B
GÎTE UN AIR D'ÉTÉ

Lynda Boucher and
Claude Gingras
8988, boul. Sainte-Anne
Château-Richer G0A 1N0
(418) 824-9210
1-888-922-8770
fax (418) 824-5645
www.unairdete.com
gite.unairdete@videotron.ca

	B&B
single	$60-80
double	$70-90
triple	$110-130
quad.	$125-145
child	$10

Taxes extra VS MC AM ER IT

Reduced rates: Oct. 1 to May 31
Open: May 1 to Oct. 31

Number of rooms	3
rooms in basement	3
shared bathrooms	1
shared wc	1

11. DESCHAMBAULT

With the St. Lawrence, the falls and Rivière Belisle at its feet, this large hundred-year-old Victorian, nicknamed "the little château", will transport you back in time with flowers, lace and a decor from days gone by. Evening meal of creative and meticulously prepared meals. Snowmobiling, sleigh rides, cross-country skiing, ice-fishing. **See colour photos.**

From Montréal or Québec City, Aut. 40, Exit 254, 1.6km to the river. Left on Rte 138 (Chemin du Roy), 2km. Left at the Inn "Chemin du Roy" sign, Rue St-Laurent.

INN
AUBERGE CHEMIN DU ROY

Francine Bouthat and
Gilles Laberge
106, rue Saint-Laurent
Deschambault G0A 1S0
(418) 286-6958
1-800-933-7040
www.cheminduroy.com

	B&B	MAP
single	$64-89	$94-119
double	$79-104	$139-164
triple	$94-119	$184-209
quad.	$134	$254
child	$12	$20-30

Taxes extra VS MC

Open year round

Number of rooms	8
rooms with private bath	8

12. L'ÎLE-D'ORLÉANS, ST-JEAN

2001 Grand Prix du Tourisme, Québec City region, and national winner of the "Silver" Grand Prix du Tourisme Québécois 2001. Located 25 min from Vieux-Québec, 400m away from the road, near the river; rooms and 1 suite with queen-size bed and balcony with river view. Full breakfast with homemade products. Several packages available.

From Québec City, Aut. 40 or 440 East twd Ste-Anne-de-Beaupré, Île d'Orléans Exit. At traffic light, straight ahead to St-Laurent and St-Jean. 2.4km past the St-Jean.

B&B
AU GIRON DE L'ISLE

Lucie and Gérard Lambert
120, chemin des Lièges
Saint-Jean, Île d'Orléans
G0A 3W0
(418) 829-0985
1-888-280-6636
fax (418) 829-1059
www.total.net/~giron
giron@total.net

	B&B
single	$75-110
double	$85-120
triple	$150
quad.	$160
child	$20

Taxes extra VS MC AM IT

Reduced rates: Sun. to thurs Oct. 15 to Dec. 15 and Mar. 1 to Apr. 30
Open year round

Number of rooms	3
rooms with private bath	3

13. L'ÎLE-D'ORLÉANS, ST-JEAN

We are 25 min from Québec City, in an ancestral home very close to the river, and near museums, theatres, handicraft boutiques, art galleries, and restaurants. Friendly atmosphere and hearty breakfast. We will do everything we can to make your stay a pleasant one. Welcome to Île d'Orléans.

From Québec City, Rte 440 East twd Ste-Anne-de-Beaupré, Île d'Orléans Exit. At the traffic light, straight ahead, 20km. On the right, corner of Chemin du Quai.

B&B
GÎTE DU QUAI

Rita and Grégoire Roux
1686, chemin Royal
Saint-Jean, Île d'Orléans
G0A 3W0
(418) 829-2278
www.inns-bb.com/quai

☀☀☀ F e P TA R.1

	B&B
single	$40
double	$53
triple	$75
child	$10-15

Reduced rates: May 1 to May 31, Oct. 1 to Oct. 31
Open: May 1 to Oct. 31

Number of rooms	3
shared bathrooms	2

🏛 🦆 🖼 🚶 🚲

14. L'ÎLE-D'ORLÉANS, ST-JEAN

Nestled on the cape and the ancestral lands of the "Audets, name Lapointes", our bicentenary house welcomes guests in a warm atmosphere. Quiet, with a view of the river that remains charming with each passing season. You will want to linger over our lavish breakfasts. A stay that allows you to discover the island and its treasures.

From Québec City, Rte 440 East, Île d'Orléans Exit. At the light, continue straight ahead, 17.7km. After Manoir Mauvide-Genest, left on hill. Go up to the white house on the right.

B&B
LA MAISON SUR LA CÔTE

Hélène and Pierre Morissette
1477, chemin Royal
Saint-Jean, Île d'Orléans
G0A 3W0
(418) 829-2971
fax (418) 829-0991
pages.infinit.net/orleans
p.morissette@videotron.ca

☀☀☀ F E P TA R.5

	B&B
single	$55
double	$60
triple	$90

Open: Apr. 1 to Oct. 31

Number of rooms	4
rooms with sink	4
shared bathrooms	2

🏛 🛏 🖼 🚶 🚲

15. L'ÎLE-D'ORLÉANS, ST-JEAN

If you're looking for a peaceful and comfortable place, our 19th century replica of an old farm house, situated on a cliff, is awaiting you. Your hosts: Yolande, Claude and Valentine (the cat).

From Québec City, Rte 138 East twd Ste-Anne-de-Beaupré, Île d'Orléans Exit. After the bridge straight ahead, 17.5km. At the B&B sign, left, the house is on your right on the cliff.

B&B
LE MAS DE L'ISLE

Yolande and Claude Dumesnil
1155, chemin Royal
Saint-Jean, Île d'Orléans
G0A 3W0
tel/fax (418) 829-1213
www.inns-bb.com/lemasdelisle
sorciere@total.net

☀☀☀ ⚿ F E 🚭 P 🐾 TA R.5

	B&B
single	$55-60
double	$60-65
triple	$90-95
quad.	$115
child	$20

VS

Reduced rates: Nov. 1 to Apr. 30
Open year round

Number of rooms	3
shared bathrooms	2

🏛 🖼 🚶 🚲 ⛷ 🔭 ⛸

16. L'ÎLE-D'ORLÉANS, ST-LAURENT

Feel the romantic charm and comfort in the rooms furnished with antiques belonging to our grandmothers. Every room has its own private bathroom in our ancestral home, dating from 1836. Our cottage totally equipped and independent can lodge as much as 6 people. Our riverside terrace, equipped with a fireplace, offers easy access to the beach where you watch the unique view. A warm, friendly and peaceful atmosphere awaits you... And what can we say about Marie's breakfasts ! They are delicious and you will never forget the taste. Our pleasure is to give you pleasure !

From Québec, Aut. 40 East or Aut. 440, twd Ste-Anne-de-Beaupré, Exit 235 Île d'Orléans. After the bridge, at light, straight ahead 7.5km.

INN
AUBERGE L'ÎLE FLOTTANTE

Marie-Pierre Feix etMichel Venkovic
1657, Chemin Royal, C.P 127
Saint-Laurent-de-l'Île-d'Orléans G0A 3Z0
(418) 828-9476
www.ileflottante.com
ileflottante@oricom.ca

	B&B
single	$80-90
double	$85-120
triple	$110-135
quad.	$150

Taxes extra VS

Reduced rates: for a long stay
Open year round

Number of rooms	5
rooms with private bath	5

17. L'ÎLE-D'ORLÉANS, ST-LAURENT

Regional Prize for Excellence "Special Favorite" 2001. Our lovely Victorian home has exquisite air-conditioned bedrooms that will delight you. Come and enjoy a royal breakfast while admiring the majestic St. Lawrence River. The beauty of the landscape property is only equaled by the melody of the birds. You will be surprised how good it feels to let yourself be pampered. At l'Oasis de Rêves (Dream Oasis), your dreams do come true.

From Québec City, Aut. 40 East twd Ste-Anne-de-Beaupré, Île d'Orléans Exit. At the traffic light, continue straight ahead, 5km past St-Laurent church.

B&B
L'OASIS DE RÊVES

Lyette Chedore and Jean Tardif
179, chemin Royal
Saint-Laurent-de-l'Île-d'Orléans G0A 3Z0
(418) 829-3473
fax (418) 829-0053
www.oasisdereves.com
info@oasisdereves.com

	B&B
single	$95-130
double	$105-140
triple	$175
child	$35

VS MC
Open: May 1 to Oct. 31

Number of rooms	3
rooms with private bath	3

18. L'ÎLE-D'ORLÉANS, ST-PIERRE

Situated next door to the oldest church in Québec, Auberge Le Vieux Presbytère is a beautiful, large ancestral home. Restaurant on site. The 150,000-ft property has American buffalo, wapitis (large deer) and ostriches. Breathtaking view. Only 15 min from Québec City. Bike rental on site.

From Québec City, Aut. Dufferin-Montmorency, Île d'Orléans Exit. Left at the light. At the village centre of Saint-Pierre, left between the two churches.

INN
AUBERGE LE VIEUX PRESBYTÈRE

Louise Lapointe and Hughes L'Heureux
1247, rue Mgr. D'Esgly
Saint-Pierre-de-l'Île-d'Orléans G0A 4E0
(418) 828-9723
1-888-828-9723
fax (418) 828-2189
www.presbytere.com

	B&B	MAP
single	$60-120	$85-135
double	$70-130	$120-170
triple	$100-155	$180-225
quad.	$115-170	$225-270
child	$20	

Taxes extra VS MC AM ER IT
Open year round

Number of rooms	8
rooms with private bath	6
shared bathrooms	1
shared wc	2

19. L'ÎLE-D'ORLÉANS, ST-PIERRE

☀☀☀ **F e P TA R1**

Located near the bridge, our B&B is 10 min from Québec City, 5 min from the Montmorency falls and 20 min from Ste-Anne-de-Beaupré. Here, comfort, cleanliness, privacy and hearty breakfasts are guaranteed! Bicycle storage. One room with private entrance and another with air conditioning. At "Crépuscule", enjoy an explosion of fall colours!

From Québec City, Aut. 40 East or 440 East, twd Ste-Anne-de-Beaupré, Exit 325 Île d'Orléans. At the traffic light at top of the hill, straight about 1km.

B&B
CRÉPUSCULE

Louise Hamel
863, rue Prévost
Saint-Pierre-de-l'Île-d'Orléans G0A 4E0
(418) 828-9425
www.inns-bb.com/crepuscule
louise.hamel3@sympatico.ca

	B&B
single	$55
double	$60-65
triple	$85
quad.	$105
child	$10

Open: Dec. 20 to Oct. 31

Number of rooms	3
rooms with private bath	3

---

20. L'ÎLE-D'ORLÉANS, ST-PIERRE

☀☀☀ **F e ⊘ P TA R1**

Welcome to the B&B "Bel Horizon", the gateway to Île d'Orléans, only 15 min from Québec City. Comfort, intimacy, complete breakfast. View of the river, facing Chutes Montmorency. 5 rooms (12 people): 2 on ground-floor, 3 on first floor, family suite, private bathroom. Ideal for family and groups. Shared bathrooms for couples (if not in a group). Reserve now!

At entrance to Québec City, Rte 440 or Aut. 40 East twd Ste-Anne-de-Beaupré, about 35km, Exit 325 Île d'Orléans. At the top of the hill, at the light, right, 1km.

B&B
GÎTE BEL HORIZON

Yvette and Paul-Émile Vézina
402, chemin Royal
Saint-Pierre-de-l'Île-d'Orléans G0A 4E0
(418) 828-9207
www.inns-bb.com/belhorizon
belhorizon@sympatico.ca

	B&B
single	$50-60
double	$65
triple	$90
quad.	$90-100
child	$20

VS MC

Reduced rates: Feb. 1 to May 1
Open: Feb. 1 to Nov. 1

Number of rooms	5
rooms with private bath	3
shared bathrooms	1

---

21. L'ÎLE-D'ORLÉANS, ST-PIERRE

☀☀☀☀ **F E P R.5**

Regional Prize for Excellence "Special Favorite" 2002. Located in one of the most beautiful spots on Île d'Orléans, nestled in a vineyard, our ancestral home invites you to relive a bit of history. Tour of the vineyard and free wine tasting. Our rooms combine modern comfort with a warm and intimate ambiance. Memorable breakfasts! Large living room with fireplace. Terrace with a view of the river and sunsets. Less than 15 min from Québec City, 20 min from Mont Ste-Anne and near the Montmorency Falls.

On Île-d'Orléans, left at the traffic light, 2km.

B&B
LA MAISON DU VIGNOBLE

Lise Roy
1071, chemin Royal
Saint-Pierre-de-l'Île-d'Orléans G0A 4E0
(418) 828-9562
fax (418) 828-1764
www.inns-bb.com/vignoble
isledebacchus@sympatico.ca

	B&B
single	$50-60
double	$65-85
triple	$90-110
quad.	$135
child	$15

VS MC

Open year round

Number of rooms	4
rooms with private bath	2
shared bathrooms	2

22. L'ÎLE-D'ORLÉANS, ST-PIERRE

A house with over 200 years of history... is cosy comfort where antique furniture and dried flowers encourage calm and relaxation. Come share authentic and refined country cooking in the intimacy of the dining room. Relax by the fire in the living room or in the garden near the farmyard.

From Québec City, Aut. 40 or 440 East twd Ste-Anne-de-Beaupré, Île d'Orléans Exit. Left at the traffic light, 3km.

INN
L'AUBERGE SUR LES PENDANTS

Chantale Vignault and
Jean-Christophe L'Allier
1463, chemin Royal
Saint-Pierre-de-l'Île-
d'Orléans G0A 4E0
(418) 828-1139
www.inns-bb.com/pendants
surlespendants@qc.aira.com

	B&B	MAP
single	$52	$79
double	$62	$116
triple	$77	$158
child	$15	$22

Taxes extra VS MC AM IT
Open year round

Number of rooms	5
shared bathrooms	2

---

23. L'ÎLE-D'ORLÉANS, STE-FAMILLE

The wind has carried us to all the continents and we've brought back the scents, great life experiences, a different way of doing things and the desire to share. Hundred-year-old house, adjoining shop, view of the river and the Laurentians, walking path, cycling, X-country skiing, snowshoeing, picnic baskets. We speak Japanese, French and English. Dinner if request.

From Québec City, Aut. 440 East twd Ste-Anne-de-Beaupré, Île d'Orléans Exit. Left at the light, straight for 13km.

B&B
AU TOIT BLEU

Loulou Germain
3879, chemin Royal
Sainte-Famille, Île d'Orléans
G0A 3P0
(418) 829-1078
fax (418) 829-3052
www.inns-bb.com/toitbleu
toitbleu@total.net

	B&B
single	$60-85
double	$65-90
triple	$85-110
quad.	$130

VS AM

Reduced rates: 10% 3 nights and more, Nov. 1 to Apr. 30
Open year round

Number of rooms	5
rooms with private bath	3
rooms with sink	2
shared bathrooms	1
shared wc	2

---

24. L'ÎLE-D'ORLÉANS, STE-PÉTRONILLE

The tip of the island is pure magic! On Île d'Orléans, the cradle of French civilization (more precisely in Sainte-Pétronille, one of the most beautiful villages in Québec), you will find Auberge La Goéliche. Our warm, personalized rooms all offer a view of the majestic St. Lawrence River. In the dining room/sunroom, discover French-style local cuisine prepared by our chef, Martin Bolduc, as well as our wine cellar, which includes products that were privately imported. **See colour photos.**

Aut. 40, Exit Pont de l'Île d'Orléans, at the lights, right to Sainte-Pétronille, follow the blue tourist signs for Auberge La Goéliche.

INN
AUBERGE LA GOÉLICHE

Pascal Bussières
22, chemin du Quai
Ste-Pétronille, Île d'Orléans
G0A 4C0
(418) 828-2248
1-888-511-2248
fax (418) 828-2745
www.goeliche.ca
infos@goeliche.ca

	B&B	MAP
single	$128-163	$155-190
double	$163-198	$220-255

Taxes extra VS MC AM ER IT

Reduced rates: on information
Open year round

Number of rooms	16
rooms with private bath	16

25. L'ÎLE-D'ORLÉANS, STE-PÉTRONILLE

☀ ☀ ☀ F E 🚭 P R.5

Enchanting setting on magical Île d'Orléans. Come discover the art of living in harmony with the past in our home, amidst a century and a half of history. The magnificent view of the majestic St. Lawrence and a visit to the Chutes Montmorency will leave you with unforgettable memories. To top it all off, we offer generous breakfasts and hospitality worthy of the finest establishments; a wonderful stay awaits you.

From Québec City, Rte 138 and Aut. 40 or 440 twd St-Anne-de-Beaupré, Île d'Orléans Exit. Right at the light after the bridge, 3.5km.

B&B
LE 91 DU BOUT DE L'ÎLE

Jeanne Trottier
91, chemin Royal,
ch. du Bout de l'Île
Sainte-Pétronille,
Île d'Orléans G0A 4C0
(418) 828-2678
www.inns-bb.com/91duboutdelile

	B&B
single	$50-55
double	$60-65
triple	$80-85

Open: Feb. 1 to Nov. 1

Number of rooms	4
rooms with sink	2
shared bathrooms	2

---

26. MONT-STE-ANNE, ST-FERRÉOL

★ ★ F E P ⇌ ✕

Once upon a time, there was a small school, a general store, a cosy inn... Just 5 min from Mont Ste-Anne and 30 min from Québec City, in an attraction-packed region, you'll discover an inn with special charm and architecture. Comfortable rooms, a warm dining room and a highly skilled chef will make your stay an experience well worth repeating!

From Québec City, Rte 138 East, 40km. In Beaupré, twd Mont Ste-Anne, Rte 360 East, 10km. Just past the church, in the heart of the village

INN
AUBERGE DU
MAGASIN GÉNÉRAL

Dominique and Martin Forgues
3470, avenue Royale
Saint-Ferréol-les-Neiges
G0A 3R0
(418) 826-3636
1-866-826-3636
fax (418) 826-0216
www.aubergedumagasingeneral.
qc.ca
martin.forgues@sympatico.ca

	B&B	MAP
single	$75	$109
double	$95	$139
triple	$105	$164
quad.	$115	$183

Taxes extra VS MC IT
Open year round

Number of rooms	10
rooms with private bath	10

---

27. MONT-STE-ANNE, ST-FERRÉOL

★ ★ F 🚭 P R.25

5min from Mont Ste-Anne and 30min from Québec City, discover our quiet, comfortable, soundproof rooms with queen-size or twin beds, sink, suite and bridal suite with therapeutic bath and TV. Sitting room with fireplace. Amazing view of Mont Ste-Anne, deep in the wilderness. Nearby: Sept Chutes, "Grand Canyon," Cap Tourmente, ski, cycling, golf, pedestrian paths, snowmobiling, horseback riding, dog-sledding. Ski packages. Antique shop on site.

From Québec City, Rte 138 East, 40km. At Beaupré, twd Mont-Ste-Anne, Rte 360, 10km. From Baie-St-Paul, Rte 138 West, 30km, and Rte 360 twd St-Ferréol. After the 7 Chutes, 3km.

B&B
LES AROLLES

Louise Desmeules
3489, av. Royale, route 360
Saint-Ferréol-les-Neiges
G0A 3R0
tel/fax (418) 826-2136
www.inns-bb.com/arolles
aubergelesarolles@
megaquebec.net

	B&B
single	$60-80
double	$70-105
triple	$90-105
quad.	$115
child	$15

Taxes extra VS MC IT
Open year round

Number of rooms	6
rooms with private bath	2
rooms with sink	3
shared bathrooms	2

28. NEUVILLE

☀ ☀ ☀ 🄵🄴⊘🄿 TA R1

200 years of history... This magnificent residence offers a splendid view of the majestic St. Lawrence River and welcomes you throughout the year. This site is ideal for relaxation, with beautiful landscapes, warm reception and personalized care that make for a pleasant stay. On-site services: spa, billiards, fireplace, "murder mystery" dinners, home theatre with satellite, piano, three-course breakfast, theme rooms, evening meal by request.

Aut. 40, Exit 281 South, Rte 138 East, 1.5km.

B&B
AU GRÉ DES SAISONS

Sophie Charrois
1117, Route 138
Neuville G0A 2R0
(418) 876-2384
www.inns-bb.com/gredessaisons
charrois@mail.com

	B&B
single	$75
double	$90
triple	$110
quad.	$130
child	$15

Taxes extra VS

Reduced rates: $10 Nov. 1 to May 1 except Chrismas holidays
Open year round

Number of rooms	4
rooms with private bath	1
shared bathrooms	1
shared wc	1

---

29. NEUVILLE

☀ ☀ ☀ 🄵🄴🄿 🍴 R8

30 min from Québec City, discover a unique agrotourism farm with emus, ostriches rheas and other animals. Large house with solarium, filled with sunshine and good times, warm ambiance. Families welcome! Special: 2 adults + 2 children $84/B&B or $125/MAP. Shop on premises. Free farm visit. Come share our passion! **Farm Stay p 72.**

Aut. 40 West or East, Exit 285 Neuville twd Pont-Rouge, Rte Gravel, about 5km, right on Petit-Capsa.

B&B
LA FERME L'ÉMEULIENNE

Émilienne Chouinard and
Jacques Houle
307, rang Petit-Capsa
Neuville G0A 2R0
(418) 876-2788
fax (418) 876-3280
www.quebecweb.com/emeu
emeu@globetrotter.net

	B&B	MAP
single	$50	$70
double	$60	$100
child	$15	$25

Taxes extra

Reduced rates: 10% Oct. 30 to Apr. 30 2 nights and more
Open year round

Number of rooms	2
shared bathrooms	1
shared wc	1

---

30. NEUVILLE

☀ ☀ ☀ ☀ 🄵🄴⊘🄿 TA R1

15 min from Québec City, in one of the prettiest villages in Québec, discover many ancestral houses. Stunning view of the St. Lawrence. Relax on the terrace, in the sunroom or near the fireplace. Air conditioned. Nearby: marina, antiques, theatre and dogsledding. Guides tours of the village and church. Bikes available.

From Montréal or Québec City, Aut. 40, Exit 285, twd Neuville, Route 138, 3km.

B&B
LA MAISON DUBUC

Madeleine and Antoine Dubuc
421, rue des Érables
Neuville G0A 2R0
tel/fax (418) 876-2573
www.inns-bb.com/dubuc
maison.dubuc@globetrotter.net

	B&B
single	$50
double	$65
child	$15

Reduced rates: 10% double occupancy 3 nights or more
Open year round

Number of rooms	2
shared bathrooms	2

31. NEUVILLE

All the charm of the country 15 min from Québec City. View of the St. Lawrence River, the perfect spot. Large property, woods, terrace with inground pool. Generous breakfast served on the terrace or in the dining room. Living room with TV, pool room. Bikes available. Large parking lot.

From Montréal, Aut. 40 East, Exit 281 Neuville, Rte 138 East, 6km. From Québec City, Aut. 40 West, Exit 298, Rte 138 West, 10.4km.

B&B
LE GÎTE DE NEUVILLE

Louise Côté and Ernest Germain
173, Route 138
Neuville G0A 2R0
(418) 876-3779
(418) 876-3060
fax (418) 876-3780
www.inns-bb.com/neuville
legitedeneuville@videotron.ca

	B&B
single	$45
double	$60
child	$15

VS IT

Reduced rates: 10% 2 nights, 15% 3 nights and more
Open year round

Number of rooms	3
shared bathrooms	1
shared wc	2

---

32. PORTNEUF

Steps away from the majestic St. Lawrence River, this beautiful stone-covered ancestral home is nestled in the Baronnie de Portneuf. More than 220 years old, this picturesque home will charm you, and you will be seduced by the tranquillity and beauty of the countryside. Spend a few moments by the fire, in the flower garden or the water garden, in the shade of our fruit trees. Feel the benefits of the spa, sauna and massage therapy for total relaxation. Healthy breakfast. Table d'hôte by reservation. **See colour photos.**

50km west of Québec City. Aut. 40, Exit 261 twd Portneuf, left on 1ère Av.

B&B
AUBERGE DE LA BARONNIE
DE PORTNEUF

Michelle Paquet-Rivière and
Denis Rivière
54, 1ère Avenue
Portneuf G0A 2Y0
(418) 286-4000
fax (418) 286-6767
www.baronnie.ca
labaronnie@globetrotter.net

	B&B	MAP
single	$60	$90
double	$70	$130

Open year round

Number of rooms	2
shared bathrooms	1
shared wc	1

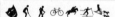

---

33. QUÉBEC

Located 5 min from Vieux-Québec and the convention centre, Abat-Jour B&B will fill your stay with unforgettable pleasant memories. Travel back in time and revel in the culture and history of Québec. Go for a bike ride on the Corridor de Cheminots, explore Domaine Maizeret, Parc Montmorency and much more. Cordial reception and personalized service. Delicious breakfasts. See you soon!

Aut. 20, Pierre-Laporte bridge or Aut. 40 twd Ste-Anne-de-Beaupré, Exit 316. At the 1st stop sign, Rue Chamfleury straight to the 8th stop sign, left De Fondville, 700m.

B&B
ABAT-JOUR B&B

Nadia El-Ghandouri
2064, rue De Fondville
Québec G1J 1X6
(418) 666-6654
(418) 265-4853
fax (418) 666-6699
www.abatjour.ca
info@abatjour.ca

	B&B
single	$52-77
double	$67-87
triple	$87-107
quad.	$107-127
child	$10

VS MC

Open year round

Number of rooms	3
rooms with private bath	2
rooms with sink	3
shared bathrooms	1
shared wc	1

34. QUÉBEC

☀☀☀ **F** **E** ⊘ **P** ⇌ **R.3**

Located in the heart of Québec City, Acacias offers luxury suites with refrigerator, microwave, cable TV and air conditioning. Complete bathroom. We are situated near all the main attractions.

From Montréal, Aut. 20, Pierre-Laporte bridge, Exit Boul. Laurier. Left on Rue Holland, left on Rue Marie Rollet. Aut. 40, right on Côte St-Sacrement, right on Rue Marie Rollet.

B&B
ACACIAS

Clément Thivierge
1336, Marie-Rollet
Québec G1S 2H2
tel/fax (418) 681-6651
www.quebecweb.com/acacias
acaciasqc@hotmail.com

B&B	
single	$65-110
double	$65-110
triple	$85-130
quad.	$105-150

Open year round

Number of rooms	3
rooms with private bath	3

---

35. QUÉBEC

☀☀☀ **F** **E** ⊘ **P** **TA** **R.1**

In Old Québec, extra muros, few steps from St-John Gate and its old walls, close to Convention Center and all services "l'Heure Douce" a cosy B&B welcomes you in its ancestral house. Confortable and charming rooms. Excellent breakfast served at your convenience. Dining room and panoramic balcony reserved to our guests. Good addresses suggested. Parking on demand.

Aut. 20, P-Laporte bridge, Boul. Laurier Exit, Rue Cartier, left, right Chemin Ste-Foy, left St-Augustin twd Richelieu. Aut. 40, Boul. Charest, twd dowtown. Right Dorchester, côte d'Abraham, right Richelieu.

B&B
ACCUEIL B&B L'HEURE DOUCE

Diane Dumont
704, rue Richelieu
Québec G1R 1K7
tel/fax (418) 649-1935
bbheuredouce.com
heuredouce@videotron.ca

B&B	
single	$55-65
double	$65-75
triple	$85-100
quad.	$110-125

Taxes extra VS
Open year round

Number of rooms	3
shared bathrooms	2

---

36. QUÉBEC

☀☀☀ **F** **e** ⊘ **P** 🐾 **R.3**

Cosy house built in 1930, near the Musée du Québec; you'll admire the river and greenery of the Plains of Abraham as you walk towards the old city. Exquisite breakfast, served in the flowery garden or the dining room. We'll chat about the history of our beautiful city and about what you like. Free parking.

From Montréal, Aut. 20, Pierre-Laporte bridge, twd downtown. 8km from the bridge, left on Av. Murray. From Aut. 40, Av. St-Sacrement South Exit, left on Chemin St-Louis, 1.3km, left on Av. Murray.

B&B
À LA CAMPAGNE EN VILLE

Marie Archambault
1160, avenue Murray
Québec G1S 3B6
(418) 683-6638
www.quebecweb.com/gpq/
alacampagneenville
marie.archambault@videotron.ca

B&B	
single	$60
double	$70
triple	$90
child	$15

Reduced rates: 3 nights or more double occupancy
Open year round

Number of rooms	2
shared bathrooms	1

37. QUÉBEC

☀☀☀☀ **F** E ⊘ **P** R.2

Discover enchantment in this beautiful, turn-of-the-century Tudor-style home, near national parks and Vieux-Québec. Top-quality lodging under a gabled roof. Private parking, sheltered in winter months. Office and internet computer facilities upon request. Discreet, personal attention to travellers' needs.

From Montréal, Aut. 20 East twd Québec City. After the Pierre-Laporte bridge, follow Boul. Laurier to old Québec. Left on Av. Moncton at the Plains of Abraham.

B&B
À LA MAISON TUDOR

J. Cecil Kilfoil
1037, avenue Moncton
Québec G1S 2Y9
(418) 686-1033
fax (418) 686-6066
www.alamaisontudor.com
ckilfoil@lamaisontudor.com

B&B	
single	$85-100
double	$90-100
triple	$105-120
child	$15

Taxes extra VS MC ER

Open year round

Number of rooms	2
shared bathrooms	1
shared wc	1

🏛 ➡ 🏃 🚲 ⛷ 🏃

38. QUÉBEC

☀☀☀ **F** E ⊘ 🐄 **TA** R.5

The B & B Au Croissant de Lune is located in the Faubourg St-Jean-Baptiste, a colourful and typical extra muros quarter bordering St-Jean Street, lively throughfare of Old Quebec,Convention Center and Parliament Hill within 200 meters. Tourist attractions, boutiques, restaurants and more at your doorstep. Varied breakfasts served in the library, cosy and comfortable rooms, terrace. A good place in the heart of a historical city!

Aut. 20, Pierre-Laporte Bridge, turn left on Cartier Street, right on Chemin Ste-Foy (becomes St-Jean Street), second Street after the church, turn right on des Zouaves , righton St-Gabriel. (B & B first house on the corner of Des Zouaves and St-Gabriel).

B&B
AU CROISSANT DE LUNE

Louise St-Laurent and
René Gilbert
594, rue Saint-Gabriel
Québec G1R 1W3
(418) 522-6366
1-866-522-6366
www.inns-bb.com/croissantdelune
aucroissantdelune@hotmail.com

B&B	
single	$70
double	$75
child	$15

VS

Open year round

Number of rooms	3
shared bathrooms	1

🏛 🐄 ➡ 🍴 🚲 ⛸ 🥾

39. QUÉBEC

☀☀☀☀ **F** E ⊘ 🚐 **TA** R.1

Give in to the sweet pleasure of living and the quiet ambiance of our Victorian house (1830), just steps away from the sights of Vieux-Québec, the Grand Théâtre and the conference centre. Spacious rooms decorated with warmth and meticulous comfort. Gourmet breakfast, parking lot.

Aut. 20, P-Laporte Bridge, Boul. Laurier Exit, 7.8km, left on Claire Fontaine, 400m, right on Burton. Aut. 40, Boul. Charest East, right on Langelier, go up Salaberry, left on St-Jean, at the 2nd light, right on Claire Fontaine and 2nd left on Burton.

B&B
AU PETIT ROI

Khalid El-Haji
445, rue Burton
Québec G1R 1Z8
tel/fax (418) 523-3105
www.oricom.ca/petitroi
petitroi@oricom.ca

B&B	
single	$55-85
double	$70-105
triple	$90-125
quad.	$105-140
child	$15

Taxes extra

Reduced rates: 1 pers./$50. and 2 pers./$65. Nov. 1 to Apr. 30, except Dec. 20 to Jan. 5 and Jan. 31 to Feb. 15

Open year round

Number of rooms	3
rooms with private bath	1
rooms with sink	1
shared bathrooms	2

🏛 🐄 ➡ 🏃 🚲 ⛸ 🥾

40. QUÉBEC

☀☀☀ F E ⊘ P R.25

In Québec City, people choose "the Pied à Terre" for its comfort and tranquillity. After a most exquisite breakfast, set off on the right foot for a walk to the heart of Vieux-Québec (35 min); the Plains of Abraham, museums, Cartier and Grande-Allée streets, Château Frontenac. Free parking. Steps away from bus routes.

Aut. 20, P-Laporte Bridge, Boul. Laurier, 6km, left on Belvédère, right on René-Lévesque, left on Casot. Or Aut. 40, Av. St-Sacrement South, left on Chemin Ste-Foy, 1.8km.

B&B
AU PIED À TERRE À QUÉBEC

Nicole Marcotte
810, rue Casot
Québec G1S 2X9
tel/fax (418) 687-1986
www.aupiedaterre.com
n.marcotte@sympatico.ca

B&B	
single	$60-70
double	$75-90
triple	$90-105
quad.	$120
child	$10

Reduced rates: 10 nights and more
Open: Mar. 15 to Nov. 1

Number of rooms	3
rooms with private bath	1
rooms with private wc	1
shared bathrooms	1

🏛 🚗 🚶 🚲 🎿

---

41. QUÉBEC

☀☀☀☀ F E ⊘ P ⟵ TA R.2

In downtown Québec City, a neighbourhood with European charm, restaurants, cafés and boutiques. Located just 2 min from the Plains of Abraham and the Museum of Québec. Old Québec City is a 10-min walk away. Gourmet breakfast. 2 parking lots free.

Aut. 20, Pierre-Laporte bridge, Boul. Laurier to downtown (Grande-Allée). 8.7km after the bridge, turn on Cartier, then left on Saunders. Or Aut. 40, Boul. Charest East, right on St-Sacrement South, left on Chemin Ste-Foy, right on Rue Cartier, right on Rue Saunders.

B&B
AUX TROIS BALCONS

Pauline and Pierre Amesse
130, rue Saunders
Québec G1R 2E3
tel/fax (418) 525-5611
1-866-525-5611
www.troisbalcons.qc.ca
amesse@troisbalcons.qc.ca

B&B	
single	$65-75
double	$75-95
triple	$95-115
child	$15

Taxes extra VS MC
Open year round

Number of rooms	3
rooms with private bath	2
rooms with sink	1
shared bathrooms	1

🏛 🚗 🚶 🚲 🎿 🎿

---

42. QUÉBEC

☀☀☀ F E ⊘ R.1

Magnificient Victorian home just steps from old Québec City in the heart of the Faubourg St-Jean-Baptiste: historic, artistic and creative. I am a professional artist. Large, well-ventilated and comfortable rooms. Copious breakfast.

Boul. Laurier twd Québec City. Near the Museum of Québec, left on Rue Cartier, 2nd traffic light, right on ch. Ste-Foy (becomes Rue St-Jean), left on Rue St-Augustin and left on Rued'Aiguillon.

B&B
B&B CHEZ PIERRE

Pierre Coté
636, rue d'Aiguillon
Québec G1R 1M5
(418) 522-2173
http://welcome.to/chezpierre
chezpierre@ca.inter.net

B&B	
single	$60-85
double	$70-100
triple	$100-125
quad.	$125-145

Taxes extra VS MC
Open year round

Number of rooms	3
rooms with private bath	2
shared bathrooms	1

🏛 🔥 🚗 🚲 🎿

43. QUÉBEC

☀☀☀☀ **F** e ⊗ **P** ▬ **R.2**

Located on a peaceful street in the heart of a lively area a short distance from the Plains of Abraham, Grande-Allée, Grand-Théâtre, and a 10 min walk from Vieux-Québec and the convention centre. A few rooms with queen-size beds and living rooms available. Hearty breakfasts. Discount for stays of three nights or longer. Free parking.

From Montréal, Aut. 20, P.-Laporte bridge, Boul. Laurier to downtown. Left on Av. de la Tour 8.8km from the bridge. Or, Aut. 40, right on Rue St-Sacrement Sud, left on Chemin St-Louis, 2.6km.

B&B
B&B DE LA TOUR

Huguette Rodrigue and André Blanchet
1080, avenue de la Tour
Québec G1R 2W7
(418) 525-8775
1-877-525-8775
www.quebecweb.com/bbdelatour
bbdelatour@qc.aira.com

	B&B
single	$55-60
double	$70-75
triple	$90
child	$15

Taxes extra

Reduced rates: 3 nights and more
Open: Jan. 5 to dec. 20

Number of rooms	4
rooms with sink	2
shared bathrooms	2

---

44. QUÉBEC

☀☀☀☀ **F** e 🐾 **TA R.3**

Right in the heart of Vieux-Québec, inside the walls and near Château Frontenac, a Québécois family welcomes you to their refined home (1888). Personalised rooms with TV and gourmet breakfasts are conducive to discovery... We will treat you the way we would like to be treated. Free Internet access.

Aut. 20, Pierre-Laporte bridge, Boul. Laurier Exit twd Vieux-Québec. After the Porte St-Louis, at the traffic light, right on Rue d'Auteuil, left on Rue Ste-Genevièvre and left on Rue des Grisons.

B&B
B&B DES GRISONS

Claudine Desbois and Jocelyn Santerre
1, des Grisons
Québec G1R 4M6
(418) 694-1461
fax (418) 694-9204
www.inns-bb.com/grisons
jsanterr@videotron.ca

	B&B
single	$60
double	$70-85

MC

Reduced rates: 3 nights and more
Open year round

Number of rooms	3
shared bathrooms	2

---

45. QUÉBEC

☀☀☀ **F** E ⊗ **P** 🐾 **TA R1**

Warm house located on a quiet street near services, restaurants, university, congress centre, hospitals, shopping centres, 5 min from the old city. Comfortable, private rooms in a simple decor. Dining room and boudoir available to guests for extra privacy. Family suite with private bathroom. Facilities for children. Private entrance, microwave, refrigerator. Storage for skis and bikes. Bus (Métro-bus) on the corner.

Aut. 20, Pierre-Laporte bridge, downtown Québec City twd Boul. Laurier. Past Université Laval, left on Av. Des Gouverneurs, left on Boul. René Lévesque, left on Madeleine-de-Verchères.

B&B
B&B LA BEDONDAINE

Sylvie and Gaétan Tessier
912, rue Madeleine-de-Verchères
Québec G1S 4K7
(418) 681-0783
www.inns-bb.com/bedondaine
bedondaine@sympatico.ca

	B&B
single	$55-65
double	$60-70
triple	$80-90
child	$15

VS

Reduced rates: low season: single ($50-$60). Double ($55-$65)
Open year round

Number of rooms	3
rooms in basement	3
rooms with private bath	2
shared bathrooms	1
shared wc	1

46. QUÉBEC

A few steps away from the Plains of Abraham and 5min (2km) from Vieux-Québec, well-decorated interior, space and tranquillity, stylish suites (room, boudoir with TV and private bathroom), central air conditioning, safe, free parking **See colour photos.**

Aut. 20, Pierre-Laporte bridge, Boul. Laurier twd downtown, Chemin St-Louis to Av. des Laurentides, 6km. Or Aut. 40, Boul. Charest West, Rue St-Sacrement South, 1.5km, left on Chemin St-Louis to Av. des Laurentides, 1.2km.

B&B
B&B MAISON LESAGE

Jean-Luc Lesage and Yves Ruel
760, chemin Saint-Louis
Québec G1S 1C3
(418) 682-9959
www.inns-bb.com/lesage
bbmaisonlesage@videotron.ca

B&B	
single	$90
double	$110

Taxes extra VS MC
Open year round

Number of rooms	3
rooms with private bath	3

---

48. QUÉBEC

Located in the heart of Québec City, at the entrance to Faubourg St-Jean-Baptiste, our B&B offers incomparable comfort, old-fashioned charm and affordable rates near the city's major attractions. Overlooking Rue St-Jean, in a trendy district filled with restaurants and shops, walking distance from Vieux-Québec, Château Frontenac, Carré d'Youville, the Capitole and fortifications, Centre des Congrès, Grand Théâtre, museums and Plains of Abraham. Five spacious rooms with private bathroom, air conditioning and warm decor. Hearty breakfast served in the quaint dining nook. Parking lot (charge) adjacent. **See colour photos.**

Aut. 20, Pont Pierre-Laporte, Exit Boul. Laurier for about 9km. Left on Turnbull, right on Rue St-Jean.

B&B
CHÂTEAU DES TOURELLES

Allen Johnston and
Marc Castonguay
212, rue St-Jean
Québec G1R 1P1
(418) 647-9136
(418) 523-5843
fax (418) 647-3096
www.chateaudestourelles.qc.ca
info@chateaudestourelles.qc.ca

B&B	
single	$85-95
double	$85-95
triple	$105-115
quad.	$125-135
child	$20

Taxes extra VS MC ER IT
Open year round

Number of rooms	5
rooms with private bath	5

---

49. QUÉBEC

This renovated Second Empire/Napoleon III-style chateau is located in the heart of Québec City's historic district. It is a unique private mansion whose refined 18th- and 19th-century furnishings are worthy of France's most beautiful residences. The family offers three exquisite rooms, central air and a luxurious, relaxing ambiance. Enjoy the quiet gardens in the inner courtyard or two front terraces and watch the activity on Faubourg Saint-Jean-Baptiste. Upon request, high tea is served in the ballroom or gardens. On site: beauty salon (hair, skin and body care; massage therapy). **See colour photos.**

Reserve or call first. Smoke-free environment.

B&B
CHÂTEAU DU FAUBOURG

André and David
429, rue St-Jean
Québec G1R 1P3
tel/fax (418) 524-2902
www.lechateaudufaubourg.com
chateaudufaubourg@caramail.com

B&B	
single	$89-99
double	$99-109
triple	$119-129

Taxes extra VS MC AM IT

Reduced rates: 10% Oct. 1 to Apr. 30. 3 nights or more from Sunday to Thursday except holidays
Open year round

Number of rooms	3
rooms with private bath	1
shared bathrooms	2
shared wc	1

49. QUÉBEC

F E P TA R.1

Prize for Excellence "Special Favorite" Regional 1999. Regional winner of Québec Tourism Grand Prizes for hospitality and customer service (1995); Classification Hébergement Québec «4 suns». Located at 5 min (1.5km) from «fortified Old Québec». Central air conditioning, pool table, bikes, parking, table d'hôte.

Aut. 20 P. Laporte bridge, or Aut. 40 East, twd Ste-Anne-de-Beaupré, Exit 316, staight ahead untill Chemin de la Canardière.

B&B
CHEZ MONSIEUR GILLES

Gilles Clavet
1720, chemin de la Canardière
Québec G1J 2E3
(418) 821-8778
fax (418) 821-8776
www3.sympatico.ca/mgilles
mgilles@sympatico.ca

B&B	
single	$90-100
double	$90-100
triple	$110-120
quad.	$130-140
child	$20

Taxes extra VS ER

Open year round

Number of rooms	**5**
rooms with private bath	3
rooms with sink	2
shared bathrooms	1
shared wc	2

50. QUÉBEC

F e P R.1

Gîte du Parc is a century-old home bathed in the tranquillity of the Montcalm area, 2 min from the Plains of Abraham, le Musée du Québec and a stone's throw from Vieux-Québec. You will be delighted by our friendly welcome, helpful tourist information on Québec City, spacious, attractively decorated rooms, copious breakfasts and free parking. **See colour photos.**

From Montréal, Aut. 20, Pierre-Laporte bridge, Exit Boul. Laurier. Left on Des Érables, then left Rue Fraser.

B&B
GÎTE DU PARC

Henriette Hamel and
René Thivierge
345, rue Fraser
Québec G1S 1R2
(418) 683-8603
fax (418) 683-8431
www.quebecweb.com/giteduparc
rene.giteduparc@sympatico.ca

B&B	
single	$75
double	$75-90
triple	$95-110

Open year round

Number of rooms	**3**
rooms with private bath	1
rooms with sink	1
shared bathrooms	1

51. QUÉBEC

F e R1

French artist's home located in "Upper Town" and in the cultural heart of Québec City. Personalised welcome, cosiness, relaxation, tranquillity and security. Special meals (for diabetics). Near most tourist attractions, shops, boutiques, restaurants.

Chemin Ste-Foy to "Vieux Québec". Left on Rue Désy. La Coule Douce is on Rue Dolbeau, 2nd street on your left.

B&B
LA COULE DOUCE

Michel Champagne
473, rue Dolbeau
Québec G1S 2R6
(418) 527-2940
fax (418) 527-0288
www.inns-bb.com/couledouce
*michelchampagne1940@
hotmail.com*

B&B	
single	$70
double	$75
triple	$100
quad.	$150

Open year round

Number of rooms	**2**
shared bathrooms	1

52. QUÉBEC

Located right near Château Frontenac, within the city ramparts. Quiet area. Superb view of the Séminaire de Québec. Hardwood floors, stone walls. Healthy breakfast in a warm setting. Parking near the house.

Aut. 20, Pierre-Laporte bridge, Boul. Laurier Exit, 10km. Left on Rue du Fort, which becomes Port-Dauphin and Des Remparts. Left on Ste-Monique, left on Laval. Aut. 40 Boul. Charest becomes St-Paul, 12km. At the light, right on Rue Légaré, left on Côte de la Canoterie, right on Ste-Famille, at the stop sign, left on Hébert, left on Ste-Monique, right on Laval.

B&B
LA MAISON LAFLEUR

Gilles Lafleur
2, rue Laval
Québec G1R 3T9
(418) 692-0685
fax (418) 692-2486
futurix.clic.net/com/lafleur
lamaisonlafleur@sympatico.ca

☀ ☀ **F E** ⊘ **R.5**

B&B	
single	$85
double	$85

VS
Open year round

Number of rooms	3
rooms with sink	3
shared bathrooms	1
shared wc	1

---

53. QUÉBEC

A luxurious, Victorian-style home whose stained-glass windows and woodwork make it an incomparable B&B. L'Hémérocalle is located near Québec City's historic and cultural attractions, 10 min walking distance from Vieux-Québec, just steps from the Plains of Abraham, the museum and Rue Cartier. Varied breakfast. Free parking.

Aut. 20, Pierre-Laporte bridge, Boul. Laurier twd downtown, Ch. St-Louis, left on Av. des Érables. Or Aut. 40, Boul. Charest East, right on St-Sacrement, to Boul. René-Lévesque, right on Av. des Érables.

B&B
L'HÉMÉROCALLE

Ghislaine Julien and Marc Dion
1196, av. des Érables
Québec G1R 2N5
(418) 527-6844
**pages.globetrotter.net/
hemerocalle**
hemerocalle@globetrotter.net

☀ ☀ ☀ ☀ **F e** ⊘ **P R1**

B&B	
single	$75
double	$95
triple	$110-120

Open year round

Number of rooms	3
rooms with private bath	3

---

54. QUÉBEC, BEAUPORT

Our B&B is located on the oldest road in Québec City, 10 min from old Québec City, 1km from the Montmorency falls, 30 min from Mont-St-Anne. Come relax in the outdoor pool and the large garden. Bike/ski shed. And what a delicious breakfast! Prize for Excellence "Special Favorite" Regional 1998. **See colour photos.**

From Québec City, Aut. 440, Exit 29, Exit 322, left on Boul. des Chutes, left at Côte Morel, right on Av. Royale, 0.5km. From Montréal, Aut. 40 East or Aut. 40 West, Rte 73 North and 40 East, Exit 322...

B&B
LA MAISON ANCESTRALE
THOMASSIN

Madeleine Guay
2161, avenue Royale
Beauport G1C 1N9
(418) 663-6067
1-877-663-6067
fax (418) 660-8616
www.inns-bb.com/thomassin

☀ ☀ ☀ ☀ **F e** ⊘ **P** ⟋ **TA R.5**

B&B	
single	$42
double	$59
triple	$76
quad.	$87
child	$15

Taxes extra
Open year round

Number of rooms	4
shared bathrooms	2

55. QUÉBEC, BEAUPORT

Sure, our ancestral house is gorgeous, but our breakfasts alone are worth the trip! Filled with paintings, our art gallery is also an artist's studio. A delight for both the eyes and the tastebuds! In addition, we're 5 min from the Montmorency falls and Vieux-Québec, 30 min from Mont Ste-Anne and Stoneham. France and Michel await you.

Aut. 40 twd Ste-Anne-de-Beaupré. Seigneuriale South Exit, right on Av. Royale. From Old Québec, Aut. Dufferin, Exit François-de-Laval, right on Av. Royale.

☀☀☀☀ **F** e ⊘ **P** R.3

B&B
LA MAISON DUFRESNE

France Collin and Michel Nigen
505, avenue Royale
Beauport G1E 1Y3
(418) 666-4004
1-877-747-4004
www.quebecweb.com/dufresne
dufresne@mlink.net

	B&B
single	$60
double	$70
triple	$90
child	$15

Taxes extra VS

Reduced rates: low season
Open year round

Number of rooms	3
rooms with sink	3
shared bathrooms	1
shared wc	1

---

56. QUÉBEC, BEAUPORT

Discover the picturesque charm of Avenue Royale, take the bike path to the Montmorency falls or explore Vieux-Québec, only 5 min from our comfortable and welcoming hundred-year-old home. Hearty breakfasts with homemade bread and jam. Large family room, pool, central air conditioning, bicycle and ski storage.

Aut. 40 East, Exit 320, right on Rue Seigneuriale and right on Av. Royale. From Vieux-Québec, Aut. 440 East, François de Laval Exit, right on Av. Royale.

☀☀☀☀ **F** E ⊘ **P** 🏊 🎿 🦌 **TA** R.2

B&B
LE GÎTE DU VIEUX-BOURG

Marielle Viel and
Benoit Couturier
492, avenue Royale
Beauport G1E 1Y1
tel/fax (418) 661-0116
www3.sympatico.ca/vieux-bourg
vieux-bourg@sympatico.ca

	B&B
single	$60-90
double	$70-90
triple	$90-110
quad.	$110-130
child	$15

Taxes extra VS

Reduced rates: Nov. 1 to Apr. 30
Open year round

Number of rooms	4
rooms with private bath	2
rooms with sink	2
shared bathrooms	1
shared wc	1

---

57. QUÉBEC, BEAUPORT

Built in 1875, Manoir Vallée will make your relive the warmth and ambiance of yesteryear. Located 5 min from Vieux-Québec and the Montmorency Falls. Relax in our spacious rooms with stone walls and a romantic decor. You will appreciate our old-fashioned breakfasts. Relaxation room, suite with kitchen.

From Montréal, Aut. 40 East, or from Côte-Nord, Aut. 40 West, Exit Rue Labelle, until Royale, right, 10th house facing "Ultramar".

☀☀☀☀ **F** E ⊘ **P** 🏊 🎿 R.2

B&B
LE MANOIR VALLÉE

Francine Huot, Kevin Strassburg,
Carlos, Rosalee and Yohan
907, avenue Royale
Beauport G1E 1Z9
(418) 660-3855
(418) 666-5421
fax (418) 660-8792
www.inns-bb.com/manoirvallee
kevenstr@total.net

	B&B
single	$65-85
double	$70-95
triple	$75-105
quad.	$90-120
child	$5

Taxes extra VS IT

Open year round

Number of rooms	4
rooms with private bath	4

58. QUÉBEC, BEAUPORT

B&B
LE PETIT MANOIR DU SAULT MONTMORENCY

	B&B
single	$60
double	$75

VS

Open year round

Number of rooms	4
shared bathrooms	2
shared wc	1

Le Petit Manoir is located on the historic site of Chute Montmorency, with the St. Lawrence River and Île d'Orléans in the backdrop. Representing living history, this 19th-century bourgeois residence have kept its original allure and character. Bordered by two peaceful streams, the property will seduce you with comfort and make you succumb to its charms. Vieux-Québec and Mont-Ste-Anne nearby.

Aut. 40 twd Ste-Anne-de-Beaupré, Exit 322, left on Boul. des Chutes, right on Côte du Moulin.

Nycole Giroux and
Jean-Pierre Morneau
63, Côte du Moulin
Beauport G1C 2L7
(418) 663-6510
fax (418) 663-8996
www.inns-bb.com/petitmanoir
petitmanoir@hotmail.com

---

59. QUÉBEC, CAP-ROUGE

B&B
À LA JOLIE ROCHELLE

	B&B
single	$50
double	$60-65

Open year round

Number of rooms	3
shared bathrooms	1
shared wc	1

Welcome to "À La Jolie Rochelle", a warm, comfortable B&B surrounded by trees and flowers. A peaceful spot 15 min away from Vieux-Québec, 3 min from bridges. Breakfast on the terrace, pond, flowered garden to enhance your stay. Our beautifully decorated rooms and bathroom are spacious and quiet. Free parking. Our hospitality and breakfasts will win you over! Your hosts, Huguette and Martin.

Aut. 20, after the bridges, Exit 133, right on Ch. St-Louis, to the end, 3km, Louis-Francœur is to the right. Or, Aut. 40 Duplessis Aut. Exit Ch. Ste-Foy, right to Louis-Francœur, 2.5km.

Huguette Couture and
Martin Larochelle
1450, rue Louis-Francoeur
Cap-Rouge, Pointe-Sainte-Foy
G1Y 1N6
(418) 653-4326
www.inns-bb.com/jolierochelle
jolierochelle@sympatico.ca

---

60. QUÉBEC, CAP-ROUGE

B&B
AU BORD DU FLEUVE

	B&B
single	$50
double	$65

Open year round

Number of rooms	2
shared bathrooms	1

(Air conditioning). A house located a stone's throw from the St. Lawrence River, on Jacques-Cartier beach, with its 2.5km of parkland along the shore. Every room offers a magnificent view of the river, the Québec City bridge, Baie de Cap-Rouge with the river and trestle bridge. Relax to the soothing rhythm of the tides in a unique setting.

Aut. 20, Pierre-Laporte bridge, Aut. Duplessis Exit, Chemin Ste-Foy Exit twd Cap-Rouge, at left. Go down the Cap-Rouge hill to the Info Tourism, left and follow the river. Aut. 40, Cap-Rouge Exit to Info Tourism...

Michel Beaudet and
Suzanne Lafond
4068, Chemin-de-la-plage
Jacques-Cartier
Cap-Rouge G1Y 1W3
(418) 658-4703
www.inns-bb.com/borddufleuve
gite-auborddufleuve@
sympatico.ca

61. QUÉBEC, CAP-ROUGE

Large house (comfort, quiet, rest) 15km from old Québec City. Hearty, all-you-can-eat breakfast. Flower-filled sunroom. Private living room. Free parking. Flower garden, whirlpool bath. Nearby: golf course, footpath, St.Lawrence River, marina, art gallery, big shopping centre. Family suite (kitchenette, private bathroom).

From Montréal, Aut. 20 East, Pierre-Laporte bridge, Chemin St-Louis West Exit to Louis Francoeur. Left on Chemin Ste-Foy, Rue St-Félix, right on Rue du Golf. Or, Rte 138 twd Cap-Rouge.

B&B
L'HYDRANGÉE BLEUE

Yvan Denis
1451, rue du Golf
Cap-Rouge G1Y 2T6
(418) 657-5609
(418) 657-5609
fax (418) 657-7918
www.inns-bb.com/hydrangeebleue
hby@sympatico.ca

B&B	
single	$55-60
double	$60-65
triple	$80-85
quad.	$100-105
child	$15

Open year round

Number of rooms	3
rooms in basement	1
rooms with private bath	1
rooms with sink	1
shared bathrooms	1

---

62. QUÉBEC, LAC DELAGE

Stay a while in an enchanting site with country-style decor, far from the city's hustle and bustle, 20 min from downtown Québec City and Parc de la Jacques-Cartier, 10min from the Stoneham and Relais du Lac-Beauport ski resorts. In summer, after your outings, fall asleep to the sounds of a waterfall; in winter, after a hearty breakfast, enjoy one of the many sports and outdoors activities offered near the B&B. And in the evening, why not lounge by the fireplace in the company of our pets!

Aut. 40, Exit 73 North twd Chicoutimi, Exit 167 3km twd Lac-Delage.

B&B
LE GÎTE DELAGEOIS

Noëlla Cabana
1, avenue des Villas
Lac-Delage G0A 4P0
tel/fax (418) 848-2058
www.inns-bb.com/delageois
gitedelageois@globetrotter.net

B&B	
single	$60
double	$70
child	$20

Reduced rates: single 2 nights and more $55/night

Open year round

Number of rooms	2
rooms with private bath	1
shared bathrooms	1

---

63. QUÉBEC, STE-FOY

In a quiet residential district, your hosts offer a daily three-course breakfast that is hearty and varied. 10min from Vieux Québec and the airport, and 5min from the bridges; near all the services and shopping centres. Air conditioning and cable TV in all rooms. Internet access available. Our outdoor swimming pool and patio await you in a landscaped garden. Free parking. We speak French, English and German.

Aut. 20, cross the bridges, Exit 133 Chemin St-Louis. Aut. 540, Exit 10 Chemin St-Louis. Aut. 73, Exit 136 Chemin St-Louis.

B&B
CHEZ ANICK ET PATRICK

Anick Loret
2742, de Montarville
Sainte-Foy G1W 1V1
(418) 651-3216
1-866-651-2003
fax (418) 651-2711
www.anickpatrick.com
info@anickpatrick.com

B&B	
single	$50-65
double	$70-85
child	$15

Reduced rates: Oct. 1 to Apr. 30

Open year round

Number of rooms	3
rooms with private bath	1
shared bathrooms	1

64. QUÉBEC, STE-FOY

☀ ☀ ☀ **F** **E** ⊘ **P** ↝ **R.3**

10 min from Old Québec City, quiet residential district, quick access to highways. Warm ambiance and reception, sitting room, comfortable rooms (queen-size bed or two twin beds) with sink, generous breakfast. Walking distance from Université Laval, big shopping centres, public transport, cinema, restaurants. Central air conditioning. Free Internet access. Free and easy parking.

From Montréal, Aut. 20, Pierre Laporte bridge, Exit Boul. Laurier, right at 5th light on Rue Jean De Quen to Rue Lapointe. Aut. 40, Exit Aut. Duplessis South, Boul. Laurier, right at 5th light...

B&B
LA MAISON LECLERC

Nicole Chabot and
Conrad Leclerc
2613, rue Lapointe
Sainte-Foy G1W 3K3
tel/fax (418) 653-8936
1-866-653-8936
www.inns-bb.com/maisonleclerc
lamaisonleclerc@bellnet.ca

	B&B
single	$45
double	$60
triple	$75
child	$15

VS MC
Open year round

Number of rooms	5
rooms in basement	2
rooms with sink	2
shared bathrooms	2

---

65. QUÉBEC, STE-FOY

F ⊘ **P** ↝ **R.5**

House located in the heart of the town of Ste-Foy, 1km from the Pierre-Laporte bridge. Very close to the largest shopping centres in Québec City, the bus terminal, the post office, banks, hospitals. Chilean-style breakfast available. We speak Spanish very well.

After the Pierre-Laporte bridge twd downtown Québec City, Boul. Laurier Exit. At the 2nd traffic light, left, right on Rue Légaré, and right again on the next street.

B&B
MAISON DINA

Dina Saéz-Velozo
2850, rue Fontaine
Sainte-Foy G1V 2H8
(418) 652-1013
www.inns-bb.com/maisondina

	B&B
single	$45
double	$55
triple	$80
child	$12

Open: June 1 to Dec. 1

Number of rooms	3
rooms in basement	2
shared bathrooms	2

---

66. QUÉBEC, STE-FOY

☀ ☀ ☀ **F** **e** ⊘ **P** ↝ **TA** **R.1**

Prize for Excellence "Special Favorite" Regional 1994-95. Canadian-style house located in a calm residential neighborhood, near services, shopping centre, public transport and expressways. 5 min from the airport and Université Laval. 10 min from old Québec City. Warm atmosphere, comfortable rooms, living room, copious breakfast, central air conditioning system. Welcome.

From Montréal, Aut. 20 East twd Québec City, Pierre-Laporte bridge, Boul. Laurier Exit. 1st traffic light, right on Rue Lavigerie, at the 3rd street, right on Rue de la Seine.

B&B
MONIQUE ET ANDRÉ
SAINT-AUBIN

Monique and André Saint-Aubin
3045, rue de la Seine
Sainte-Foy G1W 1H8
(418) 658-0685
fax (418) 658-8466
www.quebecweb.com/staubin
staubin@qbc.clic.net

	B&B
single	$50
double	$65
triple	$85
child	$15

Open year round

Number of rooms	3
shared bathrooms	3

67. QUÉBEC, SILLERY

✹✹✹✹ F E ⊘ P R.2

White, English-style house dating back to the 1930s surrounded by century-old trees. Quiet, exceptional neighbourhood. Fireplace, piano, large rooms on the second floor, king- and queen-size beds. Quality, homemade breakfast served in the dining room: terrace overlooking a wooded area. Nearby: Université de Laval, Plains of Abraham, old Québec City and just steps from famous Rue Majeure (trendy restaurants, shops, services). **See colour photos.**

Aut. 20, Pierre-Laporte Bridge, Boul Laurier twd Québec City. 3.9km from bridge right on Rue Maguire. Right on Ch. St-Louis. Aut. 40, Boul. Duplessis South Exit to Boul. Laurier...

B&B
B&B LES CORNICHES

Francine C. DuSault
2052, chemin Saint-Louis
Sillery G1T 1P4
(418) 681-9318
fax (418) 681-4028
www.inns-bb.com/corniches
fjdusault@globetrotter.net

	B&B
single	$65-85
double	$80-95
triple	$115
child	$15

VS

Open year round

Number of rooms	3
rooms with private bath	1
shared bathrooms	2

---

68. QUÉBEC, SILLERY

✹✹✹ F E ⊘ P TA R2

10min from Vieux-Québec, a warm, simple ambiance in a country setting, with a terrace offering a view of the St. Lawrence River. Lavish breakfast. Near the bike path (Le Littoral), golfing, hiking, Vieux-Québec attractions, river cruises, museums, shopping centres, dogsledding.

From Montréal, Aut. 20 East. From Rivière-du-Loup, Aut. 20 West, Aut. 73 North, Pierre-Laporte bridge, Boul. Champlain Exit 132, or Henri IV Aut., Boul. Champlain Exit. 3km East of the bridge, Exit twd Côte du Verger, 1st street on the right...

B&B
GÎTE AU CHEMIN DU FOULON

Francine and Yvon Arsenault
2521 C, Chemin du Foulon
Sillery G1T 1X6
(418) 659-1365
fax (418) 659-1736
www.inns-bb.com/chemindufoulon
auchemindufoulon@videotron.ca

	B&B
single	$45
double	$65

Open year round

Number of rooms	2
shared bathrooms	1
shared wc	1

---

69. QUÉBEC, WENDAKE

✹✹✹ F E P TA R.25

Century-old house where the past mingles with the present. Friendly atmosphere, in which Native art transports guests back in time. Breakfast with a Huron flavour. The Bear, Wolf and Turtle Rooms await you. Located in the heart of the old village of Huron-Wendat, which you can explore, 15 min from Québec City and area ski resorts. Guided tours of historic sites.

From Québec City, Aut. 73 and Aut. 369 twd Loretteville. The B&B is located on a street parallel to Boul. Bastien, right Rue Gabriel Vincent and you're there.

B&B
LA MAISON AORHENCHE

Line Gros-Louis
90, rue François Gros-Louis, C.P. 110
Wendake G0A 4V0
(418) 847-0646
fax (418) 847-4527
www.quebecweb.com/aorhenche
aorhenche@sympatico.ca

	B&B
single	$55-65
double	$75-86
triple	$95-106
quad.	$126
child	$15

Open year round

Number of rooms	3
rooms with private bath	1
shared bathrooms	1

70. ST-ALBAN

☀ ☀ ☀ **F** e ⊛ ⊘ **P** ⊷ 🐖 ✕ **TA** R1.5

Country home located in the beautiful Portneuf region, halfway between Trois-Rivières and Québec City, on the north shore of the St. Lawrence River. Come enjoy the tranquillity of a small, lovely village. We have been welcoming tourists since 1990. Homemade, all-you-can-eat breakfast and dinner by reservation. Looking forward to meeting you!

From Montréal or Québec City, Aut. 40, Exit 254 twd St-Marc-des-Carrières. Boul. Bona Dussault or Avenue Principale via a small street, straight ahead twd St-Alban. The B&B is 1.3km away from the church.

B&B
GÎTE CHEZ FRANCE

France Leduc and
Clément Perreault
87, rang de l'Église nord
St-Alban G0A 3B0
(418) 268-3440
www.inns-bb.com/chezfrance
gitechezfrance@
globetrotter.net

	B&B	MAP
single	$35	$50
double	$49	$75
triple	$69	$105
quad.	$89	$135
Open year round		
Number of rooms		3
shared bathrooms		2

🚶 🎿 🚲 ⛵ 🏃 🎿 🎣 ➤

---

71. ST-CASIMIR

☀ ☀ ☀ **F** **E** **P** 🐖 R6

This wood farmhouse dating from 1850 has preserved its authenticity. Surrounded by a maple grove, river, flower gardens and, in winter, snow, it is the ideal nature escape. Three rooms and summer kitchen where guests can savour rabbit and garden products near the wood-burning stove. Taste the flavours of spring at the traditional sugar shack. Your hosts, Gabrielle and Gaston.

From Montréal, Aut. 40 East, Exit 236, left on Rte 159, right on Rte 354 twd Saint-Casimir. From the church, travel 0.5km, right on the bridge, 6km.

B&B
GÎTE B&B POUR LES AMIS

Gabrielle Poisson and
Gaston Girard
950, rang de la Rivière Noire
St-Casimir G0A 3L0
(418) 339-2320
http://pages.globetrotter.net/
gitepourlesamis
gitepourlesamis@
globetrotter.net

	B&B	MAP
single	$35-55	$55-75
double	$45-65	$85-105
triple	$90	$150
quad.	$115	$195
Open:		
Number of rooms		3
rooms with private bath		2
shared bathrooms		1

 🐟 🚶 🚲 ⛵ 🏃 🎿 🎣 ➤

---

72. ST-GABRIEL-DE-VALCARTIER

★ ★ ★ **F** **E** ⊛ **P** ⊷ 🐖 **TA** R8

Country-style inn in the heart of the valley, 35km from Québec City. Bucolic setting and view. 200 acres of fresh air, silence, charm, serenity and joie de vivre! Well-maintained footpaths for walking, snowshoeing, cross-country skiing, bird-watching, mycology. Large terraces, gardens, tennis, pool. Multiple accommodations, comfortable cottage, studio-apt, suite, docks, kitchenette, large bed, balcony, refined and copious breakfast. Rafting, dogsledding, skidoo, glissades, special packages. Near the city, Parc Jacques-Cartier.

In Québec City, Aut. 73 and Rte 175 twd Chicoutimi, Exit 167, Rte 371, 20km.

INN
AUBERGE DU MAS
DES ÉQUERRES

Annette Légaré
171, 5ᵉ Avenue, rte 371
Saint-Gabriel-de-Valcartier
G0A 4S0
(418) 844-2424
1-877-844-2424
fax (418) 844-1607
www.auxancienscanadiens.qc.ca
/gite.html
gite@auxancienscanadiens.qc.ca

	B&B
single	$70-120
double	$90-120
triple	$110-140
quad.	$120-140
child	$20
Taxes extra VS MC	
Reduced rates: package price 2 nights and more	
Open year round	
Number of rooms	8
rooms with private bath	8

 🚶 🚲 🐎 🏃 🎿 🎣 ➤

73. ST-RAYMOND

Lovely early-20th-century brick house surrounded by equally charming neighbours. A short bike ride away from the cycling path, three strides from nature (canoeing, hiking, snowmobiling, skiing, hang-gliding...). Colours, local flavours and exotic aromas mingle here.

Aut. 40, Rte 365 North, at 1st light in the village, right after the church. By bike, St-Raymond Exit twd downtown. By snowmobile via trail 365.

INN
LA VOISINE

Odile Pelletier and
Denis Baribault
443, Saint-Joseph
Saint-Raymond G3L 1K1
(418) 337-4139
1-877-737-4139
fax (418) 337-3109
www.lavoisine.com
voisine@globetrotter.net

	B&B
single	$46-56
double	$56-66
triple	$76
child	$14

Taxes extra VS MC AM
Open year round

Number of rooms	5
rooms with private bath	1
rooms with sink	5
shared bathrooms	2
shared wc	1

74. ST-RAYMOND

Located on the lakeshore amidst lush greenery, we offer peace and relaxation. Veranda, terraces, private beach, a few min from the bike path, canoeing, golf and summer hikes. Winter is just as exciting, with access to a snowmobile path and downhill skiing 3km away. Our refined breakfast and dinner table will win you over!

From Montréal, Aut. 40 Exit 281, Rte 365 North. In St-Raymond, Rte 367 South twd Ste-Catherine. About 5km, left Ch. du Lac Sept-Îles. From Québec, Aut. 40 Exit 295, Rte 367 North twd Ste-Catherine/St-Raymond. About 10km past Duchesnay, right Ch. du Lac Sept-Îles.

Snowmobile trail 365.

INN
MANOIR DU LAC SEPT-ÎLES

Vincent Caron and
Guillaume Bouquet
3679, ch. du Lac Sept-Îles
Saint-Raymond G3L 2S3
tel/fax (418) 337-8893
(418) 951-8807
www.manoirdulacseptiles.com
*vincent@
manoirdulacseptiles.com*

	B&B	MAP
single	$40-55	$65-80
double	$55-75	$110-135
triple	$70-90	$115-170
quad.	$85-100	$180-205
child	$15	$35

Taxes extra VS MC AM IT

Reduced rates: 10 % 7 nights and more
Open year round

Number of rooms	5
rooms with private bath	5

75. STE-ANNE-DE-BEAUPRÉ

Prize for Excellence "Special Favorite" Regional 2000. Pretty country home (attic from 1909), 10 min from Mont-Ste-Anne, 20 min from Québec City, near Cap Tourmente, the Canyon and Sept Chutes. Refined breakfast (garden products) served in the solarium, with view of the river and Île d'Orléans. Cozy, carefully decorated rooms. Fireplace. Small farm: lambs, rabbits...

From Québec City, Rte 138 East twd Ste-Anne-de-Beaupré. 6km from Château-Richer, past the bee museum, at the light, Rue Paré. Right on Av. Royale.

B&B
LA MAISON D'ULYSSE

Carole Trottier and
Raymond Allard
9140, av. Royale
Ste-Anne-de-Beaupré G0A 3C0
(418) 827-8224
www.inns-bb.com/maisondulysse
lamaisondulysse@sympatico.ca

	B&B
single	$50-55
double	$65-70
triple	$85
child	$5-15

Taxes extra VS MC
Open year round

Number of rooms	4
rooms with private bath	1
rooms with sink	2
shared bathrooms	2

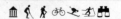

76. STE-CATHERINE-DE-LA-JACQUES-CARTIER

This B&B features a warm, cozy decor and is located near the Jacques-Cartier river, a mere 2.6km from the Centre Éco-Touristique de Duchesnay. Bike paths, golf, etc. Ideal for nature-lovers.

Aut. 40, Exit 295 Fossambault North, Rte 367 twd Ste-Catherine de la Jacques-Cartier. Left on Rte Duchesnay.

B&B
GÎTE DU SOUS-BOIS

Andrée Paradis and
Pierre Cormier
9, Route Duchesnay
Ste-Catherine-de-la-Jacques-
Cartier G0A 3M0
(418) 875-2295
www.gitedusousbois.com
gitedusousbois@aol.com

	B&B
single	$55
double	$65
child	$10

VS

Reduced rates: 3 nights and more
Open: Jan. 5 to Nov. 15

Number of rooms	3
rooms in basement	3
rooms with private bath	3

---

77. SHANNON

On the Rivière Jacques-Cartier, 15 min from the Pierre-Laporte bridge, fishers angle for trout or salmon. Relaxing, flowery setting, near Duchesnay, Village Vacances Valcartier, golfing, downhill or cross-country skiing, the Germain beach and 0.4km from the bike path. Québec City/Shannon/Rivière-à-Pierre. Pedal boat and rowboat for your relaxation.

Aut. 20 or 40, Henri IV North Exit, Rte 73, which becomes Rte 573 North, twd Val Bélair, Valcartier. In Shannon, at the Eko store, right on Rue Gosford, 1km, left on Rue Dublin, 2km, left on Rue Riverside.

B&B
LE GÎTE AU BORD
DE LA RIVIÈRE

Gaétane Bouchard-James
17, rue Riverside
Shannon G0A 4N0
(418) 844-2328
1-877-844-2323
www.inns-bb.com/borddelariviere
info@gitebordriviere.com

	B&B	MAP
single	$50-70	$70-90
double	$55-75	$95-115
child	$20	$35

VS MC AM ER

Reduced rates: 10% 2 nights and more
Open year round

Number of rooms	3
rooms in basement	1
rooms with private bath	2
shared bathrooms	1

---

78. STONEHAM, ST-ADOLPHE

Farming bed and breakfast independent of our house, near Vieux-Québec and Parc de la Jacques-Cartier. Guests are greeted with maple toffee. Hiking trails, river, lake with wriggling trout, rockery and abundant greenery. Guided tour to the maple grove and sugar shack. **Farm Stay p 72. See colour photos.**

From Québec City, Aut. 73 North twd Chicoutimi. At the end of Rte 73, do not take any Exit, but straight ahead 7km on Rte 175 to St-Adolphe Exit. Right on Rue St-Edmond, 3.5km.

B&B
AUBERGE DE LA FERME
ST-ADOLPHE

Jocelyne Couillard and
George Legendre
1035, rue Saint-Edmond
Saint-Adolphe, Stoneham
G0A 4P0
(418) 848-2879
fax (418) 848-6949
www.aubergestoneham.com
info@aubergestoneham.com

	B&B
single	$45
double	$55
triple	$75
child	$15

Taxes extra
Open year round

Number of rooms	3
shared bathrooms	2

79. CAP-TOURMENTE, MONT-STE-ANNE

F E P 〰 **TA R1 M7**

In the heart of Cap-Tourmente, 12 min from Mont Ste-Anne (view of the slopes). House with five guestrooms with private bathrooms, kitchen with dishwasher, family room with fireplace, small sitting room with cable TV, washer and dryer, pool table in the basement. Covered pool in the warm weather, hiking, cross-country skiing and mountain biking. Nearby: skiing, golf, horseback riding, casino, etc. **B&B p 229.**

From Québec City, Aut. Henri IV North, to Aut. 40 East Ste-Anne-de-Beaupré, Rte 138 East, twd St-Joachim, Cap-Tourmente.

COUNTRY HOME
L'OIE DES NEIGES

Gisèle Perron
390, ch. du Cap-Tourmente
Saint-Joachim G0A 3X0
(418) 827-5153
tel/fax (418) 827-2246
www.inns-bb.com/oiedesneiges
oiedesneiges@hotmail.com

No. houses	1
No. rooms	5
No. people	4-20
WEEK-SUMMER	$1500-2000
WEEK-WINTER	$1500-2000
W/E-SUMMER	$800-900
W/E-WINTER	$800-900
DAY-SUMMER	$450-500
DAY-WINTER	$450-500

VS
Open year round

---

80. CHÂTEAU-RICHER

★ ★ ★ **F E P** 〰 🐑 **M.2**

For your vacation, an escapade at the foot of Mont Ste-Anne. In both winter and summer, enjoy the region's activities and attractions. Near Québec City, Montmorency falls, Ste-Anne canyon, Ste-Anne-de-Beaupré basilica; a few kilometres from Charlevoix. **B&B Un air d'été p 231.**

From Québec City, Rte 138 East or Boul. Ste-Anne. Right, behind Motel Roland for information.

COUNTRY HOME
DIRECTION MONT STE-ANNE

Lynda Boucher
8988, boul. Sainte-Anne
Château-Richer G0A 1N0
(418) 824-9600
1-888-922-8770
fax (418) 824-5645
www.directionmontsteanne.com
*directionmontsteanne@
videotron.ca*

No. houses	1
No. rooms	3
No. people	10
WEEK-SUMMER	$800
WEEK-WINTER	$1500
W/E-SUMMER	$400
W/E-WINTER	$600
DAY-SUMMER	$200
DAY-WINTER	300

Taxes extra VS MC AM ER IT

Reduced rates: Oct. 14 to Dec. 20 and Apr. 22 to June 20
Open year round

---

81. MONT-STE-ANNE, ST-FERRÉOL

★ ★ ★ **F E P** 〰 🐑 **TA R.5 M.5**

Savour the tranquillity of our lovely country homes, ancestral or recent, 30 min from downtown Québec City, at the edge of Charlevoix. Dreamy, legendary spot, in a small typical Québécois town. Houses are well equipped and can comfortably accommodate 4 to 30 people, and even up to 50! We are nestled at the foot of Mt Ste-Anne, a yearound internationally renown resort. Visit us on the Internet. **See colour photos.**

1km after Mt Ste-Anne, as you enter the small town of St-Ferréol-les-Neiges.

COUNTRY HOMES
CHALETS-VILLAGE
MONT-SAINTE-ANNE

Gilles Éthier
1815, Boul. Les Neiges
St-Ferréol-Les -Neiges G0A 3R0
1-800-461-2030
tel/fax (418) 826-3331
www.chalets-village.qc.ca
gethier@chalets-village.qc.ca

No. houses	6
No. rooms	2-9
No. people	4-36
WEEK-SUMMER	$1300-3200
WEEK-WINTER	$995-7850
W/E-SUMMER	$550-2050
W/E-WINTER	$750-2800

Taxes extra VS MC IT

Reduced rates: Spring and Fall
Open year round

AGROTOURISM

Farm Explorations:

🐝 **82** MUSÉE DE L'ABEILLE - ÉCONOMUSÉE DU MIEL, Château-Richer..................... *Page 62*

🐝 **83** LAC DE PÊCHE LA SEIGNEURIE DE L'ÎSLE AUX SORCIERS,
Saint-Laurent-de-l'Île-d'Orléans .... *Page 62*

Farm Stays:

🐝 **29** LA FERME L'ÉMEULIENNE, Neuville.. *Page 72*

🐝 **78** AUBERGE DE LA FERME ST-ADOLPHE, Saint-Adolphe, Stoneham.................... *Page 72*

Farm Shops:

🐝 **84** MOULIN DU PETIT PRÉ, Château-Richer .... *Page 48*

🐝 **85** DOMAINE ORLÉANS, Saint-Pierre-de-l'Île-d'Orléans...................................... *Page 48*

Resort & nature

20 minutes *from* **Quebec City**

www.jacques-cartier.com

Regional information
1 877 844-2358

La Jacques-Cartier

For an unforgettable experience, choose from our selection of accommodations and agrotourism activities...

www.inns-bb.com
(Secure online booking service)

www.agricotours.qc.ca

Click here!

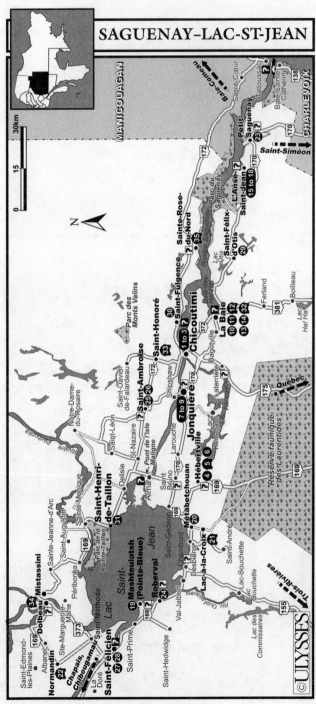

SAGUENAY–LAC-ST-JEAN

30km

15

0

N

MANICOUAGAN

CHARLEVOIX

Baie-Comeau

Sagé-Coeur

Tadoussac

138

Baie-Sainte-Catherine

Saguenay

Petit-Saguenay

23

170

Saint-Siméon

L'Anse-

Saint-Jean

170

15 to 18

Parc du Saguenay

172

Saint-Félix-

d'Otis

Sainte-Rose-du-Nord

35

Rivière Éternité

Lac Otis

29

Ferland

Boilleau

381

Lac Ha! Ha!

Saint-Fulgence

La Baie

10 11

13 14 32

Bagotville

372

Chicoutimi

1 to 3

30

Saint-Honoré

Parc des Monts-Valins

33

Saint-Ambroise

25 26

172

Saint-David-de-Falardeau

Shipshaw

Saint-Léon

Larouche

7 to 9

Jonquière

170

Laterrière

Réserve Renard

Lac Kénogami

Québec

175

Réserve faunique des Laurentides

Notre-Dame-du-Rosaire

Rivière Péribonka

St-Nazaire

Pont de l'Isle-Maligne

Saint-Bruno

Hébertville

4 5 6

169

Delisle

Alma

2

Saint-Gédéon

Métabetchouan

20

Saint-André

169

Lac-Bouchette

Lac-à-la-Croix

21

Saint-Henri-de-Taillon

31

Parc de la Pointe-Taillon

Sainte-Méthode

Sainte-Monique

169

Péribonka

Saint-Augustin

Sainte-Jeanne-d'Arc

Mistassini

Dolbeau

22

Normandin

169

Albanel

Saint-Edmond-les-Plaines

Ste-Marguerite-Marie

373

La Doré

Chapais, Chibougamau

Saint-Félicien

27 28 23

Saint-Prime

Saint-Hedwidge

Mashteuiatsh (Pointe-Bleue)

19

Roberval

24

Lac Saint-Jean

Saint-Méthode

Val-Jalbert

Desbiens

Chambord

169

Rivière Ouiatchouan

Lac des Commissaires

Lac Bouchette

155

Trois-Rivières

© ULYSSES

*The numbers on the map refer to the establishments described in the text.

1. CHICOUTIMI

☀☀☀ F e ⊘ P 🐾 R7

Finalist for Excellence "Special Favorite" Regional 2000. Overlooking a majestic fjord, this very quiet, central B&B is located in one of the most beautiful parts of the region. The rooms are cozy and the varied, abundant breakfasts are served in a solarium/dining room with a panoramic view of the river.

From Québec City, Rte 175 North twd Chicoutimi. Right on Boul. Université East, near shopping centre, left on Boul. Saguenay, 1st street on the right, Rang St-Martin, 6.8km.

B&B
À LA BERNACHE

Denise Ouellet
3647, rang Saint-Martin
Chicoutimi G7H 5A7
(418) 549-4960
fax (418) 549-9814
www.gitebernache.com
louis_martel@videotron.ca

	B&B
single	$45
double	$60
triple	$80
quad.	$100
child	$15

Open year round

Number of rooms	**4**
rooms in basement	1
rooms with sink	3
shared bathrooms	2
shared wc	1

---

2. CHICOUTIMI

☀☀☀ F ♿ P TA R2

Just east of Chicoutimi on a vast property with a commanding view of the city and the Rivière Saguenay, Le Chardonneret is a comfortable home away from home. Copious breakfasts. Various services 0.6km away: bank, pharmacy, convenience store, gas station. Welcome to my home.

From Québec City, Rte 175 North twd Chicoutimi. Right on Boul. Université East, near the shopping centre, left on Boul. Saguenay. After the Hôtel Parasol, right on Boul. Renaud. 2nd house on the left.

B&B
LE CHARDONNERET

Claire Tremblay
1253, boul. Renaud
Chicoutimi G7H 3N7
(418) 543-9336
www.inns-bb.com/chardonneret
lechardonneret@videotron.ca

	B&B
single	$40
double	$60
triple	$80
child	$15

Open: May 15 to Oct. 31

Number of rooms	**3**
rooms with sink	1
shared bathrooms	2

---

3. CHICOUTIMI

☀☀☀ F e ⊘ P 🚐 TA R4

Located in a residential neighbourhood in the north sector, 4km from downtown, our B&B offers peace and quiet and a magnificent woodland spreading behind it. Take a well-deserved break on the terrace, beneath the trees. In winter, you can snowmobile all the way to the garden since the trail is only 100m away. We will welcome you with open arms and serve you a hearty breakfast in a family atmosphere.

From Québec City, Rte 175 North twd Chicoutimi. Left on Boul. Université. Right on Boul. St-Paul twd Pont Dubuc. Past the bridge, at the top of Boul. Ste-Geneviève, right at the 1st light, Deschamps becomes Delisle. 3rd stop sign, left on Cabot, right on Boischatel.

B&B
LE GÎTE AU BOIS DORMANT

Lorraine Houde and
Lucien Girard
135, rue de Boischatel
Chicoutimi G7G 4L4
(418) 543-8751
www.legiteauboisdormant.com
lorrainelucien@videotron.ca

	B&B
single	$45-50
double	$55-60
child	$15

Open year round

Number of rooms	**3**
rooms in basement	2
shared bathrooms	2

4. HÉBERTVILLE

★★★ F E P ～⛵✕ TA

Presbytery built in 1917. Historical character and period furniture. Warm reception, intimate dining room, refined cuisine, spacious comfortable and warm rooms with full bathrooms. Conference room, peaceful, calm, inspires creativity. In the heart of the Saguenay-Lac-St-Jean region with its activities. Looking forward to your visit. **See colour photos.**

From Rte 169, don't go to the town of Hébertville, head twd Mont Lac Vert, 3km. Across from the municipal campground.

INN
AUBERGE PRESBYTÈRE
MONT LAC VERT

La Famille Bilodeau
335, rang Lac-Vert
Hébertville G8N 1M1
(418) 344-1548
1-800-818-1548
fax (418) 344-1013
www.aubergepresbytere.com

	B&B	MAP
single	$57	$76-86
double	$72	$111-131
triple	$87	$146-176
quad.	$102	$181-221
child	$5	

Taxes extra VS MC AM IT

Reduced rates: Oct. 1 to Nov. 30, Apr. 1 to June 1
Open year round

Number of rooms	6
rooms with private bath	6

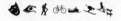

---

5. HÉBERTVILLE

☀☀☀ F P ～✕ TA R1

B&B on the farm, charming welcome. Perfect location for visiting the entire region. Come share in our family life and visit our dairy farm in the shade of Parc des Laurentides. Children welcome. Beach, mountain biking, skating and roller-blading track, fishing, playing field, downhill and cross-country skiing, ice-fishing, inner-tubes sliding. **Farm Stay p 72.**

From Parc des Laurentides, Rte 169. 1st village, Rue St-Isidore.

B&B
FERME CAROLE
ET JACQUES MARTEL

Carole and Jacques Martel
474, rue Saint-Isidore
Hébertville G8N 1L7
tel/fax (418) 344-1323
www.inns-bb.com/caroleetjacquesmartel

	B&B
single	$35
double	$45
triple	$65
quad.	$85
child	$10

Open year round

Number of rooms	3
shared bathrooms	1
shared wc	1

---

6. HÉBERTVILLE

☀☀～ F e 🚭 P ～🐎 TA R4

Visit an area where nature still offers adventure. Ancestral house in French-speaking land welcomes you year round with several activities. Halfway between Tadoussac for whale-watching (70min) and Zoo de St-Félicien (45min). We look forward to sharing pleasant family moments with you. Dinner on request. Recommended by the popular Guide Français.

From Parc des Laurentides, Rte 169 North, 6km, twd Roberval.

B&B
GÎTE BELLE-RIVIÈRE

Marie-Alice Bouchard
872, rang Caron, rte 169
Hébertville G8N 1B6
(418) 344-4345
fax (418) 344-1933
www.inns-bb.com/belle_riviere
bouchard@digicom.qc.ca

	B&B
single	$35
double	$50
triple	$70
quad.	$90
child	$12

Open year round

Number of rooms	3
rooms with sink	1
shared bathrooms	2

---

7. JONQUIÈRE

☀☀☀ F E ⊘ P ⟷ TA R.5

Finalist for the 2000-2001 Award of Excellence. This quaint English-style house from the 1900s, with original woodwork and oak staircase, is located in the historic Arvida district, near Alcan, the Manoir, the aluminium bridge, cultural activities and sports. Steps away form the Québec Issime show and bike path. In winter, snowmobiling and dogsledding on demand. Hearty breakfast served in the solarium. Professional beauty care and massage available.

From Québec City, Rte 175 North, in Chicoutimi twd Jonquière, Rte 170, 8km, right on Rue Mellon, 3km to roundabout, Boul. Saguenay twd Jonquière, about 80m, on the right.

B&B
AU MITAN

Denise F. Blackburn
2840, boul. Saguenay
Jonquière G7S 2H3
(418) 548-7388
fax (418) 548-3415
www.multimania.com/lemitan/
denisefblackburn@hotmail.com

	B&B	
single	$50	
double	$65	
child	$20	
Open year round		
Number of rooms		3
rooms in basement		1
rooms with sink		3
shared bathrooms		2

8. JONQUIÈRE

☀☀☀☀ F ⊘ P ⟷ ≋ R1

Regional Prize for Excellence "Special Favorite" 2002 and regional winner of the 2002 "People's Special Favourite" award and regional winner of the 2002 Québec Tourism Grand Prix. In the heart of the Saguenay region, 10min walking distance from downtown, soundproof rooms with two beds, sink, fan, TV. Internet, lounge with refrigerator and micro-wave. Garage for motorcycles and bicycles. For breakfast: chef's specialties served in the air-conditioned sunroom, magnificent view of the river and the unique aluminium bridge. Private beach, rowboat, pedal-boat and bike path nearby. Can ac-commodate up to 14 people.

From Québec City, Rtes 175 and 170, left twd Jonquière, 11.2km, Boul. Harvey, 2.8km, left on Rue St-Jean-Baptiste, 1.1km, left on Rue des Saules.

B&B
GÎTE DE LA RIVIÈRE
AUX SABLES

Marie and Jean Eudes Girard
4076, rue des Saules
Jonquière G8A 2G7
(418) 547-5101
fax (418) 547-6939
www.
gitedelariviereauxsables.com
marie@gitedelariviereauxsables.com

	B&B	
single	$50	
double	$60-65	
triple	$75-80	
quad.	$95	
child	$15	
Reduced rates: group 8 or more, 3 to 5 nights and more		
Open year round		
Number of rooms		4
rooms in basement		4
rooms with private bath		1
rooms with sink		2
rooms with private wc		1
shared bathrooms		2

9. JONQUIÈRE

☀☀☀☀ F E ⊘ P ⟷ 🛏 R.1

At this ancestral home in the heart of the lively downtown area, 50m away from the magnificent Parc de la Rivière-aux-Sables, we offer comfortable, carefully decorated rooms with double bed, private bathroom, living room. We provide a succulent breakfast according to your wishes, which you can enjoy on the terrace, under the shade of hundred-year-old maple trees, or in the dining room. Take advantage of little extras that make all the difference.

From Québec City, Rte 175 North and 70 West twd downtown Jonquière, Rue St-Dominique, facing the church.

B&B
LES SAISONS DE MARIE

Marie-Josée Audet and
Gérald Rathée
2518, St-Dominique
Jonquière G7X 6J7
(418) 695-7235
fax (418) 695-6228
**www.inns-
bb.com/saisonsdemarie**
mjaudet@sympatico.ca

	B&B	
single	$55-60	
double	$60-70	
child	$30	
Open year round		
Number of rooms		3
rooms with private bath		3

10. LA BAIE

★ ★ F ⊙ P ≋ ✕ TA R3

Located by the water, every room has its own private entrance, offering a superb view. Walk along the shoreline, watch the tides, discover the artist-host's granite sculptures. Evening beach campfires, for those who so desire. If nature enchants you, one day is not enough. Kayak location on site. Ice-fishing and dog-sledding packages. Restaurant on place.

From the Parc des Laurentides, Rtes 175 North and 170 East to Boul de la Grande-Baie South. After the Musée du Fjord, 5km. From St-Siméon, Rte 170 North. On the water side, a huge granite block marks the entrance.

INN
À FLEUR DE PIERRE

Colette Létourneau and
Carrol Tremblay
6788, boul. Grande-Baie Sud
La Baie G7B 3P6
(418) 544-3260
www.inns-bb.com/fleurdepierre

	B&B
single	$65
double	$70
child	$15

Taxes extra VS

Reduced rates: winter $60/2 people
Open year round

Number of rooms	3
rooms with private bath	3

---

11. LA BAIE

☀ ☀ ☀ F E ⊘ P ≋ TA R.7

15, 000 square metres of land right at the edge of the water (au bord de l'eau), in town, an outstanding location with a spectacular view, spacious rooms, on with whirlpool and one with a kitchenette. Here, the "bay" (baie) is the sea; it is a vast stretch of salt water, and its 7m tides transform the landscape. 5 min from the theatre and various activities, but in a world of its own. Hearty breakfasts, homey atmosphere.

From Parc des Laurentides, Rte 175 North, then 170 East to Boul. Grande-Baie South. 1.5km past the Musée du Fjord. You can't see the house from the road!

B&B
AU BORD DE L'EAU

Lyne Fortin and Réjean Ouellet
5208, boul. Grande-Baie Sud
La Baie G7B 3P6
(418) 544-0892
1-888-811-0892
fax (418) 544-5432
www3.sympatico.ca/rejean.
ouellet/home.html
rejean.ouellet@sympatico.ca

	B&B
single	$45-75
double	$60-90
triple	$75-105
quad.	$90-120

VS MC

Reduced rates: Sep. 15 to June 15
Open year round

Number of rooms	4
rooms with private bath	2
shared bathrooms	1

---

12. LA BAIE

☀ ☀ ☀ F e P ≋ 🐾 ✕ R2

Come live an incredible experience with the Gagné family at the "Chez Grand-Maman" B&B where you will find tranquillity in picturesque surroundings. You'll experience extraordinary things on our farm by the Baie des Ha! Ha! We will make you feel at home. **Farm Stay p 73.**

From Parc des Laurentides, Rtes 175 North and 170 East twd "Ville de La Baie", Rue Bagot. Left on Rue Victoria, about 2km. Straight ahead, 1st farm, "Alain Gagné".

B&B
CHEZ GRAND-MAMAN

Jacinthe Bouchard and
Alain Gagné
1254, chemin Saint-Joseph
La Baie G7B 3N9
(418) 544-7396
(418) 697-0517
www.inns-bb.com/grand_maman
chezgrandmaman@hotmail.com

	B&B
single	$45-50
double	$60-65
triple	$80-85
child	$10-15

Open year round

Number of rooms	3
shared bathrooms	2

13. LA BAIE

☀ ☀ ☀ **F P** 🚗 **R2**

To rediscover the charm of the countryside of long ago, drop anchor off l'Anse-à-Benjamin. Near all services: theatre, walking trails, marina, skating rink. Pleasant rooms. Enjoy our B&B winter or summer. Outfitter of fishing cabins. Packages available upon request.

From Parc des Laurentides, Rtes 175 North and 170 East twd Ville de la Baie, Rue Bagot. Left on Rue Victoria, keep right, 2km.

B&B
GÎTE DE LA PÊCHE BLANCHE

Laurence Blanchette and Jean-Claude Simard
1352, Route de l'Anse-à-Benjamin
La Baie G7B 3N9
tel/fax **(418) 544-4176**
www.inns-bb.com/pecheblanche

B&B	
single	$40
double	$50
triple	$65
child	$10
Open year round	
Number of rooms	**4**
rooms in basement	3
shared bathrooms	2

🔥 ⛷ 🏃 🛶 🐟 ➤

---

14. LA BAIE

☀ ☀ ☀ **F e P** 🐗 **TA R.1**

What a good idea it is to relax on the terrace, by the heated swimming pool, facing the fjord. Nearby: the Pyramide, a restaurant, church, convenience store, gas station, bike path and snowmobile trail, 1.5km from the Fabuleuse Histoire d'un Royaume, a peaceful place. Welcome.

Rte 75 North and 170 East, right on Boul. Grande Baie South, 1.5km. At the Durocher centre, right on Rue Mgr. Dufour. Or Rte 170 West at the light, left on Rue Mgr. Dufour. Or Rte 381, right on Chemin St-Jean and left on Mgr. Dufour.

B&B
GÎTE DE LA PYRAMIDE

Hélène Marquis and Denis Tremblay
2824, rue Mgr. Dufour
La Baie G7B 1E3
(418) 697-1997
tel/fax (418) 697-0582
royaume.com/~jessi
jessi@royaume.com

B&B	
single	$50
double	$60
triple	$70
quad.	$80
child	$10
VS MC	
Open year round	
Number of rooms	**3**
rooms in semi-basement	3
shared bathrooms	2
shared wc	1

🏛 ⛷ 🚲 ⛷

---

15. L'ANSE-ST-JEAN

☀ ☀ ☀ **F e P R1.5**

Cosy Québec-style house echoing the colours of the fjord. Breakfast in the sunroom, river and mountain view. Rest in comfortable rooms, relax and daydream to the sound of the river. Nearby: walking trails, horseback riding, sea kayaking, fjord cruises, mountain biking, salmon fishing. Françoise (the homebody) and François (the sportsman) offer simple hospitality in their green shutter house.

From Québec City, via St-Siméon, Rtes 138 East and 170 twd Anse-St-Jean. Via Chicoutimi, Rtes 175 and 170, Rue Principale de l'Anse, 3.5km.

B&B
À LA PANTOUFLARDE

Françoise Potvin and François Asselin
129, rue Saint-Jean-Baptiste
L'Anse-St-Jean G0V 1J0
(418) 272-2182
(418) 545-1099
fax (418) 545-1914
www.inns-bb.com/pantouflarde
lapantouflarde@hotmail.com

B&B	
single	$45
double	$60
triple	$75
quad.	$90
child	$15
VS MC	
Open: June 1 to Oct. 15	
Number of rooms	**3**
rooms with sink	2
shared bathrooms	2

16. L'ANSE-ST-JEAN

★★★ F E P ☒ TA

Facing the covered bridge, the inn features a large veranda off the rooms. Large living room with fireplace. Recommended (Ulysses guide and French guide) for its game, fish and seafood dishes. Direct access to snowmobile trails; skiing, fjord and ice fishing nearby. Very favourable dinner packages and off-season prices. **Ad end of this region.**

Rte 170 twd L'Anse-St-Jean, Rue St-Jean-Baptiste twd the dock. Located 0.2km from the church, in front of the covered bridge.

INN
AUBERGE DES CÉVENNES

Enid Bertrand and
Louis Mario Dufour
294, rue Saint-Jean-Baptiste
L'Anse-St-Jean G0V 1J0
(418) 272-3180
1-877-272-3180
fax (418) 272-1131
auberge-des-cevennes.qc.ca
*auberge-des-cevennes@
royaume.com*

	B&B	MAP
single	$74	$90
double	$81-101	$124-144
triple	$108	$174
quad.	$115	$204
child	$5	$12

Taxes extra VS MC IT

Reduced rates: Sep. 1 to June 24
Open year round

Number of rooms	14
rooms with private bath	14

---

17. L'ANSE-ST-JEAN

☀☀☀ F E ⊘ P TA R2

In wild nature, alongside Parc Saguenay and St-Jean river, our bed and breakfast offers spacious comfortable rooms, a cosy fireplace and an appetizing breakfast. In closeby surroundings, hiking, horseback riding, kayaking, boat cruises and fishing possibilities. In winter, fishing through the ice, alpine and cross-country skiing, etc.

From St-Siméon or Ville La Baie, on Rte 170, stop exactly at km. 71 sign. There stands Rue Côté, on Côté 1rst entry to the left.

B&B
AU GÎTE DU BARRAGE

Élisabeth Ross and
Égide Lessard
3, rue Côté
L'Anse-St-Jean G0V 1J0
(418) 272-3387
fax (418) 272-1388
augitedubarrage.com
info@augitedubarrage.com

	B&B
single	$52
double	$62

VS MC
Open year round

Number of rooms	4
rooms in basement	2
rooms with private bath	4

---

18. L'ANSE-ST-JEAN

☀☀☀☀ F E ⊘ P ≈ TA R3

"...A beautiful terrace and river behind the B&B is ideal for enjoying a good book, and offers a splendid view of the mountains. Your host offers a friendly welcome into his sunny and spacious home; beautiful rooms will help put your worried behind you. Budget-conscious travellers in search of the utmost in comfort will find it here." A French tourist. Our prices included the $2.00 taxes fee.

From Québec City via St-Siméon, Rtes 138 East and 170 twd Anse St-Jean, via Chicoutimi, Rtes 175 and 170. Rue St-Jean-Baptiste, 3.5km.

B&B
AU GLOBE-TROTTER

André Bouchard
131, rue Saint-Jean-Baptiste
L'Anse-St-Jean G0V 1J0
(418) 272-2353
fax (418) 272-1731
www.inns-bb.com/globe_trotter
andreb7@hotmail.com

	B&B
single	$45-50
double	$60-65
child	$15

VS MC
Open: May 1 to Oct. 31

Number of rooms	3
rooms with private bath	1
shared bathrooms	1

19. MASHTEUIATSH

☀☀☀ F E 🚭 P 🚤 🏊 TA R8

Located by Lac-St-Jean, in the very heart of Mashteuiatsh, Auberge Shakahikan (lake in Montagnais) offers a magnificent stay in a Canadian-style house. Nearby tourist attractions: Musée Amérindien, Val-Jalbert and the St-Félicien zoo. Mashteuiatsh is located West of Lac St-Jean, 8km North of Roberval.

From Parc des Laurentides, Rte 169 North, 1st light Roberval, right Rue Brassard and Boul. St-Joseph twd Mashteuiatsh.

B&B
AUBERGE SHAKAHIKAN

Jocelyne Paul and Len Moar
1380, rue Ouiatchouan
Mashteuiatsh G0W 2H0
(418) 275-3528
fax (418) 275-3929
www.inns-bb.com/shakahikan

	B&B
single	$50-60
double	$65-75
triple	$95
quad.	$115
child	$15

Open year round except Dec., Jan. and Feb. by reservation only

Number of rooms	5
rooms in basement	2
shared bathrooms	2
shared wc	1

20. MÉTABETCHOUAN-LAC-À-LA-CROIX

☀☀☀ F 🚭 P TA R2

Succumb to the charms of nature. A beautiful Canadian house located in the heart of majestic Lac-St-Jean. Lovely terrace on which to relax. Our guests receive a warm, simple welcome. Spacious, attractive and comfortable room with soft bed. Hearty breakfast with Fernande's homemade jam and many other treats. Swimming and bike path (3km).

From Parc des Laurentides, Rte 169 North, 10km, twd Roberval.

B&B
BELLE-VUE SUR LE LAC

Fernande and Marcel Duchesne
1436, Route 169
Métabetchouan-Lac-à-la-Croix
G8G 1A5
(418) 349-3490
(418) 480-8673
fax (418) 349-8589
www.inns-bb.com/belle_vue_sur_le_lac

	B&B
single	$40
double	$50
child	$15

Open year round

Number of rooms	2
shared bathrooms	1

21. MÉTABETCHOUAN-LAC-À-LA-CROIX

☀☀☀ F e P 🚤 ✕ R8

Century-old farmhouse where we like to keep up traditions: a toast to friends, home-made meals, cows in their pyjamas in the fall. Well-located for touring the region. Traditional recipes to be shared. Cross-country skiing on the farm and near the mountain. **Farm Stay p 73.**

From Parc des Laurentides, Rte 169, 1st Rang on the left before the village of Hébertville, 11km.

B&B
CÉLINE ET GEORGES MARTIN

Céline and Georges Martin
2193, 3ᵉ Rang Ouest
Métabetchouan-Lac-à-la-Croix
G8G 1M6
tel/fax (418) 349-2583
www.inns-bb.com/celineetgeorgesmartin

	B&B	MAP
single	$35	$50
double	$45	$75
child	$13	$18

Open year round

Number of rooms	3
shared bathrooms	1
shared wc	2

22. NORMANDIN

Recipient of the National «gold» winner Grand Prix 2000 and Regional Grand Prix 2000-2001 «Achievement» award and 1999 «Special Favorite». Welcoming you is a pleasure. Whether alone or as a couple, family or group, you are sure to be charmed by our B & B. Solarium lounge, outdoor pool. Near Véloroute des Bleuets (3km restaurant shuttle). Bike garage, special attention to cyclists. 4km from Grands Jardins. **Farm Stay p 73.**

From Parc des Laurentides, Rte 169 twd Roberval, St-Félicien. At Normandin traffic light, 3km twd St-Thomas.

B&B
LES GÎTES MAKADAN

Micheline Villeneuve and Daniel Bergeron
1728, rue Saint-Cyrille
Normandin G8M 4K5
tel/fax (418) 274-2867
1-877-625-2326
gitemakadan.cjb.net
makadan@destination.ca

	B&B
single	$50
double	$60-80
triple	$80-95
quad.	$100
child	$15

VS

Reduced rates: Oct. 15 to Apr. 15
Open year round

Number of rooms	5
rooms with private bath	1
rooms with sink	4
shared bathrooms	2

23. PETIT-SAGUENAY

This inn faces a large plot of land next to the salmon river. Here, Régine will welcome you in a rustic decor where reception is key. A warm fireplace, a delicious, reputable cuisine of fish, game and regional delicacies. Packages: whales and fjord, sea kayaking, dinghy rides, canoeing, shows. Hiking excursions in the Saguenay-St. Lawrence Marine Park. Snowmobiling, ice fishing, dogsledding. Ideal for a long stay.

From St-Siméon in Charlevoix, Rte 170 twd Chicoutimi, 50km. 100m from tourist office and 1hr from Tadoussac and Chicoutimi.

INN
AUBERGE LES 2 PIGNONS

Régine Morin
117, Route 170
Petit-Saguenay G0V 1N0
1-877-272-3091
fax (418) 272-1676
www.royaume.com/auberge-2-pignons
auberge-2-pignons@royaume.com

	B&B	MAP
single	$67	$90
double	$74	$120
triple	$99	$168
quad.	$109	$201

Taxes extra VS MC ER IT

Reduced rates: Sep. 10 to June 22
Open year round

Number of rooms	6
rooms with private bath	6

24. ROBERVAL

Come relax by splendid Lac St-Jean, a veritable inland sea. Take advantage of a well-deserved quiet moment and stretch out on our private beach near the house. It gives us great pleasure to have you as our guests.

From Parc des Laurentides, Rte 169. We are 3.5km from the Val-Jalbert bridge. From La Tuque, Rte 155 twd Chambord. Left twd Roberval, Rte 169, 10km.

B&B
LA MAISON AU TOIT ROUGE

Yolande Lalancette and Raynald Girard
1345, boul. de l'Anse, route 169
Roberval G8H 2N1
(418) 275-3290
fax (418) 275-4273
www.inns-bb.com/toitrouge

	B&B
single	$40
double	$50
child	$10

Open: May 15 to Sep. 30

Number of rooms	3
shared bathrooms	2

25. ST-AMBROISE-DE-CHICOUTIMI

Nomination Prize for Excellence 2001. Prize for Excellence "Special Favorite" Regional 2000. In the heart of Saguenay-Lac-St-Jean, a country farmhouse with a garden, flowers, farmyard, lake, and trout stream. Cozy beds, choice breakfasts and, by reservation, delicious Saguenay meals. Also, 3- to 6-day "all-inclusive" packages. In summer: fishing, blueberry picking. In winter: snowmobiling, dogsledding, skiing, ice fishing.

From Chicoutimi, Rte 172 West twd Alma. Past St-Ambroise, right twd Bégin. 5km. Right on Rang 9. We are 500m from the corner.

B&B
AUX PIGNONS VERTS

Ghislaine Ouellet and
Jean-Claude Villeneuve
925, Rang 9
Saint-Ambroise-de-Chicoutimi
G7P 2A4
(418) 672-2172
fax (418) 672-6622
**www3.sympatico.ca/
pignonsverts**
pignonsverts@sympatico.ca

B&B	
single	$40-50
double	$50-65
child	$15-25

VS

Reduced rates: 10% 3 nights and more and corporatif price
Open year round

Number of rooms	3
shared bathrooms	2

---

26. ST-AMBROISE-DE-CHICOUTIMI

Discover an enchanting and relaxing natural site. This near-century-old (1909) B&B features a warm, restful atmosphere. Rooms decorated with antique furnishings. Lavish, all-you-can-eat breakfasts. Magnificent landscape, mountains, forest, fields in which to stroll, flowers and vegetable garden. A perfect getaway from the pressures of everyday life.

Rte 172 between Chicoutimi and Alma. Twd Bégin, 3.5km along Rang des Aulnaies

B&B
GÎTE DE LA SOURCE
DES AULNAIES

Ghislaine Girard and
Laurier Sergerie
322, rang des Aulnaies
Saint-Ambroise G7P 2B4
(418) 672-2571
aulnaies.tripod.com

B&B	
single	$30-45
double	$50
child	$10

Reduced rates: Sept. 1 to May 31
Open year round

Number of rooms	3
shared bathrooms	2

---

27. ST-FÉLICIEN

10 metres from the Ashuap-mushuan River, and boasting a large terrace. What a joy to meet people from all over the world. Tourist attractions: zoo (6km), falls (5km), Val-Jalbert (20km). Located near downtown. Come meet us for a pleasant time. Special little considerations await you.

From Parc des Laurentides, Rte 169 twd Roberal to St-Félicien, located opposite "Mets Chinois". From Dolbeau, at 2nd light, left on Sacré-Coeur, located opposite "Mets Chinois".

B&B
À FLEUR D'EAU

Claudette Nadeau and
Paul Hébert
1016, rue Sacré-Coeur
Saint-Félicien G8K 1R5
(418) 679-0784
www.multimania.com/afleurdeau

B&B	
single	$50-55
double	$50-60

Reduced rates: Oct. 1 to June 1
Open year round

Number of rooms	5
rooms in basement	1
rooms with private bath	5

28. ST-FÉLICIEN

☀ ☀ ☀ F e P ⮌R2

If you like the charm of the country, you'll be enchanted by our surroundings. A warm welcome in a calming and restful atmosphere. A sitting room is at your disposal. Evenings outdoors around the campfire lead to good conversation. Healthy, generous breakfast. 3km to town, 6km to the zoo. Reduced rates: September to June. 1.5km to "Véloroute des Bleuets". Our prices included the 2.00$ taxes fee.

From Parc des Laurentides, Rte 169 twd Roberval twd St-Félicien. At the 1st traffic light, turn left on Rue Notre-Dame, 2.6km. Right on Rang Double, 0.7km.

B&B
À LA FERME HÉBERT

Céline Giroux and
J-Jacques Hébert
1070, rang Double
Saint-Félicien G8K 2N8
(418) 679-0574
fax (418) 679-4625
www.inns-bb.com/fermehebert
fhebert@destination.ca

	B&B
single	$40
double	$48-52
triple	$63
child	$10

Taxes extra

Reduced rates: 2 nights and more, Sep. 1 to June 15
Open year round

Number of rooms	3
rooms in basement	2
rooms with sink	1
shared bathrooms	2

---

29. ST-FÉLIX-D'OTIS

☀ ☀ ☀ F e 🚭 P 〜 🐾 TA R1

Country farm between La Baie and Rivière-Eternité with animals running free, flowers, decorative garden. A relaxing, rejuvenating haven where life flows with the seasons. Outdoor pool, air-conditioned house. Healthy breakfast, oven-fresh bread, wild berries. Near: Parc Saguenay, Site de la Nouvelle France and «La Fabuleuse Histoire d'un Royaume». Guided beaver-watching tour.

From Parc des Laurentides, Rtes 175 North and 170 East. From St-Siméon, Rte 170.

B&B
GÎTE DE LA BASSE-COUR

Huguette Morin
271, rue Principale
Saint-Félix-d'Otis G0V 1M0
(418) 544-8766
communities.fr.msn.ca/eet
gitebassecour@hotmail.com

	B&B
single	$45
double	$55-65
triple	$75
quad.	$85
child	$5-15

Open year round

Number of rooms	3
shared bathrooms	2

---

30. ST-FULGENCE

☀ ☀ ☀ F E P 〜 🐾 TA R.4

La Maraîchère du Saguenay, our ancestral home, our old barn and our latest addition, a tiny house similar to our old home. Warm, stunning, cosy rooms with antique furnishings. A grandiose fjord and magnificent parks nearby, Mont-Valin, Saguenay and Cap-Jaseux. Kayaking, canoeing, hiking, dogsledding, snowmobiling plus all the activities we can organise for you. Dinner available, must reserve ahead of time. See you soon.

From Chicoutimi, 8km past Dubuc bridge, Rte 172 twd Tadoussac. Left 400m after Esso station.

B&B
LA MARAÎCHÈRE DU SAGUENAY

Adèle Copeman and
Rodrigue Langevin
97, boul. Tadoussac
Saint-Fulgence G0V 1S0
(418) 674-9384
(418) 674-2247
fax (418) 674-1055
www.maraicheresaguenay.ca
infos@maraicheresaguenay.ca

	B&B
single	$55-65
double	$65-75
triple	$80-100
quad.	$95-125
child	$10-20

Taxes extra VS MC
Open year round

Number of rooms	4
rooms with private bath	2
shared bathrooms	1
shared wc	1

31. ST-HENRI-DE-TAILLON

☀☀☀ F e ⊘ P ⟵ ✕ TA R1

At L'Eau Berge du Lac, discover the charms of yesteryear. We will welcome you to our warm, charming, country-style ancestral home, built by the first pioneers. Our B&B is located near Parc de la Pointe Taillon, where there is a magnificent beach. The Véloroute des Bleuets runs along the inn, while Jardins Scullion are a mere 15min away. In winter, enjoy snowmobiling, skiing, fishing and snowshoeing. Your hosts, Julie and Daniel.

Rte 169 North, 18km from Alma and 1km from St-Henri.

B&B
L'EAU BERGE DU LAC

Julie Martel
274, Route 169
St-Henri-de-Taillon G0W 2X0
(418) 347-4864
fax (418) 668-0656
www.inns-bb.com/bergedulac
bergelac@hotmail.com

	B&B	MAP
single	$45-70	$65-90
double	$55-80	$75-120
triple	$70-95	$130-155
quad.	$85-110	$170-190

VS MC

Reduced rates: $10 for the 3rd night
Open year round

Number of rooms	4
rooms with private bath	1
shared bathrooms	2

🔥 🛏 🛶 🏃 🚲 👓 🐟 ➡

32. LA BAIE

F e ♿ P 🛏 TA R2 M2

Ancestral house from 1848 located 2km from La Baie and 12km from Chicoutimi. Near tourist activities, La Fabuleuse theatre, hiking trails, marina, cheese shop, farm, blueberry grove, bike path, ice fishing, etc. 10 apartments, 2 bathrooms. **Country Home on a Farm p 74.**

From Parc des Laurentides, Rtes 175 North and 170 East twd La Baie. At the 2nd light, continue to Rue Victoria, left, 2km along Victoria, which turns into St-Joseph. After the flashing light, the second house on the right.

COUNTRY HOME
LA MAISON DES ANCÊTRES

Judith and Germain Simard
1722, chemin Saint-Joseph
La Baie G7B 3N9
(418) 544-2925
fax (418) 544-0241
www.maisondesancetres.com
simardgermain@globetrotter.net

No. houses	1
No. rooms	5
No. people	10-12
WEEK-SUMMER	$600
WEEK-WINTER	$500
W/E-SUMMER	$300
W/E-WINTER	$250
DAY-SUMMER	$150
DAY-WINTER	150

Open year round

 🏛 🦃 🚗 🚶 🚲

AGROTOURISM

Farm Explorations:

🏠 *33* ACCUEIL DU RANDONNEUR, Saint-Honoré...*Page 63*

Farm Stays:

🏠 *5* FERME CAROLE ET JACQUES MARTEL, Hébertville ....*Page 72*

🏠 *12* CHEZ GRAND-MAMAN, La Baie ....*Page 73*

🏠 *21* CÉLINE ET GEORGES MARTIN, Métabetchouan-Lac-à-la-Croix ....*Page 73*

🏠 *22* LES GÎTES MAKADAN, Normandin ....*Page 73*

Country Home on a Farm:

🏠 *32* LA MAISON DES ANCÊTRES, La Baie...*Page 74*

Farm Shops:

🏠 *34* LA MAGIE DU SOUS-BOIS INC., Dolbeau-Mistassini ....*Page 49*

🏠 *35* FROMAGERIE LA PETITE HEIDI ENR., Sainte-Rose-du-Nord ....*Page 49*

INDEX BY NAME OF ESTABLISHMENT

6
6400 COUETTE ET CAFÉ BED & BREAKFAST, LE (MONTRÉAL)...... 214

9
91 DU BOUT DE L'ÎLE, LE (L'ÎLE-D'ORLÉANS, STE-PÉTRONILLE) 236

À
À AMOUR ET AMITIÉ (MAGOG)..100
À BON MATIN (MONTRÉAL) 209
À BONHEUR D'OCCASION (MONTRÉAL) 208
À FLEUR DE PIERRE (LA BAIE)..260
À FLEUR D'EAU (ST-FÉLICIEN) 265
À LA BELLE VIE (MONTRÉAL) 209
À LA BERNACHE (CHICOUTIMI)...257
À LA BONNE HEURE (MONTRÉAL) 209
À LA BRUNANTE (LONGUEUIL)...202
À LA CAMPAGNE EN VILLE (QUÉBEC) 239
À LA CAPITAINERIE DU PASSANT (GRANDES-PILES) 188
À LA CARTE B & B (MONTRÉAL)..210
À LA CHOUETTE (BAIE-ST-PAUL)...114
À LA CLAIRE FONTAINE (CHAMBLY)..199
À LA COLLINE AUX CHEVAUX (MAGOG) 67, 101
À LA FERME HÉBERT (ST-FÉLICIEN) 266
À LA GIRONDINE (FRELIGHSBURG) 20, 36, 52, 96
À LA JOLIE ROCHELLE (QUÉBEC, CAP-ROUGE)..247
À LA MAISON D'À CÔTÉ (MONTRÉAL) 210
À LA MAISON DREW (MAGOG)...101
À LA MAISON TUDOR (QUÉBEC) 240
À LA PANTOUFLARDE (L'ANSE-ST-JEAN) 261
À LA RÊVASSE (PERCÉ) 154
À L'ABRI DU CLOCHER (NOUVELLE) 153
À L'ABRI DU VENT (PERCÉ) 154
À L'ADRESSE DU CENTRE-VILLE (MONTRÉAL) 210
À L'ANCESTRALE B&B (MAGOG)..101
À L'ARRÊT DU TEMPS (STE-ANNE-DE-LA-PÉRADE) 191
À L'OASIS DU VIEUX-LONGUEUIL (LONGUEUIL)...203
À L'ORÉE DU MOULIN (PAPINEAUVILLE, MONTEBELLO) 225
À TOUT VENANT (MAGOG)...102

A
ABAT-JOUR B&B (QUÉBEC)..238
ACACIAS (QUÉBEC)..239
ACCUEIL B&B L'HEURE DOUCE (QUÉBEC) 239
ACCUEIL DU RANDONNEUR (ST-HONORÉ) 63
ACCUEIL LES SEMAILLES (HÉROUXVILLE)...69, 189
ANCESTRAL B&B (STE-AGATHE-DES-MONTS)..177
ANCESTRALE, L' (ST-ANDRÉ-AVELLIN)..225
ANCÊTRE DE GASPÉ, L' (GASPÉ) 148
ANNE MA SŒUR ANNE (MONTRÉAL) 217
APPARTEMENT DU CENTRE-VILLE (TROIS-RIVIÈRES) 196
APPARTEMENTS LES BONS MATINS (MONTRÉAL)...217
APPARTEMENTS TOURISTIQUES DU CENTRE-VILLE (MONTRÉAL) 217
ARCHE DE NOÉ (RAWDON) 57
AROLLES, LES (MONT-STE-ANNE, ST-FERRÉOL) 236
ATOME, L' (MONTRÉAL) 213
AU 55 TACHÉ (HULL) 222
AU BEAU-SÉJOUR (ST-LOUIS-DU-HA! HA!)..90
AU BOISÉ JOLI (ST-JEAN-PORT-JOLI)..132
AU BONHOMME SEPT HEURES (BAIE-ST-PAUL) 115
AU BORD DE L'EAU (LA BAIE) 260
AU BORD DU FLEUVE (QUÉBEC, CAP-ROUGE)..247
AU CHARME DE LA MONTAGNE (PONTIAC, LUSKVILLE) 225
AU CLOCHETON (BAIE-ST-PAUL)..115
AU COURANT DE LA MER (STE-ANNE-DES-MONTS, TOURELLE)..157
AU CROISSANT DE LUNE (QUÉBEC)...240
AU GIBIER DU ROI (MIRABEL, ST-BENOÎT)..26, 42
AU GIRON DE L'ISLE (L'ÎLE-D'ORLÉANS, ST-JEAN)..231

270. INDEX BY NAME OF ESTABLISHMENT

AU GÎT'ANN (MONTRÉAL) 211
AU GÎTE DE LA CHUTE (BOISCHATEL) 228
AU GÎTE DU BARRAGE (L'ANSE-ST-JEAN) 262
AU GÎTE LE RAYON VERT (MONTRÉAL) 211
AU GÎTE MAISON EMERY JACOB (ST-TITE) 191
AU GÎTE OLYMPIQUE (MONTRÉAL) 211
AU GLOBE-TROTTER (L'ANSE-ST-JEAN) 262
AU GRÉ DES SAISONS (NEUVILLE) 237
AU GRÉ DU VENT (LÉVIS) 128
AU GRÉ DU VENT (MAGOG) 20
AU MANOIR DE LA RUE MERRY (MAGOG) 102
AU MITAN (JONQUIÈRE) 259
AU NID D'HIRONDELLES (STE-AGATHE-DES-MONTS) 179
AU PAYS DES RÊVES (L'ISLE-VERTE) 84
AU PERCHOIR (BAIE-ST-PAUL) 116
AU PETIT BONHEUR (BAIE-COMEAU, POINTE-LEBEL) 137
AU PETIT CHÂTEAU DU LAC (ST-DONAT) 164
AU PETIT ROI (QUÉBEC) 240
AU PIED À TERRE À QUÉBEC (QUÉBEC) 241
AU PIED DE LA CHUTE (LACHUTE, ARGENTEUIL) 25
AU PIGNON SUR LE PARC (HULL) 223
AU TEMPS DES MÛRES (DUNHAM) 95
AU TERROIR DES BASQUES (RIVIÈRE-DU-LOUP) 87
AU TOIT BLEU (L'ÎLE-D'ORLÉANS, STE-FAMILLE) 235
AU VERSANT DE LA MONTAGNE (HULL) 223
AU VIEUX PRESBYTÈRE (ST-ÉLOI) 89
AU VIRAGE (MAGOG) 102
AUBE DOUCE (ST-ADOLPHE-D'HOWARD) 172
AUBERGE UNE FERME EN GASPÉSIE, L' (MÉTIS-SUR-MER, LES BOULES) 151
AUBERGE À LA CROISÉE DES CHEMINS, L' (MONT-TREMBLANT, LA CONCEPTION) ... 171
AUBERGE ALTITUDE 2000 (SUTTON) 106
AUBERGE AU BOIS D'MON COEUR (FERME-NEUVE) 168
AUBERGE AU CRÉPUSCULE (CAP-CHAT) 145
AUBERGE AU DIABLO-VERT (LA POCATIÈRE) 83
AUBERGE AU PHIL DE L'EAU (STE-MARGUERITE-DU-LAC-MASSON) 180
AUBERGE AU PIRATE 1775 (PERCÉ) 154
AUBERGE AUX NUITS DE RÊVE (STE-AGATHE-DES-MONTS) 178
AUBERGE BAIE-JOLIE (TROIS-RIVIÈRES, POINTE-DU-LAC) 194
AUBERGE BAKER (CHÂTEAU-RICHER) 230
AUBERGE CAP-AUX-CORBEAUX (BAIE-ST-PAUL) 114
AUBERGE CHARME DES ALPES (VAL-DAVID) 181
AUBERGE CHEMIN DU ROY (DESCHAMBAULT) 231
AUBERGE CHEZ IGNACE (LAC-NOMININGUE) 168
AUBERGE CHEZ MARIE-ROSES (BIC, LE) 80
AUBERGE D'ANDROMÈDE, L' (COURCELLES) 67, 94
AUBERGE DE LA BAIE-DES-CAPUCINS (CAP-CHAT, CAPUCINS) 145
AUBERGE DE LA BAIE (LES ESCOUMINS) 138
AUBERGE DE LA BARONNIE DE PORTNEUF (PORTNEUF) 238
AUBERGE DE LA FERME ST-ADOLPHE (STONEHAM, ST-ADOLPHE) 72, 253
AUBERGE DE LA GARE (STE-ADÈLE) 176
AUBERGE DE LA TOUR DU LAC (STE-AGATHE-DES-MONTS) 178
AUBERGE DE LA VISITATION (LÉVIS) 128
AUBERGE DE L'EIDER (STE-LUCE-SUR-MER) 90
AUBERGE DE L'ORPAILLEUR (VAL D'OR) 77
AUBERGE DES CÉVENNES (L'ANSE-ST-JEAN) 262
AUBERGE DES ÎLES (KAMOURASKA) 82
AUBERGE DES SABLONS (ST-IRÉNÉE) 123
AUBERGE DU MAGASIN GÉNÉRAL (MONT-STE-ANNE, ST-FERRÉOL) 236
AUBERGE DU BOURG (TROIS-RIVIÈRES) 193
AUBERGE DU CHEMIN FAISANT (CABANO) 81
AUBERGE DU GRAND FLEUVE (MÉTIS-SUR-MER, LES BOULES) 151
AUBERGE DU MAS DES ÉQUERRES (ST-GABRIEL-DE-VALCARTIER) 251
AUBERGE DU PETIT-PRÉ (CHÂTEAU-RICHER) 230
AUBERGE DU TRAPPEUR (ST-MATHIEU-DU-PARC) 190
AUBERGE DU VIEUX MOULIN (STE-ÉMÉLIE-DE-L'ÉNERGIE) 165
AUBERGE DU ZOO (GRANBY) 97
AUBERGE EDELWEISS (VAL-DAVID) 181
AUBERGE HÉRITAGE COUNTRY INN (HUNTINGDON) 201
AUBERGE LA BELLE ÉPOQUE (MONTMAGNY) 130
AUBERGE LA BONNE MINE (THETFORD-MINES) 134
AUBERGE LA BOUCLÉE (LES ÉBOULEMENTS) 121
AUBERGE LA CÔTE D'OR (PETITE-RIVIÈRE-ST-FRANÇOIS) 123
AUBERGE LA GOÉLICHE (L'ÎLE-D'ORLÉANS, STE-PÉTRONILLE) 235
AUBERGE LA GRANDE MAISON (BAIE-ST-PAUL) 114
AUBERGE LA JARNIGOINE (CHAMBLY, RICHELIEU) 200

AUBERGE LA MARÉE DOUCE (POINTE-AU-PÈRE) 86
AUBERGE LA MARGUERITE (L'ISLET-SUR-MER) 129
AUBERGE LA MUSE (BAIE-ST-PAUL) 115
AUBERGE LA PENTE DOUCE (LES ÉBOULEMENTS) 121
AUBERGE LA SABLINE (RIVIÈRE-DU-LOUP) 87
AUBERGE LA SEIGNEURIE (MATANE) 149
AUBERGE LA SOLAILLERIE (ST-ANDRÉ, KAMOURASKA) 89
AUBERGE LA SUISSE (PIKE-RIVER, ST-PIERRE-DE-VÉRONNE) 105
AUBERGE LAC DU PIN ROUGE (ST-HIPPOLYTE) 174
AUBERGE L'AIR DU TEMPS (CHAMBLY) 200
AUBERGE LE CLOS ROLLAND (STE-ADÈLE) 176
AUBERGE LE MONTAGNARD (ST-ROCK-DE-MEKINAC) 191
AUBERGE LE PETIT SÉJOUR (CHÂTEAU-RICHER) 230
AUBERGE LE SAINT-VENANT (STE-AGATHE-DES-MONTS) 178
AUBERGE LE VIEUX PRESBYTÈRE (L'ÎLE-D'ORLÉANS, ST-PIERRE) 233
AUBERGE LES 2 PIGNONS (PETIT-SAGUENAY) 264
AUBERGE LES DEUX ÎLOTS (NEWPORT) 152
AUBERGE LES SOURCES INC (LA MALBAIE) 119
AUBERGE L'ÎLE FLOTTANTE (L'ÎLE-D'ORLÉANS, ST-LAURENT) 233
AUBERGE MARCIL (LAC-AUX-SABLES) 189
AUBERGE PRESBYTÈRE MONT LAC VERT (HÉBERTVILLE) 258
AUBERGE ROCHE DES BRISES (ST-JOSEPH-DU-LAC) 175
AUBERGE SHAKAHIKAN (MASHTEUIATSH) 263
AUBERGE SOUS L'ÉDREDON (ST-SAUVEUR-DES-MONTS) 175
AUBERGE ST-MATHIAS (CABANO) 81
AUBERGE SUR LES PENDANTS, L' (L'ÎLE-D'ORLÉANS, ST-PIERRE) 235
AUBERGE VILLA BELLERIVE (LAC-NOMININGUE) 169
AUBERGE WANTA-QO-TI (ESCUMINAC, MIGUASHA) 147
AUTRUCHE DORÉE, L' (MARIEVILLE) 30
AUX DEUX MARQUISES (MONTMAGNY) 130
AUX 5 LUCARNES (BIC, LE) 80
AUX ABORDS (GRANBY) 97
AUX BERGES DE LA RIVIÈRE SIMON (MORIN-HEIGHTS) 171
AUX CHANTS D'OISEAUX (ST-JEAN-SUR-RICHELIEU) 204
AUX CHUTES (STE-FLAVIE) 158
AUX DOUCES HEURES (DUNHAM) 95
AUX JARDINS CHAMPÊTRES (MAGOG) 21, 103
AUX PÉTALES DE ROSE (CAP-DES-ROSIERS, FORILLON) 145
AUX PETITS OISEAUX (BAIE-ST-PAUL) 116
AUX PETITS OISEAUX (VAL-DES-MONTS) 226
AUX PIGNONS VERTS (ST-AMBROISE-DE-CHICOUTIMI) 265
AUX PORTES DE LA NUIT (MONTRÉAL) 212
AUX RÊVES D'ANTAN (ST-MARC-SUR-RICHELIEU) 204
AUX TROIS BALCONS (QUÉBEC) 241
AZUR (MONTRÉAL) 212
AZUR RESIDENCES DE TOURISME (MONTRÉAL) 218

B

B&B CHEZ PIERRE (QUÉBEC) 241
B&B DE LA TOUR (QUÉBEC) 242
B&B DES GRISON (QUÉBEC) 242
B&B LA BEDONDAINE (QUÉBEC) 242
B&B LE CAMPAGNARD (GRANBY) 98
B&B LES CORNICHES (QUÉBEC, SILLERY) 250
B&B MAISON LESAGE (QUÉBEC) 243
BASILIC ET ROMARIN (STE-ANNE-DES-PLAINES) 28
BELLE AU BOIS DORMANT, LA (MONT-TREMBLANT) 170
BELLE AU BOIS DORMANT, LA (ST-JOACHIM-DE-SHEFFORD) 105
BELLE ÉCHAPPÉE, LA (MAGOG) 103
BELLE MAISON BLANCHE, LA (DÉGELIS) 82
BELLE-VUE SUR LE LAC (MÉTABETCHOUAN-LAC-À-LA-CROIX) 263
BERGÈRE, GÎTE ET COUVERT, LA (TROIS-PISTOLES) 18
BERGERIE DES NEIGES (ST-AMBROISE-DE-KILDARE) 164
BERGERONNETTE, LA (BERGERONNES) 137
BONHEURS DE SOPHIE, LES (ST-SAUVEUR-DES-MONTS) 176
BONNE ADRESSE, LA (ST-FAUSTIN, LAC-CARRÉ) 173
BOUCHERVILLOISE, LA (BOUCHERVILLE) 199

C

CACHE À MAXIME, LA (SCOTT JONCTION) 40
CACHET, LE (NORTH HATLEY) 104
CAPUCINES, LES (L'ISLE-VERTE) 85
CASSIS ET MÉLISSE (ST-DAMIEN-DE-BUCKLAND) 68, 132

272. INDEX BY NAME OF ESTABLISHMENT

CÉLINE ET GEORGES MARTIN (MÉTABETCHOUAN-LAC-À-LA-CROIX)..73, 263
CHALETS-VILLAGE MONT-SAINTE-ANNE (MONT-STE-ANNE, ST-FERRÉOL).......................................254
CHANTERELLES, LES (ST-IRÉNÉE)..124
CHARDONNERET, LE (CHICOUTIMI)...257
CHÂTEAU DES TOURELLES (QUÉBEC)...243
CHÂTEAU DU FAUBOURG (QUÉBEC)..243
CHAUMIÈRE EN PAIN D'ÉPICES, LA (AYER'S CLIFF)...93
CHÈVRERIE DES ACACIAS, LA (DUNHAM)...19
CHEVRIÈRE, LA (LA POCATIÈRE)..83
CHEZ ANICK ET PATRICK (QUÉBEC, STE-FOY)..248
CHEZ BÉCASSINE (ST-ADOLPHE-D'HOWARD)...172
CHEZ GERTRUDE CENTRE DE L'ÉMEU DE CHARLEVOIX (ST-URBAIN)...............................55, 68, 125
CHEZ GRAND-MAMAN (LA BAIE)...73, 260
CHEZ GRAND-MÈRE ZOIZEAUX (STE-LUCIE-DES-LAURENTIDES)...180
CHEZ GRAND'PAPA BEAU (TROIS-RIVIÈRES)...194
CHEZ MARIE B&B (GRANBY)..98
CHEZ MARTHE-ANGÈLE (STE-ANNE-DES-MONTS)...157
CHEZ MONSIEUR GILLES (QUÉBEC)...244
CHEZ NICOLE (MATANE, ST-ULRIC)...150
CIDRERIE FLEURS DE POMMIERS, LA (DUNHAM)..36
CLAIREVALLÉE (BIC, ST-FABIEN)..80
CLAIRIÈRE DE LA CÔTE, LA (L'ANNONCIATION)...25, 69, 169
CLÉ DES CHAMPS, LA (HOPE TOWN, PASPÉBIAC)..148
CLOS DE LA MONTAGNE (MONT-ST-GRÉGOIRE)..44
CLOS DES ÉPINETTES, LE (MONTRÉAL)...214
CONCLUSION, LA (STE-ANNE-DES-PLAINES)...28
CORPORATION D-TROIS-PIERRES/FERME ÉCOLOGIQUE (PIERREFONDS)...61
COULE DOUCE, LA (QUÉBEC)...244
CRÉPUSCULE (L'ÎLE-D'ORLÉANS, ST-PIERRE)..234

D

DIRECTION MONT STE-ANNE (CHÂTEAU-RICHER)..254
DOMAINE AUX CROCOLLINES (LAC-SIMON, CHÉNÉVILLE)..224
DOMAINE DE LA CHEVROTTIÈRE (DUNHAM)..35
DOMAINE DE LA TEMPLERIE (HUNTINGDON)...30, 202
DOMAINE DU BON VIEUX TEMPS (RIMOUSKI, ST-NARCISSE)..87
DOMAINE FÉLIBRE (STANSTEAD)..38
DOMAINE ORLÉANS (L'ÎLE-D'ORLÉANS, ST-PIERRE)..48
DOMAINE SUR LA COLLINE B&B (COWANSVILLE)..94
DOUCES ÉVASIONS (ST-ANSELME)...130

E

EAU BERGE DU LAC, L' (ST-HENRI-DE-TAILLON)...267
EAU BERGE, L' (LA MALBAIE)..120
EIDER MATINAL, L' (ST-IRÉNÉE)...124
ÉLEVAGE DE LA BUTTE AUX CAILLES (ST-HILARION)..54
ÉLEVAGES RUBAN BLEU, LES (ST-ISIDORE-DE-LAPRAIRIE)..45, 59
ENTRE MER ET MONTS (BAIE-STE-CATHERINE)..117
ENTREMONT, L' (ST-FAUSTIN, LAC-CARRÉ)...173
ÉRABLIÈRE DES PATRIOTES (L'ASSOMPTION)...57
ÉRABLIÈRE L'AUTRE VERSAN (STE-HÉLÈNE)..47
ESCAPADE B&B, L' (AYLMER)..221
ÉTAPE CHEZ MARIE-THÉRÈSE ET GÉRARD LEMAY, L' (ST-JÉRÔME)..174
ÉTOILE DE MER, L' (NEW RICHMOND)...153
ÉVASION MONTRÉAL (MONTRÉAL)..218
ÉVEIL SUR LE LAC, L' (ST-HIPPOLYTE)..174

F

FERME 5 ÉTOILES (SACRÉ-COEUR)..69, 139, 142
FERME CAROLE ET JACQUES MARTEL (HÉBERTVILLE)..72, 258
FERME CAVALIER (ST-SIXTE)..32
FERME DE BELLECHASSE (GATINEAU)...71, 222
FERME DE CATHERINE, LA (ST-ANDRÉ-D'ARGENTEUIL)..27
FERME DE LA BERCEUSE, LA (WICKHAM)...67, 111
FERME DE LA BUTTE MAGIQUE (ST-FAUSTIN, LAC CARRÉ)..58
FERME DU WAPITI, LA (FRELIGHSBURG)..53
FERME GUY RIVEST (RAWDON)..41
FERME JEAN DUCHESNE (ST-PIE)...59
FERME KOSA (ST-RÉMI-DE-NAPIERVILLE)..31
FERME LA BISONNIÈRE (ST-PROSPER-DE-CHAMPLAIN)..43
FERME LA COLOMBE (ST-LÉON-DE-STANDON)..24

FERME L'ÉMEULIENNE, LA (NEUVILLE)..72, 237
FERME MARTINETTE, LA (COATICOOK) 19, 35, 52, 107
FERME PAYSAGÉE, LA (ST-JEAN-DE-DIEU) 66, 90
FERME PÉDAGOGIQUE MARICHEL (STE-AGATHE-DE-LOTBINIÈRE) 56
FERME VACANCES HÉLÈNE WILLE (ÎLE-NEPAWA) 74, 78
FINESSES DE CHARLEVOIX, LES (LES ÉBOULEMENTS) 39
FLEUR EN BOUCHÉE (ST-MAJORIQUE) 22
FROMAGERIE AU GRÉ DES CHAMPS (ST-JEAN-SUR-RICHELIEU) 45
FROMAGERIE LA PETITE HEIDI ENR. (STE-ROSE-DU-NORD)...49

G

GÎTE À CLAUDIA (ST-SIMON) 70, 205
FARM STAYS DU RANG (STE-VICTOIRE-DE-SOREL) 71, 206
GÎTE À L'ANCRAGE (BAIE-ST-PAUL) 116
GÎTE ANSE-AU-SABLE (COLOMBIER) 138
GÎTE AU BOIS DORMANT, LE (BATISCAN) 188
GÎTE AU BOIS DORMANT, LE (CHICOUTIMI)..257
GÎTE AU BORD DE LA RIVIÈRE, LE (SHANNON) 253
GÎTE AU CHEMIN DU FOULON (QUÉBEC, SILLERY) 250
GÎTE AU PETIT BONHEUR (KAMOURASKA)...83
GÎTE AU TOIT ROUGE (DÉGELIS)...82
GÎTE AU VIEUX BAHUT (LÉVIS) 128
GÎTE AUX CHAMPS DES ELFES (STE-AGATHE-NORD) 179
GÎTE AUX P'TITS OISEAUX (JOLIETTE) 163
GÎTE B&B POUR LES AMIS (ST-CASIMIR) 251
GÎTE BAIE-JOLIE (TROIS-RIVIÈRES, POINTE-DU-LAC) 195
GÎTE BEL HORIZON (L'ÎLE-D'ORLÉANS, ST-PIERRE) 234
GÎTE BELLE-RIVIÈRE (HÉBERTVILLE)..258
GÎTE BELLEVUE (MONT-JOLI)..151
GÎTE CHEZ DESPARD (PERCÉ) 155
GÎTE CHEZ FRANCE (ST-ALBAN) 251
GÎTE CHEZ MIMI, LE (STE-AGNÈS-DE-DUNDEE)...70, 205
GÎTE CHEZ NICO (TROIS-PISTOLES) 91
GÎTE CHUTE COUETTE ET CAFÉ (NOTRE-DAME-DU-PORTAGE) 85
GÎTE DE LA BAIE (ST-SIMÉON, BAIE-DES-ROCHERS) 125
GÎTE DE LA BASSE-COUR (LES ÉBOULEMENTS) 121
GÎTE DE LA BASSE-COUR (ST-FÉLIX-D'OTIS)..266
GÎTE DE LA BELLE ÉPOQUE (ST-JEAN-PORT-JOLI)...132
GÎTE DE LA GARE, LE (ST-FAUSTIN, LAC-CARRÉ) 173
GÎTE DE LA MAISON LEVESQUE (NEW RICHMOND) 152
GÎTE DE LA PÊCHE BLANCHE (LA BAIE) 261
GÎTE DE LA POINTE (POINTE-AU-PÈRE) 86
GÎTE DE LA PYRAMIDE (LA BAIE)...261
GÎTE DE LA RIVIÈRE AUX SABLES (JONQUIÈRE) 259
GÎTE DE LA SEIGNEURIE, LE (LOUISEVILLE) 190
GÎTE DE LA SOURCE DES AULNAIES (ST-AMBROISE-DE-CHICOUTIMI) 265
GÎTE DE LA VALLÉE, LE (CAUSAPSCAL) 146
GÎTE DE L'ÎLE (L'ÎLE-PERROT)..202
GÎTE DE L'OIE DES NEIGES (CAP-TOURMENTE, MONT-STE-ANNE) 229, 254
GÎTE DE NEUVILLE, LE (NEUVILLE) 238
GÎTE DELAGEOIS, LE (QUÉBEC, LAC DELAGE) 248
GÎTE DES AMÉRIQUES (STE-ADÈLE) 177
GÎTE DES FLEURS (ST-ALEXANDRE, KAMOURASKA)..88
GÎTE DES ÎLES (MATANE)...149
GÎTE DES JARDINS DE LA MONTAGNE (ST-JOSEPH-DU-LAC) 175
GÎTE DES ROSES, LE (DRUMMONDVILLE) 110
GÎTE DES SOMMETS (MATANE, ST-RENÉ) 69, 150
GÎTE DU CAP BLANC (PERCÉ) 155
GÎTE DU CAPITAINE (BAIE-STE-CATHERINE)..118
GÎTE DU LIÈVRE (STE-MARGUERITE-DU-LAC-MASSON) 180
GÎTE DU LYS, LE (BLAINVILLE) 168
GÎTE DU MANOIR KANE (SHAWINIGAN) 192
GÎTE DU MARIGOT (LAVAL, PONT-VIAU)...185
GÎTE DU MOULIN À VENT (PERCÉ, STE-THÉRÈSE)..156
GÎTE DU PARC (QUÉBEC) 244
GÎTE DU PHARE DE POINTE-DES-MONTS, LE (BAIE-TRINITÉ) 137
GÎTE DU QUAI (L'ÎLE-D'ORLÉANS, ST-JEAN)..232
GÎTE DU SOUS-BOIS (STE-CATHERINE-DE-LA-JACQUES-CARTIER) 253
GÎTE DU SUD, LE (SHAWINIGAN-SUD) 193
GÎTE DU TEMPS QUI PASSE (LA MACAZA) 169
GÎTE DU VACANCIER (LES ÉBOULEMENTS) 122
GÎTE DU VIEUX-BOURG, LE (QUÉBEC, BEAUPORT)...246
GÎTE E.T. HARVEY (LA MALBAIE)..119
GÎTE ET COUVERT LA MARIE-CHAMPAGNE (MONT-TREMBLANT, LAC-SUPÉRIEUR) 171

GÎTE FANNY ET MAXIME (HULL)..223
GÎTE HISTORIQUE L'ÉMERILLON (GASPÉ)..147
GÎTE HONEYS (GASPÉ)..147
GÎTE ÎLE BIZARD (L'ÎLE-BIZARD)...208
GÎTE LA BERCEUSE (CACOUNA)...81
GÎTE LA CANADIENNE (GASPÉ)...148
GÎTE LA CINQUIÈME SAISON (MONTRÉAL)..212
GÎTE LA MAISON BLANCHE (ISLE-AUX-COUDRES)..118
GÎTE LA MAISON ROSE (CAP-DES-ROSIERS, FORILLON)..146
GÎTE LA NICHÉE (STE-ANNE-DE-PORTNEUF)..139
GÎTE LA TOURELLE (WARWICK)..111
GÎTE LA TREMBLANTE (MONT-TREMBLANT)..170
GÎTE LA VILLA DU VIEUX CLOCHER (PADOUE)..153
GÎTE L'ANCESTRAL (GRAND-MÈRE)...188
GÎTE LAUZIER (AYER'S CLIFF)...93
GÎTE LE NOBLE QUÊTEUX (BAIE-ST-PAUL)..117
GÎTE L'ÉCUREUIL (PETITE-RIVIÈRE-ST-FRANÇOIS)..123
GÎTE LES BOULEAUX (NEW RICHMOND)...152
GÎTE LES COLIBRIS (BAIE-ST-PAUL)..117
GÎTE LES LEBLANC (CARLETON)..146
GÎTE LES PECCADILLES (EASTMAN)...96
GÎTE L'ESTRAN (STE-ANNE-DES-MONTS)..157
GÎTE MAISON JACQUES (PIERREFONDS)..216
GÎTE MASYPA (COWANSVILLE)..94
GÎTE NICOLAS LE JARDINIER (CAP-SANTÉ)..229
GÎTE SAINT-LAURENT (TROIS-RIVIÈRES)..194
GÎTE SAINT-MICHEL, LE (ST-MICHEL-DES-SAINTS)...165
GÎTE UN AIR D'ÉTÉ (CHÂTEAU-RICHER)..231
GÎTE VILLA DES ROSES (LES ÉBOULEMENTS)...122
GÎTE/AUBERGE LA GIROUETTE DES GLOOR (STE-ADÈLE)..177
GÎTES MAKADAN, LES (NORMANDIN)..73, 264
GRANDE OURSE, LA (L'ISLE-VERTE)..84
GRENOUILLÈRE DES TROIS VILLAGES, LA (STANSTEAD)..106
GUIMONTIÈRE, LA (STE-ANGÈLE-DE-MÉRICI)..156

H

HALTE DU VERGER, LA (NOTRE-DAME-DU-PORTAGE)..85
HAZELBRAE FARM (HOWICK)...70, 201
HÉBERGEMENT ROSALINE (ÉTANG-DU-NORD)..161
HÉMÉROCALLE, L' (QUÉBEC)..245
HÉRITAGE VICTORIEN (MONTRÉAL)...213
HYDRANGÉE BLEUE, L' (QUÉBEC, CAP-ROUGE)...248

I

INTERMIEL (MIRABEL, ST-BENOÎT)..58
IRIS BLEU, L' (BOLTON)...93

J

JARDIN DE GIVRE, LE (MATANE, ST-LÉANDRE)..149
JARDIN DES MÉSANGES, LE (ST-CYPRIEN)...68, 131
JARDINS DE LA GARE, LES (VAL-MORIN)...181
JARDINS DE RÊVES (MONTEBELLO)...224
JARDINS DE VINOY, LES (VINOY, CHÉNÉVILLE)..71, 226
JARDINS DES TOURTEREAUX DE LA FERME LA COLOMBE (ST-LÉON-DE-STANDON)............................56

L

LAC DE PÊCHE LA SEIGNEURIE DE L'ÎSLE AUX SORCIERS (L'ÎLE-D'ORLÉANS, ST-LAURENT).............62

M

MAGESTIK, LE (MANSONVILLE)...104
MAGIE DU SOUS-BOIS INC., LA (DOLBEAU-MISTASSINI)..49
MAISON ANCESTRALE THOMASSIN, LA (QUÉBEC, BEAUPORT)...245
MAISON ANCESTRALE, LA (L'ISLE-VERTE)...84
MAISON AORHENCHE, LA (QUÉBEC, WENDAKE)..250
MAISON AU TOIT BLEU, LA (ST-ALEXANDRE, KAMOURASKA)..89
MAISON AU TOIT ROUGE, LA (ROBERVAL)..264
MAISON BÉRUBÉ, LA (RIMOUSKI, BIC)...66, 86
MAISON BLANCHE, LA (LAC-MÉGANTIC)..99
MAISON BON REPOS (AYLMER, BRECKENRIDGE)...221

MAISON CAMPBELL, LA (MAGOG) 103
MAISON DE L'ANCÊTRE, LA (LOUISEVILLE) 190
MAISON DE L'ENCLOS, LA (ROSEMÈRE) 182
MAISON DE L'ERMITAGE, LA (ST-JEAN-PORT-JOLI) 133
MAISON DE MLLE BERNARD, LA (CAP-SANTÉ) 229
MAISON DE MON ENFANCE, LA (RIVIÈRE-DU-LOUP, ST-ANTONIN) 88
MAISON DES ANCÊTRES, LA (LA BAIE) 74, 268
MAISON DES GALLANT (STE-LUCE-SUR-MER) 91
MAISON DES LACS, LA (WOTTON) 107
MAISON DES LECLERC, LA (STE-MARTHE-DU-CAP) 192
MAISON DINA (QUÉBEC, STE-FOY) 249
MAISON DU JARDINIER, LA (LOUISEVILLE) 196
MAISON DU VIGNOBLE, LA (L'ÎLE-D'ORLÉANS, ST-PIERRE) 234
MAISON DUBUC, LA (NEUVILLE) 237
MAISON DUCHARME, LA (CHAMBLY) 200
MAISON DUCLAS, LA (GRANBY) 98
MAISON DUFOUR-BOUCHARD, LA (LA MALBAIE) 119
MAISON DUFRESNE, LA (QUÉBEC, BEAUPORT) 246
MAISON D'ULYSSE, LA (STE-ANNE-DE-BEAUPRÉ) 252
MAISON FLEURIE, LA (STE-ANNE-DE-PORTNEUF) 139
MAISON FORTIER (TADOUSSAC) 140
MAISON FRIZZI, LA (LA MALBAIE) 120
MAISON GAUTHIER ET LES SUITES DE L'ANSE (TADOUSSAC) 140
MAISON HARVEY-LESSARD, LA (TADOUSSAC) 140
MAISON HINGSTON 4335 (MONTRÉAL, NOTRE-DAME-DE-GRÂCE) 216
MAISON HOVINGTON (TADOUSSAC) 141
MAISON JAUNE, LA (MONTRÉAL) 213
MAISON LAFLEUR, LA (QUÉBEC) 245
MAISON LEBREUX, LA (PETITE-VALLÉE) 156, 159
MAISON LECLERC, LA (QUÉBEC, STE-FOY) 249
MAISON MARTIN, LA (ST-MARTIN) 133
MAISON MC CRACKEN (DANVILLE) 95
MAISON NORMAND, LA (ST-ANTOINE-DE-TILLY) 131
MAISON SOUS LES ARBRES, LA (SHAWINIGAN) 192
MAISON SOUS LES LILAS, LA (LA MALBAIE) 120
MAISON SOUS L'ORME, LA (LÉVIS) 129
MAISON SUR LA COLLINE, LA (GATINEAU) 222
MAISON SUR LA CÔTE, LA (L'ÎLE-D'ORLÉANS, ST-JEAN) 232
MAISON SUR LE LAC, LA (ST-DONAT) 164
MAISON TRUDEL (HÉROUXVILLE) 189
MALARDS, LES (CONTRECOEUR) 201
MANOIR BÉCANCOURT (BÉCANCOUR) 110
MANOIR DES CÈDRES (HULL) 224
MANOIR D'IVRY B&B (STE-AGATHE-NORD) 179
MANOIR D'ORSENNENS (LAC-MÉGANTIC) 100
MANOIR DU LAC SEPT-ÎLES (ST-RAYMOND) 252
MANOIR VALLÉE, LE (QUÉBEC, BEAUPORT) 246
MAPIROL (STE-CATHERINE-DE-HATLEY) 105
MARAÎCHÈRE DU SAGUENAY, LA (ST-FULGENCE) 266
MARCHAND DE SABLE, LE (TERREBONNE) 165
MAS DE L'ISLE, LE (L'ÎLE-D'ORLÉANS, ST-JEAN) 232
MATINS DE ROSIE, LES (FARNHAM) 96
MONIQUE ET ANDRÉ SAINT-AUBIN (QUÉBEC, STE-FOY) 249
MOULIN DU PETIT PRÉ (CHÂTEAU-RICHER) 48
MUSÉE DE L'ABEILLE - ÉCONOMUSÉE DU MIEL (CHÂTEAU-RICHER) 62

N

NIAPISCA (STE-MARIE) 134
NICHOUETTE, LE (LES ÉBOULEMENTS) 122
NID D'AMOUR (VAL-MORIN) 182
NOTRE CAMPAGNE D'ANTAN (ST-APOLLINAIRE) 131
NOTRE MAISON SUR LA RIVIÈRE (LAVAL, ST-FRANÇOIS) 185

O

O' P'TITS OIGNONS (ST-JULIEN) 133
OASIS (DRUMMONDVILLE, ST-CYRILLE) 111
OASIS DE RÊVES, L' (L'ÎLE-D'ORLÉANS, ST-LAURENT) 233
OIE DES NEIGES, L' (CAP-TOURMENTE, MONT-STE-ANNE) 254

P

PACANE ET POTIRON CAFÉ COUETTE (VERDUN) 216

PANORAMA, LE (MATANE, ST-LUC) 150
PETIT MANOIR DU SAULT MONTMORENCY, LE (QUÉBEC, BEAUPORT) 247
PETITE CHARTREUSE, LA (ST-ALPHONSE-RODRIGUEZ) 163
PETITE MONET, LA (JOLIETTE) 163
PIEDS DANS L'EAU, LES (L'ISLET-SUR-MER) 129
PIERRE ET DOMINIQUE (MONTRÉAL) 215
POMMIER D'ARGENT, LE (GATINEAU) 32
POUR UN INSTANT (LAVAL, FABREVILLE) 186
PRESBYTÈRE, LE (PERCÉ) 155
P'TITE BALEINE, LA (BERGERONNES) 138
P'TITS POMMIERS, LES (SHAWINIGAN-SUD) 193

Q
QUAI DU RÊVE, LE (L'ÎLE-BIZARD) 208

R
RABOUILLÈRE, LA (ST-VALÉRIEN) 31, 60, 70, 205
REFUGE DU POÈTE, LE (LONGUEUIL) 203
REFUGE DU VOYAGEUR, LE (BOISCHATEL) 228
RÉGALIN, LE (ST-EUSTACHE) 27
REGARD SUR LE FLEUVE (BÉCANCOUR, ST-GRÉGOIRE) 110
RIVIÈRE AU BOIS DORMANT, LA (AYLMER) 221
ROCHERS, LES (RIVIÈRE-DU-LOUP, ST-PATRICE) 88
RONDINS, LES (MIRABEL, ST-SCHOLASTIQUE) 26
ROYAL CHAMPÊTRE, LE (BOISCHATEL) 228
RUÉE VERS GOULD, LA (GOULD) 97
RUSTIQUE, LE (ST-IRÉNÉE) 124

S
SAISONS DE MARIE, LES (JONQUIÈRE) 259
SAVEURS OUBLIÉES, LES (LES ÉBOULEMENTS) 23
SECOND SOUFFLE, LE (MONT-TREMBLANT) 170
SÉJOUR NADEAU (COATICOOK) 74, 107
SHÉZELLES (MONTRÉAL) 215
SOLEIL LEVANT (TROIS-RIVIÈRES, POINTE-DU-LAC) 195
SONNEZ LES MATINES (BOUCHERVILLE) 199
STUDIO MARHABA (ST-LAURENT) 218
SUCRERIES DES AÏEUX, LES (RAWDON) 41

T
TABLE DE LA SEIGNEURIE, LA (LOUISEVILLE) 29
TU-DOR, LE (LAC-BROME, FULFORD) 99

U
UN TEMPS D'ARRÊT (ROUGEMONT) 203
UNE FLEUR AU BORD DE L'EAU (GRANBY) 99

V
VALLÉE DES CERVIDÉS, LA (LA MALBAIE) 39, 54
VERGER CIDRERIE LARIVIÈRE (ST-THÉODORE-D'ACTON) 46
VICTORIENNE, LA (MONTRÉAL) 214
VICTORINES DU LAC, LES (LAC-MÉGANTIC) 100
VIGNOBLE ARTISANS DU TERROIR (ST-PAUL-D'ABBOTSFORD) 46
VIGNOBLE DE LA RIVIÈRE DU CHÊNE (ST-EUSTACHE) 42
VIGNOBLE DIETRICH-JOOSS (IBERVILLE) 44
VIGNOBLE LE CEP D'ARGENT, LE (MAGOG) 37
VIGNOBLE LES CHANTS DE VIGNES, LE (MAGOG) 37
VILLA DES CHÊNES, LA (PIKE-RIVER) 104
VILLA DU MOULIN (ISLE-AUX-COUDRES) 118
VIREVENT, LE (ST-MARC-SUR-RICHELIEU) 204
VOISINE, LA (ST-RAYMOND) 252

Z
ZÈBRE, LE (MONTRÉAL) 215
ZIBOU, LE (OKA) 172

LOCATION INDEX

A

AYER'S CLIFF 93
AYLMER...221
AYLMER, BRECKENRIDGE 221

B

BAIE-COMEAU, POINTE-LEBEL 137
BAIE-SAINTE-CATHERINE 117, 118
BAIE-SAINT-PAUL.......................... 114, 115, 116, 117
BAIE-TRINITÉ...137
BATISCAN...188
BÉCANCOUR...110
BÉCANCOUR, SAINT-GRÉGOIRE....................................110
BERGERONNES 137, 138
BIC, LE 80
BIC, SAINT-FABIEN 80
BLAINVILLE..168
BOISCHATEL...228
BOLTON...93
BOUCHERVILLE...199

C

CABANO 81
CACOUNA..81
CAP-CHAT 145
CAP-CHAT, CAPUCINS..145
CAP-DES-ROSIERS, FORILLON 145, 146
CAP-SANTÉ...229
CAP-TOURMENTE, MONT-SAINTE-ANNE 229, 254
CARLETON 146
CAUSAPSCAL..146
CHAMBLY... 199, 200
CHAMBLY, RICHELIEU..200
CHÂTEAU-RICHER.......................... 48, 62, 230, 231, 254
CHICOUTIMI...257
COATICOOK 19, 35, 52, 74, 107
COLOMBIER...138
CONTRECOEUR..201
COURCELLES..67, 94
COWANSVILLE 94

D

DANVILLE...95
DÉGELIS 82
DESCHAMBAULT 231
DOLBEAU-MISTASSINI..49
DRUMMONDVILLE...110
DRUMMONDVILLE, SAINT-CYRILLE................................111
DUNHAM 19, 35, 36, 95

E

EASTMAN...96
ESCUMINAC, MIGUASHA..147
ÉTANG-DU-NORD 161

F

FARNHAM...96
FERME-NEUVE...168
FRELIGHSBURG 20, 36, 52, 53, 96

G

GASPÉ...147, 148
GATINEAU...32, 71, 222
GOULD..97
GRANBY...97, 98, 99
GRANDES-PILES...188
GRAND-MÈRE..188

H

HÉBERTVILLE...72, 258
HÉROUXVILLE..69, 189
HOPE TOWN, PASPÉBIAC..148
HOWICK..70, 201
HULL..222, 223, 224
HUNTINGDON..30, 201, 202

I

IBERVILLE..44
ÎLE-NEPAWA..78
ISLE-AUX-COUDRES..118

J

JOLIETTE..163
JONQUIÈRE..259

K

KAMOURASKA..82, 83

L

LA BAIE...73, 260, 261, 268
LA MACAZA..169
LA MALBAIE...39, 54, 119, 120
LA POCATIÈRE...83
LAC-UX-SABLES...189
LAC-BROME, FULFORD..99
LACHUTE, ARGENTEUIL..24
LAC-MÉGANTIC...99, 100
LAC-NOMININGUE..168, 169
LAC-SIMON, CHÉNÉVILLE..224
L'ANNONCIATION..25, 69, 169
L'ANSE-SAINT-JEAN...261, 262
L'ASSOMPTION..57
LAVAL, FABREVILLE...186
LAVAL, PONT-VIAU...185
LAVAL, SAINT-FRANÇOIS..185
LES ÉBOULEMENTS...23, 39, 121, 122
LES ESCOUMINS..138
LÉVIS...128, 129
L'ÎLE-BIZARD...208
L'ÎLE-D'ORLÉANS, SAINTE-FAMILLE...235
L'ÎLE-D'ORLÉANS, SAINTE-PÉTRONILLE..235, 236
L'ÎLE-D'ORLÉANS, SAINT-JEAN...231, 232
L'ÎLE-D'ORLÉANS, SAINT-LAURENT..62, 233
L'ÎLE-D'ORLÉANS, SAINT-PIERRE...48, 233, 234, 235
L'ÎLE-PERROT..202
L'ISLET-SUR-MER...129
L'ISLE-VERTE..84, 85
LONGUEUIL...202, 203
LOUISEVILLE...29, 190, 196

M

MAGOG..20, 21, 37, 67, 100, 101, 102, 103
MANSONVILLE..104

MARIEVILLE 30
MASHTEUIATSH..263
MATANE 149
MATANE, SAINT-LÉANDRE..149
MATANE, SAINT-LUC...150
MATANE, SAINT-RENÉ..69, 150
MATANE, SAINT-ULRIC...150
MÉTABETCHOUAN-LAC-À-LA-CROIX 73, 263
MÉTIS-SUR-MER, LES BOULES...151
MIRABEL, SAINT-BENOÎT 26, 42, 58
MIRABEL, SAINT-SCHOLASTIQUE 26
MONTEBELLO 224
MONT-JOLI 151
MONTMAGNY 130
MONTRÉAL 208, 209, 210, 211, 212, 213, 214, 215, 217, 218
MONTRÉAL, NOTRE-DAME-DE-GRÂCE 216
MONT-SAINTE-ANNE, SAINT-FERRÉOL 236, 254
MONT-SAINT-GRÉGOIRE..44
MONT-TREMBLANT 170
MONT-TREMBLANT, LA CONCEPTION 171
MONT-TREMBLANT, LAC-SUPÉRIEUR 171
MORIN-HEIGHTS 171

N
NEUVILLE 72, 237, 238
NEW RICHMOND 152, 153
NEWPORT...152
NORMANDIN...73, 264
NORTH HATLEY 104
NOTRE-DAME-DU-PORTAGE...85
NOUVELLE..153

O
OKA 172

P
PADOUE 153
PAPINEAUVILLE, MONTEBELLO 225
PERCÉ...154, 155
PERCÉ, SAINTE-THÉRÈSE..156
PETITE-RIVIÈRE-SAINT-FRANÇOIS..123
PETITE-VALLÉE 156, 159
PETIT-SAGUENAY 264
PIERREFONDS...61, 216
PIKE-RIVER 104
PIKE-RIVER, SAINT-PIERRE-DE-VÉRONNE...105
POINTE-AU-PÈRE 86
PONTIAC, LUSKVILLE 225
PORTNEUF 238

Q
QUÉBEC....................................... 238, 239, 240, 241, 242, 243, 244, 245
QUÉBEC, BEAUPORT 245, 246, 247
QUÉBEC, CAP-ROUGE...247, 248
QUÉBEC, LAC DELAGE...248
QUÉBEC, SAINTE-FOY 248, 249
QUÉBEC, SILLERY...250
QUÉBEC, WENDAKE..250

R
RAWDON 41, 57
RIMOUSKI, BIC..66, 86
RIMOUSKI, SAINT-NARCISSE 87
RIVIÈRE-DU-LOUP 87

RIVIÈRE-DU-LOUP, SAINT-ANTONIN 88
RIVIÈRE-DU-LOUP, SAINT-PATRICE 88
ROBERVAL 264
ROSEMÈRE 182
ROUGEMONT 203

S

SACRÉ-COEUR 69, 139, 142
SAINT-ADOLPHE-D'HOWARD 172
SAINT-ALBAN 251
SAINT-ALEXANDRE, KAMOURASKA 88, 89
SAINT-ALPHONSE-RODRIGUEZ 163
SAINT-AMBROISE-DE-CHICOUTIMI 265
SAINT-AMBROISE-DE-KILDARE 164
SAINT-ANDRÉ, KAMOURASKA 89
SAINT-ANDRÉ-AVELLIN 225
SAINT-ANDRÉ-D'ARGENTEUIL 26
SAINT-ANSELME 130
SAINT-ANTOINE-DE-TILLY 131
SAINT-APOLLINAIRE 131
SAINT-CASIMIR 251
SAINT-CYPRIEN 68, 131
SAINT-DAMIEN-DE-BUCKLAND 68, 132
SAINT-DONAT 164
SAINTE-ADÈLE 176, 177
SAINTE-AGATHE-DE-LOTBINIÈRE 56
SAINTE-AGATHE-DES-MONTS 177, 178, 179
SAINTE-AGATHE-NORD 179
SAINTE-AGNÈS-DE-DUNDEE 70, 205
SAINTE-ANGÈLE-DE-MÉRICI 156
SAINTE-ANNE-DE-BEAUPRÉ 252
SAINTE-ANNE-DE-LA-PÉRADE 191
SAINTE-ANNE-DE-PORTNEUF 139
SAINTE-ANNE-DES-MONTS 157
SAINTE-ANNE-DES-MONTS, TOURELLE 157
SAINTE-ANNE-DES-PLAINES 28
SAINTE-CATHERINE-DE-HATLEY 105
SAINTE-CATHERINE-DE-LA-JACQUES-CARTIER 253
SAINTE-ÉMÉLIE-DE-L'ÉNERGIE 165
SAINTE-FLAVIE 158
SAINTE-HÉLÈNE 47
SAINT-ÉLOI 89
SAINTE-LUCE-SUR-MER 90, 91
SAINTE-LUCIE-DES-LAURENTIDES 180
SAINTE-MARGUERITE-DU-LAC-MASSON 180
SAINTE-MARIE 134
SAINTE-MARTHE-DU-CAP 192
SAINTE-ROSE-DU-NORD 49
SAINT-EUSTACHE 27, 42
SAINTE-VICTOIRE-DE-SOREL 11, 206
SAINT-FAUSTIN, LAC CARRÉ 58
SAINT-FAUSTIN, LAC-CARRÉ 173
SAINT-FÉLICIEN 265, 266
SAINT-FÉLIX-D'OTIS 266
SAINT-FULGENCE 266
SAINT-GABRIEL-DE-VALCARTIER 251
SAINT-HENRI-DE-TAILLON 267
SAINT-HILARION 54
SAINT-HIPPOLYTE 174
SAINT-HONORÉ 63
SAINT-IRÉNÉE 123, 124
SAINT-ISIDORE-DE-LAPRAIRIE 45, 59
SAINT-JEAN-DE-DIEU 66, 90
SAINT-JEAN-PORT-JOLI 132, 133
SAINT-JEAN-SUR-RICHELIEU 45, 204
SAINT-JÉRÔME 174
SAINT-JOACHIM-DE-SHEFFORD 105
SAINT-JOSEPH-DU-LAC 175

SAINT-JULIEN 133
SAINT-LAURENT 218
SAINT-LÉON-DE-STANDON 24, 56
SAINT-LOUIS-DU-HA! HA! 90
SAINT-MAJORIQUE 22
SAINT-MARC-SUR-RICHELIEU 204
SAINT-MARTIN 133
SAINT-MATHIEU-DU-PARC 190
SAINT-MICHEL-DES-SAINTS 165
SAINT-PAUL-D'ABBOTSFORD 46
SAINT-PIE 59
SAINT-PROSPER-DE-CHAMPLAIN 43
SAINT-RAYMOND 252
SAINT-RÉMI-DE-NAPIERVILLE 31
SAINT-ROCK-DE-MEKINAC 191
SAINT-SAUVEUR-DES-MONTS 175, 176
SAINT-SIMÉON, BAIE-DES-ROCHERS 125
SAINT-SIMON 70, 205
SAINT-SIXTE 32
SAINT-THÉODORE-D'ACTON 46
SAINT-TITE 191
SAINT-URBAIN 55, 125
SAINT-VALÉRIEN 31, 60, 68, 70, 205
SCOTT JONCTION 40
SHANNON 253
SHAWINIGAN 192
SHAWINIGAN-SUD 193
STANSTEAD 38, 106
STONEHAM, SAINT-ADOLPHE 72, 253
SUTTON 106

T

TADOUSSAC 140, 141
TERREBONNE 165
THETFORD-MINES 134
TROIS-PISTOLES 18, 91
TROIS-RIVIÈRES 193, 194, 196
TROIS-RIVIÈRES, POINTE-DU-LAC 194, 195

V

VAL D'OR 77
VAL-DAVID 181
VAL-DES-MONTS 226
VAL-MORIN 181, 182
VERDUN 216
VINOY, CHÉNÉVILLE 71, 226

W

WARWICK 111
WICKHAM 67, 111
WOTTON 107

INDEX BY TOURIST REGION

ABITIBI-TÉMISCAMINGUE

☐ **INNS**
    VAL D'OR
        AUBERGE DE L'ORPAILLEUR...77

☐ **COUNTRY HOME ON A FARM**
    ÎLE-NEPAWA
        FERME VACANCES HÉLÈNE WILLE...74-78

BAS-SAINT-LAURENT

☐ **INNS**
    BIC, LE
        AUBERGE CHEZ MARIE-ROSES..80
    CABANO
        AUBERGE DU CHEMIN FAISANT..81
    KAMOURASKA
        AUBERGE DES ÎLES...82
    POINTE-AU-PÈRE
        AUBERGE LA MARÉE DOUCE..86
    ST-ANDRÉ, KAMOURASKA
        AUBERGE LA SOLAILLERIE...89
    ST-ÉLOI
        AU VIEUX PRESBYTÈRE...89
    STE-LUCE-SUR-MER
        AUBERGE DE L'EIDER..90

☐ **FARM STAYS**
    RIMOUSKI, BIC
        LA MAISON BÉRUBÉ...66-86
    ST-JEAN-DE-DIEU
        LA FERME PAYSAGÉE..66-90

☐ **BED & BREAKFASTS**
    BIC, LE
        AUX 5 LUCARNES...80
    BIC, ST-FABIEN
        CLAIREVALLÉE...80
    CABANO
        AUBERGE ST-MATHIAS..81
    CACOUNA
        GÎTE LA BERCEUSE...81
    DÉGELIS
        GÎTE AU TOIT ROUGE...82
        LA BELLE MAISON BLANCHE..82
    KAMOURASKA
        GÎTE AU PETIT BONHEUR...83
    LA POCATIÈRE
        AUBERGE AU DIABLO-VERT..83
        LA CHEVRIÈRE...83
    L'ISLE-VERTE
        AU PAYS DES RÊVES..84
        LA GRANDE OURSE...84
        LA MAISON ANCESTRALE..84
        LES CAPUCINES...85
    NOTRE-DAME-DU-PORTAGE
        GÎTE CHUTE COUETTE ET CAFÉ..85
        LA HALTE DU VERGER..85
    POINTE-AU-PÈRE
        GÎTE DE LA POINTE..86
    RIMOUSKI, ST-NARCISSE
        DOMAINE DU BON VIEUX TEMPS...87
    RIVIÈRE-DU-LOUP
        AU TERROIR DES BASQUES..87
        AUBERGE LA SABLINE..87
    RIVIÈRE-DU-LOUP, ST-ANTONIN
        LA MAISON DE MON ENFANCE..88
    RIVIÈRE-DU-LOUP, ST-PATRICE
        LES ROCHERS..88

ST-ALEXANDRE, KAMOURASKA
GÎTE DES FLEURS 88
LA MAISON AU TOIT BLEU 89
STE-LUCE-SUR-MER
MAISON DES GALLANT 91
ST-LOUIS-DU-HA! HA!
AU BEAU-SÉJOUR 90
TROIS-PISTOLES
GÎTE CHEZ NICO 91

☐ COUNTRY-STYLE DINING
TROIS-PISTOLES
LA BERGÈRE, GÎTE ET COUVERT 18

EASTERN TOWNSHIPS

☐ INNS
LAC-MÉGANTIC
LES VICTORINES DU LAC 100
MANOIR D'ORSENNENS 100
MAGOG
AUX JARDINS CHAMPÊTRES 103
PIKE-RIVER, ST-PIERRE-DE-VÉRONNE
AUBERGE LA SUISSE 105

☐ FARM EXPLORATIONS
COATICOOK
LA FERME MARTINETTE 52
FRELIGHSBURG
À LA GIRONDINE 52
LA FERME DU WAPITI 53

☐ FARM STAYS
COURCELLES
L'AUBERGE D'ANDROMÈDE 67-94
MAGOG
À LA COLLINE AUX CHEVAUX 67-101

☐ BED & BREAKFASTS
AYER'S CLIFF
GÎTE LAUZIER 93
LA CHAUMIÈRE EN PAIN D'ÉPICES 93
BOLTON
L'IRIS BLEU 93
COWANSVILLE
DOMAINE SUR LA COLLINE B&B 94
GÎTE MASYPA 94
DANVILLE
MAISON MC CRACKEN 95
DUNHAM
AU TEMPS DES MÛRES 95
AUX DOUCES HEURES 95
EASTMAN
GÎTE LES PECCADILLES 96
FARNHAM
LES MATINS DE ROSIE 96
FRELIGHSBURG
À LA GIRONDINE 96
GOULD
LA RUÉE VERS GOULD 97
GRANBY
AUBERGE DU ZOO 97
AUX ABORDS 97
B&B LE CAMPAGNARD 98
CHEZ MARIE B&B 98
LA MAISON DUCLAS 98
UNE FLEUR AU BORD DE L'EAU 99
LAC-BROME, FULFORD
LE TU-DOR 99
LAC-MÉGANTIC
LA MAISON BLANCHE 99
MAGOG
À AMOUR ET AMITIÉ 100
À LA MAISON DREW 101
À L'ANCESTRALE B&B 101

À TOUT VENANT...102
AU MANOIR DE LA RUE MERRY 102
AU VIRAGE..102
LA BELLE ÉCHAPPÉE...103
LA MAISON CAMPBELL 103
MANSONVILLE
LE MAGESTIK...104
NORTH HATLEY
LE CACHET..104
PIKE-RIVER
LA VILLA DES CHÊNES..104
STANSTEAD
LA GRENOUILLÈRE DES TROIS VILLAGES...106
STE-CATHERINE-DE-HATLEY
MAPIROL...105
ST-JOACHIM-DE-SHEFFORD
LA BELLE AU BOIS DORMANT...105
SUTTON
AUBERGE ALTITUDE 2000..106

□ **COUNTRY HOMES**
COATICOOK
LA FERME MARTINETTE...107
WOTTON
LA MAISON DES LACS...107

□ **COUNTRY HOMES ON A FARM**
COATICOOK
SÉJOUR NADEAU 74-107

□ **FARM SHOPS**
COATICOOK
LA FERME MARTINETTE..35
DUNHAM
DOMAINE DE LA CHEVROTTIÈRE 35
LA CIDRERIE FLEURS DE POMMIERS 36
FRELIGHSBURG
À LA GIRONDINE..36
MAGOG
LE VIGNOBLE LE CEP D'ARGENT...37
LE VIGNOBLE LES CHANTS DE VIGNES 37
STANSTEAD
DOMAINE FÉLIBRE..38

□ **COUNTRY-STYLE DINING**
COATICOOK
LA FERME MARTINETTE..19
DUNHAM
LA CHÈVRERIE DES ACACIAS...19
FRELIGHSBURG
À LA GIRONDINE..20
MAGOG
AU GRÉ DU VENT..20
AUX JARDINS CHAMPÊTRES 21

CENTRE-DU-QUÉBEC

□ **INNS**
BÉCANCOUR
MANOIR BÉCANCOURT...110

□ **FARM STAYS**
WICKHAM
LA FERME DE LA BERCEUSE 67-111

□ **BED & BREAKFASTS**
BÉCANCOUR, ST-GRÉGOIRE
REGARD SUR LE FLEUVE...110
DRUMMONDVILLE
LE GÎTE DES ROSES...110
DRUMMONDVILLE, ST-CYRILLE
OASIS 111
WARWICK
GÎTE LA TOURELLE..111

☐ **COUNTRY-STYLE DINING**
   ST-MAJORIQUE
      FLEUR EN BOUCHÉE 22

CHARLEVOIX

☐ **INNS**
   BAIE-ST-PAUL
      AUBERGE CAP-AUX-CORBEAUX 114
      AUBERGE LA GRANDE MAISON 114
      AUBERGE LA MUSE 115
      AUX PETITS OISEAUX 116
   LA MALBAIE
      AUBERGE LES SOURCES INC 119
      L'EAU BERGE 120
   LES ÉBOULEMENTS
      AUBERGE LA BOUCLÉE 121
      AUBERGE LA PENTE DOUCE 121
   PETITE-RIVIÈRE-ST-FRANÇOIS
      AUBERGE LA CÔTE D'OR 123
   ST-IRÉNÉE
      AUBERGE DES SABLONS 123
      LE RUSTIQUE 124

☐ **FARM EXPLORATIONS**
   LA MALBAIE
      LA VALLÉE DES CERVIDÉS 54
   ST-HILARION
      ÉLEVAGE DE LA BUTTE AUX CAILLES 54
   ST-URBAIN
      CHEZ GERTRUDE CENTRE DE L'ÉMEU DE CHARLEVOIX 55

☐ **FARM STAYS**
   ST-URBAIN
      CHEZ GERTRUDE CENTRE DE L'ÉMEU DE CHARLEVOIX 68-125

☐ **BED & BREAKFASTS**
   BAIE-STE-CATHERINE
      ENTRE MER ET MONTS 117
      GÎTE DU CAPITAINE 118
   BAIE-ST-PAUL
      À LA CHOUETTE 114
      AU BONHOMME SEPT HEURES 115
      AU CLOCHETON 115
      AU PERCHOIR 116
      GÎTE À L'ANCRAGE 116
      GÎTE LE NOBLE QUÊTEUX 117
      GÎTE LES COLIBRIS 117
   ISLE-AUX-COUDRES
      GÎTE LA MAISON BLANCHE 118
      VILLA DU MOULIN 118
   LA MALBAIE
      GÎTE E.T. HARVEY 119
      LA MAISON DUFOUR-BOUCHARD 119
      LA MAISON FRIZZI 120
      LA MAISON SOUS LES LILAS 120
   LES ÉBOULEMENTS
      GÎTE DE LA BASSE-COUR 121
      GÎTE DU VACANCIER 122
      GÎTE VILLA DES ROSES 122
      LE NICHOUETTE 122
   PETITE-RIVIÈRE-ST-FRANÇOIS
      GÎTE L'ÉCUREUIL 123
   ST-IRÉNÉE
      L'EIDER MATINAL 124
      LES CHANTERELLES 124
   ST-SIMÉON, BAIE-DES-ROCHERS
      GÎTE DE LA BAIE 125

☐ **FARM SHOPS**
   LA MALBAIE
      LA VALLÉE DES CERVIDÉS 39
   LES ÉBOULEMENTS
      LES FINESSES DE CHARLEVOIX 39

☐ **COUNTRY-STYLE DINING**
    LES ÉBOULEMENTS
        LES SAVEURS OUBLIÉES 23

CHAUDIÈRE-APPALACHES

☐ **INNS**
    L'ISLET-SUR-MER
        AUBERGE LA MARGUERITE 129
    MONTMAGNY
        AUBERGE LA BELLE ÉPOQUE 130
    THETFORD-MINES
        AUBERGE LA BONNE MINE 134

☐ **FARM EXPLORATIONS**
    STE-AGATHE-DE-LOTBINIÈRE
        FERME PÉDAGOGIQUE MARICHEL 56
    ST-LÉON-DE-STANDON
        JARDINS DES TOURTEREAUX DE LA FERME LA COLOMBE 56

☐ **FARM STAYS**
    ST-CYPRIEN
        LE JARDIN DES MÉSANGES 68-131
    ST-DAMIEN-DE-BUCKLAND
        CASSIS ET MÉLISSE 68-132

☐ **BED & BREAKFASTS**
    LÉVIS
        AU GRÉ DU VENT 128
        AUBERGE DE LA VISITATION 128
        GÎTE AU VIEUX BAHUT 128
        LA MAISON SOUS L'ORME 129
    L'ISLET-SUR-MER
        LES PIEDS DANS L'EAU 129
    MONTMAGNY
        AUX DEUX MARQUISES 130
    ST-ANSELME
        DOUCES ÉVASIONS 130
    ST-ANTOINE-DE-TILLY
        LA MAISON NORMAND 131
    ST-APOLLINAIRE
        NOTRE CAMPAGNE D'ANTAN 131
    STE-MARIE
        NIAPISCA 134
    ST-JEAN-PORT-JOLI
        AU BOISÉ JOLI 132
        GÎTE DE LA BELLE ÉPOQUE 132
        LA MAISON DE L'ERMITAGE 133
    ST-JULIEN
        O' P'TITS OIGNONS 133
    ST-MARTIN
        LA MAISON MARTIN 133

☐ **FARM SHOPS**
    SCOTT JONCTION
        LA CACHE À MAXIME 40

☐ **COUNTRY-STYLE DINING**
    ST-LÉON-DE-STANDON
        FERME LA COLOMBE 24

CÔTE-NORD

☐ **INNS**
    BAIE-TRINITÉ
        LE GÎTE DU PHARE DE POINTE-DES-MONTS 137
    BERGERONNES
        LA BERGERONNETTE 137
    LES ESCOUMINS
        AUBERGE DE LA BAIE 138
    TADOUSSAC
        MAISON GAUTHIER ET LES SUITES DE L'ANSE 140

☐ **FARM STAYS**
    SACRÉ-COEUR
        FERME 5 ÉTOILES 69-139

☐ **BED & BREAKFASTS**
    BAIE-COMEAU, POINTE-LEBEL
        AU PETIT BONHEUR 137
    BERGERONNES
        LA P'TITE BALEINE 138
    COLOMBIER
        GÎTE ANSE-AU-SABLE...138
    STE-ANNE-DE-PORTNEUF
        GÎTE LA NICHÉE 139
        LA MAISON FLEURIE...139
    TADOUSSAC
        LA MAISON HARVEY-LESSARD...140
        MAISON FORTIER 140
        MAISON HOVINGTON 141

☐ **COUNTRY HOMES**
    SACRÉ-COEUR
        FERME 5 ÉTOILES 142

GASPÉSIE

☐ **INNS**
    CAP-CHAT, CAPUCINS
        AUBERGE DE LA BAIE-DES-CAPUCINS..145
    ESCUMINAC, MIGUASHA
        AUBERGE WANTA-QO-TI 147
    GASPÉ
        L'ANCÊTRE DE GASPÉ 148
    MATANE
        AUBERGE LA SEIGNEURIE 149
    MÉTIS-SUR-MER, LES BOULES
        AUBERGE DU GRAND FLEUVE 151
        L'AUBERGE UNE FERME EN GASPÉSIE 151
    PERCÉ
        AUBERGE AU PIRATE 1775...154
    PETITE-VALLÉE
        LA MAISON LEBREUX 156

☐ **FARM STAYS**
    MATANE, ST-RENÉ
        GÎTE DES SOMMETS...69-150

☐ **BED & BREAKFASTS**
    CAP-CHAT
        AUBERGE AU CRÉPUSCULE...145
    CAP-DES-ROSIERS, FORILLON
        AUX PÉTALES DE ROSE...145
        GÎTE LA MAISON ROSE..146
    CARLETON
        GÎTE LES LEBLANC 146
    CAUSAPSCAL
        LE GÎTE DE LA VALLÉE 146
    GASPÉ
        GÎTE HISTORIQUE L'ÉMERILLON..147
        GÎTE HONEYS 147
        GÎTE LA CANADIENNE 148
    HOPE TOWN, PASPÉBIAC
        LA CLÉ DES CHAMPS...148
    MATANE
        GÎTE DES ÎLES 149
    MATANE, ST-LÉANDRE
        LE JARDIN DE GIVRE...149
    MATANE, ST-LUC
        LE PANORAMA 150
    MATANE, ST-ULRIC
        CHEZ NICOLE 150
    MONT-JOLI
        GÎTE BELLEVUE..151
    NEW RICHMOND
        GÎTE DE LA MAISON LEVESQUE 152

GÎTE LES BOULEAUX 152
L'ÉTOILE DE MER 153
NEWPORT
AUBERGE LES DEUX ÎLOTS 152
NOUVELLE
À L'ABRI DU CLOCHER 153
PADOUE
GÎTE LA VILLA DU VIEUX CLOCHER 153
PERCÉ
À LA RÊVASSE 154
À L'ABRI DU VENT 154
GÎTE CHEZ DESPARD 155
GÎTE DU CAP BLANC 155
LE PRESBYTÈRE 155
PERCÉ, STE-THÉRÈSE
GÎTE DU MOULIN À VENT 156
STE-ANGÈLE-DE-MÉRICI
LA GUIMONTIÈRE 156
STE-ANNE-DES-MONTS
CHEZ MARTHE-ANGÈLE 157
GÎTE L'ESTRAN 157
STE-ANNE-DES-MONTS, TOURELLE
AU COURANT DE LA MER 157
STE-FLAVIE
AUX CHUTES 158

☐ **COUNTRY HOMES**
PETITE-VALLÉE
LA MAISON LEBREUX 159

ÎLE-DE-LA-MADELEINE

☐ **BED & BREAKFASTS**
ÉTANG-DU-NORD
HÉBERGEMENT ROSALINE 161

LANAUDIÈRE

☐ **INNS**
STE-ÉMÉLIE-DE-L'ÉNERGIE
AUBERGE DU VIEUX MOULIN 165

☐ **FARM EXPLORATIONS**
L'ASSOMPTION
ÉRABLIÈRE DES PATRIOTES 57
RAWDON
ARCHE DE NOÉ 57

☐ **BED & BREAKFASTS**
JOLIETTE
GÎTE AUX P'TITS OISEAUX 163
LA PETITE MONET 163
ST-ALPHONSE-RODRIGUEZ
LA PETITE CHARTREUSE 163
ST-AMBROISE-DE-KILDARE
BERGERIE DES NEIGES 164
ST-DONAT
AU PETIT CHÂTEAU DU LAC 164
LA MAISON SUR LE LAC 164
ST-MICHEL-DES-SAINTS
LE GÎTE SAINT-MICHEL 165
TERREBONNE
LE MARCHAND DE SABLE 165

☐ **FARM SHOPS**
RAWDON
FERME GUY RIVEST 41
LES SUCRERIES DES AÏEUX 41

LAURENTIDES

☐ **INNS**
FERME-NEUVE
AUBERGE AU BOIS D'MON COEUR 168

LAC-NOMININGUE
    AUBERGE CHEZ IGNACE 168
    AUBERGE VILLA BELLERIVE 169
MONT-TREMBLANT, LA CONCEPTION
    L'AUBERGE À LA CROISÉE DES CHEMINS 171
STE-ADÈLE
    AUBERGE LE CLOS ROLLAND 176
STE-AGATHE-DES-MONTS
    AUBERGE AUX NUITS DE RÊVE 178
    AUBERGE DE LA TOUR DU LAC 178
    AUBERGE LE SAINT-VENANT 178
STE-AGATHE-NORD
    MANOIR D'IVRY B&B 179
STE-MARGUERITE-DU-LAC-MASSON
    AUBERGE AU PHIL DE L'EAU 180
ST-FAUSTIN, LAC-CARRÉ
    LA BONNE ADRESSE 173
ST-HIPPOLYTE
    AUBERGE LAC DU PIN ROUGE 174
ST-JOSEPH-DU-LAC
    AUBERGE ROCHE DES BRISES 175
ST-SAUVEUR-DES-MONTS
    AUBERGE SOUS L'ÉDREDON 175
VAL-DAVID
    AUBERGE CHARME DES ALPES 181
    AUBERGE EDELWEISS 181
VAL-MORIN
    LES JARDINS DE LA GARE 181

☐ **FARM EXPLORATIONS**
    MIRABEL, ST-BENOÎT
        INTERMIEL 58
    ST-FAUSTIN, LAC CARRÉ
        FERME DE LA BUTTE MAGIQUE 58

☐ **FARM STAYS**
    L'ANNONCIATION
        LA CLAIRIÈRE DE LA CÔTE 69-169

☐ **BED & BREAKFASTS**
    BLAINVILLE
        LE GÎTE DU LYS 168
    LA MACAZA
        GÎTE DU TEMPS QUI PASSE 169
    MONT-TREMBLANT
        GÎTE LA TREMBLANTE 170
        LA BELLE AU BOIS DORMANT 170
        LE SECOND SOUFFLE 170
    MONT-TREMBLANT, LAC-SUPÉRIEUR
        GÎTE ET COUVERT LA MARIE-CHAMPAGNE 171
    MORIN-HEIGHTS
        AUX BERGES DE LA RIVIÈRE SIMON 171
    OKA
        LE ZIBOU 172
    ST-ADOLPHE-D'HOWARD
        AUBE DOUCE 172
        CHEZ BÉCASSINE 172
    STE-ADÈLE
        AUBERGE DE LA GARE 176
        GÎTE DES AMÉRIQUES 177
        GÎTE/AUBERGE LA GIROUETTE DES GLOOR 177
    STE-AGATHE-DES-MONTS
        ANCESTRAL B&B 177
        AU NID D'HIRONDELLES 179
    STE-AGATHE-NORD
        GÎTE AUX CHAMPS DES ELFES 179
    STE-LUCIE-DES-LAURENTIDES
        CHEZ GRAND-MÈRE ZOIZEAUX 180
    STE-MARGUERITE-DU-LAC-MASSON
        GÎTE DU LIÈVRE 180
    ST-FAUSTIN, LAC-CARRÉ
        LE GÎTE DE LA GARE 173
        L'ENTREMONT 173

ST-HIPPOLYTE
L'ÉVEIL SUR LE LAC 174
ST-JÉRÔME
L'ÉTAPE CHEZ MARIE-THÉRÈSE ET GÉRARD LEMAY 174
ST-JOSEPH-DU-LAC
GÎTE DES JARDINS DE LA MONTAGNE 175
ST-SAUVEUR-DES-MONTS
LES BONHEURS DE SOPHIE 176

☐ **COUNTRY HOMES**
ROSEMÈRE
LA MAISON DE L'ENCLOS 182
VAL-MORIN
NID D'AMOUR 182

☐ **FARM SHOPS**
MIRABEL, ST-BENOÎT
AU GIBIER DU ROI 42
ST-EUSTACHE
VIGNOBLE DE LA RIVIÈRE DU CHÊNE 42

☐ **COUNTRY-STYLE DINING**
LACHUTE, ARGENTEUIL
AU PIED DE LA CHUTE 25
L'ANNONCIATION
LA CLAIRIÈRE DE LA CÔTE 25
MIRABEL, ST-BENOÎT
AU GIBIER DU ROI 26
MIRABEL, ST-SCHOLASTIQUE
LES RONDINS 26
ST-ANDRÉ-D'ARGENTEUIL
LA FERME DE CATHERINE 27
STE-ANNE-DES-PLAINES
BASILIC ET ROMARIN 28
LA CONCLUSION 28
ST-EUSTACHE
LE RÉGALIN 27

LAVAL

☐ **BED & BREAKFASTS**
LAVAL, PONT-VIAU
GÎTE DU MARIGOT 185
LAVAL, ST-FRANÇOIS
NOTRE MAISON SUR LA RIVIÈRE 185

☐ **CITY HOMES**
LAVAL, FABREVILLE
POUR UN INSTANT 186

MAURICIE

☐ **INNS**
STE-ANNE-DE-LA-PÉRADE
À L'ARRÊT DU TEMPS 191
ST-ROCK-DE-MEKINAC
AUBERGE LE MONTAGNARD 191
TROIS-RIVIÈRES
AUBERGE DU BOURG 193
TROIS-RIVIÈRES, POINTE-DU-LAC
AUBERGE BAIE-JOLIE 194

☐ **FARM STAYS**
HÉROUXVILLE
ACCUEIL LES SEMAILLES 69-189

☐ **BED & BREAKFASTS**
BATISCAN
LE GÎTE AU BOIS DORMANT 188
GRANDES-PILES
À LA CAPITAINERIE DU PASSANT 188
GRAND-MÈRE
GÎTE L'ANCESTRAL 188
HÉROUXVILLE
MAISON TRUDEL 189

LAC-AUX-SABLES
    AUBERGE MARCIL 189
LOUISEVILLE
    LA MAISON DE L'ANCÊTRE...190
    LE GÎTE DE LA SEIGNEURIE...190
SHAWINIGAN
    GÎTE DU MANOIR KANE..192
    LA MAISON SOUS LES ARBRES..192
SHAWINIGAN-SUD
    LE GÎTE DU SUD...193
    LES P'TITS POMMIERS 193
STE-MARTHE-DU-CAP
    LA MAISON DES LECLERC...192
ST-MATHIEU-DU-PARC
    AUBERGE DU TRAPPEUR..190
ST-TITE
    AU GÎTE MAISON EMERY JACOB 191
TROIS-RIVIÈRES
    CHEZ GRAND'PAPA BEAU..194
    GÎTE SAINT-LAURENT...194
TROIS-RIVIÈRES, POINTE-DU-LAC
    GÎTE BAIE-JOLIE 195
    SOLEIL LEVANT..195

☐ **COUNTRY HOMES**
    LOUISEVILLE
        LA MAISON DU JARDINIER..196

☐ **CITY HOMES**
    TROIS-RIVIÈRES
        APPARTEMENT DU CENTRE-VILLE..................................196

☐ **FARM SHOPS**
    ST-PROSPER-DE-CHAMPLAIN
        FERME LA BISONNIÈRE...43

☐ **COUNTRY-STYLE DINING**
    LOUISEVILLE
        LA TABLE DE LA SEIGNEURIE...29

MONTÉRÉGIE

☐ **INNS**
    CHAMBLY, RICHELIEU
        AUBERGE LA JARNIGOINE 200
    HUNTINGDON
        AUBERGE HÉRITAGE COUNTRY INN 201

☐ **FARM EXPLORATIONS**
    ST-ISIDORE-DE-LAPRAIRIE
        LES ÉLEVFAGES RUBAN BLEU...59
    ST-PIE
        FERME JEAN DUCHESNE...59
    ST-VALÉRIEN
        LA RABOUILLÈRE..60

☐ **FARM STAYS**
    HOWICK
        HAZELBRAE FARM 70-201
    STE-AGNÈS-DE-DUNDEE
        LE GÎTE CHEZ MIMI 70-205
    STE-VICTOIRE-DE-SOREL
        FARM STAYS DU RANG..71-206
    ST-SIMON
        GÎTE À CLAUDIA..70-205
    ST-VALÉRIEN
        LA RABOUILLÈRE...70-205

☐ **BED & BREAKFASTS**
    BOUCHERVILLE
        LA BOUCHERVILLOISE...199
        SONNEZ LES MATINES...199
    CHAMBLY
        À LA CLAIRE FONTAINE...199
        AUBERGE L'AIR DU TEMPS...200
        LA MAISON DUCHARME...200

CONTRECOEUR
LES MALARDS 201
HUNTINGDON
DOMAINE DE LA TEMPLERIE 202
L'ÎLE-PERROT
GÎTE DE L'ÎLE 202
LONGUEUIL
À LA BRUNANTE 202
À L'OASIS DU VIEUX-LONGUEUIL 203
LE REFUGE DU POÈTE 203
ROUGEMONT
UN TEMPS D'ARRÊT 203
ST-JEAN-SUR-RICHELIEU
AUX CHANTS D'OISEAUX 204
ST-MARC-SUR-RICHELIEU
AUX RÊVES D'ANTAN 204
LE VIREVENT 204

☐ **FARM SHOPS**
IBERVILLE
VIGNOBLE DIETRICH-JOOSS 44
MONT-ST-GRÉGOIRE
CLOS DE LA MONTAGNE 44
STE-HÉLÈNE
ÉRABLIÈRE L'AUTRE VERSAN 47
ST-ISIDORE-DE-LAPRAIRIE
LES ÉLEVAGES RUBAN BLEU 45
ST-JEAN-SUR-RICHELIEU
FROMAGERIE AU GRÉ DES CHAMPS 45
ST-PAUL-D'ABBOTSFORD
VIGNOBLE ARTISANS DU TERROIR 46
ST-THÉODORE-D'ACTON
VERGER CIDRERIE LARIVIÈRE 46

☐ **COUNTRY-STYLE DINING**
HUNTINGDON
DOMAINE DE LA TEMPLERIE 30
MARIEVILLE
L'AUTRUCHE DORÉE 30
ST-RÉMI-DE-NAPIERVILLE
FERME KOSA 31
ST-VALÉRIEN
LA RABOUILLÈRE 31

MONTRÉAL (RÉGION DE)

☐ **FARM EXPLORATIONS**
PIERREFONDS
CORPORATION D-TROIS-PIERRES/FERME ÉCOLOGIQUE 61

☐ **BED & BREAKFASTS**
L'ÎLE-BIZARD
GÎTE ÎLE BIZARD 208
LE QUAI DU RÊVE 208
MONTRÉAL
À BON MATIN 209
À BONHEUR D'OCCASION 208
À LA BELLE VIE 209
À LA BONNE HEURE 209
À LA CARTE B & B 210
À LA MAISON D'À CÔTÉ 210
À L'ADRESSE DU CENTRE-VILLE 210
AU GÎT'ANN 211
AU GÎTE LE RAYON VERT 211
AU GÎTE OLYMPIQUE 211
AUX PORTES DE LA NUIT 212
AZUR 212
GÎTE LA CINQUIÈME SAISON 212
HÉRITAGE VICTORIEN 213
LA MAISON JAUNE 213
LA VICTORIENNE 214
L'ATOME 213
LE 6400 COUETTE ET CAFÉ BED & BREAKFAST 214
LE CLOS DES ÉPINETTES 214

LE ZÈBRE 215
PIERRE ET DOMINIQUE 215
SHÉZELLES 215
MONTRÉAL, NOTRE-DAME-DE-GRÂCE
MAISON HINGSTON 4335 216
PIERREFONDS
GÎTE MAISON JACQUES 216
VERDUN
PACANE ET POTIRON CAFÉ COUETTE 216

☐ **CITY HOMES**
MONTRÉAL
ANNE MA SŒUR ANNE 217
APPARTEMENTS LES BONS MATINS 217
APPARTEMENTS TOURISTIQUES DU CENTRE-VILLE 217
AZUR RESIDENCES DE TOURISME 218
ÉVASION MONTRÉAL 218
ST-LAURENT
STUDIO MARHABA 218

OUTAOUAIS

☐ **FARM STAYS**
GATINEAU
FERME DE BELLECHASSE 71-222
VINOY, CHÉNÉVILLE
LES JARDINS DE VINOY 71-226

☐ **BED & BREAKFASTS**
AYLMER
LA RIVIÈRE AU BOIS DORMANT 221
L'ESCAPADE B&B 221
AYLMER, BRECKENRIDGE
MAISON BON REPOS 221
GATINEAU
LA MAISON SUR LA COLLINE 222
HULL
AU 55 TACHÉ 222
AU PIGNON SUR LE PARC 223
AU VERSANT DE LA MONTAGNE 223
GÎTE FANNY ET MAXIME 223
MANOIR DES CÈDRES 224
LAC-SIMON, CHÉNÉVILLE
DOMAINE AUX CROCOLLINES 224
MONTEBELLO
JARDINS DE RÊVES 224
PAPINEAUVILLE, MONTEBELLO
À L'ORÉE DU MOULIN 225
PONTIAC, LUSKVILLE
AU CHARME DE LA MONTAGNE 225
ST-ANDRÉ-AVELLIN
L'ANCESTRALE 225
VAL-DES-MONTS
AUX PETITS OISEAUX 226

☐ **COUNTRY-STYLE DINING**
GATINEAU
LE POMMIER D'ARGENT 32
ST-SIXTE
FERME CAVALIER 32

QUÉBEC (RÉGION DE)

☐ **INNS**
CHÂTEAU-RICHER
AUBERGE BAKER 230
AUBERGE DU PETIT-PRÉ 230
AUBERGE LE PETIT SÉJOUR 230
DESCHAMBAULT
AUBERGE CHEMIN DU ROY 231
L'ÎLE-D'ORLÉANS, STE-PÉTRONILLE
AUBERGE LA GOÉLICHE 235
L'ÎLE-D'ORLÉANS, ST-LAURENT
AUBERGE L'ÎLE FLOTTANTE 233

L'ÎLE-D'ORLÉANS, ST-PIERRE
AUBERGE LE VIEUX PRESBYTÈRE 233
L'AUBERGE SUR LES PENDANTS 235
MONT-STE-ANNE, ST-FERRÉOL
AUBERGE DU MAGASIN GÉNÉRAL 236
ST-GABRIEL-DE-VALCARTIER
AUBERGE DU MAS DES ÉQUERRES 251
ST-RAYMOND
LA VOISINE 252
MANOIR DU LAC SEPT-ÎLES 252

☐ **FARM EXPLORATIONS**
CHÂTEAU-RICHER
MUSÉE DE L'ABEILLE - ÉCONOMUSÉE DU MIEL 62
L'ÎLE-D'ORLÉANS, ST-LAURENT
LAC DE PÊCHE LA SEIGNEURIE DE L'ÎSLE AUX SORCIERS 62

☐ **FARM STAYS**
NEUVILLE
LA FERME L'ÉMEULIENNE 72-237
STONEHAM, ST-ADOLPHE
AUBERGE DE LA FERME ST-ADOLPHE 72-253

☐ **BED & BREAKFASTS**
BOISCHATEL
AU GÎTE DE LA CHUTE 228
LE REFUGE DU VOYAGEUR 228
LE ROYAL CHAMPÊTRE 228
CAP-SANTÉ
GÎTE NICOLAS LE JARDINIER 229
LA MAISON DE MLLE BERNARD 229
CAP-TOURMENTE, MONT-STE-ANNE
GÎTE DE L'OIE DES NEIGES 229
CHÂTEAU-RICHER
GÎTE UN AIR D'ÉTÉ 231
L'ÎLE-D'ORLÉANS, STE-FAMILLE
AU TOIT BLEU 235
L'ÎLE-D'ORLÉANS, STE-PÉTRONILLE
LE 91 DU BOUT DE L'ÎLE 236
L'ÎLE-D'ORLÉANS, ST-JEAN
AU GIRON DE L'ISLE 231
GÎTE DU QUAI 232
LA MAISON SUR LA CÔTE 232
LE MAS DE L'ISLE 232
L'ÎLE-D'ORLÉANS, ST-LAURENT
L'OASIS DE RÊVES 233
L'ÎLE-D'ORLÉANS, ST-PIERRE
CRÉPUSCULE 234
GÎTE BEL HORIZON 234
LA MAISON DU VIGNOBLE 234
MONT-STE-ANNE, ST-FERRÉOL
LES AROLLES 236
NEUVILLE
AU GRÉ DES SAISONS 237
LA MAISON DUBUC 237
LE GÎTE DE NEUVILLE 238
PORTNEUF
AUBERGE DE LA BARONNIE DE PORTNEUF 238
QUÉBEC
À LA CAMPAGNE EN VILLE 239
À LA MAISON TUDOR 240
ABAT-JOUR B&B 238
ACACIAS 239
ACCUEIL B&B L'HEURE DOUCE 239
AU CROISSANT DE LUNE 240
AU PETIT ROI 240
AU PIED À TERRE À QUÉBEC 241
AUX TROIS BALCONS 241
B&B CHEZ PIERRE 241
B&B DE LA TOUR 242
B&B DES GRISON 242
B&B LA BEDONDAINE 242
B&B MAISON LESAGE 243
CHÂTEAU DES TOURELLES 243
CHÂTEAU DU FAUBOURG 243

CHEZ MONSIEUR GILLES 244
GÎTE DU PARC 244
LA COULE DOUCE 244
LA MAISON LAFLEUR 245
L'HÉMÉROCALLE 245
QUÉBEC, BEAUPORT 245
LA MAISON ANCESTRALE THOMASSIN 246
LA MAISON DUFRESNE 246
LE GÎTE DU VIEUX-BOURG 246
LE MANOIR VALLÉE 247
LE PETIT MANOIR DU SAULT MONTMORENCY 247
QUÉBEC, CAP-ROUGE 247
À LA JOLIE ROCHELLE 247
AU BORD DU FLEUVE 248
L'HYDRANGÉE BLEUE 248
QUÉBEC, LAC DELAGE 248
LE GÎTE DELAGEOIS ....
QUÉBEC, SILLERY 250
B&B LES CORNICHES 250
GÎTE AU CHEMIN DU FOULON ....
QUÉBEC, STE-FOY 248
CHEZ ANICK ET PATRICK 249
LA MAISON LECLERC 249
MAISON DINA 249
MONIQUE ET ANDRÉ SAINT-AUBIN ....
QUÉBEC, WENDAKE 250
LA MAISON AORHENCHE ....
SHANNON
LE GÎTE AU BORD DE LA RIVIÈRE 253
ST-ALBAN 251
GÎTE CHEZ FRANCE ....
ST-CASIMIR 251
GÎTE B&B POUR LES AMIS ....
STE-ANNE-DE-BEAUPRÉ 252
LA MAISON D'ULYSSE ....
STE-CATHERINE-DE-LA-JACQUES-CARTIER 253
GÎTE DU SOUS-BOIS ....

☐ **COUNTRY HOMES**
CAP-TOURMENTE, MONT-STE-ANNE
L'OIE DES NEIGES 254
CHÂTEAU-RICHER
DIRECTION MONT STE-ANNE 254
MONT-STE-ANNE, ST-FERRÉOL
CHALETS-VILLAGE MONT-SAINTE-ANNE 254

☐ **FARM SHOPS**
CHÂTEAU-RICHER
MOULIN DU PETIT PRÉ 48
L'ÎLE-D'ORLÉANS, ST-PIERRE
DOMAINE ORLÉANS 48

SAGUENAY-LAC-SAINT-JEAN

☐ **INNS**
HÉBERTVILLE
AUBERGE PRESBYTÈRE MONT LAC VERT 258
LA BAIE
À FLEUR DE PIERRE 260
L'ANSE-ST-JEAN
AUBERGE DES CÉVENNES 262
PETIT-SAGUENAY
AUBERGE LES 2 PIGNONS 264

☐ **FARM EXPLORATIONS**
ST-HONORÉ
ACCUEIL DU RANDONNEUR 63

☐ **FARM STAYS**
HÉBERTVILLE
FERME CAROLE ET JACQUES MARTEL 72-258
LA BAIE
CHEZ GRAND-MAMAN 73-260
MÉTABETCHOUAN-LAC-À-LA-CROIX
CÉLINE ET GEORGES MARTIN 73-263

NORMANDIN
LES GÎTES MAKADAN 73-264

☐ **BED & BREAKFASTS**
CHICOUTIMI
À LA BERNACHE ....
LE CHARDONNERET 257
LE GÎTE AU BOIS DORMANT 257
HÉBERTVILLE
GÎTE BELLE-RIVIÈRE... 257
JONQUIÈRE
AU MITAN... 258
GÎTE DE LA RIVIÈRE AUX SABLES 259
LES SAISONS DE MARIE 259
LA BAIE
AU BORD DE L'EAU 259
GÎTE DE LA PÊCHE BLANCHE 260
GÎTE DE LA PYRAMIDE 261
L'ANSE-ST-JEAN
À LA PANTOUFLARDE... 261
AU GÎTE DU BARRAGE... 261
AU GLOBE-TROTTER.. 262
MASHTEUIATSH
AUBERGE SHAKAHIKAN 262
MÉTABETCHOUAN-LAC-À-LA-CROIX
BELLE-VUE SUR LE LAC 263
ROBERVAL
LA MAISON AU TOIT ROUGE.. 263
ST-AMBROISE-DE-CHICOUTIMI 264
AUX PIGNONS VERTS ....
GÎTE DE LA SOURCE DES AULNAIES... 265
ST-FÉLICIEN
À FLEUR D'EAU... 265
À LA FERME HÉBERT 265
ST-FÉLIX-D'OTIS 266
GÎTE DE LA BASSE-COUR..
ST-FULGENCE
LA MARAÎCHÈRE DU SAGUENAY.. 266
ST-HENRI-DE-TAILLON
L'EAU BERGE DU LAC... 267

☐ **COUNTRY HOMES À LA FERME**
LA BAIE
LA MAISON DES ANCÊTRES 74-267

☐ **FARM SHOPS**
DOLBEAU-MISTASSINI
LA MAGIE DU SOUS-BOIS INC... 49
STE-ROSE-DU-NORD
FROMAGERIE LA PETITE HEIDI ENR. 49

EVALUATION FORM:
INNS, BED & BREAKFASTS, CITY AND COUNTRY HOMES

Your opinion is important for the continued EXCELLENCE of our guide.

In order to continue to improve the network and the quality of the services it offers, please send your comments and suggestions to:

Fédération des Agricotours
C.P. 1000, succ. M,
Montréal, Québec
H1V 3R2

Win a free stay!

Each year, Agricotours bestows an award of EXCELLENCE to several of its members. The selection is based on clients' comments; we therefore invite you to fill out the following form to show your appreciation and get the chance to win a free stay at one of our members' establishments!

HOW DO YOU RATE YOUR STAY?

RECEPTION
Friendliness and availability of hosts, special considerations

YOUR ROOM
Comfort of beds, overall comfort of room, cleanliness, quality of bedding

MEALS
Quality of food and presentation, flexibility of serving times

HOUSE
Comfort, cleanliness, decor, overall impression of the site

BATHROOM
Facilities, cleanliness

COMMENTS AND SUGGESTIONS

OVERALL APPRECIATION

Excellent   ☐   Good   ☐

Very good   ☐   Poor   ☐

FOR OUR RECORDS

1. Name of establishment: _____

2. Region: _____

3. Date of stay: _____

4. Did you know this establishment was accredited by Agricotours?
    ☐ Yes   ☐ No (go to question 6)

5. Did you choose this establishment for that reason?
    ☐ Yes   ☐ No   If not, then why?
    _____

6. Is this your first experience in this type lodging ?
    ☐ Yes   ☐ No   If not, how many times? _____

    How did you hear about the *Inns and Bed & Breakfasts in Québec* guide?
    _____

7. Do you have Internet access?
    ☐ Home   ☐ Work   ☐ No

8. Did you book by:
    ☐ Internet (e-mail, reservation service, etc.) ☐ Telephone
    ☐ Other, please specify: _____

9. Respondant's age group:
    ☐ Under 20   ☐ 40-49   ☐ 70 and over
    ☐ 20-29   ☐ 50-59
    ☐ 30-39   ☐ 60-69

10. Level of schooling: _____

11. Profession: _____

EVALUATION FORM: COUNTRY STYLE DINING

Your opinion is important for the continued EXCELLENCE of our guide.

In order to continue to improve the network and the quality of the services it offers, please send your comments and suggestions to:

Fédération des Agricotours
C.P. 1000, succ. M,
Montréal, Québec
H1V 3R2

Win a free stay!

Each year, Agricotours bestows an award of EXCELLENCE to several of its members. The selection is based on clients' comments; we therefore invite you to fill out the following form to show your appreciation and get the chance to win a free stay at one of our members' establishments!

HOW DO YOU RATE YOUR STAY?

WELCOME
Friendliness and availability of hosts, special considerations

MEALS
Quality of food and presentation, freshness, variety

DINING ROOM
Comfort, cleanliness, decor

OVERALL IMPRESSION
Exterior of the house, buildings, grounds

FARM TOUR
Content, exchanges, communication skills

_____

COMMENTS AND SUGGESTIONS

_____
_____
_____
_____

OVERALL APPRECIATION

Excellent	☐	Good	☐
Very good	☐	Poor	☐

FOR OUR RECORDS

1. Name of establishment: _____

2. Region: _____

3. Date of stay: _____

4. Did you know this establishment was accredited by Agricotours?
   ☐ Yes   ☐ No (go to question 6)

5. Did you choose this establishment for that reason?
   ☐ Yes   ☐ No   If not, then why?
   _____

6. Is this your first experience in this type lodging ?
   ☐ Yes   ☐ No   If not, how many times? _____

7. How did you hear about the *Inns and Bed & Breakfasts in Québec* guide?
   _____

8. Do you have Internet access?
   ☐ Home   ☐ Work   ☐ No

9. Respondant's age group:
   ☐ Under 20   ☐ 40-49   ☐ 70 and over
   ☐ 20-29   ☐ 50-59
   ☐ 30-39   ☐ 60-69

10. Level of schooling: _____

11. Profession: _____

EVALUATION FORM: FARM SHOPS AND FARM EXCURSIONS

Your opinion is important for the continued EXCELLENCE of our guide.

In order to continue to improve the network and the quality of the services it offers, please send your comments and suggestions to:

Fédération des Agricotours
C.P. 1000, succ. M,
Montréal, Québec
H1V 3R2

Win a free stay!

Each year, Agricotours bestows an award of EXCELLENCE to several of its members. The selection is based on clients' comments; we therefore invite you to fill out the following form to show your appreciation and get the chance to win a free stay at one of our members' establishments!

HOW DO YOU RATE YOUR STAY?

RECEPTION
Friendliness and availability of hosts

ENTERTAINMENT
Content, exchanges, communication skills

FACILITIES
Sanitary installations, parking, reception area, buildings, signs

SERVICES
Reservations, information, payment

COMMENTS AND SUGGESTIONS

_____
_____
_____
_____
_____
_____

OVERALL APPRECIATION

Excellent ☐   Good ☐

Very good ☐   Poor ☐

FOR OUR RECORDS

1. Name of establishment: _____

2. Region: _____

3. Date of stay: _____

4. Did you know this establishment was accredited by Agricotours?
   ☐ Yes   ☐ No (go to question 6)

5. Did you choose this establishment for that reason?
   ☐ Yes   ☐ No   If not, then why?
   _____

6. Is this your first experience in this type lodging ?
   ☐ Yes   ☐ No   If not, how many times? _____

7. How did you hear about the *Inns and Bed & Breakfasts in Québec* guide?
   _____

8. Do you have Internet access?
   ☐ Home   ☐ Work   ☐ No

9. Respondant's age group:
   ☐ Under 20   ☐ 40-49   ☐ 70 and over
   ☐ 20-29   ☐ 50-59
   ☐ 30-39   ☐ 60-69

10. Level of schooling: _____

11. Profession: _____